An Actological Theology

ACTOLOGICAL EXPLORATIONS

A series of books that understand reality as action in changing patterns. Also in this series

Actology: Action, change and diversity in the western philosophical tradition

Two streams run through western philosophy: one characterized by Being, beings, the unchanging, the static, and the unitary, and the other by Action, actions, the changing, the dynamic, and the diverse. This book explores the 'Action' stream as it has wound its way through the Western philosophical tradition, and enables us to see ourselves, the universe and God as action in changing patterns rather than as beings that change.

Mark's Gospel: An actological reading

The second book in the series reads Mark's Gospel in the light of an actological understanding of reality. So it understands God, Jesus, and ourselves, as action, change, and diversity. The result is a unique and somewhat unexpected reading of the text, and a distinctive theology to match.

Actological Readings in Continental Philosophy

The third book in the series continues the journey begun in the first. Understanding reality as action in changing patterns casts new light on the writings of a variety of Continental philosophers and raises and answers some significant new questions.

An Actology of the Given

The fourth book discusses anthropology, continental philosophy, biblical texts, social policy, and a variety of givens, to enable us to explore the concepts of the gift, givenness, giving, and so on, in the light of reality understood as action in changing patterns.

An Actological Metaphysic

The fifth book studies a wide variety of metaphysical concepts, such as causality, time, and space, in the light of reality understood as action in changing patterns

An Actological Theology

MALCOLM TORRY

RESOURCE *Publications* · Eugene, Oregon

AN ACTOLOGICAL THEOLOGY

Copyright © 2024 Malcolm Torry. All rights reserved. Except for brief quotations in critical publications or reviews, no part of this book may be reproduced in any manner without prior written permission from the publisher. Write: Permissions, Wipf and Stock Publishers, 199 W. 8th Ave., Suite 3, Eugene, OR 97401.

Resource Publications
An Imprint of Wipf and Stock Publishers
199 W. 8th Ave., Suite 3
Eugene, OR 97401

www.wipfandstock.com

PAPERBACK ISBN: 979-8-3852-1975-9
HARDCOVER ISBN: 979-8-3852-1976-6
EBOOK ISBN: 979-8-3852-1977-3

VERSION NUMBER 05/28/24

All Scriptural quotations are taken from the New Revised Standard Version of the Bible (Anglicized Version), copyright 1989, 1995 by the Division of Christian Education of the National Council of the Churches of Christ in the United States of America. Used by permission. All rights reserved.

Contents

Preface and acknowledgements | vii

Introduction to An Actological Theology | xiii

Chapter 1	Connections: Philosophy and apologetics	1
Chapter 2	Connections: Apologetics and theology	26
Chapter 3	An actological God	46
Chapter 4	A suffering God	73
Chapter 5	Beginning with Jesus of Nazareth	96
Chapter 6	Grace in the Scriptures	117
Chapter 7	Grace after the New Testament	139
Chapter 8	The City of God	166
Chapter 9	An actological Trinity	181
Chapter 10	The reconciling God	196
Chapter 11	An actological church	207
Chapter 12	Doing Christianly	227
Chapter 13	An actological Bible	244
Chapter 14	An actology of religions	255
Chapter 15	Conclusions	266

Bibliography | 273

Subject Index | 289

Names Index | 305

Scripture Index | 309

Preface and acknowledgements

IN 1974 I ATTENDED lectures in the philosophy of religion and experienced Plato for the first time. The following year I studied systematic theology and was reading works by the early theologians Justin Martyr and Origen. It felt as if I was reading Plato, and it all felt rather arid. I married, we moved to South London, I worked in Brixton's Supplementary Benefit office for two years, I encountered some rather different theology when I studied for a master's degree in twentieth-century theology, we moved to Durham for a year where I trained for ordination, and I then found myself back in South London undertaking a curacy at the Elephant and Castle. A Platonic theology about the static, the unchanging, and the unitary had little to say to the dynamic, the changing, and the diversity that I was increasingly experiencing. What was to be done?

In 1985, a Church of England commission published *Faith in the City*, and in its theological chapter—which I was not surprised to discover had been an afterthought—I found a God "infinitely transcendent," with no suggestion that God suffered in and with a suffering urban world, or with suffering human beings: and I was again reminded of Plato.[1] At the same time I was attending a theological society convened by the Very Rev'd David Edwards, Provost of Southwark Cathedral: so I prepared for it a short paper that suggested that because our society was increasingly characterized by change and diversity, and decreasingly by sameness and the unchanging, the Church's theology needed to be expressed in terms of change and diversity. Life was busy, and further exploration of the idea had to wait until a period of sabbatical leave in 1994. The outcome was an essay, on which both Professor Robin Gill and David Atkinson (then Canon Missioner in the Diocese of Southwark, and subsequently Archdeacon of Lewisham and Bishop of Thetford) offered valuable comment; and that essay subsequently became a series of articles that Bill Jacob, Archdeacon of Charing Cross and Editor

---

1. Archbishop of Canterbury's Commission on Urban Priority Areas, *Faith in the City*, 70.

of *Theology*, published in the journal. I am most grateful to all of those who contributed in various ways to the writing and publication of those articles.

The first article, "On Completing the Apologetic Spectrum,"[2] suggested that in a context in which the changing and the diverse are becoming more important categories than the unchanging and the unitary, the Church's apologetics, and therefore the metaphysic (in the sense of a "system of metaphysics"[3]) underlying its theology, needed to reflect that trend. The Western philosophical tradition has for two thousand years given priority to the unchanging, to the static, to rest (as opposed to movement), to the unitary, to being, and to Being—being itself—and Christian theology has largely followed suit. Now a different conceptual structure—or perhaps, better, an additional conceptual structure—might be required if we are to express the Christian Faith in today's world: a metaphysic, or foundational conceptual framework, that prioritizes change, the dynamic, movement, diversity, action, and Action: action itself.

A further article followed: "Action, Patterns and Religious Pluralism."[4] Just as a Being metaphysic has always needed some way to express the change that we experience, so an Action metaphysic needs to express the continuities that we experience. In this second article I suggested that "patterns of action" or "action in patterns" might be a useful way to do this.

I have always been most grateful to St. John's College, Cambridge, for the hospitality that it has extended to me over many years. Most years for the past forty years I have spent three nights at St. John's to enable me to immerse myself in the Cambridge libraries; and the college has also offered occasional longer periods of residence. On one of my annual visits the Dean of Chapel, the Rev'd Andrew Macintosh, asked whether I might like to visit a former Master of the College who had moved into a care home in South London near to where I was Vicar of St. Catherine's, Hatcham, at New Cross. At the age of ninety John Boys Smith still had a lively mind, and we held an interesting discussion about process theology. He died soon after. On my next visit to Cambridge I discovered that the only theological or philosophical publication listed in the University Library catalogue under his name was a booklet that he had written in 1930, *Christian Doctrine and the Idea of Evolution*.[5] The booklet's contents were in many ways ahead of their time. Further research revealed that Boys Smith's son, Stephen Boys Smith, still possessed a holdall containing many of his father's sermons:

2. Torry, "On Completing the Apologetic Spectrum."
3. Oxford English Dictionary.
4. Torry, "Action, Patterns and Religious Pluralism."
5. Boys Smith, *Christian Doctrine and the Idea of Evolution*.

so I edited and published the sermons with an introduction, and had the 1930 booklet reprinted as an appendix.[6] The third *Theology* article was an abridged version of the introduction to the edited sermons.[7]

In 2004 Keith Trivasse employed what he called "Torry's model" in a somewhat too adulatory fashion to discuss the relationship between Muhammad and the Christian Faith.[8] This inspired further thought on my part, which led to my next article, "Testing Torry's Model,"[9] which distinguished my "action in patterns" conceptual framework from the conceptual framework underlying process theology, and also related my framework to recent scientific developments. A final article, "'Logic' and 'Action': two new readings of the New Testament,"[10] asked how the conceptual framework might work as a lens through which to interpret passages from the fourth gospel.

That last article was written in 2006 and published in 2008, and for nearly ten years after that I hardly thought about metaphysics. Being Team Rector of the Parish of East Greenwich, Co-ordinator of the Greenwich Peninsula Chaplaincy, Director of the Citizen's Income Trust, and a Visiting Senior Fellow at the London School of Economics, researching and writing on reform options for the benefits system and on the management of religious and faith-based organizations, was quite enough.

For over forty years I have been involved in the debate about Basic Income—an unconditional income for every individual—and in 2014 that debate began to demand rather a lot of my time. I was doing too much, so I retired early from the full-time ministry in order to concentrate on the research and writing that the Basic Income debate was demanding of me, and also to make time to revisit the subject-matter of the *Theology* articles. Those articles contained the sketchiest of surveys of the Western philosophical tradition, so to explore that tradition in more depth seemed like the obvious place to start. I was therefore pleased to be accepted as a candidate for the Archbishop's Examination in Theology. I was initially intending to complete a Ph.D. thesis, but the demands that the Basic Income debate were making on me made it necessary to rein in my ambition and to submit a thesis for the degree of Master of Philosophy. In relation to the thesis I am most grateful to Cambridge University Library, the library of St. John's College, Cambridge, the library of King's College, London, and

---

6. Boys Smith, *The Sermons of John Boys Smith*.
7. Torry, "A Neglected Theologian."
8. Trivasse, "May the Prophet Muhammad Be a Prophet to Christianity?"
9. Torry, "Testing Torry's Model."
10. Torry, "'Logic' and 'Action.'"

Gladstone's Library, for hospitality, and to my two supervisors, Professors George Newlands and Simon Oliver.

I eventually found the time to expand the MPhil thesis into a book, *Actology: Action, Change and Diversity in the Western Philosophical Tradition*, that Wipf and Stock kindly published under their "Resource" imprint, and I remain grateful for the interest that Matt Wimer, George and Emily Callihan, Savanah Landerholm and others at Wipf and Stock have shown in what has become the "Actological Explorations" series.

Following the publication of *Actology*, the pandemic provided some time that could only be used for reading and writing, so I took the opportunity to write *Mark's Gospel: An Actological Reading*: the gospel interpreted through an understanding of reality as action in changing patterns. This became the second book in the "Actological Explorations" series.

Undertaking the Lambeth research degree and writing *Actology* had revealed a significant knowledge gap, which I began to fill by undertaking a master's degree in continental philosophy at Staffordshire University. I subsequently expanded the module essays, dissertation, and my contributions to student-led study groups, into two books, *Actological Readings in Continental Philosophy* and *An Actology of the Given*: the third and fourth members of the "Actological Explorations" series. I am most grateful to Professor David Webb and Drs Patrick O'Connor and Bill Ross for helping me to navigate what I experienced as the biggest intellectual challenge that I have ever faced, and am only sorry that Bill died suddenly and too young soon after I completed the degree so that I couldn't send him copies of the books that he had helped to make possible.

For forty years I had fitted whatever philosophical studies I could find time for around the full-time ministry of the Church of England and the research and organizational activity demanded by the Basic Income debate: but by 2022 there were increasing numbers of researchers and activists involved in what is now a global debate about the desirability and feasibility of giving everyone an unconditional income, so it was time for some of us who had been involved since the beginning of the modern Basic Income movement to step aside and allow a new generation the social space that it needed. I returned to voluntary part-time ministry in the Church of England as Priest in Charge of St Mary Abchurch in the City of London, and to some further work on actology: an understanding of reality as Action rather than Being, and as action in changing patterns rather than as beings that change. *Actology*, *Actological Readings in Continental Philosophy*, and *An Actology of the Given*, had all set out from the writings of a variety of philosophers, both to understand their philosophies on the basis that reality is action in changing patterns, and to enable what they had written to inform the construction of an actology. It was time to take a different approach, so *An Actological Metaphysic* employed both philosophical and scientific texts to study a wide variety of metaphysical concepts in the light of reality understood as action in changing patterns in order to construct something like a systematic actology—the "something like" here being a recognition that the change and diversity inherent to any actology means that any particular actology that we might create will be of partial, brief, and local relevance, so that the next moment a new actology will be required. This book, *An Actological Theology*, employs a similar method to *An Actological Metaphysic*: that is, it understands a variety of theological writings and themes on the basis that reality is action, the dynamic, movement, change, and diversity, and it employs what it discovers to construct something like a systematic theology, again on the understanding that the theology constructed can only be of partial, brief, and local relevance.

As well as those individuals mentioned above, numerous individuals have contributed to the development of the ideas to be found in the "Actological Explorations" series by their willingness to discuss them with me. There are too many to mention, and I cannot remember all of them: but particularly significant contributions have been made at various stages by John Byrom, Stephen Sykes, James Bogle, Renford Bambrough, Jed Davis, chaplains of the South London Industrial Mission, members of the congregations of St. Catherine's, Hatcham, St. George's, Westcombe Park, and Holy Trinity, Greenwich Peninsula, participants in seminars held in relation to the Archbishop's Examination in Theology, and staff and students of Staffordshire University's continental philosophy department. I am more than grateful to those who made possible several periods of study leave of varying lengths: staff members and officers of the parishes that I have served for their willingness to shoulder additional burdens; Bishops of Woolwich for permissions to take sabbaticals; St. John's College for appointing me a Fellow Commoner for a term; and particularly my wife Rebecca and children Christopher, Nicholas, and Jonathan for their unfailing support.

I am still most grateful to all of the people mentioned above for their encouragement and help along the way.

Introduction to
An Actological Theology

This volume forms the sixth and probably final part of the "Actological Explorations" series.

THE FIRST BOOK IN THE SERIES, *Actology: Action, change and diversity in the Western philosophical tradition*, published in 2020—not actually labelled "Actological Explorations" because there was no series when it was published—sought the thin stream of diversity, Action, action, change, and the dynamic as it coursed its way through the history of Western philosophy, frequently submerged by the alternative stream about the unitary, Being, beings, the unchanging, and the static, and then asked what that stream might offer to the creation of an actology: an understanding of reality as action in changing patterns rather than as beings that change.

The second book in what was by then a "series" was a somewhat different project, made possible by the acres of time set free for writing by Covid-19: *Mark's Gospel: An actological reading*, published in 2022. This was what it said it was: a way of reading Mark's Gospel with reality understood as action in changing patterns rather than as beings that change. Then followed two volumes that trace the "Action" stream through continental philosophy: *Actological Readings in Continental Philosophy* and *An Actology of the Given*, both published in 2023—the former a reading of a variety of philosophers through the lens of reality understood as action in changing patterns, and the latter a more focused volume that understands the "givenness" explored by Husserl, Heidegger, Levinas, Derrida, and Jean-Luc Marion as a "giving" rather than as a "gift." Again, the journey through the philosophical tradition not only understands that tradition in a new way, but also asks what that philosophy might have to contribute to the construction of an actology: a philosophy that understands reality as action in changing patterns.

All of those volumes did philosophy by setting out from a wide diversity of texts written by a variety of philosophers in order to understand their authors' philosophies in a particular way and to seek the resources with which to build an actological tradition. The volume previous to this one, *An Actological Metaphysic*, and this volume, start from a different place: they ask what metaphysics and theology might look like if reality were to be understood as action in changing patterns rather than as beings that change. We have of course encountered a wide variety of philosophers and other scholars as we have constructed our new metaphysic, and we shall encounter a variety of philosophers and theologians as we construct an actological theology, but we are here mining the texts for what they might contribute to an understanding of the particular metaphysical and theological concepts that we are discussing, rather than reading them in order to understand what their authors might have to offer to the construction of an actology.

There was far too much metaphysical and theological material to get into a single volume: hence *An Actological Metaphysic* and *An Actological Theology*: but that does not avoid the question as to how the subject matter of the two volumes should have been divided. Is a division between "metaphysics" and "theology" a purposeful statement that the secular and the sacred cannot be discussed together, or is it a somewhat arbitrary attempt to divide material into two books of roughly equal length? It has to be the latter. The ubiquitous dynamic and diverse character of an actological understanding of reality as action in changing patterns implies and promotes an extreme and radical non-dualism and non-reductionism in which there can be no divisions between the physical and the mental, the spiritual and the secular, and so on. This means that any division of material into different volumes can only be entirely practical, and that there will be plenty of overlap between them, and sometimes repetition as well. Metaphysics raises theological questions and theology raises metaphysical questions, particularly when we consider such concepts as the origin of the universe.

A further question relates to the order in which the volumes have been written. The order in which the reader will find the volumes might be regarded as a recognition that an actological metaphysic might provide a useful basis for discussion of our experience and understanding of God, the ultimate reality: for if God does not relate to our experience of the world, or to the metaphysical questions that we cannot avoid asking, then there is nothing theological to discuss. The alternative order would have recognized that God, as ultimate reality, is inevitably the basis for all other reality, and therefore for any understanding of it. The reader should not regard the order in which the volumes have appeared as in any sense indicative of a conceptual ordering, and certainly not of any order of priority. It would be more relevant to regard the order in which the books have been published as entirely arbitrary.

Readers might find it useful to see discussed here a particular difference that they might notice between *An Actological Metaphysic* and *An Actological Theology*. This book, *An Actological Theology*, employs a similar method to *An Actological Metaphysic*: that is, it understands a variety of theological writings on the basis that reality is action, the dynamic, movement, change, and diversity, and it employs what it discovers to construct something like a systematic theology, again on the understanding that the theology constructed can only be of partial, brief, and local relevance. However, to use the word "systematic" at all in this theological context might be misguided. When we studied metaphysics we were able to order a number of concepts and discuss each of them in turn from both philosophical and scientific points of view. Such boundary-drawing is impossible when it comes to theology because although we might be able to discuss in something like an orderly fashion a history of apologetics or a list of theories of the atonement, as soon as we begin to discuss God we are attempting the impossible. Just as Heidegger could discuss Being only in the context of my own being in the world, so we can only discuss Action—action itself, and the source of all action—in terms of the action in changing patterns of which we have some primary or secondary experience. God, who must be Action, action itself, and the action in changing patterns that might constitute God, and who must be the focus of our explorations, remains out of sight and out of reach. The necessarily partial, local, and brief nature of any actological exploration is thus compounded into the impossible, partial, local, and brief nature of any actological theology, so any attempt at systematization might mislead. A book needs to be written, so something needs to be said, and whenever we attempt to say anything at all a certain amount of tentative systematization is inevitable: but readers might find that the somewhat discursive nature of much that they will find in this volume will be more representative of the actological theology that we need than will be any of the more systematic elements.

As for the title: *An Actological Theology* suggests that the book will understand theology through an actological lens—that is, on an understanding of the basis of reality as Action, action, change, diversity, movement, and the dynamic. The indefinite article is as important as the "Actological" and the "Theology" because it makes it clear that there might be many more actological understandings of theology than the reader will find here. This we should expect, because the very act of constructing systems of metaphysics and theology on an actological basis is immediately defeated by that basis itself, because any systematic structure that might be proposed, if understood actologically, will be merely a momentary snapshot of a dynamic reality. In an actological context, any system is constantly dissolved and reformed, if we can call such an entity a "system," which means that any systematic characteristics of the theology will be changing patterns of action. The reader will find here ubiquitous attempts at systematic treatment of both metaphysics and theology but will not be surprised when these collapse into change and diversity. It is an *actological* theology that is offered here, not an ontological theology.

Although not essential to an understanding of the actological theology contained in this volume, readers might wish to refer to chapters 1 and 2 of *An Actological Metaphysic*. There will be found a chapter on definitions and a chapter that describes the actological journey as it is contained in the first four volumes of the "Actological Explorations" series.

Following this introduction—the first part of which repeats the first part of the introduction to *An Actological Metaphysic*—this volume gives two chapters to the discussion of connections between philosophy and apologetics and between apologetics and theology. It then launches into the construction of an actological theology. Chapter 3 asks how God might be understood actologically, and chapter 4 finds that an actological God must be a suffering God. Chapter 5 asks what theology might look like if we start with Jesus of Nazareth, and then follow two chapters that return to a discussion of a concept explored in *An Actology of the Given*: "grace," studied in chapter 6 through actological readings of the Hebrew and Christian scriptures, and in chapter 7 through a study of subsequent discussion of the concept. Chapter 8 asks whether "City of God" might be more appropriate than "Kingdom of God" in an actological context; chapter 9 explores the Trinitarian God actologically; and chapter 10 understands reconciling activity as constitutive of God. In chapter 11 the Church is understood actologically; chapter 12 asks how we might "do Christianly" rather than "being Christians"; chapter 13 reads the Bible actologically; and chapter 14 offers an actology of the diversity of religions. Chapter 15 offers a few conclusions.

Chapter 1

Connections
Philosophy and apologetics[1]

Thesis: An actological understanding of reality requires an actological apologetics

INTRODUCTION

Paul uses the word *apologeisthai* (from *apologeomia*, "to speak in defence, to defend oneself"[2]) to describe the defense speech that he is to make before King Agrippa.[3] Like that highly theological speech, all theology is to some extent apologetics: a spoken or written defense of the Christian Faith. "Apologetics" does not mean apologizing for writing about God—although the ethos of our times frequently invites such a reaction. It means offering reasons for belief in God, which in turn means relating what we write about God to the thought-world within which we communicate. As Alan Richardson puts it:

> Apologetics deals with the relationship of the Christian faith to the wider sphere of [our] "secular" knowledge—philosophy, science, history, sociology, and so on—with a view to showing that

---

1. I am grateful to participants in an Archbishop's Examination in Theology seminar held on the 17th June 2016 for useful comments on an essay on which some of this chapter is based.
2. Liddell and Scott, *An Intermediate Greek-English Lexicon*.
3. Acts 26:2–23; Milbank, "An Apologia for Apologetics," xiii–xiv.

faith is not at variance with the truth that these enquiries have uncovered.[4]

A paradox emerges. If apologetics is to connect with today's society and its culture, and with a variety of disciplines as they are conducted today, then it must be framed in their languages and thought-forms, so one of the tasks of apologetics must be to defend those languages and thought-forms and to map such different language games as the cosmological, scientific, philosophical, theological, and literary, onto each other,[5] on the basis that all language is analogical.[6] However, there is also something distinctive about the Christian Faith, and therefore about the thought-forms and language in which it must be framed, so that language and those thought-forms might need to be defended against other disciplines' prevailing thought-forms and languages. As John Milbank puts it,

> this shifting location between the defence against the world on the one hand, and defence of worldly nomos [law] and worldly logos [reason] on the other, is not really a tension between Christianity and something else, but rather a tension constitutive of Christianity as refusing the Gnostic or the Marcionite path[7]

—that is, a tension entirely coherent with the doctrine of the incarnation: that no longer is there a boundary between God and flesh, or, more generally, between God and a contingent world of action in changing patterns.

But things are not as simple as that, for all of the ways in which the Christian Faith has been framed have relied on the conceptual structures of their times. There is no pure Christian language. In particular, the language of the New Testament is shaped by the thought-forms of its time: so Jesus' parables, the first chapter of the fourth gospel, Paul's speech before Agrippa, and Paul's letters to the churches, are all informed by the thought-forms of their times: thought-forms from which the Christian Faith can never be abstracted. To construct new conceptual structures is no doubt risky, but it is not that the choice that we face is one between the Christian Faith expressed through a risky new conceptual framework and the Christian Faith per se. The choice is between the Christian Faith expressed through the conceptual structures of previous times, and the Christian Faith expressed through an understanding of reality as action in changing patterns in which verbs will

---

4. Richardson, *Christian Apologetics*, 19.
5. Gibson, *God and the Universe*.
6. Gibson, *God and the Universe*, 22–23, 251–52.
7. Milbank, "An Apologia for Apologetics," xviii.

be generally more relevant than nouns: so we might find ourselves speaking of believing Christianly (a verb, qualified by an adverb) rather than of Christian Faith (a noun, qualified by an adjective). Whatever the risk, better the employment of a conceptual structure attuned to our own times than one that has little connection with them: and maybe those new thought-forms will end up expressing to some extent the character of the Kingdom of God, just as thought-forms from the past have been influenced by the Kingdom of God to which they gave utterance in their own time.

God is Action, action in changing patterns, and diverse, so the question is: To what extent can theology be diverse? In different contexts, "God" will mean different things. Thus "God" is changed by a changing context, and so God is changed: for we have no access to reasoning about God apart from employing the word "God" and relating that word to other words. Thus God is not only diverse, but is also an organic entity, evolving along with the cosmos and inseparable from its evolution:[8] so we can no longer give meaning to the concept of an unchanging God. And as we are diverse, and each of us is diverse across time and space, so what we understand by "God" is diverse, and God is diverse. We can no longer give meaning to the concept of a unitary God, for there is no means whereby we might discuss such an idea.

CHOICES

Whether individually or corporately, we have always chosen what we mean by "God," and if the images and concepts that arise in our minds when we use the word "God" are not the result of our choosing then they are the result of somebody else's choosing.

In every culture, and in every church, the variety of meanings of the word "God," and the limits to that variety, are arrived at by a corporate process of making choices between ancient images and modern ones, and of choosing connections between the ancient and the modern. Consensus emerges through a process of slow evolution that is influenced by the evolutions of philosophy, literature, history, political science, and economics, in the same way as in the natural and human sciences new conceptual structures are created by a complex process of choice among ancient and modern possibilities and of influence from other disciplines. Occasionally an individual's choices will be determinative of a discipline's direction for a few years (as with Einstein's influence on physics), but generally there are no sudden conversions: new models and new connections slowly replace

8. Deane-Drummond, *Christ and Evolution*.

more traditional ones by a process of synthesis of new with old in order to create a new framework that might appear to bear little relationship with previous modes of thought. Paradigms shift,[9] and paradigms within which we understand paradigm shifts might shift as well.

There is nothing absolute about any philosophical statement, any economic law, any scientific theory, or any theological system:[10] they are all the results of myriads of choices made individually and corporately from amongst traditional models and the multiple diverse new possibilities invented on the basis of experience and in relation to trends in other disciplines. Every choice contains an element of the arbitrary, and there is no guarantee that developments will cohere with each other to give a satisfying overall structure. There are no final systems, and energy should not be wasted in seeking them.

This does not mean that commitment is impossible. It is rational for groups and individuals, and indeed whole societies, to commit themselves to particular ways of viewing history, to particular brands of philosophy, to scientific theories, to economics based on particular assumptions, to theologies with particular structures, and to ways of life more or less based on any of those, as long as the commitment remains tentative and open to revision. This is no less true of philosophical, scientific, or political commitments, as it is of theological commitment.[11] Without commitment to particular models or ways of life, further exploration becomes difficult to undertake individually and impossible corporately; and sanity is difficult to maintain if every possible variable is permanently in flux. Commitment to a view of history or to a philosophical framework is essential if new thinking is to happen and to be communicable. However, for individuals and for groups, conversions are always possible (either rapidly or by slow synthesis)[12] as new experience chips away at accepted models, and new images and connections take their place.

If traditional definitions of God become meaningless, then we need to choose new definitions as theological starting-points: we need conversions—that is, we need to make new choices among the options available. However, no healthy conversion leaves the past behind, so when new definitions of God are offered, they are rarely completely new, and they should not be expected to be. In a secular world, in which religious thought-forms and

---

9. Kuhn, *The Structure of Scientific Revolutions*.

10. Cartwright, *The Dappled World*.

11. Allen, "Faith and the Recognition of God's Activity."

12. James, *The Varieties of Religious Experience*; Moscovici, "Toward a Theory of Conversion Behavior"; Sargent, *Battle for the Mind*.

religious institutions are becoming irrelevant to public life, it is not surprising that individual religious belief increases in intensity as a defense against the disintegration of the social fabric, or that new attempts at definitions of God are less and less new. What is required in such circumstances is a radical destruction of those definitions of God that are generally meaningless, and the choice of a God that can be generally meaningful, even if that God has strong connections with some previous definition. In short: for the time being, we might need to leave behind a theism that was once reasonably well understood within a Being-based ontology, and seek out a God relevant to and communicable within a reality that we increasingly understand within an action in changing patterns actology, and if possible a God who retains some connection with previous definitions—reimagined actologically—in order to retain coherence at the same time as enhancing the diversity.

Conversions can occur in many directions: from one kind of Christian faith to another; out of atheism into Christian faith; out of Christian faith into atheism; out of one brand of politics into another; or out of one relationship and into another. Such conversion experiences need to be carefully examined and evaluated, for they have a large part to play in the people that we have become and the people that we might become, and our conversions will inevitably affect other people, and theirs will affect us. To mitigate any damage done by a conversion, to care for anyone damaged by it, and to internalize what has occurred, can be a healing process, for that process can help to integrate us around the new connections that we have created between experience, convictions, and actions. And just as we exercise choice in many areas of our lives, so we can exercise choice here. We do have some control over our various conversions. We can evaluate where a potential conversion might be going, and if it might damage other people or ourselves then we can steer it into a different path. To stop it might be futile, but where it leads will be partly up to us.

We live in a culture in which "choice" is important. This implies a complex process: a collapse of traditional authority meaning that we have to make our own choices in areas of our lives in which we they used to be made for us; and the increasing number of options among which choices have to be made means that we contract out our decision-making and are easily influenced: and those institutions and individuals that influence us will often be serving their own ends and so will be treating us and other human beings as means rather than ends. Both this process and the concept of choice will inevitably inform our conversions, our actions, our beliefs, and our definitions of God. In particular, we shall each need to choose what we mean by "God" if God is to be meaningful to us in a society in which choice is a significant concept, and we shall have to take care to make our own choices if they are not to be made for us. In fact, we always have chosen what we mean by "God," unless others have made the choice for us: but now that process must become explicit, for only a conscious and deliberate choosing of our God will give to us a God whom we can worship and enjoy and who can give hope to us and to our society. There are no absolutes, so there is no necessity to choose as our God anything or anyone in particular. The choice will be constrained by choices made in the past and by our current experience, but still the choice is ours to make, individually and along with others who also understand the necessity to make such decisions.

And the choice will need to be made over and over again, because if we believe that we have arrived, and that hope has been fulfilled, then we shall have found a fixed and unitary object, a being, a thing, and thus not reality. Both alone and in the company of others we must make choices by employing transitory models, and then we must abandon them for new ones: and that will enable us still to hope, for we shall know that we have not found. In particular, we must be honest with ourselves. If we think that we have arrived somewhere, or that we have found God, then we need to remind ourselves that we might have found a previously buried part of ourselves—which means that we cannot avoid the conclusion that the same happened to some of those whom we regard as the greatest saints. But then perhaps we have met God—for if God is to come to us, then it can only be in the form of human ideas, emotions, and words. Nothing else will connect. So we must choose, not only where to look, but also what we think we might have found in this moment and in this place. There will be no conclusion to the journey: but the journey is real.

In relation to today's thought-forms, and the choices now facing us, it is particularly the discipline of philosophy with which I shall be concerned in this chapter, although later on I shall wander briefly into other disciplines in order to suggest additional lines of enquiry. Philosophy has to be the first discipline to be tackled because it is so closely connected with our society's culture, both as a barometer of that culture, and as a contributor to it. If we can construct a philosophy that enables us to express Christian believing, that reflects our society's character, that connects with philosophy's history and contemporary configuration, and that connects with the trajectories of other disciplines, then we shall have constructed a useful framework within which to do apologetics.

APOLOGETICS, PHILOSOPHY, AND METAPHYSICS

But what is the character of today's philosophy? We live in the midst of a variety of "language games."[13] There is no single big story that contains all of the stories that we tell about ourselves and about our world.[14] There is unremitting diversity, with different philosophical frameworks jostling for position: everything from Jacques Derrida's *différance*[15] to Iris Murdoch's Platonic "good."[16] This situation presents us with an opportunity. In a context of multiple language games, it is easier to exercise the imagination[17] than it would be within a more monochrome philosophical context: so it will be both possible and entirely legitimate to construct a *"paralogie"*—a new reasoning, a new language—that runs alongside existing philosophical, scientific, and other language games.[18]

It has frequently been difficult to do apologetics. It was particularly difficult during the 1940s, during the reign of logical positivism following the publication of A.J. Ayer's *Language, Truth and Logic*.[19] Ayer attempted to eliminate metaphysics by insisting that all philosophy is analysis: but at least the agenda was clear. Today the philosophical agenda is far from clear; we find value in a variety of philosophical frameworks; and Christian apologetics has to fight on so many fronts that it is tempted to retreat into a previous worldview (and often a fourth-century one) and into biblical studies, church history, and liturgy. These are all interesting areas of research, but they are not the apologetics that we need. What is required is a conceptual structure within which we can express Christian believing and everything else, and so within which we can relate Christian believing to everything else and everything else to Christian believing.

I take it as axiomatic that Christian apologetics is the most important task facing Christian theology today; that in order to do apologetics

---

13. Wittgenstein, *Philosophische Untersuchungen / Philosophical Investigations*, § 7, 5; Lyotard, *La Condition Postmoderne*, 20–24.

14. Davison, "Christian Reason and Christian Community," 17.

15. Jacques Derrida's *différance* "n'est pas, n'existe pas, . . . différance . . . se disloque sans cesse dans une chaîne de substitutions différentes"; *différance* "is not, does not exist ..... [It] unceasingly dislocates itself in a chain of differing and deferring solutions": Derrida, *Marges de Philosophie*, 6, 28; *Margins of Philosophy*, 6, 26: so it is an open question as to whether *différance* should appear in a list of philosophical frameworks.

16. Murdoch, *Metaphysics as a Guide to Morals*, 511: "I attach . . . great importance to the concept of a transcendent good as an idea . . . essential to both morality and religion."

17. Davison, "Introduction," xxv–xxvi.

18. Lyotard, *La Condition Postmoderne*, 98.

19. Ayer, *Language, Truth and Logic*.

we need to create, or to rediscover, systematic theologies in tune with our contemporary philosophical diversity; and that in order to do that we need to construct what we might call theological metaphysics that resonate with the philosophical agendas of our time. And further: for the time being, I shall take it that the world in which we live, the philosophy that we do, and the ways in which we think, should for the time being be characterized by diversity and by the dynamic rather than by the unitary and the static, even if we later go on to find new value in a conceptual framework characterized by the unitary and the static.

In defense of the different parts of that statement: Apologetics has always been the most important task facing Christian theology for at least two reasons: a) if we are not doing apologetics, then Christian believing and the Church lose touch with the world around them, and the Christian gospel will be neither proclaimed nor heard; and b) apologetics has always been the womb of Christian theology: the place where the conceptual structures that nurture our faith are given birth. In this sense, all theology is apologetics understood as an ordered defense of the Christian Faith.[20] Not every theologian would agree with this. Donald MacKinnon, who understood religious discourse as "the language which seems to hesitate between the frankly metaphysical and the actually descriptive,"[21] and who believed that a proper task of the philosopher is to understand theological language that tries to reconcile "opposed elements in our spiritual and intellectual inheritance,"[22] nevertheless thought that "apologetic concern . . . is the death of serious theologizing, and . . . equally of serious work in the philosophy of religion."[23] I take the opposite view. Apologetic concern is the birth of serious theologizing, and equally of serious work in the philosophy of religion.

There is of course much good apologetics that is not systematic theology. Poetry, novels, sermons, music, drama, and the visual arts, can all be Christian apologetics. The recent revival of interest in passion plays is particularly welcome.[24] However, if Christian believing and Christian theology are to connect with other conceptual structures, then we need relevant conceptual structures within which to do theology: structures of philosophical and theological ideas that we can find our ways around—"cathedrals of the mind."[25] If we are to construct the kinds of consistent arguments for Chris-

---

20. Milbank, "An Apologia for Apologetics," xvi-xvii.
21. MacKinnon, *The Borderlands of Theology*, 7.
22. MacKinnon, *The Borderlands of Theology*, 18.
23. MacKinnon, *The Borderlands of Theology*, 28.
24. Torry, *Mediating Institutions*, 100, 132–36.
25. Gilson, *The Philosophy of St. Thomas Aquinas*, 193.

tian believing that apologetics has always demanded, then we shall need conceptual structures within which ideas and narratives can connect both with each other and with ideas and narratives in the public realm, and we shall need those conceptual structures to be able to relate constructively to a wide diversity of philosophical, scientific, and other disciplines, however tentative and temporary those structures might have to be. Perhaps more of a marquee than a cathedral.

If the fundamental understanding of reality on which our theologies are built is not that on which the secular world's ideas and narratives are constructed, then communication will not occur: so if our Christian theology is constructed on the basis of the static and the unitary, and the narratives flowing through philosophical, scientific, and other disciplines in the contemporary world are based on an understanding of reality structured around ideas of a diverse and dynamic cosmos, then the theologies that we create, and the narratives and ideas of the world that flow around us, will find few if any points of contact. It is therefore clear that we must do metaphysics: that is, we must study reality itself,[26] and we must employ and elaborate a metaphysic that will do the connecting that we need.

"Metaphysics" means "after physics," but it only got that name because Aristotle wrote his *Metaphysics* after he wrote his *Physics*. "Prophysics" would be a better term—"before physics"—because logically the study of reality itself is the necessary basis for study of any particular reality. Because metaphysics is the science of reality itself, Charles Hartshorne can suggest that metaphysical truths are truths "that no experience can contradict" and that every experience must "illustrate";[27] and that "a metaphysical truth must fit any conceivable experience."[28] And while metaphysics might always of necessity be speculative, we can at least claim—in A.N. Whitehead's words—that "speculative philosophy is the endeavour to frame a coherent, logical, necessary system of general ideas in terms of which every element of our experience can be interpreted."[29] Metaphysics is therefore bound to have considerable practical importance, particularly when, as John Cobb suggests, "reason that is in intention autonomous is employed to construct a conceptual structure within which Christianity might not only survive but also thrive."[30]

---

26. Grayling, "Metaphysics: Introduction," 183: "Metaphysics is the branch of philosophy which is concerned with the ultimate nature of reality."
   27. Harteshorne, *The Logic of Perfection*, 285.
   28. Harteshorne, *Creative Synthesis and Philosophic Method*, 19.
   29. Whitehead, *Process and Reality*, 4; *Process and Reality: corrected edition*, 3.
   30. Cobb, *The Structure of Christian Existence*, 150.

Because it is metaphysics that we need to do, it is the metaphysical aspects of philosophers' work that we shall need to study: that is, those aspects of their philosophy that seek to understand the nature of reality itself. We have done some of that metaphysical work in the book previous to this one in the "Actological Explorations" series: but here we must do some metaphysics more directly related to the apologetic task.

So apologetics is itself theology, and the particular aspect of the apologetic task in which we shall be most interested will be its attempt to create, in company with relevant philosophy, a conceptual structure within which to understand Christian believing, the nature of reality, and the world around us. But how to do that? We shall begin as Paul began in Athens, employing conceptual structures already well developed within our philosophical tradition:[31] so we shall need to do as Maurice Blondel did, and construct out of the philosophical palate of our time a metaphysic—a conceptual structure within which to understand reality—that we can employ to express the Christian Faith in today's world. A hundred years ago Blondel chose an action-centered metaphysic in order to create an apologetics focused on human action, because that was the need at the time. Our world is even more characterized by change, action, movement, the dynamic, and diversity, than was Blondel's, so we would do well to employ his insights as we create our own metaphysic: but however much we shall benefit from philosophy from the past, our world is constantly new, so we shall also need to construct afresh, and that we shall attempt to do as this book progresses.

This all sounds rather systematic, and it is. We might object that a diverse and dynamic world implies that systematic metaphysics, and systematic theologies that we might build on them, are precisely what we do not need in such a situation. I disagree. If we do not construct a systematic, coherent, and relevant understanding of reality, then we shall find ourselves building our theologies on systematic conceptual structures from previous eras, and we shall therefore fail to connect with today's diverse and dynamic conceptual structures. And there is no harm in developing systematic conceptual structures if we recognize that they are necessarily tentative and temporary, and if we are ready to abandon them and to build afresh as soon as that is required, which it soon will be.

Christianity started as a Judaic sect functioning in Aramaic and Hebrew and in relation to Jewish religion and culture, but it soon found itself propelled into a largely Gentile world and functioning in Greek, Latin, and a wide variety of other languages, cultures, and philosophies,

---

31. Acts 17:28.

thus relativizing everything.[32] It is far from insignificant that, unlike the Qur'an, the Christian Bible is translatable. The original Hebrew and Greek remain authoritative, of course, and any good translator will translate out of them: but Jesus' disciples were expected to take the Christian Faith to "all nations,"[33] and therefore to translate the Faith into a variety of nations' languages, and so into their cultures.[34] Sometimes a hegemony has had to be challenged, as when the Reformation challenged the Latin and Thomist hegemony of the medieval Catholic Church, and when the Roman Catholic Church had to fight similar battles at the Second Vatican Council, but generally—even when the Church has infiltrated societies on the coat-tails of armed colonizers—evangelists have attempted to express the Faith in terms of the languages and cultures in which they have found themselves.[35] Lamin Sanneh describes Christianity as a "dynamic translation movement,"[36] and is surely correct when he suggests that translation into a new language always results in "a fresh discourse."[37] When the originally Jewish Church encountered the Gentile world and the Greek language, it could not help encountering Greek philosophy as well: so the Christian Faith could not help being reshaped both by the Greek language and by Greek philosophy. And so with every philosophy and every language: there is no "core" of the Christian Faith that is somehow inviolate. The whole becomes a "fresh discourse." As Hans Küng has recognized, Christianity has passed through a variety of paradigms—the early Christian apocalyptic paradigm; the early church Hellenistic paradigm; the mediaeval Roman Catholic paradigm; the Reformation Protestant paradigm; the Enlightenment modern paradigm; and the contemporary ecumenical paradigm. He identifies an "essence" of Christianity constituted by the recognition of "Jesus the Christ" as the decisive event of revelation and as God's Messiah and Son:[38] but given the radical nature of each paradigm shift and its accompanying shifts in the meanings of words, it is difficult to see how such words as "Christ" and "Son" can be regarded as representing an unchanging "essence." Our task is perhaps even more substantial than we might have thought, because what is now clearly required is a fresh metaphysic that connects both with changing Christian believing and with the changing world in which we live, and

32. Sanneh, *Translating the Message*, 1.
33. Matthew 28:19.
34. Sanneh, *Translating the Message*, 47.
35. Sanneh, *Translating the Message*, 124–25.
36. Sanneh, *Translating the Message*, 175.
37. Sanneh, *Translating the Message*, 192.
38. Küng, *Christianity*.

then an evolving Christian theology—but always one with deep roots in the tradition, just as the metaphysic that we might construct will have deep roots in the Western philosophical tradition and in the now long history of continental philosophy.

There are many ways of categorizing different conceptual or philosophical frameworks: historically; along such spectra as that between realism and nonrealism; or geographically. In the context of this book I shall be employing a "static—dynamic" spectrum,[39] while recognizing that this is only one among many possibilities; and I shall be recognizing that it is a complex spectrum, as we have discovered in other books in the "Actological Explorations" series. In our diverse world we need a variety of different metaphysics, and a variety of theologies, in tune with different points along this spectrum, the points on the spectrum being defined by the degree of reality attributed to the dynamic, and, conversely, the degree of unreality attributed to the static: but that does not mean that we shall not be making a decision as to where to concentrate. For two thousand years the Church has been concentrating its theological efforts between the "static" end of the spectrum and the area around the middle of it, so the "dynamic" end has suffered serious neglect. This is unfortunate, because it is the "dynamic" end that will be particularly relevant to the world in which we live: so the important philosophical task facing us here is the construction of systematic metaphysical structures at the "dynamic" end of the spectrum and then the employment of those structures as we develop an actological theology. Such structures will not of course be all that there is to be said about philosophy or metaphysics, and the theologies that we construct on them will not be the only theologies that we shall need: but the relative philosophical and theological neglect that this end of the spectrum has suffered means that this is where we now need to concentrate our attention.

A "Sainsbury Wing" of a world—one made up, like the Sainsbury's extension to London's National Gallery, of a variety of past and present styles—might require a "Sainsbury Wing" of philosophy and a "Sainsbury Wing" of theology: but we might also need to build a new "cathedral of the mind" at the extreme dynamic end of the static/dynamic spectrum: or at least a marquee that will last long enough to do some useful work.

---

39. Malcolm Torry, "On Completing the Apologetic Spectrum," 108–10.

A BRIEF HISTORY OF APOLOGETICS

Avery Dulles[40] suggests that there are three periods in the history of apologetics. Much early apologetics was defensive, proving that Christianity was not harmful to the State, to public morals, or to the pursuit of truth; subsequent apologetics has generally been "offensive," that is, an attempt to persuade and convert (I prefer the term "positive"); and more recently, apologetics has been aimed at Christians' own doubts. But most apologetics has related to all three tasks, and generally to the pursuit of intellectual honesty; and this is as true of the New Testament as of any other theological literature.

The New Testament

In the apostolic preaching, and thus in the gospels, memories of events, theological reflection on those events, imaginative story-telling, and apologetic arguments, are inextricably combined, and any boundary-drawing would be highly artificial.[41] To take one example: Luke's Gospel could well have been written with a variety of purposes in mind:[42] to defend the Christian Faith against contemporary accusations; to commend the Faith to a cosmopolitan, and particularly to a Gentile and Roman, world; and to ground Christian faith in a history of salvation and thus to answer doubts related to the delay of Christ's second coming. Thus at the beginning of theological history we find all three types of apologetics listed by Dulles.

The Acts of the Apostles contains some explicitly apologetic material,[43] recommending the Faith on the basis of historical events and relating the Christian Faith to the history of Israel and to the prophetic literature. Much of the material of the New Testament letters relates to Christians' theological problems—and so, in 1 Thessalonians 4 and 1 Corinthians 15, Paul deals with problems related to Christians dying before Christ returns; and the letter to the Hebrews is aimed at Christians and others who might need to be convinced that Christian faith both fulfils and replaces the promises and requirements contained in the Hebrew Scriptures.

Thus many of the New Testament documents address Dulles' three apologetic agendas: but this should not be taken to mean that their authors always had clear purposes in mind, nor that we can be sure what they were.

40. Dulles, *A History of Apologetics*, xv.
41. Dulles, *A History of Apologetics*, 2.
42. Evans, *Saint Luke*, 104–11.
43. Acts 2:14–36; 3:11–26; 7:1–53; 10:34–43; 17:16–34.

Dennis Nineham suggests that Mark had no single clear aim in view when he wrote his Gospel,[44] but that it is possible to discover a variety of purposes: for instance, Mark suggested that Jesus was the Messiah understood as a suffering servant rather than as a victorious figure, and that his Messiahship was hidden on purpose—a useful explanation as to why there was no widespread early knowledge of it. Mark wanted to give encouragement to early Christians who were already suffering persecution; he wanted to provide material for preachers who wished to discuss Jesus' humanity; and he wanted to provide liturgical and catechetical material for Christians in Rome, and material for missionary preachers.[45] These and other concerns determined Mark's choice of material, and the order in which he put it. Thus the Gospel, in its content and in its structure, is apologetic.

John's Gospel relates the Christian tradition to a Hellenistic (Greek-influenced) Jewish worldview; the first letter of John and the letter to the Ephesians tackle questions relating to mystery religions; and the Pastoral Epistles (the letters to Timothy and the letters of James and Peter) tackle a variety of theological questions, and particularly those related to persecution.

Further study of the New Testament would reveal that all of it is in some sense apologetic, and theological in that context, rather than theological and therefore apologetic.

The Church Fathers

Justin Martyr's aim was civil tolerance for the Christian religion, and to this end he constructed a theology on the basis of a Platonic *Logos*, a "word" that informs everyone's reason without them knowing it, a "word" that Justin believed had become flesh in Jesus Christ, and thus a "word" that could form a bond between Christ, Christians, and the life of society.[46] John's Gospel had employed *Logos* terminology, but Justin's thoroughgoing Platonic framework (a framework in which the ultimately real is in a different world from the world that we inhabit) gave to Christian theology a Platonic bias from which it has never recovered. Thus a particular apologetic purpose has defined the theological agenda for two thousand years, rather suggesting that a new apologetic purpose will be required if we are to reduce the dominance of Platonic thoughtforms.

---

44. Nineham, *Saint Mark*, 29–34.

45. Cranfield, *The Gospel According to Mark*, 14.

46. Justin Martyr, "First Apology," 46; "Second Apology," 8-10; Stevenson, *A New Eusebius*, 62–69; Daniélou, *A History of Early Christian Doctrine*, vol. II, 40–48.

Clement's outlook was more pastoral, but it was just as Platonic: "The Word was not hidden from any; He is a universal light; He shines on all men . . . let us hasten to salvation, to the new birth. Let us, who are many, haste to be gathered together into one love corresponding to the union of the One Being."[47] Clement's apologetics is defensive (he defends Christians against the charge of atheism); it is positive, recommending faith in Jesus the "minstrel" (for music was an important element in the Greek culture of the time); and it employs Old and New Testament material against other religions, partly in order to strengthen Christians' faith.

Much of Origen's apologetics was defensive and mainly against Celsus's attacks on the Christian Faith: for instance, in answer to the accusation that the Christians had plagiarized Greek philosophers, Origen suggested that the Christian Faith and earlier philosophers agreed, not because Christians had plagiarized the philosophers, but because God had already revealed to the philosophers, by his *Logos*, "Word," what he was later to reveal through his Son Jesus. None of this, however, is purely defensive: it is also positive pastoral theology, intended to promote the spiritual growth of the Church.[48]

The greatest early apologist was Augustine, and it is largely from him that we learn our own strategy: the creation of a conceptual framework, from within which we can understand the Christian tradition and relate it to the world that we live in and to the people that we are. In one sense, the process was easier for Augustine than it is for us. Platonism was the philosophical air that he breathed.[49] Earlier in his life Augustine had attached himself to a Manichaean sect: followers of Mani who believed our task and destiny to be to escape from this world into another, spiritual world—a highly Platonic religion. Augustine immersed himself in neoplatonic philosophy, and then converted to the Christian Faith: but in one sense there was no conversion, because the Manichean religion, Platonism, and the Christian tradition to which Augustine attached himself, all assumed a realm of reality more important than this world of our experience. Significant biblical passages for Augustine were 2 Cor. 4:18: "We look not at what can be seen but at what cannot be seen; for what can be seen is temporary, but what cannot be seen is eternal"; and 1 John 2:15: "Do not love the world or the things in the world.

---

47. Clement, "Protrepticus," 195.

48. Origen, *Contra Celsum*; Monaci Castagno, "Origen the Scholar and Pastor", 75: "In the homilies, the allegorical interpretation was only partly in function of the construction of a theological system; it was used above all to build up an immense symbolic repertory of the spiritual growth of the soul, its progressive detachment from passions, and its drawing closer to God."

49. Augustine, *Confessions*, 152–55.

The love of the Father is not in those who love the world."[50] But following his conversion the Platonism was tempered with a sense of history: and it is from the existence and experience of the Church that Augustine argues for the historicity of Jesus' resurrection; it is from prophecy's fulfilment that he argues for Christian faith; and it is from the history of God's relationship with Israel and the Church that he argues against paganism.[51] However, the Platonic framework takes over again when Augustine insists that we can know nothing until God enlightens our minds with knowledge of the eternal realm. The Church, the Bible, and our own experience are certainly authorities, but their witness is to an unchanging and superior world, and they are not fundamentally about this one: and in Augustine's magisterial *City of God*, a Platonist dualism is clear in the distinction between the City of God and the City of this world.[52]

As Dulles says,

> with Clement and Origen, and even more with Eusebius, Theodoret and Augustine, the overriding problem concerns the relationship between Christianity and Platonism in its various forms. The leading apologists are almost unanimous in opting for a synthesis of Biblical faith with classical culture.[53]

The danger of this approach, as Dulles sees it, is an individualistic and otherworldly religion that risks not representing the world-changing nature of the gospel: but at least these early apologists were trying to connect the gospel with reality as they understood it: that is, they were doing apologetics, as Dulles concludes:

> Christian apologists must remain eternally indebted to the Fathers of the Church for their boldness in seeking to relate the Biblical revelation to the whole of human culture, human philosophy, and human history.[54]

The middle ages

Anselm's (1033-1109) ontological argument for God's existence assumes that God's existence needs to be proved by rational means, and is thus a

---

50. 2 Cor. 4:18; 1 John 2:15, NRSV; Augustine, *Of True Religion*, 1:4.
51. Augustine, *Of True Religion*, 3:5; *City of God*, xxii, 5.
52. Augustine, *City of God*.
53. Dulles, *A History of Apologetics*, 71.
54. Dulles, *A History of Apologetics*, 71.

new turn in apologetics, for it gives to our reason an authority greater than other more traditional authorities. The argument goes: If God is that than which nothing greater can be conceived, then God must exist, for to exist is greater than not to exist.[55] The argument fails because existence is not a predicate. It is true that an argument for necessary existence does succeed, for that can be regarded as a predicate: but this only proves that if God exists then God exists necessarily, which does not prove God's existence. Even though both forms of the argument fail, they set the agenda for all subsequent apologetics, an agenda that the thirteenth century Thomas Aquinas pursued when he formulated his cosmological and teleological arguments for God's existence. The cosmological argument argues that everything has a cause, so there must be a cause of the universe as a whole, and this cause must be God; and the teleological argument finds design in the world, concludes that there must therefore be a designer, and decides that this is God.[56] But neither of these arguments can do more than merely suggest that there might be a first cause and a designer: there can be no proof, as either the first cause is in this world, and thus itself needs a cause, or it is not in this world and thus cannot cause anything in it; and in any case, the cause and the designer are not necessarily the supreme being, for whose existence the ontological argument is needed.[57]

Aquinas thought that the ontological, cosmological, and design arguments succeeded, but he knew that this was not sufficient support for Christian apologetics in an era when people were beginning to question the Church's prominent position in society, and in which universities were being founded and the natural sciences were being pursued largely independently of the Church's authority. Aristotle's philosophy became available via Arabic philosophical literature, and Aquinas employed many of Aristotle's concepts to construct systematic theology that would nourish believers' faith and defend Christian Faith against attack from a variety of religious and secular positions. An important element in Aquinas's apologetics was the distinction that he drew between truths known by reason (truths that include God's existence) and truths known by revelation (for instance, the doctrine of the Trinity).[58] Thus reason is an autonomous authority within its own sphere of interest, and the Scriptures and the Church are another within their sphere of interest, with the Bible being used to complete a worldview based on

55. Descartes, *Meditations*, 3, in *Discourse on Method*, 117–33; Hick, *Arguments for the Existence of God*; Barth, *Anselm*.

56. Kenny, *The Five Ways*.

57. Kant, *The Critique of Pure Reason*, The Transcendental Dialectic, Book II, chapter 3, "The Ideal of Pure Reason."

58. Copleston, *Aquinas*, 111–55; Gilson, *The Philosophy of St. Thomas Aquinas*.

Aristotle and his Arabian commentators. In one sense this is not apologetics, for it distances the Christian tradition (known by revelation) from the intellectual environment of the time (the sphere of reason), thus formalizing a divide that had always existed to some extent, but which previous apologists had attempted to bridge. Now Aquinas had located the divide at the heart of theology, thus marginalizing apologetics and compounding the difficulties which apologists were to experience during the next five hundred years as they struggled to catch up with a fast-changing world in which neither blind faith (such as Pascal's "the heart has its reasons") nor quasimathematical proofs were likely to be persuasive.

The modern period

As we approach the modern period, we find the Cambridge Platonists in the seventeenth century returning to an earlier strategy by attempting to relate the Christian tradition to contemporary concerns with reason and morality by expounding a Platonist God revealed through the use of human reason and served through moral effort. As John Smith put it,

> Seek for God within thine own soul . . . God runs through all created Essence, containing the Archetypal Ideal of all things in himself . . . A soul that is truly God-like, a Mind that is enlightened from the same Fountain, and hath its myriad senses affected with the sweet relishes of Divine Goodness, cannot but everywhere behold itself in the midst of that Glorious Unbounded Being who is indivisibly everywhere.[59]

William Paley and Bishop Butler revived teleological arguments for God's existence that David Hume then dismissed;[60] during the nineteenth century, Friedrich Schleiermacher employed the notion of "dependence" in order to do apologetics among the "cultured despisers of religion";[61] Maurice Blondel, as well as exploring the notion of "action," created apologetics around our desire for fulfilment and our inability to satisfy that desire;[62] and Søren Kierkegaard recommended a "leap of faith" and strove for a radical distinction between Christian faith and objectivity. For Kierkegaard, we

---

59. Smith, *Select Discourses*, 2–3, 434.
60. Hume, *Dialogues Concerning Natural Religion*.
61. Schleiermacher, *The Christian Faith*; Sykes, *Friedrich Schleiermacher*, 29.
62. Blondel, *L'Action*; *Action*.

cannot talk about Christianity, only about being a Christian: Christianity is a mystery to be lived, and not something to be understood.[63]

Rudolf Bultmann was an important exponent of existentialist theology: that is, like Kierkegaard, he regarded faith as "decision," and believed there to be a qualitative distinction between God and any understanding that we might have of God. Thus revelation comes as "God's word," and this word is an event summoning us to "authentic existence": Heidegger's phrase. The decision is a gift, as is God's word, and is not something that we can isolate and discuss as an object. Bultmann believed that by demythologizing the Bible's message—that is, by freeing it from its mythological first-century language—we can make revelation's character clearer to our world.

Bultmann believed that Heidegger's treatment of *Dasein* ("being-there") in his *Being and Time*[64] offered an understanding of humanity that Christian theology can employ in order to do apologetics. Some questions arise: Is Heidegger's description of "authentic" and "inauthentic" existence an accurate expression of the way that we live? If not, can we use this terminology to do apologetics? If the answers to both of these questions is "yes," then are we still relating to the Christian tradition? Bultmann's ambiguous use of important theological terms such as "Jesus" suggests that his theology is not apologetics, because at any one time it relates either to our world, or to the Christian tradition, but not to both.[65]

Theologians before and since Bultmann have employed the language of contemporary philosophy in order to make connections.[66] However, philosophical language games are restricted to religious and academic élites, they change, and they are frequently themselves disconnected from other language games: and perhaps more seriously, the concepts and structures within which the Christian Faith are expressed can end up betraying it: so at both ends the apologetics relationship might be broken. Bultmann's existentialism, focused on the individual's decision-making in the present, was only a partial reflection of German and French culture, and an extremely partial one of British culture, so his apologetics never achieved widespread consent: and neither could it handle the importance of history to the Christian tradition. This is not to say that Bultmann's attempt to rebuild Christian

---

63. Kierkegaard, *Concluding Unscientific Postscript*; Perkins, *Søren Kierkegaard*.

64. Heidegger, *Being and Time*; Torry, *Actological Readings in Continental Philosophy*, 72–96.

65. Torry, "Two Kinds of Ambiguity"; Bultmann, *Essays Philosophical and Theological*, 133; Bultmann, *Faith and Understanding*, 265; Roberts, *Rudolf Bultmann's Theology*, 105–7.

66. Bultmann, *Existence and Faith*, 288; Bultmann, *Faith and Understanding*; MacQuarrie, *An Existentialist Theology*.

theology around a new philosophical framework was not a significant project. It was: and while this book might be looking in very different philosophical directions, it follows Bultmann's strategy of seeking a conceptual framework within which the Christian tradition can connect with the world in which we live.

John MacQuarrie, like Bultmann, valued Heidegger's philosophy, but for him the important part was the part for which the material on *Dasein* was intended to be the preliminaries, but which Heidegger never completed: the work on "Being." For MacQuarrie, Being is not a being: it is the ground of being, and that to which all beings relate. It is a "letting be."[67] By this means, MacQuarrie hoped to bring Christian talk about God into the twentieth century. The concepts are interesting, and offer us an "ontological" rather than an "existentialist" theology,[68] but they do not relate well to how we see the world, or to the Christian tradition, unless that tradition is identified with its strong Platonic strain—in which case we are no nearer to freeing the tradition from its dominant and somewhat debilitating Platonism than we were before MacQuarrie wrote.

The same might be said of Teilhard de Chardin's seminal work,[69] in which the "Omega point" towards which the universe is evolving is best viewed as a scientific hypothesis. Teilhard's achievement is an overall vision that encompasses the material world, living beings, the human mind, and potentially God, in an evolutionary scheme influenced by Maurice Blondel:[70] but about the Omega point Teilhard himself asked whether this was still the Christ of the gospels or some other.[71] The vision gives theological significance to the secular, and secular significance to the theological, and thus creates the conditions for an apologetics that is a dialogue between the Christian tradition and a secular world: but unless there is a conceptual framework within which the Omega point can make sense in our world, rather than in some future world, the apologetics is still missing an essential connection.

There was much popular apologetics during the twentieth century: from Geoffrey Studdert Kennedy with his "comrade God,"[72] through C.S.

---

67. MacQuarrie, *Principles of Christian Theology*, 105–10.
68. MacQuarrie, *An Existentialist Theology*.
69. Teilhard de Chardin, *The Phenomenon of Man* 283–86.
70. King, *Christ in All Things*, 70.
71. Jacques Maritain, *The Peasant of the Garonne*, New York: 1968, translated by Michael Cuddily and Elizabeth Hughes from *Le Paysan de la Garonne*, Paris: 1966, 23, quoted in Dulles, *A History of Apologetics*, 224–25.
72. Studdert Kennedy, *The Unutterable Beauty*, 30–31.

Lewis with his allegorical tales,[73] to Billy Graham with his appeal to our sense of guilt,[74] and the Alpha Course's[75] invitation to belonging and to certainty. But there has also been plenty of reflection on the method of apologetics, and particularly on the relationship between fact and interpretation. As Dulles suggests,

> the twentieth century has seen more clearly than previous periods that apologetics stands or falls with the question of method. In the past few decades apologetical science has merged to an increasing degree with the epistemology of religious knowledge. It is in this difficult area that the most important work remains to be done:[76]

and it is in this difficult area that Tom Roberts explores the relationship between historical method and Christian faith, for "if some or all of the events upon which Christianity has been traditionally thought to be based could be proved unhistorical, then the religious claims of Christianity would be seriously jeopardized."[77] Herbert Butterfield expresses the relationship between Christianity and history in more positive terms:

> Christianity is an historical religion . . . it presents us with religious doctrines which are at the same time historical events or historical interpretations. In particular it confronts us with the questions of the Incarnation, the Crucifixion and the Resurrection, questions which may transcend all the apparatus of the scientific historian—as indeed many other things do—but which imply that Christianity in any of its traditional and recognizable forms has rooted its most characteristic and daring assertions in that ordinary realm of history with which the technical student is concerned.[78]

It is the positive relationship between Christianity and history that makes apologetics possible, and the problems that historical methods have with unique events that make the relationship between historical study and Christian faith problematic and therefore apologetics somewhat difficult.

---

73. Lewis, *The Lion, the Witch and the Wardrobe*, and several others by the same author.
74. Graham, *Peace with God*.
75. Alpha International.
76. Dulles, *A History of Apologetics*, 246.
77. Roberts, *History and Christian Apologetics*, vii.
78. Butterfield, *Christianity and History*, 3.

If Karl Barth is an apologist—and it might be that his theological position, even more than Bultmann's, rules out connections between our reason and God's revelation, and so precludes apologetics as a possibility—then he takes a very different attitude to historical method. For Barth, it is God's freedom that establishes the Scriptures as the bearer of revelation,[79] so any connection with events in history becomes somewhat less relevant. There is thus a pre-eminent story for Barth, and other worldviews must be measured against it, which again makes apologetics difficult, for apologetics requires some kind of positive relationship between Christian faith and a variety of worldviews.

Alister McGrath, a theologian in the British evangelical tradition, has taken seriously two of the strands within apologetics introduced at the beginning of this chapter. For him, Christian apologetics is "a presentation and defence of [the Christian Faith's] claims to truth and relevance in the great market-place of ideas."[80] Different cultures define different gaps between Christian faith and culture, and so different "points of contact" must be used in order to construct bridges. McGrath suggests "a sense of unsatisfied longing," "the ordering of the world," "human morality," "existential anxiety and alienation," and "awareness of finitude and mortality," as points of contact in our culture, and that the apologist's task is to find related points of contact in the Christian tradition and then to build bridges—as if Christian faith is itself a conceptual framework that remains permanently the same, unaffected by shifting cultures and languages. Thus "enlightenment rationalism" is a rival to Christian faith, suggesting that Christian faith is its own conceptual framework; and similarly with "postmodernism":

> Sadly, the intellectual shallowness of much postmodernism perhaps obliges the apologist to stoop low in order to respond. Happily, there are indications that postmodernism is unlikely to remain a significant feature of our cultural landscape. But while it does, the apologist must be able to respond to its outlook.[81]

But even if "postmodernism" as a movement ceases to be part of the landscape, it will leave behind its effects, just as glaciers leave behind glacial valleys. Nothing will ever be the same again. The medieval systematic theologies, the "cathedrals of the mind,"[82] that McGrath hankers after, are gone forever; and if someone wants to be an apologist then they will need to

---

79. Ford, *Barth and God's Story*, 138.
80. McGrath, *Bridge-building*, 9.
81. McGrath, *Bridge-building*, 229.
82. Gilson, *The Philosophy of St. Thomas Aquinas*, 193.

recognize that the task is to relate the Christian tradition to contemporary culture if the tradition is to be expressed in terms of that culture and not in opposition to it: otherwise the tradition will not connect with our life today, there will be little "transformative potential,"[83] and there will be no real apologetics.

Diogenes Allen is more positive towards postmodernism, believing that it opens the way for reappropriation of traditional beliefs and morality. He thus offers "a case for the truth of Christian belief, without directly examining and refuting the various reasons people have today for becoming relativists."[84] But relativism is part of the culture that we inhabit, and if apologetics does not connect with it positively, then it won't be apologetics. Allen's argument is

> that the natural world's existence and order point to the possibility of God; that our own needs, unless deliberately restrained, lead us to search for what is ultimate; and that conviction concerning the reality of God comes from the actual experience of divine grace, frequently made possible through the witness of the Bible and a believing community.[85]

This could have been an argument employed by Augustine—but we are not living in Augustine's times, and new expressions of the Christian Faith are now needed, based on a conceptual framework informed by the world in which we live, a framework that might act as the map on which we might be able to locate the points in the tradition and in our world through which bridges might be built.

The diversity of the agenda that the Church faces as it contemplates its mission is well recognized by David Bosch, who regards the situation as a "crisis": that is, as both dangerous and an opportunity. He knows that there has been a paradigm shift in our understanding of ourselves, of the nature of reality, and of the world that we live in, but suggests that there have been paradigm shifts before and that the Church's mission has generally adapted successfully.[86] The new pluralism means that the Church's mission must be as diverse as human experience,[87] and Bosch offers a list of actions that the Church might take as it becomes a Church for others, seeks justice, undertakes evangelism, contextualizes itself and its message, liberates the oppressed, and co-operates with others with similar agendas.

83. Gilson, *The Philosophy of St. Thomas Aquinas*, 265.
84. Allen, *Christian Belief in a Postmodern World*, 9.
85. Allen, *Christian Belief in a Postmodern World*, 19.
86. Bosch, *Transforming Mission*, 4.
87. Bosch, *Transforming Mission*, 10.

"Mission is 'Action in Hope.'"[88] Yes: but the strictly apologetic agenda has still not been addressed in relation to the paradigm shift that Bosch has correctly identified.

An instructive piece of apologetics in action is that undertaken by Vincent Donovan among the Masai: instructive because cross-cultural in ways in which much of the apologetics that we have studied has not been. Here we have a three-cornered relationship: Donovan's culture; the Masai culture; and the Christian tradition. In this context, and more generally, Donovan believes that what is required is apologetics "undertaken by a gospel-oriented community, of transcultural vision, with a special mandate, charism, and responsibility of spreading and carrying that gospel to the nations of the world, with a view of establishing the Church of Christ";[89] and he knows that whatever is being done should always be questioned and revised, and that in the process of evangelization the evangelist is changed, the Masai are changed, and the Christian Faith is changed—though he would not have put it quite like that.

CONCLUSIONS

It is always risky to express the Christian Faith within new conceptual structures, because doing so affects the very heart of the Christian Faith. There is no impermeable boundary between doctrine and apologetics. And so, for instance, "of the same substance,"[90] which was a new theological concept not found in the New Testament, was employed by early Christian councils to express the divinity of Jesus Christ in a way that would unite bishops who differed over the relationship between Jesus and God. This would have been useful apologetics at the time:[91] but we are still saying "of the same substance"[92] over one and a half millennia later, even though almost nobody now understands the nuances of the term "substance" as it was used then. We are constantly in need of new concepts that connect with contemporary thought-forms, of which philosophy can sometimes be a useful barometer, and that at the same time both connect with and develop Christian doctrine. Throughout this chapter we have found the concepts of diversity, action, and patterns evidenced in the stream of Western philosophy, and we have

---

88. Bosch, *Transforming Mission*, 498.

89. Donovan, *Christianity Rediscovered*, 194.

90. *homoousion*, the neuter form of *homoousios*, is formed out of *homos*, "same," and *ousía*, "substance."

91. Stevenson *A New Eusebius*, 358–68.

92. *ousia*, "substance": *homoousion*, "of the same substance."

occasionally found them helpful as we have tried to express the life of the universe, society, individuals, and God. More such concepts will be needed as the world changes, and only widespread experiment will yield results.

As we have seen, during both the medieval and the modern periods arguments for the existence of God have been significant elements of the apologetic tradition. Do we still need them? The actology with which we are now operating suggests not. If God is a verb, and if God is grace, and if God is action in changing patterns as well as being Action and the source of all action, then there is no thing to exist: there is action and not substance. If the verb is the primary building-block of language, then we can say "God is no thing," "God is grace," and "God is love," and we can find the question "Does God exist?" an impossible question to ask as well as to answer. It is the Action and the diverse action in changing patterns that constitute God that we need to communicate within a world characterized by action, change, and diversity.

Chapter 2

Connections
Apologetics and theology

Thesis: An actological apologetics implies and generates an actological theology.

INTRODUCTION

In this chapter we shall develop further our discussion of apologetics by asking about its connections with theology. Maurice Blondel's early book *L'Action* was in many ways the inspiration for the ideas behind the first book in the "Actological Explorations" series, *Actology: Action, Change and Diversity in the Western Philosophical Tradition*, and in this chapter we shall employ his *Letter on Apologetics* to stimulate our discussion of the relationship between theology and apologetics.

BLONDEL ON APOLOGETICS

In 1896 Maurice Blondel, whose philosophy of action we study in *Actology: Action, Change and Diversity in the Western Philosophical Tradition*, wrote a *Lettre sur les Exigences de la Pensée Contemporaine en Matière d'Apologétique et sur la Méthode de la Philosophie dans l'Étude du Problème Religieux:*[1] a

---

1. Blondel, *Lettre sur les Exigences de la Pensée Contemporaine*, 5–95.

title generally translated into English as the *Letter on Apologetics*,[2] because that was the major concern of this rather long letter to the Director of the *Annales de Philosophie Chrétienne*. Here we do not need to recount the detail of the debate to which this "letter" contributed: but what we shall be interested in is Blondel's discussion of the relationship between philosophy and apologetics, because that might inform the task that this book is tackling.

Blondel sets out from six related axioms:

- science is not directly useful to either philosophy or theology;
- we cannot turn historical facts into apologetic proofs;[3]
- any moral argument for Christianity "lacks demonstrable force for the unbeliever" but can be "convincing for the believer";[4]
- faith is a gift, so no apologetics can communicate or create it.[5]
- But that leaves the relationship between religion and philosophy still to be determined "[since] religion is not to be simply a philosophy, and philosophy is not to be absorbed in any way by religion." [6]
- The only relationship possible is that philosophy sees the supernatural as necessary but impracticable for us. "The one [theology] declares to be gratuitously given what the other [philosophy] can only postulate ... so that they coincide not by overlapping but because one is empty and the other full."[7]

Blondel believes that for the philosopher the supernatural "appears indispensable and at the same time inaccessible."[8] According to Blondel, there is no such thing as a Christian philosophy in the sense of an amalgam of philosophy and Christian theology.[9] Philosophy's role is to understand

2. Blondel, *The Letter on Apologetics*.

3. Blondel, *Lettre sur les Exigences de la Pensée Contemporain*, 9–10; Blondel, *The Letter on Apologetics*, 132–33.

4. "*pour l'incroyant . . . est destituée de force démonstrative, pour le croyant elle doit être probante*": Blondel, *Lettre sur les Exigences de la Pensée Contemporain*, 20; Blondel, *The Letter on Apologetics*, 139.

5. Blondel, *Lettre sur les Exigences de la Pensée Contemporain*, 13; Blondel, *The Letter on Apologetics*, 134.

6. Blondel, *Lettre sur les Exigences de la Pensée Contemporain*, 34; Blondel, *The Letter on Apologetics*, 151.

7. Blondel, *Lettre sur les Exigences de la Pensée Contemporain*, 42; Blondel, *The Letter on Apologetics*, 160.

8. *apparaît comme « nécessaire » en même temps qu'inaccessible*: Blondel, *Lettre sur les Exigences de la Pensée Contemporain*, 43; Blondel, *The Letter on Apologetics*, 161.

9. Blondel, *Lettre sur les Exigences de la Pensée Contemporain*, 54; Blondel, *The*

thought and action, to recognize that its conclusions are insufficient, to open us up to the possibility of Christian faith, and then to leave the field clear for Christian theology.[10] Theology begins where philosophy finds itself inadequate. However, Blondel also recognizes that once theology is filling the gap left by philosophy, philosophy still retains a role. We still need to understand theology, and we need to understand our actions in the light of that theology—faith needs reason just as much as reason needs faith[11]— and it is entirely understandable that the philosophy with which Blondel reasoned about Christian theology should now be understood as an attempt at Christian philosophy.[12]

Theological philosophy / philosophical theology

When we compare what we have discovered about Blondel's philosophy of action and his theology in *L'Action* and *L'Être et les Êtres*[13] with what he writes in the *Letter on Apologetics*, we discover that the philosophy and the theology inform each other rather than the theology determining the philosophy in a unidirectional manner. While the steps that Blondel takes from his philosophical study of action to his discussion of Christian theology, and from his later study of beings and Being to Christian theology, could be interpreted as driven by Christian theology rather than by the philosophy of action that had led him to the threshold of Christian faith, the way in which God coheres with the action-shaped philosophy that preceded the theological steps suggests that the philosophy was in practice at least influencing, if not determining, the theology, and was not simply using philosophical methods as a means of understanding. And similarly: the choices that Blondel made over which philosophical ideas and language to employ had roots in the theology that he intended to write. All of this is surely inevitable. If the same person is doing both philosophy and theology, and if the same language is being used for both philosophy and theology, then there will inevitably be a complex and intimate relationship between the theology and the philosophy, and that relationship will reach into the

---

Letter on Apologetics, 171.

10. Blondel, *Lettre sur les Exigences de la Pensée Contemporain*, 66–70; Blondel, *The Letter on Apologetics*, 181–84.

11. Blondel, *Lettre sur les Exigences de la Pensée Contemporain*, 80–81; Blondel, *The Letter on Apologetics*, 193.

12. English, *The Possibility of Christian Philosophy*.

13. Torry, *Actology*, 103–13.

deep roots of both disciplines. Andrew Davison might wish the theology to rule the philosophy,[14] and he is surely right to suggest that

> apologetics concerns faith's appeal to reason . . . [and so] requires a Christian understanding of reason . . . a theological account of reason is part of what we offer with the gospel . . . [and so] a new way to understand everything:[15]

but our theological language is inevitably shaped by the philosophical currents of our own and of previous eras: a process that we might wish to understand, but not one from which we would ever be able to escape. The philosophy of which Blondel and every theologian makes use will be chosen largely for theological reasons,[16] and, in relation to Blondel's philosophy, to understand beings, Being, and all of reality, in terms of action, and then to use "action" language of God, will be bound to create a theology largely shaped by a philosophy of action.

However, theology and philosophy are still not the same. They start out from different presuppositions, and their methods, although similar, are not identical. As each of them steps further into the other's territory, their statements will inevitably become increasingly analogical and therefore tentative. The same is true of every other relationship between theology and another discipline—for instance, between theology and the physical or biological sciences, between theology and history, and between theology and such social sciences as psychology and sociology. This makes the apologist's task difficult, to say the least: for it is precisely across such complex relationships, and on the contested and shifting boundaries between theology and other disciplines, that apologetics needs to be done; and because apologetics is where theology is given birth, the essentially tentative and ambivalent nature of apologetics will give to theology the same tentative and ambivalent character. As John Milbank puts it:

> Apologetics . . . lies at the heart of faith and of theology . . . and . . . it introduces into that heart something complexly cautious and even ambivalent.[17]

According to the Acts of the Apostles, when Paul was doing apologetics in Athens, he quoted from the two Greek poets Epimenides and Aratus: "in

14. Davison, "Introduction," xxvii.
15. Davison, "Introduction," xxv.
16. I am not aware of anyone choosing logical positivism as a basis for theological construction—which is not to say that there has been no discussion of the relationship between logical positivism and theology: Price, "Logical Positivism and Theology."
17. Milbank, "An Apologia for Apologetics," xvii.

[him] we live and move and have our being," and "we too are his offspring."[18] This is true apologetics: the building of connections between Christian theology and a philosophical tradition, to the benefit and the complexification of both. The apologists of the next couple of centuries followed suit. Justin Martyr's First and Second Apologies[19] were designed to recommend Christians to the Roman Empire as virtuous and godly citizens, and one of the methods employed was to connect the Christian Faith to contemporary culture. A particularly clear example is the connection that Justin Martyr drew between the New Testament use of "Word," *Logos*, and Greek philosophy's use of the same idea. According to Justin, *Logos*, the "Word," was a "seed," *sperma*, "implanted," *emphutos*, in the whole human race, and so was available to Greek Philosophers as well as being the Word incarnate in Jesus Christ. The philosophers only knew *apo merous*, "in part," and what they knew they had learnt from Moses in Egypt (including the Platonic Forms[20]): but still, the *Logos* was a useful point of contact between the culture of the day and the Christian Faith.[21] Alfred North Whitehead wrote that "the safest general characterization of the European philosophical tradition is that it consists of a series of footnotes to Plato,"[22] and Keith Ward wonders whether Christian theology might also be termed "a series of footnotes to Plato." He decides against, but recognizes that the Christian tradition has been heavily influenced by Plato and his followers, and he does not find that problematic.[23] Sebastian Kim finds that the ways in which the Bible has been understood in Africa, India, and Korea, have been largely determined by those countries' cultures and philosophies. Such cultural and philosophical determination of Christian theology would appear to be simply a fact.[24] However, the question arises as to whether the way in which Christian apologists framed their theology in terms of Greek thought-forms has enabled

---

18. Acts 17:28, NRSV: Epimenides' *Krētica* has to be reconstructed from Latin translations. Rendel Harris's reconstruction of the original Greek text of "for in you we live and move and have our being" is *en gar soi zōmen kai kinumethēde kai esmen*. See Harris, "A Further Note on the Cretans," 336; "St. Paul and Epimenides," 350. "For we also are his offspring" is from Aratus, *Phaenomena*, I. The Greek text reads *tou gar kai genos*: the *tou* refers to *Dios*, normally translated "Zeus."

19. Justin, "First and Second Apologies."

20. Justin, "Hortatory Address to the Greeks," 285; "Second Apology," quoted in Daniélou, *A History of Early Christian Doctrine*, 43.

21. Justin, "Second Apology," quoted in Daniélou, *A History of Early Christian Doctrine*, 41–42.

22. Whitehead, *Process and Reality*, 63; Whitehead, *Process and Reality: Corrected edition*, 39.

23. Ward, "Plato and his Legacy."

24. Kim, *Theology in the Public Sphere*, 27–56.

those thought-forms to distort the Christian gospel. The third century theologian Tertullian thought so. In his *De Praescriptione Haereticorum* he discusses the Greek philosophers Heraclitus, Plato, Zeno, and Aristotle, and those Christian theologians influenced by them, and then he asks:

> What then has Athens in common with Jerusalem? What has the Academy in common with the Church?[25] What have heretics in common with Christians? Our principles are from the "Porch" of Solomon,[26] who himself handed down that the Lord must be sought in simplicity of heart.[27] Away with those who bring forward a Stoic or Platonic or dialectic Christianity. We have no need of speculative inquiry after we have known Christ Jesus; nor of search for the Truth after we have received the Gospel. When we become believers, we have no desire to believe anything besides; for the first article of our belief is that there is nothing besides which we ought to believe.[28]

We might find ourselves in agreement with Tertullian if we study the way in which the concept of a "soul" has come to occupy an important place in Christian doctrine. A separable soul is not a biblical idea: it is an idea that developed within Greek philosophy. Take, for example this passage in Plato's *Phaedo*:

> We believe, do we not, that death is the separation of the soul from the body, and that the state of being dead is the state in which the body is separated from the soul and exists alone by itself and the soul is separated from the body and exists alone by itself? Is death anything other than this?[29]

By the fifth century we find the apologist Theodoret asking us to "learn the truth of the divine teachings: the body's formation by God, the immortal nature of the soul."[30] Tertullian would have had nothing to do with such apologetics, and neither should we—except as an object lesson in how philosophy-driven apologetics can come to contradict the Christian Faith. However, it is not always obvious when we have crossed that line, and, if we do cross it, whether we have crossed it in a place that matters. Sometimes

---

25. Tertullian is replicating the literary structure of 1 Corinthians 1:20 and 2 Corinthians 6:14–16.
26. John 10:23; Acts 3:2, 12.
27. Wisdom of Solomon, 1:1.
28. Tertullian, *On the Prescription of Heretics*, 7–13.
29. Plato, *Phaedo*, 64c, 4–9.
30. Theodoret, "Apology."

it will not be clear that an important line has been crossed until much later. This means that any attempt to do apologetics will run the risk that our employment of conceptual structures relevant to the world in which we live will result in distortions of the Faith, and that that risk is unavoidable. However much apologetics might take us into complex and often compromising territory, not to do apologetics would consign the Christian Faith and the Church to complete irrelevance: which is why apologetics has always been something that the Church does. To do apologetics, along with all of its risks, both donates remarkable gifts to numerous disciplines, and to the world around us, and at the same time provides theology with a constant supply of new directions to follow.[31] And here by "theology" I do not mean simply systematic theology. René Descartes wrote his *Meditationes*, which contain a proof for the existence of God, for two purposes that in his mind were intimately related: as apologetics, and as devotional theology: so at the end of the third Meditation he writes this:

> But before I examine this with more attention, and pass on to the consideration of other truths that may be evolved out of it, I think it proper to remain here for some time in the contemplation of God himself—that I may ponder at leisure his marvellous attributes—and behold, admire, and adore the beauty of this light so unspeakably great, as far, at least, as the strength of my mind, which is to some degree dazzled by the sight, will permit.[32]

So we must commit ourselves, knowing the risks, and knowing that neither philosophy nor theology, nor any relationship between them, can say all that there is to be said about God, about the universe that we live in, or about ourselves. What theology and philosophy might be able to achieve is to deliver a conceptual structure that can both facilitate future apologetics and perhaps take us on a journey into the foothills of the mystery of God.

Whether Blondel is right when he suggests that the journey begins philosophically and ends theologically, we can perhaps say that the beginning of the journey on which this book will take us will be more philosophical than theological, and that the journey might become more theological than philosophical by the end: but, as Blondel suggests, it will remain philosophical throughout, and, because we shall be doing philosophy because we want to do theology, it will be theological throughout as well. In that spirit, we shall embark on a journey into a theology informed by a philosophy of Action, action, change, and diversity, and see where that takes us, but

---

31. Conrad, "Moments and Themes in the History of Apologetics."
32. Descartes, *Meditationes de Prima Philosophia*, Meditation III, §39.

not with any confidence that either our theological or our philosophical language will be adequate to the task, and in the constant knowledge of the risks that we shall be taking. As Hilary of Poitiers has put it:

> The errors of heretics and blasphemers force us to deal with unlawful matters, to scale perilous heights, to speak unutterable words, to trespass on forbidden ground. By faith alone we must constantly fulfil the commandments to worship the Father, to venerate with him the Son, always abounding in the Spirit: but at the same time we must stretch our inadequate language into the inexpressible, and add our own errors to those of others, as we risk putting into human words what should remain hidden in the soul.[33]

As we undertake this journey, we might find not only that apologetics and theology framed in terms of action categories can relate to the changing world in which we live, but also that "apologetics" changes its meaning in a similar direction: that is, it becomes more about human action and less about word-based theology. It is possible to identify shifts in the questions addressed by contemporary apologetics, from "Is it true?" to "Does it work?" to "Why should I care?"[34] It is the first of those shifts in which

---

33. Hilary of Poitiers, *De Trinitate*, II. 2: "Sed compellimur haereticorum et blasphemantium vitiis, illicita agere, ardua scandere, ineffabilia eloqui, inconcessa praesumere. Et cum sola fide expleri quae praecepta sunt oporteret, adorare videlicet Patrem, et venerari cum eo Filium, sancto Spiritu abundare; cogimur sermonis nostri humilitatem ad ea quae inenarrabilia sunt extendere, et in vitium vitio coartamur alieno: ut quae contineri religione mentium oportuissent, nunc in periculum humani eloquii proferantur." The *New Advent* website of Catholic resources translates the passage thus: "But the errors of heretics and blasphemers force us to deal with unlawful matters, to scale perilous heights, to speak unutterable words, to trespass on forbidden ground. Faith ought in silence to fulfil the commandments, worshipping the Father, reverencing with Him the Son, abounding in the Holy Ghost, but we must strain the poor resources of our language to express thoughts too great for words. The error of others compels us to err in daring to embody in human terms truths which ought to be hidden in the silent veneration of the heart." The same translation is found in *The Nicene and Post-Nicene Library of the Fathers*, series 2, vol. IX, 52. A different translation of the last part of the passage, "We are compelled to attempt what is unattainable, to climb where we cannot reach, to speak what we cannot utter. Instead of the bare adoration of faith, we are compelled to entrust the deep things of religion to the perils of human expression," appears in Atwell, *Celebrating the Seasons*, 293, and in multiple other sources, including Gore, *The Incarnation of the Son of God*, 115; Ramsey, *The Gospel and the Catholic Church*, 127; and McGrath, *A Scientific Theology*, 45 (referencing Gore, *The Incarnation of the Son of God*, 105–6, so presumably the Charles Scribner edition). The English translation in the text is the author's, and benefits from both of the above translations.

34. Stephen Proudlove, a presentation at an Archbishop's Examination in Theology seminar held on the 17th June 2016.

I am interested here. Involving someone in an event can be more effective apologetics, and more revelatory, than any words that might be said. This is the implicit theory behind such contemporary developments as "Messy Church": biblically-based all-age craft activity. Christian faith is a way of life that encompasses worship, prayer, practical action, study, and much else: it is action into which we are socialized, and it is communities to which we belong. Involving people in Christian action, broadly understood, might be much more effective practical apologetics than any spoken or written words.

Myron Bradley Penner has drawn a similar conclusion. At the heart of his argument is the conviction that since the Enlightenment, human reason has formed an "objective-universal-neutral-complex,"[35] that any modern apologetics that is framed in terms of rational argument regards human reason thus understood as authoritative, and that therefore such apologetics is an argument for the "objective-universal-neutral-complex" paradigm. It is "secular apologetics,"[36] and "may actually perpetuate forms of modern nihilism by accepting the basic assumptions that drive it."[37] We might not entirely agree with Penner. His "either/or" approach forgets that the doctrines of creation and of the incarnation commit the Christian to positive relationships between God, God's Spirit, God's Word, and human reason, and it also minimizes the extent to which the world is now somewhat short of reason, of *Logos*, so that an appeal to reason might now be an important contribution that Christian apologetics can and ought to make.[38] However, we can agree with Penner's positive suggestions that

> what our age needs is not a scientific or theoretical answer to intellectual challenges of belief but a personal response to the spiritual problems of people who have been unable to receive and have faith. This response, of course, must be Christian lives shaped by biblical and theological categories, and articulated responsibly with intellectual acumen and philosophical sophistication.[39]

Being a Christian is what we do, and Christian lives bear witness: that is, it is an activity. We make truth (together) rather than find it dispassionately.[40] This is the kind of apologetics that we find in Francis Spufford's

---

35. Penner, *The End of Apologetics*, 32.
36. Penner, *The End of Apologetics*, 36.
37. Penner, *The End of Apologetics*, 73.
38. Cheetham, "Bishop Richard writes."
39. Penner, *The End of Apologetics*, 88.
40. Penner, *The End of Apologetics*, 97.

Unapologetic:[41] a stream of consciousness exploration of what it means for him to be a Christian. Only very occasionally does Spufford appeal to rational argument, and when he does it is usually in a footnote. What the reader experiences is a lived Christian faith, with an invitation to attempt one's own. Spufford is no stranger to words, and words, of course, are as much actions as is much else that we do: so the Christian who bears witness might also "simultaneously speak the language of their tradition and [be] fluent in the language of the world."[42] It is therefore inconsistent of Penner to distance himself from the idea that "truth requires a metaphysics."[43] If the world can provide a metaphysics that enables the Christian to "speak the language of their tradition" at the same time as being "fluent in the language of the world," then that metaphysic will be of service to the kind of "action" apologetics that Penner has in mind.

Reality is action, movement, the dynamic, change, and diversity, and a conceptual framework that recognizes this will serve an action-based apologetics more effectively than a framework based on categories of being, the static, rest, the unchanging, and the unitary. We shall therefore find that an "action" metaphysic will not only help us to create a word-based apologetic that connects with the philosophy and culture of our age, but that it will also enable us to ground an action-based apologetic in usable theory.

CONCLUSION

We might object that it is not the task of Christian theology to notice how the world is changing and to adapt itself accordingly, but is rather to understand "the faith that was once for all entrusted to the saints,"[44] and if necessary to stand against the ways in which we now understand ourselves and the universe in which we live. The problem here is that in order to express the Christian Faith we shall always need to employ some kind of conceptual structure, and if we do not positively choose an appropriate one, then we might find ourselves using one of which earlier theologians ought to have been more critical, rather than a different one through which we might be better able to do apologetics that is faithful to "the faith that was once for all entrusted to the saints."[45] The problem is particularly acute in a world in which theological language games are increasingly isolated from other

41. Spufford, *Unapologetic*.
42. Penner, *The End of Apologetics*, 103.
43. Penner, *The End of Apologetics*, 132.
44. Jude 1:3, NRSV.
45. Jude 1:3. NRSV.

language games—and this goes for countries and cultures still overtly religious, in which the religious language games might be widespread, but in which they might also have little connection with other language games.[46] Conversion from one language game to another is always possible: but because that does not necessarily repair the loss of connections between them, different language games can function in isolation from each other within an individual mind, within a community, or within an institution: and where different language games do not relate to each other, communication cannot occur.

All of this raises the important question as to whether the Christian tradition changes. If connections between the language of that tradition and other language games change all the time, and the meanings of words also change all the time—as the same word in a different context will always mean something different—then we cannot avoid the conclusion that the Christian tradition changes. This is not the problem that we might have thought, and it might in fact be inevitable, necessary, and useful. First of all, as John Henry Newman pointed out nearly two hundred years ago, the Christian tradition *does* evolve as well as exhibiting continuity;[47] secondly, human religious experience, for instance, that of "the holy", routinely undergoes a "process of rationalization and moralization";[48] and thirdly, as David Bentley Hart points out,

> faith ... must begin from the supposition that the inadequacy of even the most necessary and inevitable formulations of doctrine is proof of the reality of the "essential" truth to which the tradition bears witness; and it must regard the persistence of the tradition's inner search for fuller understanding as evidence of that "antecedent finality" that makes even these imperfect resolutions at once possible and recognizable in their imperfection. ... the proof that any tradition is a living one is precisely that it does not fiercely cling to every aspect of what it has inherited, but instead exhibits an often astonishing ruthlessness in shedding the past, out of obedience to some still more original spiritual imperative. ... The tradition exists as ... handed over to future elaboration, reconstruction, adaptation, and reconceptualization.[49]

Perhaps the safest approach is to have available a variety of evolving conceptual structures that we can constantly test for their faithfulness to the

---

46. Kerr, *Theology after Wittgenstein*, 28–29, 145–46.
47. Newman, *An Essay on the Development of Christian Doctrine*.
48. Otto, *The Idea of the Holy*, 115.
49. Hart, *Tradition and Apocalypse*, 101, 105, 130.

evolving Christian tradition and for their relevance to the changing modern world. This would be to learn from the Apostle Paul, who in his letter to the Church in Galatia[50] employed conceptual structures that would have been familiar to contemporary Jews, and somewhat different conceptual structures during his visit to Athens.[51]

For two thousand years Christian theology has been significantly influenced by a metaphysical understanding of reality as Being, beings, the unchanging, rest, and unity, and of change and diversity within that fundamental understanding. The world in which we now live invites us to exercise a hermeneutics of suspicion. And so, for instance, Sebastian Kim explains the way in which liberation theology[52] has offered a critique of the ways in which the Bible has been used by dominant groups in society to consolidate their power. New ways of reading, from within the liberation theologians' own context, and from a Marxist perspective, have generated different theologies.[53] As we are here attempting an actological theology, liberation theology might be a particularly useful tradition to revisit because it is normally written in terms of activity rather than in static terms, and in terms of a Kingdom of God in which the poor shall be first, and in which justice and peace will be found, and thus the Kingdom of God proclaimed and lived by Jesus. Gustavo Gutteriérez distinguishes three levels of meaning of "liberation":

> political liberation, the liberation of man throughout history, liberation from sin and admission to communion with God. . . . These three levels mutually effect each other, but they are not the same. . . . they are all part of a single, all-encompassing salvific process . . . Nothing escapes this process, nothing is outside the pale of the action of Christ and the gift of the Spirit.[54]

As Jeffrey Eaton puts it at the end of a discussion of liberation theology, "it is God's creative activity with which we have to do when we are engaged in the cause of liberating love."[55]

If we, too, bring our understanding of today's world, and of reality as action, change, and diversity, to the construction of Christian theology, then we shall construct Christian theology different from that generated by a metaphysic based on being, the unchanging, and the unitary. But we must

50. Galatians 3, 4.
51. Acts 17:16–34.
52. Gutiérrez, *A Theology of Liberation*.
53. Kim, *Theology in the Public Sphere*, 40–47.
54. Gutiérrez, *A Theology of Liberation*, 176–77.
55. Eaton, "Divine Action and Human Liberation," 229.

not rest there. We must go on to critique that conceptual structure, and to question every previous and current way of thought, and to test yet more methods for creating Christian theology and apologetics, as the liberation theologians have done in their own context. Not that we should necessarily abandon completely previous ways of thought. Pendulums swing, wheels turn, and a conceptual structure that currently has little purchase on the contemporary world, and is proving unproductive for apologetics, might one day prove to be useful. So this book offers an alternative to the "being" and "things that change" paradigm, but not a replacement of it. We are constructing an alternative "system of meaning,"[56] and, like all such systems, it will develop its own rules and relationships. Different systems might belong in a single category of "systems," but reliable comparison of one system of meaning with alternative systems—for instance, a comparison of a system based on being, the unchanging, and the unitary, with one based on action, change, and diversity—is always going to be difficult, because each of us lives within a particular system of actions, words, and meanings, and each system can only evaluate on its own terms. Perhaps all that we can say at this stage is that the world in which we now live might require us to emphasize a relatively neglected conceptual structure rather than a previously more dominant one, at least for the time being.

After all, if everything—or rather, every changing pattern of action, and every bundle of changing patterns of actions—is action, with its source in Action, then all of it is action in changing patterns: and the meaning of "action in patterns," and of "action in changing patterns," changes along with everything else. There will be no still point where we can stand to survey the shifting landscape: either to survey the conceptual structure that we are using, or a different one. All we can do is test by experience: by using different conceptual structures—different metaphysics—and asking whether they enable us to express the Christian Faith faithfully in our own context.

I am no advocate of frenetic activity on the part of Christians, theologians, or anyone else, but I know cultural change when I see it. If we are to do apologetics in such a new situation, then the way in which theology changes will be more important than its content at any particular time and place, and the way in which the Church changes will be more important than the way that it happens to be at any point in time.

We began with the suggestion that all theology is apologetics. It is: but it is possible to distinguish between apologetics and more systematic theology, the latter being a subsequent partial, brief, and local systematization

---

56. Krieger, "Religion and the System of Meaning," 102–3.

of theology that starts out as apologetics;[57] although the systematizing will itself be culture-driven, so perhaps the most systematic of theology cannot be described as anything other than apologetics. David Atkinson[58] suggests that apologetics is like a seed catalogue, trying to persuade the outsider that the blooms are worth buying, whereas systematic theology is like Kew Gardens: a systematic map of the data. Yes: but they are the same plants, merely expressed in different formats; and the creators of the seed catalogue might well have visited Kew Gardens, and the gardeners of Kew no doubt use a seed catalogue occasionally. So it might be best to regard apologetics and systematic theology as snapshots of different parts of the cycle: apologetics being the more active and relational part, within which the tradition and culture react against and change each other; and systematic theology being a momentary stepping back to take a look at what's happening. So maybe a better analogy would be that apologetics is the gardening, the apologist is the gardener, and systematic theology is the photo and the systematic theologian the photographer.

As we have studied the concept of apologetics, and the history of apologetics, we have come to understand the importance of conceptual frameworks, and particularly of the Platonic, which has held such a dominant position in Western culture and thus in Christian apologetics and theology for nearly two thousand years. No doubt Platonism has been of some benefit to the Christian Faith. During the early years it enabled bridges to be built between a prevailing culture within which Platonism seemed to the intelligentsia to be a natural expression of the way that reality was: but it is so no longer, and apologists need to grapple afresh with the concepts of our own time. This means that Alan Richardson's book *Christian Apologetics* might not deserve that title, because it does not grapple with contemporary thought-forms: indeed, Richardson believed that

> one advantage which the Christian apologist possesses in an age which is not dominated by any one type of metaphysical outlook is that he is freed from the temptation of trying to come to terms with the reigning thought-system of the day and consequently of subordinating the distinctive faith-principle of Christianity to that of an alien philosophy.[59]

---

57. Jenson, in his *Systematic Theology*, defines the gospel in terms of Jesus' resurrection as an event, and then goes on to discuss hermeneutics. But the event has always been expressed in language and so has always been hermeneutics, meaning that from the beginning the very heart of the Christian faith has been apologetics.

58. In private correspondence.

59. Richardson, *Christian Apologetics*, 37.

Richardson does not seem to realize that the "faith-principle" can only be expressed in the thoughtforms of some time and place, and that if it is not expressed in terms of contemporary thoughtforms then it will be expressed in terms of archaic forms of thought.

In order to do apologetics we must relate the Christian tradition, in all of its changing variety, to the diverse and changing cultural currents of our times, and to the fact of that diversity: and in order to do that systematically we shall need to express both the tradition and our culture in terms of a conceptual framework that can express the nature of our culture and the richness of the tradition. The kind of conceptual framework represented by the "Actological Explorations" series might or might not be appropriate to the task: but what is essential is that we should experiment theologically in relation both to the Christian tradition and to the world today, for otherwise the Church's boundaries will close, and apologetics will become an invitation to participate in a closed and isolated language game rather than a proclamation of the Good News that the Kingdom of God is in our midst and will arrive. We must cross boundaries: "between language and experience, between interpretation and text, . . . between philosophy and theology," and "between knowledge and faith."[60]

Apologetics is itself theology, and the particular aspect of the apologetic task in which we shall be most interested will be its attempt to create a conceptual structure within which to understand the Christian Faith, the nature of reality, and the world around us: a conceptual structure that will enable the boundary-crossing that we require. But how to do that? We need to begin as Paul began in Athens, employing conceptual structures already well developed within our philosophical tradition.[61] We shall then need to do as Maurice Blondel did and construct out of the philosophical traditions of our time a conceptual structure within which we can understand the whole of reality and that we can employ to express the Christian Faith in today's world. A hundred years ago Blondel chose an action-centered metaphysic in order to create an apologetics focused on human action, because that seemed to him to be the need at the time. Our world is even more characterized by change and action than was Blondel's, which is why we employ his insights in the service of the metaphysic that we have constructed in *An Actological Metaphysic*,[62] and that we shall employ in this sixth volume of

---

60. Vanhoozer and Warner, "Introduction," 13.
61. Acts 17:28.
62. Torry, *An Actological Metaphysic*.

the "Actological Explorations" series: an approach encouraged by the recent "turn to drama" in both philosophy and theology.[63]

But the requirement is the same: just as Paul "handed over" to the Corinthian Christians the action in patterns of the Eucharist,[64] along with the words that Jesus spoke at his last meal with his disciples before his death, so we must "hand over" the action in patterns that have been handed over to us. Those patterns will constantly change, but they will also bear a family likeness to each other: always the same drama, but with every performance different. Both the tradition that is handed over, and the handing over of the tradition—the process of apologetics—will be action in changing patterns, so will be both in continuity with what has gone before, and forever new.

And as we do apologetics, and apologetics constantly changes, so philosophy, theology, and the Church, will all change. Following a period during which philosophy has risked becoming linguistics and a deconstruction site, the conceptual structure that we are developing here offers a new and positive focus—action in changing patterns—with which to understand the whole of reality and therefore philosophy itself. The sciences and the arts might become equally different, with the universe and everything in it understood in terms of action in changing patterns, and the arts understood as networks of changing patterns of action. Christian theology will be able to remain incarnational if it understands God, Jesus, the Holy Spirit, and ourselves, in terms of action in changing patterns; the Word of God will be experienced as an active, changing, and diverse Word; the risen Christ might become the action in changing patterns that constitute the Body of Christ; we might welcome diversity; and grace might take center stage. The Eucharist will continue to constitute the Church; the Church might be more shaped by grace than it has ever been; and it might therefore contribute to the shaping of our society as a community of grace, and as a promise of the Kingdom of God that will be constituted by the changing patterns of action that we find in Jesus who is our God.

> Tradition is nothing if it is not a movement through time, repeating and recreating in time the realization of the divine presence in the forms and media of the present . . . It is not and cannot be an attempt to freeze the flow of time, but, rather, must ever be seeking the deeper rhythm in time itself that makes of time a potential sacrament of eternity. This rhythm is complex and

---

63. Vanhoozer, "Once More into the Borderlands"; Vanhoozer and Warner, "Introduction," 8.

64. 1 Corinthians 11:23: "handed over": *paredōka*: the same word used for the "handing over"—often translated "betrayed"—of Jesus "into the hand of sinners" (Mark 14:41) (Pattison, *A Short Course in Christian Doctrine*, 114).

elusive, but there is no reason to suppose that it is not as likely to make itself known in moments of great and intense change as in interludes of apparent calm.[65]

However different the sciences, the arts, philosophy, theology, and everything else might look if understood actologically, differences will remain: but the common actology will also mean new connections between them. Tom McLeish has understood some existing connections between science, wisdom literature, religion, and theology;[66] and Simon Oliver has researched the way in which the concept of "motion" has, until recently, straddled the boundary between science and theology.[67] These are connections that it would be easier to conceptualize if science, wisdom literature, religion, and theology, were all to be understood as action in changing patterns; and the same is true of connections between philosophy and theology, science and philosophy, and so on.

I have argued that apologetics is the relating of the Christian tradition to our culture, that theology is apologetics, that apologetics is theology, and that an appropriate conceptual framework is needed. I have discussed our culture and found that it is best described in terms of action, diversity, and change. Here, and in other books in the "Actological Explorations" series, I have suggested a conceptual framework of "action in changing patterns," or "changing patterns of action"; I have located this framework within the western philosophical tradition; and I have tested it against longstanding metaphysical concerns. I have now surveyed a variety of attempts at apologetics, and related them to our conceptual framework, and I have begun to construct an apologetics based on this framework. In subsequent chapters I shall develop a more systematic theology, and in particular the pattern of action that we call "grace": a discussion already begun in *An Actology of the Given*.[68] A flexible metanarrative is slowly emerging, within which narratives might evolve.

Throughout, God is Action, and God is the still point, and God is action in changing patterns (and God is other spectra too: between diversity and singularity, and between change and changelessness). There is no need to jettison one conceptual framework when we begin to experiment with another. Jesus is human action and divine action: that is, his patterns of action are God's patterns of action, and this is his unity with his Father:[69]

---

65. Pattison, *A Short Course in Christian Doctrine*, 116.
66. McLeish, *Faith and Wisdom in Science*.
67. Oliver, *Philosophy, God and Motion*.
68. Torry, *An Actology of the Given*.
69. Jesus used "Father" of God, so when speaking of Jesus' relationships with God

and we might eventually return to the concept of "substance" as a way of understanding relationships within the Trinity. But for the time being we shall concentrate on the development of an actology within which the Holy Spirit is God's action today;[70] the Trinity is a shifting unity of action in changing patterns, and a diversity of persons, each of whom is defined by their activity; and the Church is Jesus' action today, so the Eucharist defines the Church. Revelation is of action that is God, and revelation is action that communicates God, so revelation is the God who is revealed, and God is God's revelation. As Bonhoeffer puts it: "All that pertains to personal appropriation of the fact of Christ is not a priori, but God's contingent action on human beings. . . . the reference of revelation to human consciousness is, in character, an act."[71]

And with God, Jesus, the Spirit, the Trinity, revelation, the Church, the believer, and the world in relation to God, there are changing patterns of action, and they relate to each another, and this is their relationships and their atonement: but only in God are the ends of the spectra to be found: the dynamic, the static, the diversity, the unitary, the change, and the changelessness: so only in God is the chaos (the transcendence) that gives birth to the patterns of action that are revealed and are the revelation (the immanence), and we experience them as grace, as death and resurrection, and so on.

The Kingdom of God is patterns of action that constitute God, now, and in eternity—and because nothing escapes change and diversity, "eternity" is now an interesting concept. Evil is patterns of action to which we give birth, and that are given birth by the entanglements of the diverse and changing patterns of action that constitute the universe: they are not patterns originated within God; and the transformation that God achieves is the transformation of these patterns within the action that is God. As Robert Jenson puts it,

> I will have other possible masters than God, and in the contingency of the fall love some of them instead of God. This evil is indeed both certain and a feature of the permeability to others by which I am a person at all. . . . And when all communities are brought into the community of the Kingdom, I will be cured without being eradicated.[72]

---

his Father, his *Abba*, we shall use "Father" language; but in other contexts we shall use "Mother" interchangeably with "Father" on the basis that the analogy relates God's relationship with us to the experience of good parenting.

70. Ramsey, *Models for Divine Activity*, 7.
71. Bonhoeffer, *Act and Being* 58–59.
72. Jenson, *On Thinking the Human*, 72.

A God so intimate with the evil and suffering of the universe clearly cannot be impassible in any normal sense of the word, but can be "serene" in the sense of not

> overwhelmed, so that he is able to accept and to absorb and even to transmute into good all the sufferings of his creatures. It is not that he is untouched by these sufferings, but that he has the power and capacity to take them on himself and not be destroyed by them.[73]

God, being plural as well as one, is known diversely and in ever changing ways, and the many religions relate to these changing patterns; and still Jesus is unique in the oneness of his relationship with the action that is God, then and thus now.

Prayer is the relating of the patterns of action that are our minds to the patterns of action that are God, and we change God and God changes us; and maybe the mystics glimpse the ends of the spectra: though maybe they don't, quite. Both Plato and Aristotle regarded contemplation as the highest virtue, and as the way of life to be pursued by the philosopher; and Hegel read and valued mystical writings. So might we, for even though the mystics might not have arrived at the ends of the spectra, they express them, and experience the radically still and also the radically active. And all of this suggests that the sea is the appropriate image for God: Chaos, patterns, moving, beautiful, necessary, overwhelming.

God, pattern upon pattern, change that changes the change that we think we know about, the relativity of all relativity, relating to us and we to you, as all is change (and you are the deepest reality, our reality and yours) so we seek you in all of it, and in the transforming of all of it, as you are changing pattern of action upon changing pattern of action.

Our words belong to these patterns of action, so not only is this book a raid on the inarticulate, but it is the inarticulate ambushing itself. It isn't good enough: of course it isn't; but in order to praise you we must speak; if there is to be mention of you, we must speak; and if we are to seek you, we must speak. From within the changing patterns of action that constitute ourselves we reach across to those that you are: but knowing that you are action itself, and stillness itself, and countless patterns of action, changing, and relating.

But there is evil and injustice, and this is why we pray: seeking some redress, some justice, some rescue; our only hope being that you are the one in whom there is all change so that all that enslaves us shall be transformed

---

73. MacQuarrie, *The Humility of God*, 69.

into new patterns of action. But still we seek the origin of the evil, and we find it in you, in your letting go: and you let go so that ever new patterns might emerge.

Some patterns destroy others, or twist them: so we hope for resurrection. Jesus is a pattern of action belonging to those patterns that we are and to those that you are, and the transformation is begun in him, leading us into hope, for thus it shall be, as the whole created order and we ourselves are transformed, seeking and knowing new changing patterns of action; and we pray to know the ends of the spectrum, the total action and the total stillness, and we pray to know the ends of every spectrum; and we pray that every pattern that crushes new patterns of action shall itself be transfigured into the patterns of action that are Jesus and the Kingdom of God.

Shall we be conscious of this? Shall it be us? I pray so: so that those who have suffered deeply shall know their justification, and the martyrs their vindication, and all of us a judgment. And what is our consciousness? It is a self-reflexive pattern of action: circular in action, constantly affected by itself, and related to many others: and this is in God and shall be in God. These changing patterns of action will not be lost. None of it is ever lost, just as every pattern of action affects every other forever, and Jesus' every pattern of action affects every other changing pattern of action forever (and consciously, too, as the Church becomes his changing pattern of action): so none of it is lost, but all is in God and shall be in God, taken up into that vast, unimaginable Action, with its pattern upon pattern, all of it changing (and in its midst a stillness?), so that God shall be all in all.

In his book *God and Realism* David Byrne presents us with a challenge:

> Theology cannot be sensibly conceived to be a realist discipline. Its reflections give no sign of being controlled by an object external to itself. It does not give us ever more reliable beliefs about the divine. It is not a science of God in that sense. Criticisms have been offered of one response to this realisation: liberal, theological pragmatism. Plenty of room is left for alternative accounts of the nature and basis of theological reasoning.[74]

Subsequent chapters of this book will understand reality as action in changing patterns, and will understand God as Action, as the source of all action, and as particular changing patterns of action. The reader will decide whether this actological understanding of reality responds adequately to Byrne's challenge.

---

74. Byrne, *God and Realism*, 178.

Chapter 3

An actological God

Thesis: God is Action—action itself—and the source of all action; God is also constituted by changing patterns of action that God chooses; and Jesus is a human being and is also changing patterns of action that are changing patterns of action that constitute God.

INTRODUCTION

"Theology" is a combination of two Greek words, *logos*, meaning "reason," "account," or "word," and *theos*, "god": so "words about God." In relation to Christian theology, the term "doctrine" is sometimes used, from the Latin "doctrina," meaning "teaching" or "instruction." As George Pattison suggests,

> we can treat the word "teaching" either as a noun or as a verb, either as a "what," a thing or a substance of some sort, or a practice, an activity, a doing. Now, I do not wish to claim here that all nouns are ultimately reducible to verbs or that language in general is better understood as expressing the turbulently interactive "verbal" process of life, of doing and being-done-to, acting and suffering, rather than as a conglomeration of labels attached to static objects. I do find such an approach attractive, but to justify it as a general thesis about language would involve a long and uncertain philosophical detour. I do, however, think that it will help us to see important aspects of Christian doctrine if we think of the word "doctrine" itself in verbal terms. For if

we do so, then doctrine becomes something rather more than a fixed body of "saving knowledge." It becomes the expression of a willed and passionate movement of life.[1]

As readers will recognize, I would wish to claim that "all nouns are ultimately reducible to verbs" and that language "is better understood as expressing the turbulently interactive 'verbal' process of life, of doing and being-done-to, acting and suffering." Whether or not this book is the "long and uncertain philosophical detour" that Pattison has in mind, it would certainly cohere with the theme of the book if we were to treat "doctrine" as expressing a process, and the content—if "content" is any longer the best word—as better expressed in terms of action in patterns than in terms of objects that might change. At the heart of that content will of course be God: a God understood as Action, as the source of all action, and as action in changing patterns.

> Knowing God is not, for Christian theology, a matter of getting a clear overview of God. It is a matter of knowing oneself to be addressed by one who is free and so cannot be tied down or boxed in.[2]

We are action in changing patterns; God is action in changing patterns; God is active towards us. But to know is not simply to passively receive, however much of a gift the revelation might be.

> For one to know God is . . . not simply to recognise oneself as addressed lovingly by God. For to know God is for one to respond to that address and be transformed by it. One truly knows God only when one has God's love for the world working through one. One knows God by becoming in this world what God is Godself . . . The word "God" in Christian theology refers first and foremost to the source of the love that addresses the world in Jesus Christ.[3]

So Christian theology is all about the action that is God and the action that is ourselves, and the source of that theology is clear: Jesus Christ. The action in changing patterns that is Jesus Christ is action in changing patterns that is God. This means that Jesus is the revelation of God, and the Bible is a witness to that revelation. As Higton puts it, "Christian theology looks to Jesus Christ as its holy book."[4]

---

1. Pattison, *A Short Course in Christian Doctrine*, 6.
2. Higton, *Christian Doctrine*, 36.
3. Higton, *Christian Doctrine*, 38–39, 44.
4. Higton, *Christian Doctrine*, 48.

To employ such terms as "doctrine" and "systematic theology" might be to suggest that theology is a science. It is not, because its statements are not falsifiable. Theology is an art, and everyone who speaks of God contributes to the art's development, contributes to an evolving tradition, and at the same time receives from that tradition some of the tools required for theological work, work that is true for us if it reflects our experience. Or perhaps, better than regarding theology as either a science or an art, we should see it is a craft, as building construction: as the construction of a cathedral of the mind—or, as we have suggested before, as a flexible marquee. We have unpacked the poles, walls, pegs, and guy ropes from the bag, so we are ready to build: that is, we are ready to employ our framework in the cause of apologetics and then to construct a theology of God as Action, action, movement, change, the dynamic, and diversity, and as some specific changing patterns of action. But there are many ways to build a marquee. To return to the cathedral analogy: We have built the foundations, and gathered a few of the stones, so we are ready to build. Medieval builders built the foundations and the crypt and then built from the center outwards, as that was the only way they knew to keep the building standing as they built it. Gaudi took a different approach with *La Sagrada Familia* in Barcelona: he began with existing foundations and an existing crypt, and then began with the walls. The pillars and the roof were then designed to stand on their own as they were being built. Similarly, there are different ways of ordering theology: that is, words about God. I shall begin in two different places, rather like Gaudi. I shall begin with God, and I shall then begin again with Jesus.

The first thing to be clear about in relation to an actological understanding of God is that we are embarking on a thought experiment. Two and a half thousand years ago Parmenides and Plato bequeathed to us an ontology: an understanding of reality as Being and as beings that change. When Christianity emerged in the context of Judaism it was quickly Hellenized—"Greekized"—and so came to understand God as Being and as the source of all being. This encouraged the view that God did not change, or at least the very heart of God did not change. There was another stream in early Greek philosophy: Heraclitus's action-based philosophy. We can still trace a thin actological stream through Western philosophy, and occasionally it has emerged in Christian theology, but it has usually been comprehensively submerged by a Platonic ontology. This leaves open the question as to what Christian theology would have looked like if Plato had gone with Heraclitus rather than with Parmenides: if Plato had regarded reality as Action and as action in changing patterns. The Hellenization of Christian theology would then have led to an understanding of God as Action, as the source of all action, and as particular changing patterns of action, and we would be assuming that God changes rather than that God does not. We would have understood that God might be moved by our prayers, and that a genuine relationship with God might be possible.⁵ Relationship implies mutual entanglement, and therefore mutual change, so an actological theology might offer a far deeper understanding of relationship with God than an ontology could ever achieve. But does an actological theology stand up to scrutiny when evaluated against two thousand years of Christian tradition?

The first test of a theology has to be that God is unique, and that it is impossible to confuse God with anything else. There is no problem doing this within our conceptual structure. Each of us, and everything else, is action in patterns. Only God is pure action—Action; and only God is pure being—Being. In this book we are employing an "action" paradigm, but the same would apply to a "being" paradigm. If we think in terms of distinctions, only God occupies both the Action and Being sides of the distinction: action itself, and the "still point":⁶ so God's uniqueness is that God is defined in relation to both sides of the fundamental distinction, whereas we and everything else are defined only in relation to particular changing patterns of action and particular objects that change.

Nothing can be omitted from our account. God is Action and action in changing patterns; everything is action in changing patterns; and all of it is related: events to language, language to mathematics, mathematics to living organisms, living organisms to the world, the world to the smallest particle that we know about, and all of it to God. In a cathedral, the nave is where such meeting between disciplines occurs. We shall be starting with the chancel: with where action and language related to God are focused; but always keeping in mind that no cathedral is complete until it has both nave and chancel. In some modern cathedrals, such as Liverpool's Roman Catholic Cathedral, they are, quite properly, the same space: so we shall sometimes discuss God in the midst of everything else, and sometimes alone: but always remembering that everything is action in changing patterns, including God, whatever else God might be—or rather, however else God might happen. We have already done some of this work while we were testing our actology against a variety of disciplines; and in other books in the series we have already related a variety of disciplines to God as we have explored the works of a number of philosophers: so in this section we must right the balance, and begin with God.

The discussion contained in the preceding books in the "Actological Explorations" series, and in the previous two chapters of this book, is

---

5. Torry, *Actology*.
6. Eliot, *Four Quartets*, 15: "Burnt Norton," line 62.

rudimentary in the extreme, for we are exploring the meaning of a new idea against the massive backdrop of the Western philosophical tradition. Further development of the paradigm will be needed as we continue to work on such problems as the reconciliation of noumena and phenomena, and of how to understand the fundamental realities of the universe. And there will be much more discussion required of our conceptual framework's relationships to the sciences, and particularly to quantum mechanics, where the framework's explanatory economy might come into its own in the clearest possible way as light and everything else is understood as action, and the regularities that we experience (the speed of light, general relativity, and so on) are understood as shifting patterns, the changing of the patterns itself being patterned by changing patterns, thus setting up a vortex that might be a tentative foundational explanation.

An important example of apologetic theology inspired by quantum mechanics, and conceptually close to an actological understanding of reality, is Diarmuid O'Murchu's:

> Life is sustained by a creative energy, fundamentally benign in nature, with a tendency to manifest and express itself in movement, rhythm, and pattern. Creation is sustained by a superhuman, pulsating restlessness, a type of resonance vibrating throughout time and eternity.[7]

It might be thought that causal divine action—termed "special divine action" by Nicholas Saunders—would be easier to incorporate into the uncertainties at the heart of quantum mechanics than into a less "porous" ontological and particulate universe, but Saunders concludes that quantum theory makes this no easier to achieve than does any previous scientific paradigm,[8] and that "on the terms of our current understanding of quantum theory, incompatibilist non-interventionist quantum [special divine action] is not theoretically possible."[9] Saunders comes to much the same conclusion in relation to chaos theory,[10] and also in relation to whether the known context-specific variations in natural laws leave sufficient space for special divine action to fill the gaps.[11] As Saunders points out, "such a wide range of doctrine is dependent on a coherent account of God's action in the

---

7. O'Murchu, *Quantum Theology*, 55.
8. Saunders, *Divine Action and Modern Science*, 125–26.
9. Saunders, *Divine Action and Modern Science*, 172.
10. Saunders, *Divine Action and Modern Science*, 205–6.
11. Saunders, *Divine Action and Modern Science*, 211–13.

world, and we simply do not have anything other than bold assertions and a belief that [special divine action] takes place."[12]

For now, we shall turn to the task of theology and apologetics, but by doing that we shall not be leaving behind discussion of everything else, for apologetics requires a constant relating to every other discipline, which means that theology does as well. By employing an action in patterns framework in apologetics we shall be at the cutting edge of our understanding of reality, rather than lagging behind everyone else, as apologetics has often done; and by joining in the exploration of new possibilities, we shall know God, our world, and ourselves, we shall do the action which is God today, and we shall be Christians today—and only for today, for tomorrow it will be different.

And in case we do not recognize the significance of our paradigm shift, from the primacy of being to the primacy of action, we only need to see that this shift is itself action, and that it affects everything: and so everything will change for us as we pursue this new agenda in apologetics. We shall understand God, the world, time, space, ourselves, language, cause, freedom—and everything else—in terms of an actology with action at its heart: and so it will be as if Heraclitus had informed the last two millennia of Western philosophy rather than Parmenides and Plato. In a changing world all theology is apologetics, all apologetics changes, and all theology changes—and if we are in any way relating to God, then God changes, and is changed by our apologetics. No longer shall we understand God's *actus*, "action", as analogous to non-causal intentional action, and in particular we shall not regard it as analogous to the act of understanding, and so perhaps close to the "actuality" of being,[13] but instead as changing patterns of action that God chooses will constitute God, who is Action itself.

It might assist the reader if I offer a brief overview of where the theology that we shall develop on the basis of the actology might take us:

To suggest that God is Action as well as Being is to suggest that change is as fundamental to the nature of God as is not changing. It might therefore be as appropriate to speak of God as suffering as of God not suffering; and "creation" might be better understood as constant diverse action in changing patterns than as a one-off event, with the patterning of the action perhaps understood as an informational ordering of otherwise entirely chaotic action:[14] although in the absence of knowledge that we do not possess, precisely which of the changing patterns of action that constitute the cosmos

---

12. Saunders, *Divine Action and Modern Science*, 215.
13. Burrell, *Aquinas*, 117, 173.
14. Dembski, *Being as Communion*.

are directly those that constitute God, and which are those that evolve from the existing changing patterns of action that constitute the cosmos, must remain an eternal mystery.[15]

If God is understood as Action, and therefore as action in changing patterns, and each of us is understood as action in changing patterns, then Jesus is action in changing patterns, and a Christology might therefore be constructed in terms of changing patterns of action rather than in terms of ontological identity. The Holy Spirit might be understood in a similar way: and an "action in patterns" conceptual framework might begin to make more sense of a relational Trinity than can a "things that change" ontology. A "things that change" ontology struggles to reconcile an economic Trinity (the way in which we experience God as Trinity) with an essential Trinity (the way that God is as Trinity), whereas an "action in patterns" metaphysic can more easily reconcile an economic Trinity—experienced as action in changing patterns—with a Trinity understood in terms of Action and of action in changing patterns. As John Robinson puts it, if the Trinity is understood as three "modes of being" of the one God, then the modes of being are "modes of being-in-relation, modes of the sort of existence which God has, modes of 'Thou' existence"[16]—a reference to Martin Buber's understanding of interpersonal relationships as "I-Thou" rather than "I-It":[17] an understanding of relationships that Buber extended to our relationship to God,[18] but not one that he would himself have applied to the three persons of the Trinity.

Robinson goes on: "Perhaps 'modes of loving' comes nearest to what is required. They are ways in which God is eternally personal."[19] But these are less "modes of being" than they are "modes of action," and both in his doctoral dissertation, *Thou who Art*, and in his other work, Robinson distances himself from a Platonic ontology and employs a more personalist and relational I-Thou conceptual framework, as much rooted in personal experience of I-Thou relationships as in academic study of the concept.[20]

If we understand God, ourselves, and everything else, in terms of action in changing patterns, then we might be more able to understand God's action in the world than we can in the context of a theology in which God is understood as Being and as not changing. The Church's task then becomes

15. Deane-Drummond, *Christ and Evolution*, 25.
16. Robinson, *Thou who Art*, 333.
17. Buber, *I and Thou*.
18. Von Balthasar, *Martin Buber and Christianity*, 113.
19. Robinson, *Thou who Art*, 333.
20. Kee, *The Roots of Christian Freedom*, 67–68, 184.

the seeking of God's action and choosing to join in, creating changing patterns of action that reflect the action in changing patterns that is God active in the world: and so the Church itself becomes an apologetics, as it represents the changing patterns of action that constitute God. This is how Michael Ramsey saw the relationship between the Church and the Christian Faith when he described his book *The Gospel and the Catholic Church* "as a study of the Church, and its doctrine, and unity and structure, in terms of the Gospel of Christ crucified and risen."[21] He expected the changing patterns of action that constituted the Church to reflect the changing patterns of action that constitute God as we find them revealed in the life, suffering, death, and resurrection of Jesus Christ. If the Church's changing words about God communicate the changing patterns of action that are God, then the Church communicates a constantly changing Christian doctrine: and we shall find ourselves doing apologetics appropriate to a changing world. How such a new apologetics will relate to other faiths, to the natural and social sciences, and to contemporary philosophy, will be important subjects for us to study.

We shall begin our substantive study of the theological implications of an actology by asking how we might understand God as Action, as the source of all action, and as particular changing patterns of action.

GOD

So far, no theology has located itself at the "Action" or "radically dynamic" end of the spectrum: there has always been a static element, an unchanging pole to God, a "substance," however "spiritual." George Pattison asks the question:

> In so far as we can say anything about God, there is no obvious reason why it is necessary to deny some analogue to time and history in the divine life. How can we in fact avoid doing so if we also wish to speak of God as living or dynamic? Is the insistence on God's timeless eternity really intrinsic to Christianity's historical witness . . . ? Our experience is that time means change . . . To be creatures of time is to be creatures subject to change, dissolution and, finally, death. But if that is generally true of our human experience, can we simply assume that it is true also for God? Do we really honour God less by speaking of God as living

---

21. Ramsey, *The Gospel and the Catholic Church*, 5.

in a dynamic, forward or progressive movement, than by repeating the mantra about changelessness or timelessness?[22]

According to Hans Küng, the God we find in the Jewish Scriptures, the Christian Old Testament, is a "living God," a "God of liberation," who "reveals himself in history as he who is: as he who will be, guiding, helping, strengthening," and who is "not less than a person," but is "superpersonal. . . . God is one who faces me, whom I can address."[23] For John Oman, a statement that God is "personal" is

> a statement about the nature of the God who deeply respects and so constitutes human freedom, who relates to men and women . . . as parent to child; and who, like the prodigal's father, allows us to squander our inheritance if we so choose, but waits for us to come to ourselves so that we can be welcomed home with the power of forgiving love.[24]

Nicholas Berdyaev's God experiences conflict—although there is still a final programmed resolution;[25] John Zizioulas's exploration of the Cappadocian Fathers' theology leads to a concept of "Being as Communion" within which God's "substance" "has no true being apart from communion";[26] for Dietrich Bonhoeffer,

> God remains always the Lord, always subject, so that whoever claims to have God as an object no longer has *God*; God is always the God who "comes" and never the God who "is there" . . . God remains free, nonobjective, pure act;[27]

and Dorothee Sölle writes of God in terms of action: of God as "the mutual, significant, actively experienced relationship to life—God happens";[28] "God is not in heaven; he is hanging on the cross . . ."[29] Both on the cross, and in general, "Christ plays God's role in the world—that and nothing else is what incarnation means . . ."[30] In a similar manner, Don Cupitt has freed us

---

22. Pattison, *A Short Course in Christian Doctrine*, 30.
23. Küng, *Does God Exist?* 613–34.
24. Bevans, *John Oman and his Doctrine of God*, 80.
25. Berdyaev, *The Beginning and the End*, 247–49.
26. Zizioulas, *Being as Communion*, 17.
27. Bonhoeffer, *Act and Being*, 85, 87.
28. Sölle, *Thinking about God*, 185; *Gott Denken*, 242: "Die gegenseitige, sinngewisse, handelnd gelebte Beziehung zum Leben—Gott geschieht. God happens." "God happens" is in English and in italics in the German original.
29. Sölle, *Suffering*, 148; *Leiden*, 182: "Gott ist nicht im Himmel, er hängt am Kreuz."
30. Sölle, *Christ the Representative*, 141–42; *Stellvertretung*, 161–62: "Christus spielt

from "any absolute Beginning, Ground, Presence or End, in the traditional metaphysical sense,"[31] but his "God," who is "the sum of our values representing to us their ideal unity, their claims upon us and their creative power,"[32] leaves us with a somewhat introverted notion with little of the dynamic about it.[33] Both Sölle and Cupitt have been inspired by the mystics' Negative Way[34] which has led them into some vital ground-breaking—but a further step is needed: a more systematic treatment of Christian theology in terms of the primacy of the dynamic, and of the dynamic as the real,[35] to match the kind of philosophical framework that we find in Heraclitus, Bergson, and Blondel: an actology of Action, action, change, movement, diversity, and the generally dynamic. Such a conceptual framework might provide a better context than an ontology within which to argue for the continuing meaningfulness of an objective metaphysical God.[36]

For Maurice Blondel,

> Is it not at least necessary to say that a being is not only that which it appears to be at a particular moment or in a particular place, but that to know it, and legitimately to affirm [its existence and/or nature], we ought to put together the totality of all of its becoming? Yes, it is.[37]

Becoming as constituting being finds echoes in Paul Tillich's theology, although ambiguously. Take, for example, "the power to be":

> In the act of the courage to be the power of being is effective in us, whether we recognize it or not. Every act of courage is a manifestation of the ground of being . . . By affirming our being we participate in the self-affirmation of being-itself. . . . If we know it, we accept acceptance consciously. If we do not know it, we nevertheless accept it and participate in it. And in our acceptance of that which we do not know the power of being is

---

Gottes Rolle in der Welt—nichts anderes bedeutet Inkarnation . . . auch wir können nun Gott füreinander spielen."

31. Cupitt, *The Long-Legged Fly*, 7.
32. Cupitt, *The Sea of Faith*, 269.
33. For Cupitt's own understanding of his theological journey see Cowdell, *Atheist Priest?* ix–x.
34. Sölle, *Hinreise*, 103–8; *The Inward Road and the Way Back*, 81–84; Cupitt, *Taking Leave of God*.
35. Torry, "On Completing the Apologetic Spectrum."
36. Ward, *Holding Fast to God*.
37. Blondel, *L'Être et les Êtres*, 92.

manifest to us. Courage has revealing power, the courage to be is the key to being-itself.[38]

Alistair Macleod suggests that

> the ontological language in which [Tillich] consciously formulates his basic doctrines is not only inessential but also presents a formidable obstacle to the very comprehension of what he has to say. So far as "de-ontologisation" of these doctrines is a possibility, it is the course which must be followed by the sympathetic interpreter of Tillich if the undoubted insights scattered throughout his writings are to be rescued.[39]

We might rephrase the passage above from *The Courage to Be* as follows: "In the act of the courage to be we enact being as becoming . . ." All over Tillich's writings, and particularly *The Courage to Be* and *The Shaking of the Foundations*, we find action in changing patterns. Again we might rephrase: "we accept accepting . . . the courage to act is the key to Action." Mcleod is looking in the right direction. Tillich would have achieved significantly enhanced consistency if he had substituted an actology for his ontology. "*Simply accept the fact that you are accepted!*"[40] is all verbs: accepting of accepting.

We might take a similar approach to Colin Gunton's *Act and Being*, in which he suggests that God's attributes "reveal certain forms of action as an expression in time of the eternal being of God . . . All of these forms of action come together in the career of Jesus, who is God's sovereignty, mercy, justice, love, patience and holiness in action."[41] Jesus is indeed God's sovereignty, mercy, justice, love, patience, and holiness, but these forms of action do not "express the eternal being of God" but rather reveal the reality of God as action in changing patterns, and in particular of God active in the time that is a foundational element of God's creative activity.[42] There is no unchanging layer of "being" underlying the changing patterns of action, whether our changing patterns of action or God's. Gunton suggests that the "distinctive forms of action of the persons" of the Trinity bring "to the fore the distinctive forms of action of the persons each in relation to the other two: originating, becoming incarnate, perfecting."[43] All of it is action in changing patterns, and none of it is static and unchanging being.

---

38. Tillich, *The Courage to Be*, 175–76.
39. Macleod, *Tillich*, 155.
40. Tillich, *The Shaking of the Foundations*, 163. Italics in the original.
41. Gunton, *Act and Being*, 119.
42. Burrell, "Divine Practical Knowing," 98–101.
43. Gunton, *Act and Being*, 145.

At the heart of the theology required is God, understood as Action—that is, the source of all action—and also as patterns of action that relate to the patterns of action that constitute ourselves, the universe, and everything else: or rather, to the patterns of action that constitute every event, every action, and every pattern of action. To say that God is Action is to say that God is the source of all action, and that God is the totality of action, encompassing all action in its source, Action. It is also to say that God can choose to be constituted by particular patterns of action, so we might say that the name of God "harbors an event, and that theology is the hermeneutics of that event."[44] Because God's transcendence is necessary to the definition of God, the changing patterns of action that constitute God—the constantly changing event of God—are of God's choosing, and these patterns of action are affected by our patterns of action, and by the patterns of action that constitute the universe, and by any other pattern of action, as a matter of God's choice. So God can and does choose to be patterns of action that are intertwined with those that constitute all of us. Within a "Being" ontology this would imply that

> the weak force of God settles down below in the hidden interstices of being, insinuated into the obscure crevices of being ... the disordering order of what disturbs being from within, like an anarchic interruption that refuses to allow being to settle firmly in place. The name of God is the name of an event transpiring in being's restless heart, creating confusion in the house of being, forcing being into motion, mutation, transformation, reversal.[45]

Within an actology a higher degree of coherence might be possible, for then the already dynamic changing patterns of action that constitute God, and the already dynamic changing patterns of action that constitute the universe and ourselves, entangle with each other. Some of those changing patterns of action we call suffering, so God suffers along with every human being, animal, and planet that suffers, and that suffering changes God's patterns of action as it changes ours. God chooses those patterns of action that will define who God is—or rather, what God does: and then these will change. Every pattern of action of which God is the source will then do its own changing, and new patterns of action will emerge, and they will relate to the patterns of action that are what God does. So every aspect of God's creation—of God's constant creating—might be described as a waterfall: as action in many and changing patterns.

44. Caputo, *The Weakness of God*, 2.
45. Caputo, *The Weakness of God*, 9.

So to say that God is particular patterns of action is to say that God is changing patterns of action and that the changing is by God's constant permission—which is itself a changing pattern of action. We might apply the word "grace" to a pattern of action that is God's chosen pattern of action,[46] but only on condition that the meaning of the word will constantly change, and that the pattern of action so named constantly changes; and we might apply the word "judgement" to a pattern of action that is God's chosen pattern of action, but only on the same conditions. And if these are indeed changing patterns of action that are God's, and that therefore define who God is, then they will be constantly and eternally God: for God is Action and changing patterns of action, and although God might unchoose a pattern of action, that pattern remains forever a changing pattern of action that constitutes God. It is also to say that wherever we find those particular patterns of action, we find God. If we find those patterns of action in Jesus, then there is God; and if we find them active in the world and in the Church, then there is the Holy Spirit, and there is God; and if we find them active in constant creativity, then there is the Creator, and there is God. So we find a number of patterns of action ascribed to Jesus in the New Testament: grace, love, forgiveness, healing, welcoming, and faith, where faith is both the faith that Jesus has in God, and the faith that we have in him.[47]

God happens. God is happening. "God" is a verb:[48] so we can say that "God" means "to happen." God is the source of all happening, and of the possibility of all happening. This language of God mirrors the "Being" language of a rather different metaphysical understanding of reality.

God "lets be": And although that looks rather passive, it is a verb, and so belongs in a theology in which God is understood as changing patterns of action, and as Action, rather than one in which God is Being, relates to beings, and is revealed and spoken of in "being" language. However, the outcome of the "letting be" is "being," which we now understand as less than real, as the patterning in which actions are experienced. Rather, God "lets happen:" God constantly gives birth to happening, and allows all manner of happening to emerge. "God lets become" would be a way of putting this that would recognize "being" in the way that Blondel understood it: that is, as

---

46. Torry, *An Actology of the Given*, 118–152.

47. Galatians 2:16: "*dia pisteōs Jesu Christou*"; Philippians 3:9: "*dia pisteōs Christou.*" In both of these places the translation should be "the faith of Christ": it is a simple genitive, as in Mark 5:34 and 10:52: "*hē pistis sou sesōken sē.*" Colossians 1:4—"*tēn pistin humōn en Christō*"—and Colossians 2:5—"*tēs eis Christon pisteōs*"—the *en*, "in", and *eis*, "into", making it clear that in those passages it is our faith in Christ that is being discussed.

48. Poland, "If God *is* a Verb, then we are 'human becomings,'" 5.

action, as becoming: as "presencing" rather than as "presence."[49] As Julian of Norwich puts it:

> He showed me a little thing, the size of a hazelnut, in the palm of my hand, and it was as round as a ball. I looked at it with my mind's eye and I thought, "What can this be?" And answer came, "It is all that is made." I marvelled that it could last, for I thought it might have crumbled to nothing, it was so small. And the answer came into my mind, "it lasts and ever shall because God loves it."[50]

God loves changing patterns of action into happening.

In the Christian tradition, God is a "God who . . . ,"[51] with the "who" followed by a verb:[52] "The God who made the world and everything in it";[53] "It is God who justifies";[54] "God who shows mercy";[55] "God who gives the growth";[56] "the same God who activates";[57] "God who raises the dead";[58] "God who is at work in you."[59] God is a God who acts: but more than that, God is Action. The covers of the books in the "Actological Explorations" series all contain an image of a waterfall: imagery that is looking increasingly appropriate. As George Pattison puts it:

> Sometimes the great religious vision of the Greek philosophers, a vision in which the created universe emanated or flowed out of God, has been described as the vision of a frozen waterfall. Everything comes from and returns to God in an eternally completed cycle in which nothing new ever really happens. But wasn't it part of the impact of Christianity to unfreeze the

---

49. Hemming, *Postmodernity's Transcending*, 10.

50. Julian of Norwich, *Enfolded in Love*, 3.

51. Paula Gooder made this point in an address to a Southwark Diocesan clergy conference.

52. The "God who . . ." in the English translation generally translates a Greek genitive participle construction: so the consistency is perhaps clearer in the English than in the original Greek.

53. Acts 17:24, NRSV.

54. Romans 8:33, NRSV.

55. Romans 9:16, NRSV.

56. 1 Corinthians 3:7, NRSV.

57. 1 Corinthians 12:6, NRSV.

58. 2 Corinthians 1:9, NRSV.

59. Philippians 2:13, NRSV.

waterfall, to bring movement into the universe, and to open the gate to novelty?[60]

The world is in God: that is, the changing patterns of action that constitute the universe are taken into God: not unchanged, of course, but constantly changed by the changing patterns of action that are God, and in the constant action-generating Action that God is. This is not pantheism, for God is not just the universe: but might "panentheism" be a legitimate way to express the relationship between God and the universe? Panentheism "affirms that although God and the world are ontologically distinct and God transcends the world, the world is 'in' God ontologically":[61] but perhaps that isn't quite right either. The action in patterns that constitute ourselves and the universe are immediately changed in contact with the action in patterns that are God, so they are no longer as they were. Perhaps "panmutatentheism": "all changed in God." To quote Pattison again: "Even the suffering of this evolving universe is somehow to be taken into and reconciled within the all-encompassing life of God;"[62] and conversely, as Paul Janz puts it, it is

> at the dynamically causal limits of sensibility of sensible embodiment at the *centre of life*, that we must encounter Christian transcendence as a present reality in space and time *today*, or more exactly that we must encounter revelation as the divine causality in the world today.[63]

God is Action, the source of action, and action itself, as well as being particular patterns of action, an infinity of which might not be remotely like those that constitute the universe: but God is active in and throughout the universe: there is a "harmonic" of God throughout it. But still God is no thing. Within a Being metaphysic, God is not simply a being, but is rather the source and ground of all being, and similarly, within an actology, God is not simply an action, but is rather the source and ground of all action. However, if we are to say anything at all specific about God, then we have to say that God is particular changing patterns of action, and particularly in the Christian tradition we have to say that because Jesus is God living a human life, he reveals particular changing patterns of action as constituting God. And it is here, as Paul Ricoeur points out, that we find perhaps the most significant difference between a God who is Being and a God who is

---

60. Pattison, *A Short Course in Christian Doctrine*, 30.
61. Cooper, *Panentheism*, 18.
62. Pattison, *A Short Course in Christian Doctrine*, 55.
63. Davies et al., *Transformation Theology*, 86. Italics in the original.

the great actant in a history of deliverance. The greatest contrast between the God of Israel and that of Greek philosophy perhaps resides here. The theology of traditions knows nothing of the concepts of cause, of ground, of essence; instead it speaks of God in agreement with the historical drama instituted by the acts of deliverance reported by the narrative. This way of speaking about God is no less meaningful than that of the Greeks; it is a theology . . . in the form of a Heilsgeschichte [history of salvation].[64]

In both the Hebrew and the Christian Scriptures, God is revealed by action and is defined by action: God rescued Israel,[65] God raised Jesus from the dead,[66] and so on. The "drama" of the Judaeo-Christian tradition explored by Hans Urs von Balthasar in his *Theodrama*[67] has far too often been submerged by an understanding of God as unchanging Being: but as Vanhoozer and Warner suggest, Christian theology is now seeing a "'turn' to embodied action and, more specifically, to drama, such that theological doctrines state acts, not simply facts, and direct us to participate in these acts."[68] In the theological world, turns to the literary forms and historical traditions of narrative, to cultural and more generally collective practice, and to hermeneutics, have now been followed by a "turn to drama" that "involves speech, story, practice", that "demands that we act with others with whom we share a particular situation,"[69] and that knows that "we grasp reality when we are touched lovingly by it":[70] a turn evidenced in both philosophy and theology, and thus a development that can enable a certain amount of border-crossing between the two.[71] "Drama" implies

---

64. Ricoeur, *From Text to Action*, 136; *Du Texte à l'Action*, 88-89: "*le grand Actant d'une histoire de délivrance. C'est là sans doute que réside le plus grand contraste entre le Dieu d'Israël et celui de la philosophie grecque; la théologie des traditions ne connaît rien des concepts de cause, de fondement, d'essence; elle parle de Dieu en accord avec le drame historique instauré par les actes de délivrance que le récit rapporte. Cette manière de parler de Dieu n'est pas moins significative que elle des Grecs; c'est une théologie en forme de Heilsgeschichte.*" The a of "actant" ought to have been capitalized in the English translation; and, as we have shown, Greek philosophy is more diverse than Ricoeur makes out. Perhaps he hasn't read Heraclitus.

65. Joshua 24:10; 1 Samuel 10:18; 12:11; 2 Samuel 12:7; Psalm 81:7.

66. Acts 2:24; 3:7; 10:40; 13:30; Romans 10:9; Galatians 1:1; Ephesians 1:20; Colossians 2:12; 1 Peter 1:21.

67. Von Balthasar, *Theodrama: IV: The Action*; Wigley, *Balthasar's Trilogy*, 103-12.

68. Vanhoozer and Warner, "Introduction," 8.

69. Vanhoozer, "Once More into the Borderlands," 43.

70. Jenson, *On Thinking the Human*, 58.

71. Vanhoozer, "Once More into the Borderlands," 53.

not only an event controlled by a script, and therefore always the same, but rather constantly changing performances: and so in relation to theology, the turn to drama implies *changing* patterns of action: "new creation,"[72] "a new spirit,"[73] "a new thing,"[74] "new teaching,"[75] "a new commandment,"[76] "a new covenant,"[77] "new birth,"[78] "a new name,"[79] "new life,"[80] "the new self,"[81] "one new humanity,"[82] "the new and living way,"[83] "the new Jerusalem,"[84] "new heavens and a new earth"[85]—always new.[86]

God reveals God: in creation, in Jesus, in the Holy Spirit, through the Church, which includes the Bible, which is a crystallization of the earliest Christians' experiences of God. The patterns of action that we might call "revelation" are themselves patterns of action that constitute God, so what is revealed is God. It was God who was revealed to Moses in fire and earthquake, and not some separable epiphany;[87] and it is God who was and is revealed in Jesus. As George Patterson puts it, the inner conversation that constitutes God as a Trinity of three persons

> is their being itself, their life itself. It is the divine being or existence itself that is being sustained, kept going, and, quite simply, "existing" by virtue of this divine conversation. Divine communication is self-communication, communication of the divine being, held open and sustained as a threefold "Thou"; it is the communication of the personal truth that is God's way of being.[88]

72. 2 Corinthians 5:17; Galatians 6:15, NRSV.
73. Psalm 51:10, NRSV.
74. Isaiah 43:19, NRSV.
75. Mark 1:27; Acts 17:19, NRSV.
76. Luke 22:20; 1 John 2:8.; 2 John 5, NRSV.
77. Luke 22:20; 1 Corinthians 11:25; 2 Corinthians 3:6; Hebrews 8:8; 8:13; 9:15; 12:24, NRSV.
78. 1 Peter 1:3, NRSV.
79. Revelation 2:17; 3:12, NRSV.
80. Romans 7:6, NRSV.
81. Ephesians 4:24; Colossians 3:10, NRSV.
82. Ephesians 2:15, NRSV.
83. Hebrews 10:20, NRSV.
84. Revelation 3:12; 21:2, NRSV.
85. Isaiah 65:17; 66:22; 2 Peter 3:13; Revelation 21:1, NRSV.
86. Davies et al., *Transformation Theology*, 93.
87. Exodus 3:1-6; 19:18.
88. George Pattison, *A Short Course in Christian Doctrine*, 38–39: cf. Buber, *I and Thou*.

God is action and God is diverse, so to identify Jesus as God is to identify a particular bundle of patterns of action with God: but by God we also mean Action, that is, action itself, and pattern upon pattern of action: an unimaginable ferment that no words can capture, for words assume some kind of fixity. God is chaos, a fertile and creative constant changing, in which nothing is ever the same. And the chaos is doubly unimaginable because there is not even a semi-rigid time-continuum within which it occurs. So we shall find it hard to conceptualize God—which is as it should be.

Within God patterns emerge: the patterns that we call matter, and others too. In matter, the particles and their relations are not things, and they are not fixed in any way: they are action—but there are regularities, temporary likenesses—before they are again swallowed up in the chaos to which God gives birth, and in the changing patterns that emerge in the chaos, all of which continues to constitute God, who might also be understood as the ultimate observer required to enable the wave functions of the universe to collapse into the action in patterns that we call matter.[89] There is a spectrum in God, from the totally unpatterned to the relatively patterned; the heart of the mystery is the depth of the chaos and its relation to the patterned; and the problem is the relationship between our need to explain, our inability to describe chaos, and our use of the word "pattern," on which perhaps we have placed too great a weight, but which we cannot do without.

Does there also emerge a stillness within God: an end-point to the spectrum? If so, then between the stillness and the chaos are strung the changing patterns, from the fleeting to the settled—although again our language fails us, for we are assuming a fixed "time" within which these things occur, when there is not one—for any "time" is a relation between changing patterns of action, it is a pattern that is secondary to patterns, and it changes and is relative to the patterns—it is a changing pattern of changing patterns, it is in God: emerging from and engulfed in God.

God gives birth to pattern upon pattern, all of them changing, action upon action, and they are God—and the patterns change each other, and new patterns emerge that are not God, for they are not patterns which are God—although they cannot leave God alone, and God cannot leave them alone, for every action and every pattern of action affects every other. And so God remains the origin and the end of all action, the chaos within which the patterns emerge, and the chaos that relates to them all, changing them all—and still all of this is mere imagery, a struggling to say something, just something, so that we are not totally silent in response to the God who is pure action.

---

89. Ward, *The Evidence for God*, 79.

There is no proof that such a God as this exists. The traditional arguments for God's existence[90] assume that there is always something that does not change. But do they need to? The ontological argument assumes that that than which nothing greater can be conceived must exist, for to exist is better than not to exist. But existence is not a predicate, and there is no perfect action, so in terms of our new paradigm the argument cannot begin, let alone reach a conclusion.

The cosmological argument suggests that because there is something, that something must have a cause: and here we can argue that because there is action there must be some source of action: some "Action." Similarly, the teleological argument argues that there is order and therefore a source of that order; and we can argue that there are patterns, and therefore a source of such patterns. So the cosmological and teleological arguments between them can offer us an argument for patterns of action, and for a source of all action, which we might call God. These arguments are not, of course, proofs. Proof is no longer possible, for everything changes, and there are no certainties. But these arguments map a tradition; they offer possibilities; and they invite further exploration of what they suggest. Above all, their conclusions are rational, they cohere with the new paradigm within which we are working, and they contribute to that paradigm's development. They might not lead us to certainty, but they are certainly scientific.

None of our models will be adequate to the reality of God, and perhaps all any one model can hope to do is to function as a critique of other models: in which case a theology constructed on the basis of an actology will function as a critique of a theology constructed on the basis of being, rest, the static, the unchanging, and Being.

We might benefit from understanding God in terms of action in patterns—and the Christian tradition, and maybe other faith traditions, might benefit: but language remains human language, and it is not even adequate to express the reality of ourselves and of the world around us, let alone God. We can attempt to express this by saying that God is Action, the source of all action, and not just particular actions: but then, if we are to say anything at all about God, and particularly if we are to remain faithful to the Christian tradition, we have to discuss God in relation to particular changing patterns of action. We might suggest that God's changing is a perfect changing, and that ours is not: but we would still have to use the same language, and the meanings and connections of that language change constantly, so we would still be struggling to recognize God's transcendence. God's perfection, God's transcendence, is no longer God's omnipotence: it is a perfect and

---

90. Hick, *Arguments for the Existence of God*.

transcendent compassion, a feeling with, and a constant reconciliation and transfiguration within the heart of God and ultimately of all things. And perhaps it is still omnipresence, but now understood as omnihappening: a complete involvement in all of the universe's changing patterns of action, experiencing the suffering as well as the joy, the destruction as well as the creation, and transfiguring it.

Such a God has pastoral implications in relation to both human and institutional relationships. If God is affected by us, and we are affected by God, and if turbulent change is the route to new and beautiful order, then we shall value the gods in whom we and other people trust, and we shall bring them into relationship with God, who is Action and the source of all action; we shall put an end to authoritarian dogma, and welcome a changing diversity of belief; we shall experience our relationship with God as action in changing patterns, and thus God as action in changing patterns; we shall welcome the changing diversity of faiths and denominations, and the possibility of real and thus fruitful dialogue; and we shall value tentative commitments: for multiple commitments to multiple particular theological positions is a requirement of diversity, and the tentativeness of every commitment is a requirement of God understood as Action, as the source of action, and as action in changing patterns. This is precisely the kind of God that we require in a secular, diverse, and active world; it is the God (and its implications) that our new conceptual framework offers to us; it is the God revealed across human history, in the scriptures of the world's faiths, and particularly in the Christian scriptures; and it is the God who is coming to birth in the Church if only we have eyes to see.

The word "God" has a variety of meanings, reflecting the diversity of God; and those meanings change, reflecting the action in changing patterns framework that constitutes both God and ourselves. There is no identifiable and definable element that is consistent throughout every actual or conceivable use of the word "God," but there are family resemblances between the uses and meanings of "God": or rather, a family of family resemblances, as each religious tradition can be regarded as containing a family of uses—although of course similarities can be discovered between members of different families. So it is as legitimate to use the language of diversity as it is to use that of the unitary, to be equivocal as to be univocal, to speak of God as complex as to speak of God as simple, to think of God as many as to think of God as one: so in the context of our actology, it makes less sense to speak of God as the One than it does to speak of God as the Many.

And in the midst of the diversity of God is God the Creator, to whom we now turn.

GOD THE CREATOR

The universe is a universe of activity. There is no substance, no essence. It is a thing to which every thing belongs: it is an object, and it is a subject. It is full of patterns, of similarities, of likenesses: and language (which belongs to it) relates to it as one thing to another, as object to subject and subject to object—and it is all action, patterned action, with the patterns constantly changing. The universe is action in patterns that change.

In chapters 3 and 4 of *An Actological Metaphysic* we have explored philosophical and scientific perspectives on the origin of the universe and on the changing patterns of action that continue to constitute it. Here we shall seek some theological perspectives.

It has been suggested that a singularity, a brief perturbation, gave birth to matter, space, time, and everything else; and we might now be clearer as to the nature of such a singularity. In the unstructured chaos of action, in the "formless void,"[91] in which there is no time and no space, no duration and no distance (because they require patterns of action as well as chaotic action), a pattern emerges, by accident, by some necessity in the Action itself, or by God's will, or by all of these. Far from being a creation *ex nihilo*, "from nothing," this is a "becoming":[92] "moving patterns come into existence with time."[93] And because there is one pattern there is another. As order exploded through the action, a universe emerged, creating space and time as it went—creating "rhythm"[94]—with the edge of space and of the universe at the edge of the patterns. The universe's expansion is still expansion into the chaos (though to use the word "chaos" suggests that there is some "thing" there when there cannot be things in any sense in the absence of pattern, space, and time). In this sense the first chapter of the book of Genesis is really quite accurate:

> In the beginning when God created the heaven and the earth, the earth was a formless void and darkness covered the face of the deep, while a wind from God swept over the face of the waters. Then God said, "let there be light"; and there was light . . .[95]

Either the chaos will eventually repossess the universe from its edges (a collapse back into chaos) or the patterns will go on spreading, and multiplying and spreading, without limit, pushing outwards the boundaries of space and

---

91. Genesis 1:1, NRSV.
92. Keller, *Face of the Deep*.
93. Peacocke and Pederson, *The Music of Creation*, 12.
94. Peacocke and Pederson, *The Music of Creation*, 13.
95. Genesis 1:1–3a, NRSV.

time, for there is none of either space or time if there are no patterns in the action.

The universe and everything in it evolves, with an evolution that itself changes. Evolution is sometimes rapid, sometimes slow; sometimes there are patterns, sometimes there are not. And every star, every planet, every black hole, every asteroid, every galaxy—and everything else, including the dark matter that we are only now beginning to comprehend—is action, and it evolves, with a changing evolution, and no one thing is the same as any other: although there might be likenesses that we try to express with our changing language, a language itself changing because it belongs to a changing universe.

We construct a world by what we do, and the action that is ourselves, and the action that is the world around us, combine to create changing patterns of action that affect us and that affect the universe. Everything affects everything else: there is no end to the implications of a changing pattern of action.

And God is the universe's creator in the sense that God is pure action and is changing patterns of action, layer upon layer, and this God gives birth to the action that is the universe, and it changes God and God changes it. Not just once, but eternally. It is not that God has created and left the universe to evolve on its own. As John Polkinghorne suggests:

> God's purposive action within the flexibility of process may be expected to bear some analogy with our human experience of willed activity, for which we know that there must be such flexibility, since we exercise it all the time.[96]

And God, as the source of all action, may be expected to bear some analogy with the action in patterns that we are and that the universe is.[97] It is not that God is an object exercising purposive action. The action is God and God is Action and is action in changing patterns. It is more true of God than it is of us that God is action.

It is no surprise that this action in patterns that we call "creation" is so often likened to music.

> There can be no scientific account of the very existence of a universe of this kind because all-that-is is contingent, all could have been otherwise. It is in response to such questions that we affirm that the world does not just happen to be ... God is the supreme Creator-Composer, the incomparable Improviser. ... And what

---

96. Polkinghorne, *Science and Providence*, 25.
97. Alston, "How to Think about Divine Action," 63–70.

> emerges is a fugue, with both order and surprise: or perhaps it is jazz. . . . God sings the blues with us, humming along with our words of pain and despair . . . We learn the music of creation by practising in an ensemble, with other voices learning their parts along with us.[98]

The universe is a changing pattern of action, emerging from God, and still embraced by God, the pure action that constantly changes the patterns of action that we call "the universe," which is pattern upon pattern, action upon action, layer upon layer, every pattern of action changing every other. Just like a composer, "God . . . is in, with, and under all-that-is and all-that-goes-on."[99] Nothing is still, for there is no still point in the universe, just as there is no absolute chaos in the universe. There are patterns that are not God, for the patterns change each other, and so new patterns emerge (and straight away this happens, once two patterns emerge in God and relate to each other)—and these are not God but neither are they strangers to God, whom they constantly change, for every pattern of action affects every other.

And the universe is patterns of action building into broader patterns, and yet broader ones, from what we call the microscopic to what we call the macroscopic, every level changing every other. Yes, there are stabilities within these patterns, but they are action all the same. Nothing is still, there are no particles, and there are no things, except in so far as we use those words to describe relatively stable patterns. At the atomic level these patterns are the quanta, the predictable forms in which the action that we call electrons, protons and neutrons find themselves, just as when we blow a tin whistle certain frequencies dominate in the chaotic movement of the air inside it. But it is all action and change. And similarly, force is action in changing patterns, gravity is action in changing patterns, interparticle forces are action in changing patterns, and all other wave motions are action in changing patterns. It works, it multiplies, the self-reinforcing patterns multiply, and we are the result, and we can watch it and describe it (and at the same time cannot avoid changing it)—and we can use language to express for ourselves this reality that is action in changing patterns. It is because it works that it's here, that the chaos has given birth to relatively stable patterns of action: but not to being, not to the static. And it might all change again, when the universe collapses, or even if it does not, or in another universe in which action gives birth to new patterns, entirely new patterns, and different orders emerge from the chaos: and all of it has its

---

98. Peacocke and Pederson, *The Music of Creation*, 5, 9, 30, 51, 53.
99. Peacocke and Pederson, *The Music of Creation*, 23.

origins in God, who creates; and all of it changes the patterns of action that constitute God.

In chapter 7 of *An Actological Metaphysic* we proposed an actological understanding of time as multiple unidirectional changing patterns into which action falls. Patterns of action are embedded within each another, and so we say that some are of short duration, and some of long, and all of it relates to multiple different unidirectional changing patterns of action, for time is relative and multiple. The universe evolves as patterns of action change each other and patterns emerge in the changing; and minds evolve, and so do languages and cultures: and galaxies, stars and planets all evolve—and it is action upon action, reflecting the nature of God: it is all made in God's image, and yet it is not God, for the patterns change each other and they do not all emerge from the Action, action itself, and changing patterns of action, that is God. The ferment relates to every action, and to every changing pattern of action, just as every action relates to every other within what we call the universe. So God is the creator, not just in the sense that all action and all patterns of action that give birth to new patterns of action have their origin in God, but also in the sense that what is created is not God, even though it is intimately related to everything that is God: or rather, to everything that God does.

What our language can grasp, and what our concepts can understand, are the relatively settled patterns within the universe—what we call things that change. So we find it relatively easy to believe, with Polkinghorne, that

> all free action, ours or God's, depends upon "gaps," the inherent incompleteness which makes openness possible, just as the resultant flexibilities require for their lasting significance that they be exercised within a generally reliable environment.[100]

But is there a "generally reliable environment"? Yes, to some extent. Some patterns of action change more slowly than others; and order constantly emerges out of the chaos of action, just as it does for multiple complex dynamical systems. But it is not that there is, on the one hand, a stable environment, and, on the other, God's action in the gaps in that. It is all action, it is all action in changing patterns, and God is the source of action, God is Action, and God relates to all of the action in patterns. There are no nongaps. As Polkinghorne suggests, "there is no reason to think that the physical world is so structured that God's particular activity is excluded from

---

100. Polkinghorne, *Science and Providence*, 34.

it."[101] The physical world is action in changing patterns, with all of which God is engaged. Gap is ubiquitous.

For thousands of years we have conceptualized the universe as an essentially unchanging object within which change occurs, but here we are understanding reality as action in patterns: patterns of action that do not change in settled ways as they emerge from the clash of pattern upon pattern, or perhaps emerge anew from within the ferment that is God as God relates to every action, bringing new actions and new patterns to birth. Here everything is miracle. It is not that there is a "natural" and a "supernatural," as departments of reality sealed off from each other: for if reality was like that then we would know nothing of the supernatural, it could not function as an explanation of the natural, and it would get us no nearer to explaining miracles than a presupposition that all there is is the natural world so miracles cannot happen.[102] There are not two categories of reality: the reality is action, within which we experience changing patterns, and therefore within which there is no clear division between an ordered environment and miracles. All there is is rates of change: although having said that, the idea of a rate of change can only be used analogously, because it assumes a fixed environment within which rates of change can be measured. There is no such thing. There is simply action in changing patterns.

Everything is changing patterns of action that we cannot grasp: the fleeting patterns, the patterns that we find it difficult or impossible to relate to, the patterns so different from the patterns that we identify as ourselves: the dark matter, the miracle, the unique, the mystery—these are all the relatively ungraspable: although in fact every action and every pattern is "other," there are no two the same, there is no identity, for we ourselves change, and so does everything else, and so does every relationship between every changing pattern of action. Thus between them the universe and God create the most phenomenal, indescribable, ungraspable chaos—the total chaos in and from God alone, and layers of changing patterns in God and in the universe, all changing each other, with new patterns emerging all the time—so nothing is ever the same, and Action, the utter chaos, action itself, and the changing patterns of action that constitute the heart of God and out of which God lets patterns of action go, is a continual ferment of creation. God sends it all out, and takes it all in, reviving it, sending it back renewed, changing pattern of action upon changing pattern of action.

God creates. First comes the chaos; then God's Spirit creates pattern, or order; and then the sun, the moon, the earth, and all the rest emerge—in

---

101. Polkinghorne, *Science and Providence*, 44.
102. Nowell-Smith, "Miracles," 253.

a remarkably correct order.[103] So what is the relationship between unordered action and God? Does God create that as well? Perhaps that is not necessary: because if God is Action, then God is automatically the source of action: God and action are coeternal. It is the explosion of patterns that is the creative moment: and forever after that, God's creativity has been at work, generating patterns in the action, constantly being the source of all action, and always "in movement," working at "a creation still unfinished."[104]

John Haught has found that Teilhard de Chardin increasingly felt that understanding God as "being"

> does not connect comfortably with the dramatic new scientific sense of a world still in the process of *becoming*. . . . Evolution . . . demands that we think of God as attracting the world into being from out of the future . . . drawing the whole cosmos forward into the realm of the not-yet.[105]

CONCLUSIONS

In a structured systematic theology, "the nature of God" is generally an early category. However, as we have seen, a rather different conception of God has emerged as we have studied those philosophers who have worked with something like an "action in patterns" conceptual framework.[106] Here we find a God thoroughly engaged with a changing and diverse world, and thus also changing and diverse: God as Action, the source of action; God as Action, "action itself"; and God as action in changing patterns. We should therefore speak of "the action of God" rather than "the nature of God," with "the action of God" not understood as a subsidiary issue in relation to God's Being or being, but as the primary reality of God, with anything unchanging, static, or being-related, being understood as a secondary and contingent phenomenon. Peacocke and Pederson suggest that there is "permanence as a pattern of change, change in permanence."[107] Might it not be more consistent to say that there is permanent change?

David Goodbourn[108] questions whether to lose "substance" language is to lose the actor who acts, and is thus to lose intentionality. "If God is pure

---

103. Genesis 1:1—2:3
104. Mayne, *The Enduring Melody*, 121.
105. Haught, *The Cosmic Vision of Teilhard de Chardin*, 87.
106. Torry, *Actology*; *Actological Readings in Continental Philosophy*; and *An Actology of the Given*.
107. Peacocke and Pederson, *The Music of Creation*, 14.
108. In private correspondence. David Goodbourn was General Secretary of

action, then what are we adding to anything by using the language of God? . . . If God is action, rather than an actor who acts, what difference does it make to describe some action as God?" I would respond that to define God in terms of action is to begin with God, and that God defined by action, and by particular patterns of action, is as definite a God as any other. So this is the approach that we shall continue to pursue.

Churches Together in Britain and Ireland.

Chapter 4

A suffering God

Thesis: Evil and sin are action in changing patterns, and God suffers along with Jesus, us, and all of the created order.

INTRODUCTION

Evil and sin are action in changing patterns and so are as real as anything else. In this chapter we shall ask about the origins of evil, God's relationship with evil, and God's suffering of evil.

GOD, GOOD, EVIL, AND SIN

We call "good" those patterns of action that emerge from God, and evil some of the patterns of action that emerge from relationships between the patterns of action that constitute God and other patterns of action, such as those that constitute us, when those new patterns of action become increasingly unlike any patterns of action that constitute God. Just as God changes—we might say "changes perfectly"—so goodness must change, because if God is God then the action in changing patterns that constitute God must also constitute goodness. Goodness, or the Good, is not some unchanging datum, and is certainly not an independent permanent criterion by which we might be able to measure the goodness of God. The changing patterns of action that constitute God are what reveal the nature of goodness: a goodness that is therefore just as much action in changing patterns as is God and as are we ourselves.

So where does evil come from? It is not that God allows evil, as Polkinghorne suggests:[1] evil is inevitable, and God is a "fellow sufferer"[2] in the midst of it all.

> The open flexibility of the world's process affords the means by which the universe explores its own potentiality, humankind exercises its will, and God interacts with his creation.[3]

The dilemma is often put as Antony Flew has put it:

> Either God cannot abolish evil or he will not: if he cannot then he is not all-powerful; if he will not then he is not all-good.[4]

Flew recognizes that a "human free will" response is not an adequate response in relation to natural evil, and neither is the argument that such goods as forgiveness require there to have been evil to be forgiven, for the cost of different kinds of evil falls on the victims of the evil, and whether it falls on God as well is not relevant. Flew suggests that God could have created people in such a way that they would always choose to do good and not evil, so not to have done that is reprehensible.[5] And God could have created us virtuous, in which case there would not even have been discussion of the possibility that God might have allowed evil to flourish so that we could be educated in goodness.

Good and evil are not things, and they are not fixed, for God changes, so the changing patterns of action that emerge from God change, and the changing patterns of action that we are change. "Good" is a changing pattern of action, and so is evil—and both are defined by their relationship to the character of God, which in relation to us and the created order is changing patterns of action as well as Action, the source of all action.

But there will also be stability, for it is patterns that we are discussing, so we should expect God to exhibit continuity as well as change, and the same must be true in relation to ourselves. God is not the same God as God was a year ago, and I am not exactly the same person that I was a year ago. The Cutty Sark in Greenwich is no longer the Cutty Sark that once sailed East to collect a cargo of tea and get it back to the UK before other boats could do so. It's been repaired and repaired, and a few years ago it was largely rebuilt following a fire. Is it still the Cutty Sark? Few of the cells,

---

1. Polkinghorne, *Science and Providence*, 67.
2. Polkinghorne, *Science and Providence*, 68.
3. Polkinghorne, *Science and Providence*, 67.
4. Flew, "Divine omnipotence and human freedom," 144.
5. Flew, "Divine omnipotence and human freedom," 53.

molecules, and particles out of which we are built are the same as those of ourselves as newborn children. So does each of us possess an identity? Yes, if we understand "identity" to mean the action in changing patterns that we experience as ourselves at this moment. Tomorrow my identity will be different, although there might be identifiable family resemblances: that is, the patterns of action might be similar from one moment to another, and possibly from one month to another; and I can remember aspects of my former life: changing patterns of action that we can entangle with other changing patterns of action.

We are changing patterns of action, good actions are like each other, and evil actions are like each other: but the definitions of the likenesses will change, so we shall never be able to pin down these ideas. All we can do is seek the patterns of action that constitute God, and do them, and attempt to know which are the actions that are God by their likeness to others that we believe constitute God: but we shall never be sure, for the patterns of action that constitute God change, and we change, so our relating to God's changing patterns of action changes, and we are left arguing among ourselves as to which actions are good and which are evil: for God relates to all of it: "he commanded and raised the stormy wind, which lifted up the waves of the sea. . . . he made the storm be still, and the waves of the sea were hushed."[6]

Owen Thomas has pointed out that the idea of "double agency"— that "in one event both the divine and creaturely agents are fully active"[7]—can be found in the theologies of Thomas Aquinas, Friedrich Schleiermacher, and Karl Barth, and he gives the example of Paul's first letter to the Corinthians: "But by the grace of God I am what I am, and his grace towards me has not been in vain. On the contrary, I worked harder than any of them—though it was not I, but the grace of God that is with me."[8] Even if the "agency" in "double agency" is here analogical to human agency,[9] the fact that the changing patterns of action that constitute God are entangling with those that constitute ourselves and the created order implies a usage less analogical than might be the case if we were to be understood as beings that change and God was to be understood as unchanging Being. This difference encourages us to radicalize the idea of double agency into what we might call "multiple agency," or perhaps "infinite agency": the idea that every changing

---

6. Psalm 107:25, 29.

7. Thomas, "Recent Thought on Divine Agency," 46.

8. 1 Corinthians 15:10, NRSV; Thomas, "Recent Thought on Divine Agency," 49.

9. Forsman, "'Double Agency' and Identifying Reference to God"; McLain, "Narrative Interpretation and the Problem of Double Agency," 160; Tracy, "Narrative Theology and the Acts of God."

pattern of action is ultimately entangled with every other, and that God, as Action, as the source of all action, and as particular changing patterns of action, is entangled with all of it. "That God appears among us and must be understood is grounded in our experience and worldedness,"[10] and at the same time the universe and ourselves, in our worldedness, appear in God, whose understanding is grounded in God's experience. God is not a stranger to any of it, so evil actions change God, and God changes them, so the patterns that are evil can become good, because the patterns change and the patterns that are good and are God change, so the evil will change and become good: but then there will be new evil actions because patterns of action that are good will relate to each other and will give birth to patterns of action that corrupt good patterns—and because novelty inevitably arises wherever changing patterns of action entangle with each other, as well as in new changing patterns of action that constitute God,[11] patterns of action very far from the patterns that constitute God can emerge (and they do), but even these change God and God changes them.

Will there ever be closure? Will the changing come to an end? No—for then there would be no God. But the question leads us to ask whether perfection is even conceivable. The problem here is that if a state that we might choose to call perfection were ever to be reached, in order for it to remain perfection it would be essential that it would not change: but then it would be less than real, and it would have nothing to do with changing patterns of action, and so nothing to do with God or with ourselves. Such a "perfection" would be pointless. If God is Action, and is changing patterns of action, and we are changing patterns of action, then perfection has to be constituted by patterns of action, change, movement, diversity, and the dynamic. It might be true that such a definition is likely to meet resistance, for we are insecure beings, and however much we enjoy journeying, we want to know that we shall arrive. But what if there is no arrival? What if our relationships with one another, and our relationship with God, are constantly changing and have no final end-point but rather a continual changing? Can we manage without a finality of some kind? Without a final judgment? Can we bear to abandon hope for a final vindication in which suffering is healed, evil is conquered, and the perpetrators of evil are judged and the evil cleansed? With a God-is-subject theology or a God-is-object theology we have real problems thinking about evil: its purpose, its roots, its final end: but what happens to it if God is letting-become?—if God is in process? Then God too suffers the evil, and indeed is suffering; God is gracious self-giving, and

---

10. Hemming, *Postmodernity's Transcending*, 244-45.
11. TeSelle, "Divine Action," 88.

receives the evil and transforms it; and we are action in changing patterns, and time is not linear or a datum, but is movement, and we need no longer conceive of eternal life as a state but as changing patterns of action: the action which is remembering, the action which is cleansing, the action which is healing, an action which is only alive when it is changing—and so there is no eschaton but there is symphony.

How we are to speak of such things I don't know, for language is fluid in relation to language, and there is no reference to changing patterns of action that are not language, so there cannot even be analogy, let alone reference, for analogy assumes a normative use of a word upon which to base an analogical use. No, we can only tell stories—or rather, we can tell stories, and we no longer need to restrict ourselves to mere description, for in the context of a theology of action, in the context of Wittgenstein and Derrida, in the context of Bergson, Blondel, and Whitehead, and in the context of Jesus of Nazareth, the storyteller, the primary mode of theology is the story: it is the creative art of the writing of the text or of the telling of the narrative. The story will no longer have a happy ending, or a tragic ending: it will have no ending. Isn't that the way in which Mark ends his gospel when the women run from the empty tomb, "for they were terrified"?[12]

The journey, the pilgrimage—whether simply there, or there and back:[13] this is the normative story of the Christian tradition, for the tradition reveals a God who is action, and a cosmos that is patterned action, from the smallest particle to the entirety of the universe: and who can tell what other realms of patterned action there might be? It is difficult to speak of other realities when reality is viewed as states of affairs, for states of affairs cannot interpenetrate—the language-game won't let them: but the same is not true of changing patterns of action, and of patterns of action relating to each other, for patterns of action interpenetrate and affect one another, so that we can speak joyfully, and without fear, of realms of action that we cannot yet experience, but can only glimpse obliquely: and we can hope, and our hope is a Christian hope that brings about what is hoped for, and the hoped-for is created by what is hoped for, for the hoped-for and the hoper and the hope are intertwining changing patterns of action.

So will the evil ever be destroyed? Will there one day be only good actions? No—for that would mean that patterns of action would no longer be relating to each other and generating new changing patterns of action. Will evil actions be transformed? Yes—they are transformed, and they shall

---

12. Mark 16:8. Author's translation.

13. See Bunyan, *The Pilgrim's Progress*, for the one-way pilgrimage, and Sölle, *The Inward Road and the Way Back*, and Bruce Reed, *The Dynamics of Religion*, for "there and back" models.

be, for God enfolds patterns of action that are evil in patterns of action that are good, and transfigures the evil ones so that they become new changing patterns of action, changing patterns of action of the character of the changing patterns of action that constitute God. As Dennis Nineham puts it in his commentary on Mark 8:27–9:1, in which Jesus predicts his own and his disciples' suffering: "One day God would judge this world and bring this age to an end, transforming whatever in it was capable of being transformed, and transferring it to the conditions of his realm."[14]

There is no "good" and no "evil" in themselves, and there is no essence or substance of "the good." There is no other world in which there is some absolute good. There are only the many different uses of the words "good" and "evil" applied to elements of the great diversity of human experience— and an action at one time and place will be "good," and a similar action at another time and place will be "evil," and an action can be both good and evil, or neither, and we are left to choose between actions that are all mixtures of good and evil. Standards change, ethics change. There might well be patterns, similarities, family likenesses, between codes of behavior in one time and place and codes of behavior in another, but there is still no unchanging "good" and thus no unchanging "evil"—and at any one time and place some people will find only good in an event, and some only evil, and some a mixture of the two.

For all of us, concepts of good and evil relate to what we believe about God, and if God changes and God is action, then good is action that is God's action and evil is action that is somehow opposed to action that is God. So if God is grace, then generous self-giving is good, and selfishly to grasp to oneself is evil, and the meanings and the actual practice of these definitions will change constantly.

The kinds of patterns of action that we call evil, and the kinds that we call good, certainly change: but the action in changing patterns is real, and so good and evil are real enough, with the different good changing patterns of action bearing family resemblances to each other, and the different evil actions or patterns of action bearing family resemblances to each other. In many circumstances it might be possible to say that the good is action: new patterns, new changing relationships; and that the evil is the static—for it cannot breed life. Thus the universe is good, God is the ultimate good, Jesus is good—and we are a mixture of good and evil. And if we are the objects of evil actions, then we suffer; and if we do evil to another person then we sin, our action is our sinful action, and it will cause suffering to ourselves, to others, to the planet, to animals, to God, or to any or all of those.

---

14. Nineham, *Saint Mark*, 228.

There are, of course, evil changings: and we shall often experience as evil those changing patterns of action that close down future changing. But even these processes, in a larger context, might be taken up into the change that is God and might contribute to new and life-enhancing patterns that also change and that relate to the God in whom there is no stillness. And similarly, our sin is whatever stifles possibilities, whatever promotes the static, the dead (which will be different in different contexts). We sin when we close off possibilities for new changing patterns of action, for others, for ourselves, or for God.

But we need stability, so we need to sin; we need patterns, and so we need to sin: and perhaps this need for stability is our "original sin": a fact of life rather than a matter of choice, for we need stability within which to change; but let us at least make out of our sinful patterns of action new possibilities that permit the possibility of yet more new changing patterns of action. Thus there will be some goodness in all of it, some righteousness. To seek innovation is to tackle sin at its roots, for it is to be godlike.

This all rather suggests that there are no permanent moral norms, but rather that in every new age we need to seek out those changing patterns of action that promote possibilities for new action, rather than return to norms from a previous age which in this age might promote a stultifying rigidity.

Whether we were to decide that particular changing patterns of action might be described as good or evil, God will love them, for that is the nature of grace: and God will transform both evil and good in order to create new diversity, and, we hope, a universe increasingly without evil, a new universe that will not be the old one but that will be the old one changed (for the risen Christ still bears the scars of the nails[15]). This is our hope: a hope for the Kingdom of God. But to what extent will our own action in patterns bring about the Kingdom of God for which we hope? Should we be optimistic about human nature, and regard ourselves as capable of contributing to the creation of utopia? Or should we be pessimistic—or perhaps realistic—and recognize that all that we can hope for is sufficient control over our evil tendencies to enable human society not to disintegrate entirely?

In the book of Genesis, Eve looks at the tree of the knowledge of good and evil, which she and Adam had been told not to touch:

> When the woman saw that the tree was good for food, and that it was a delight to the eyes, and that the tree was to be desired to make one wise, she took of its fruit and ate; and she also gave some to her husband, who was with her, and he ate.[16]

15. John 20:19–29.
16. Genesis 3:6, NRSV.

Let us blame neither Eve nor Adam, for they were intent only on seeking knowledge for the betterment of themselves and of their world. They were reaching for mature autonomy. We might legitimately applaud their decision to eat the apple: but their new knowledge destroyed their innocence and propelled them into a new existence in which hard work had to be done, in which hard decisions had to be made, and in which hard consequences had to be endured. The attempt to create utopia had brought about the destruction of utopia. And so it has always been, whatever the political label the utopianism has carried: the attempt to create utopia inevitably brings with it a release of unpredictable and often evil consequences, and we end up having to turn our minds to pragmatic and morally ambiguous policies in order to limit the damage done by our utopianism. It was E.F. Schumacher who warned against seeking final solutions in any sphere of human endeavor,[17] for a final solution is never that, and the pursuit of it can distract us from making constructive changes, and can blind its seekers to their own destructive tendencies. In any case, an action in changing patterns conceptual framework necessarily forbids a final solution: for the achievement of one would be the end of action, change, and diversity, and would result in an absolute death of reality. We can and must pursue the Kingdom of God: a community constituted by action in changing patterns that conforms to the patterns of action that constitute God—so both God and God's Kingdom never "arrive" anywhere: there is a perfect permanent changing. And it is in the pursuit of that that pragmatic and changing patterns of action are required. So the pursuit of utopia properly understood, and the seeking of pragmatic policies that will limit the damage that we do and will move us a step or two towards a Kingdom of God characterized by grace—by generous giving—are both required, and they need each other.

A good example of optimism about human nature is the fifth-century British monk Pelagius. In reply to Pelagius's belief that we can choose to do good things, Augustine wrote: "These [Pelagians] are such opponents of the grace of God . . . that without it, as they believe, man can do all the commandments of God."[18] This was a caricature of Pelagius's beliefs, and in the midst of controversy we all caricature others' ideas and become caricatures of ourselves—but, all the same, there was an important point at stake: Are we able to choose good ends and to pursue them by good means? Or are we so riddled with an "original sin" that the most that we can hope for is to be forgiven for the evil that we do, and that anything that is good is a gift from outside ourselves? Augustine rightly understood that his concentration on

17. Schumacher, *Small is Beautiful*, 54, 216.
18. Augustine, *De Haeresibus*, §88.

sin could easily lead to total neglect of the body politic, so he propounded his doctrine of the "two cities": of the City of God, that realm in which God's grace operates and to which the Church bears witness; and of the City of this world—that political realm in which the activity of the State and of its citizens might keep some control over the effects of sin.

Augustine's "two cities" dualism led to Luther's "two kingdoms" theology, which ultimately legitimated Germany's National Socialism and led to its blessing by large parts of the Church. But however much there was wrong with Augustine's obsession with sin, Pelagius's ideas were naïve and thus possibly more debilitating in the longer term: as have been those of many English-speaking theologians and philosophers since then. Such an optimistic character was Walter Rauschenbusch, an American theologian at the beginning of this century, and the father of what came to be known as the Social Gospel movement. He said this:

> For the first time in religious history we have the possibility of so directing religious energy by scientific knowledge that a comprehensive and continuous reconstruction of social life in the name of God is within the bounds of human possibility.[19]

Rauschenbusch believed that a corporate change of mind was both necessary and possible, and that even the business world had the capacity to value every human being associated with it. An "organism of mutual service"[20] was a human possibility, and American "progress" and democracy were important means of bringing this about. He did not seem to understand that American "progress" was largely a result of the exploitation of the Caribbean, nor that American democratic processes were heavily influenced by economic factors: but, to his credit, he did encourage Americans, and particularly the churches, to regard themselves as change-agents, and to believe that their activity could make a difference to American society.

It was this kind of optimism against which Reinhold Niebuhr rebelled when as a pastor in Detroit during the Great Depression he abandoned both the Social Gospel and socialism and began his lifelong campaign on behalf of realism. His first major work was titled *Moral Man and Immoral Society*,[21] and it carried the message that when people with good intentions get together to carry out by good means a project with good ends, then the result inevitably ends up being tainted with evil. "The higher the aspirations

---

19. Rauschenbusch, *Christianity and the Social Crisis*, 209.
20. Rauschenbusch, *A Theology for the Social Gospel*, 109.
21. Niebuhr, *Moral Man and Immoral Society*.

rise the more do sinful pretensions accompany them."[22] Niebuhr quite rightly saw that individual ethics and social ethics have very little to do with each other.

> A sharp distinction must be drawn between the moral and social behavior of individuals and of social groups, national, racial and economic; and . . . this distinction justifies and necessitates political policies which a purely individualistic ethic must always find embarrassing.[23]

Social conflict is inevitable, and coercion is essential in any society that hopes for a tolerable corporate way of life.

Niebuhr's writings are littered with such words as "equality" and "liberty," but these words are never meant to describe realizable social conditions: they are always "regulative principles,"[24] unrealizable ideals necessary as the "final dyke against relativism."[25] Approximations to the ideal are all that will ever be possible, and social ethics will always be a matter of choosing between different shades of grey. "Let those who are revolted by . . . ambiguities have the decency to retire to the monastery, where medieval perfectionists found their asylum."[26]

Niebuhr, like Rauschenbusch, supported democratic political processes, but for a different reason. He agreed with Rauschenbusch that democracy was made possible by our idealism, but he did not have Rauschenbusch's faith that democracy would achieve a better society. What he did believe was that the tendency of our activity to corrupt society required democratic processes to minimize the effects of our inevitable manipulation of institutions for our own benefit. Niebuhr was a lifelong student of industry, and believed a democratic state and strong trades unions to be necessary brakes on the ability of large corporations to exploit workers, consumers, and the environment. Niebuhr was the theologian of the balance of power, and in this aspect of his thought his Lutheran heritage played a vital part. However, he thought Augustine and Luther to have been wrong to divide the community of pure self-giving from the community in which self-love and contending interests needed to be controlled by the State's coercion,[27] and he sought to make the former community, and other religious frames of

---

22. Niebuhr, *An Interpretation of Christian Ethics*, 96.
23. Niebuhr, *Moral Man and Immoral Society*, xi.
24. Niebuhr, *The Godly and the Ungodly*, 64.
25. Niebuhr, *Christian Realism and Political Problems*, 164.
26. Niebuhr, *Christianity and Power Politics*, 175.
27. Niebuhr, *Moral Man and Immoral Society*, 233–34.

reference,[28] into a regulative principle which would at least slightly inform those means by which the politics of pessimism tried to arbitrate between conflicting interests in a corrupt society. An optimistic assessment of human nature is a necessary source of energy when it comes to challenging traditional forms of authority and social structure: but the optimism, left to its own devices, will destroy itself and its social project. It needs to be balanced by realism about our individual and collective self-interest. By the end of his career as a theologian, political philosopher, and statesman, Niebuhr believed the United States to have reached a situation wanted by neither realists nor idealists, but which at least kept tolerable order: the politics of universal franchise and some well-organized trades unions between them controlling to some extent the worst abuses of excessive economic power. But the recognition of the possible ironies and tragedies of a social project did not deter Niebuhr from advocating action: he understood the dangers of the United States entering the Second World War, but before the Japanese raid on Pearl Harbor he was asking the American churches to abandon their pacifism and to participate in a war that seemed to him less evil than the threat of a Nazi-dominated Europe. Similarly, he believed democracy to be necessary, even though it creates ironies, as every democratic process is in the end dominated by those with economic power, and so itself finally legitimates the authority of economic power.

We need both Pelagius and Augustine, both Rauschenbusch and Niebuhr. Whichever element of each of those pairs is more amenable to our own attitudes, we would be well advised to give attention to the other: for each of us needs to be both optimistic and pessimistic at the same time, and each of us needs to be both utopian and realistic. Realism requires us to recognize that nowhere that we might arrive can possibly be an ideal position, so we must constantly move on. Society must be always action, and the patterns of action always changing. And utopianism requires movement in the direction of the currently chosen aim: but in the recognition that the aim will change, so the direction must change. And then realism will again recognize a diversity of aims, and even more complex changes in the patterns of action, just some of which might come to resemble the changing patterns of action that constitute God.

---

28. Niebuhr, *The Godly and the Ungodly*, 4.

A SUFFERING GOD

In memoriam

Here I cannot avoid writing in the first person:

After a curacy at the Elephant and Castle in South London, and five years as an industrial chaplain with the South London Industrial Mission, in 1988 I became Vicar of St Catherine's, Hatcham, in New Cross, also in South London. The worship was centered on the Eucharist, children had for some years been made to feel welcome, and innovation was accepted as normal. Before I arrived, the bishops had sent a questionnaire asking the parish about the policy that it wished to follow in relation to children receiving communion. The Parochial Church Council replied that they wished to continue to admit children to communion at the age of seven—a practice permitted in the Diocese of Southwark since 1975—but that they did not regard that policy as definitive: the implication being that some wished to see smaller children receive communion: for were they not baptized? My own interest in seeing the parish's worship as a welcoming experience, when combined with this similar interest in the parish, led fairly quickly to parents being encouraged to share their bread with their children at the altar rail: a practice that had become more common amongst parish churches and cathedrals up and down the country.

But then Charmaine, Antoinette, and Justine joined the congregation: three sisters aged ten, eight, and four. They came without their parents, simply because they wanted to come, and they brought their friends. And there they were, at the communion rail, with their hands held out, and no adults with them to share the bread for which they were asking.

I explained about being admitted to communion and about the classes we held once a year, but they weren't interested in classes: they were interested in joining in, and in any case Justine was too young to be admitted to communion. Sometimes a nearby adult would share their bread with the sister nearest to them, but this still left out the others; and so I took my dilemma to the Parochial Church Council: How could I refuse to give the consecrated bread to these children? How dare I allow them to be excluded and discriminated against simply because they had no parent with them? The Parochial Church Council understood, so I went to see Peter, Bishop of Woolwich, who listened carefully, could not give permission, but understood—and I began to share the consecrated bread with the three girls and their friends and to give the consecrated bread to all of the young children myself rather than leaving it to their parents to share theirs. James, Daniel, and Robin, other priests who lived in the parish and who presided occasionally, began to do likewise.

It was on Sunday the 17th of December 1989 that I first gave Charmaine, Antoinette, and Justine pieces of bread as I passed along the communion rail. And on the night of Friday the 22nd of December, Charmaine, Antoinette, and Justine died in a fire at their home. I went to see the children's grandmother, and their mother, and there was nothing to say except "How can God do this?" A heavy grief affected the whole parish and congregation; at every Christmas service the same news had to be given; and at the girls' funeral just after Christmas I couldn't avoid saying "If you still believe in a God of love . . ." Most of the congregation filed past the open coffins, even though they had been warned that the children's bodies had been burned in the fire, and the grief was audible as people wept and their mother screamed. The thankfulness was both expressed and felt, of course, because the children's very different personalities had enriched all of us, and I for one shall never forget them, nor ever forget that day and the looks of the passers by as the three hearses with three coffins drove through London streets to the cemetery. And amongst the mixed emotions which the tragedy has left behind is the knowledge that I would have found it difficult to forgive myself if the children had died before I had enabled them to participate in the Eucharist: if I had not allowed them to share in the actions that constitute us as the body of Christ. As it is, they participated with the rest of us in the banquet that foreshadows that Kingdom beyond words for which we hope.[29]

And what of God? Every ghastly tragedy carries the same lesson, but it can take personal involvement to bring home to us an understanding that we ought to have developed already: and the lesson that those terrible events in 1989 brought home to me is that it is no longer possible to worship an unmoved God. I had for a long time been aware of the difficulty of doing theology after Auschwitz, and that some attempts appeared to insulate God from the theological consequences of vast suffering: such as Ulrich Simon's *Theology of Auschwitz*, which draws multiple parallels between theological terms and the experience of the concentration camps, but does not allow its reflections to get too close to the heart of God.[30] After the events of Christmas 1989 my inability to worship a God who controls events and is unmoved by them was no longer merely cerebral. The only God possible for me became one intimately involved in the patterns of action that constitute the universe, and one who experiences the universe's suffering: a God

---

29. Torry, "A place at the table."
30. Ulrich Simon, *A Theology of Auschwitz*.

who is changed by the constantly changing patterns of action as much as God changes them: a God characterized by grace, by an accepting, gracious activity—a God who can be spoken of only in terms of gift, of giving and receiving, and never again in terms of power and might.

Whilst one understood the platitudes expressed over sandwiches after the three girls' funeral—"He only takes the best," "He loved them so much that he took them"—they were utterly inadequate. The children did not die in their sleep, gently taken. They died terrified, surrounded by flame and smoke, unable to escape from the inferno. It is no longer possible to believe in a God who, whilst able to stop it, chose not to do so, or in one who constantly chooses, or has taken an immutable choice, not to interfere in a world for which God is responsible. I cannot believe in a God who is a moral monster, a psychopath, but only in one powerless to stop the tragedy, powerless to stop any tragedy—and a God who grieves that that is so, whose heart goes out to those who suffer, and who suffers the agony with us: a God who accepts the world's pain and is changed by it to the core of God's being—or rather, to the core of God's action—and whose coming is one of penitence and the desire for reconciliation. It is such a God that we can love with a love that is

> patient . . . kind . . . not envious or boastful or arrogant or rude. It does not insist on its own way; it is not irritable or resentful; it does not rejoice in wrongdoing, but rejoices in the truth. It bears all things, believes all things, hopes all things, endures all things.[31]

One of the sisters' friends said to me, "I can't believe in God any more?" She didn't want me to reply, so I didn't: and in any case I could no longer believe in the God in whom she had ceased to believe. After the 22nd of December 1989 the only God in whom I can believe is one who cannot stop the pain, one who is vulnerable to the world's agony, and one whose character is grace: a reconciling, gracious activity. And then, having believed in this God, I can begin to believe in a God who accepts and transforms the changing patterns of action that are the suffering, the evil, and the sin: not to negate them, and not to forget them, but to send them out again as transfigured new changing patterns of action. God does not forget Charmaine, Antoinette, and Justine. God has suffered with them their intense pain and their deaths, and carries those into new changing patterns of action in the Kingdom of God

---

31. 1 Corinthians 13:4–6.

A GOD WHO SUFFERS

For Mark Vernon, agnosticism might be the only legitimate response to the evil and suffering of the world;[32] and Albert Camus concluded that an almighty God and a suffering humanity can only lead to either atheism or rebellion, and that the only other option is a suffering God.[33] It is this option that we explore in this chapter.

God has taken a risk in creating a universe—indeed, God constantly takes risks as God continually creates the universe—because

> accidents are an inevitable consequence of there being a world sufficiently complex for life to exist. Hence suffering is unavoidable. God's omniscience is unchallenged because, although he knows all that can be known about the good and bad, the original act of creating carried with it certain implications which must have been recognized and could not be altered now without self-contradiction. God could and did take upon himself, in Jesus, the consequences of his decision to create in the first place.[34]

Suffering is an action to or within us that closes off possibilities, that stops us acting or changing, that destroys relationships, that stifles newness. The pattern of action that we call "pain" is suffering, the pattern of action that we call "grief" is suffering. No one instance of suffering is like any other, but there are similarities.

We suffer, other animals suffer, the planet suffers, the universe suffers, Jesus suffers, the risen Christ suffers, the Spirit of God suffers, and God suffers: and so God knows suffering, knows death itself, and goes with us into our suffering. Whenever we suffer, whether we choose to or not, that pattern of action is a pattern of action intimately connected with the patterns of action that constitute God: and just as God has brought healing and new goodness out of the suffering that is Jesus' suffering and therefore God's suffering, so God brings healing and new goodness out of the suffering that is our suffering: although clearly not always in the life that we now experience, in which much suffering goes on and on and results in death. So there must be a new life offered, generously offered, in which newness can be brought out of suffering, for otherwise God's creative action is an evil action, it is sin, and it is unforgivable because there is no transfiguration. As Bruce Epperly puts it:

32. Vernon, *Science, Religion and the Meaning of Life*.
33. Camus, *L'Homme Révolté*, 53.
34. Bartholomew, *God, Chance and Purpose*, 241.

> The world contributes to and shapes God's experience. Rather than turning inward in narcissistic self-absorption . . . God is completely oriented toward the world. God embraces every moment of experience intimately, feeling its joy and sorrow, and responding with new and life-giving possibilities.[35]

"Suffering" means a person's (or anything else's) destruction or corruption by evil patterns of action. It is all the harder to bear because such evil has emerged from the good, and ultimately from God. And the fact that God transforms evil is no comfort. Suffering, like everything else, is action in changing patterns—it changes us, and we change the suffering, as many people of course do. And suffering changes, because every pattern of action is different, every person is different, each person is constantly different, and every evil action is different. No suffering is ever the same as any other.

One person's suffering affects everyone and everything else. Every changing pattern of action affects every other, every relationship between patterns of action affects every other, and suffering is a relationship between an evil pattern of action and a personal pattern of action, so every example of suffering affects every other pattern of action, particularly those in close relationship to the suffering. So we are changed by others' suffering, and we suffer.

The fact that God is Action, and the source of all action, makes God ultimately responsible for the changing patterns of action that emerge from God's "letting happen." Having given birth to action, and to changing patterns of action, those patterns of action will continue to change. Just as one of God's patterns of action is choosing, so it is one of ours: so there is also a sense in which each of us is responsible for the patterns of action that we might call "evil" or "sin." We choose to do evil, and we choose to sin. However, the possibility of that has been chosen by God: and the world of tectonic plates and thus of earthquakes, and the world of bacteria and viruses, and thus of disease, are changing patterns of action to which God has given birth. These are God's responsibility.

How should we respond to this? By deciding that God is not good, as the film *The Trial of God* depicts Jews in a concentration finding when they put God on trial? By recognizing that all language is analogy, particularly when applied to God, so to understand God as suffering is now necessary[36] but does not necessarily imply everything relating to suffering as the concept might apply to us?[37] Perhaps we should simply refuse to

---

35. Epperly, *Process Theology*, 49.
36. Doctrine Commission, *Contemporary Doctrine Classics*, 79, 123–27, 365–66.
37. Ward, *The Concept of God*, 196, 202, 207–8.

respond? Or perhaps we should pretend that there is some other source of action?—in which case God would not be Action, and the source of all action, and would not be God. Or perhaps we should say that God remains the source of changing patterns of action, that the Kingdom of God is and will be patterns of action that will repattern all patterns of action into still changing patterns of action that no longer entail suffering, thus redeeming every changing pattern of action? The last of those options is a possibility, and the most hopeful, because the transfiguration of all patterns of action across all of their changings and relationships, and across all of time and space—which are of course changing patterns of action—will automatically enfold everything into the redemption process: every person and their suffering and death will be transfigured, and the whole of creation, across time and space, and across every conceivable universe, will be brought within the Kingdom of God.

God is good, and God is not good:

> I form light and create darkness,
> I make weal and create woe;
> I the Lord do all these things.[38]

God is violent, and God makes peace. Joshua slaughtered the inhabitants of the city of Ai at God's command:[39] a characteristic action of a God who specialized in anger:

> Now therefore, O kings, be wise;
>   be warned, O rulers of the earth.
> Serve the Lord with fear,
>   with trembling kiss his feet,
> or he will be angry, and you will perish in the way;
>   for his wrath is quickly kindled.[40]

But the violence was matched by a somewhat paradoxical peacemaking, to which the anger was a means to the peaceful end:

> He shall judge between the nations,
>   and shall arbitrate for many peoples;
> they shall beat their swords into ploughshares,
>   and their spears into pruning-hooks;
> nation shall not lift up sword against nation,
>   neither shall they learn war any more.[41]

38. Isaiah 45:7, NRSV.
39. Joshua 8.
40. Psalm 2:10–12, NRSV.
41. Isaiah 2:4, NRSV.

God is the source of every pattern of action, and of the patterns that generate new patterns, and so of freedom. There is no simplicity here: there is extreme complexity, complexity itself, and action itself. There is here no human soul that is in any sense the same as God. There is diversity, as every aspect of the created order exercises its freedom of action, and its freedom to change its patterns of action. God is not looking for a community of reflections of God: the Kingdom of God is rather a community of diversity and of changing patterns of action, and it is all of that to which God relates. But the inevitable consequence is suffering, and all we can hope for is that there was no alternative, and that redemption, completion, healing, maturity, unity—and continuing freedom—will be the direction in which patterns of action change. God is responsible for cancer, earthquake, war, famine, torture, oppression, unemployment, and crucifixion. God has made us free to do evil because that is the only way to create a community of free, individual, changing patterns of action, of whom God can be one. If there could have been any other way to create that Kingdom of God, then God would have chosen it: but there is no other way; there is no other way in which we can be free, free to love God, to love one another, and to understand love as the very character of God.

The idea that God the Creator suffers was once regarded as a heresy: "Patripassionism"; and early in the third century of the Christian era Tertullian accused Praxeas of "crucifying the Father."[42] No: the Father was not crucified. It was Jesus who was crucified—but his suffering is God's suffering, and the Creator's intimate relationship with every changing pattern of action (including those that constitute God) involves God in the whole of the world's suffering as well as in Jesus' suffering. Such a depth of suffering is beyond our imagining. So Tertullian recognized that God suffers analogously to human suffering: an analogy that begins with God, and not with us: for it is God's suffering that is a perfect suffering, and our sufferings therefore have to be understood in an analogous relationship to God's.

> And this, therefore, is to be deemed the likeness of God in man, that the human soul have the same emotions and sensations as God, although they are not of the same kind; differing as they do both in their conditions and their issues according to their nature. Then, again, with respect to the opposite sensations—I mean meekness, patience, mercy, and the very parent of them all, goodness—why do you form your opinion of the divine displays of these (from the human qualities)? For we indeed do

---

42. Tertullian, *Adversus Praxean*, 1; in *Tertullian's Treatise against Praxeas*, edited by E. Evans (London: SPCK, 1948), 123.4–125.3, quoted in McGrath, *The Christian Theology Reader*, 261.

not possess them in perfection, because it is God alone who is perfect. So also in regard to those others—namely, anger and irritation. We are not affected by them in so happy a manner, because God alone is truly happy, by reason of His property of incorruptibility. Angry He will possibly be, but not irritated, nor dangerously tempted; He will be moved, but not subverted. . . . All these affections He is moved by in that peculiar manner of His own, in which it is profoundly fit that He should be affected; and it is owing to Him that man is also similarly affected in a way which is equally his own.[43]

As we have suggested, the primary analogy stems from "the love of God . . . expressed through Jesus in an act of complete divine self-giving which is also perfect self-affirmation."[44] And if this "love of God" is to mean anything, then God is a God who suffers: "God was in Christ reconciling the world by experiencing Jesus' pain as God's own pain. . . . God fully experiences the pain of the world, including Jesus' death on the cross."[45] God suffers from God's own suffering in Jesus, and also from God's immediate relationship with every example of suffering, and with every evil action and every sinful action, so the greatest suffering is God's: as Geoffrey Studdert Kennedy puts it, God's is "the hardest part."[46] God relates to every pattern of action, so to every relationship between an evil pattern of action and any other pattern of action—so God's suffering is unimaginable: and it would be better to say that God's suffering is the definition of suffering, and that we and the universe share in God's suffering.

Studdert Kennedy is not the only modern Christian writer to have explored the possibility of God's suffering, although his thoroughgoing theology of a suffering God was the first to treat the idea as central to theological construction, was unique in its time, and was a forerunner of much theology that evolved during the twentieth century.[47] In the seventeenth century Thomas Traherne wrote that "God . . . is happy in you when you are happy, as parents in their children. He is afflicted in all your afflictions."[48] Particularly in the UK, and during the early twentieth century, a stream of theological thought developed that could be identified as "passibilism": "the doctrine

---

43. Tertullian, *Adversus Marcionem*, book II, 16, 6-7. Cf. Daniel Castelo, "A Crisis in God-Talk."

44. Newlands, *Theology of the Love of God*, 141.

45. Epperly, *Process Theology*, 51.

46. Studdert Kennedy, *The Hardest Part*.

47. Parker, *A Seeker after Truths*, 173-74; Torry, *Actology*, 176-88.

48. Traherne, *Centuries of Meditations*, I, 51-53.

that God is passible, or suffers."⁴⁹ Michael Brierley identifies four strands to the passibilist tradition: 1. A suffering Jesus reveals a suffering God; 2. God is love, so God suffers; 3. God is immanent in the world, so suffers as we and the world suffer; 4. God can only be moral if God suffers⁵⁰—although there are not hard and fast boundaries between the strands. One theologian whose work spanned the second and third categories was C.E. Rolt, who was much influenced by Henri Bergson:⁵¹

> God's true victory consists in the power to endure apparent defeat and failure throughout all time, and still to hope unchanged through the strength of his own patient eternity. If he could not endure this last and uttermost pang, His love would not be omnipotent.⁵²

Michael Brierley calls this "divine passivity."⁵³ It is not. Rolt's God is defined by love, and might equally be said to be love. "God is Love, and this Love is itself His power."⁵⁴ This is an active patience, not a passive one, and it is patience in the context of an intimate relationship with humanity and the cosmos. As Argyris Nicolaidis puts it:

> This relational mode of existence, which has been associated with creative growth, novelty, and free development, is qualified as agape. Agape . . . is the very principle of existence: relating in a creative manner. [God is love] signifies that God is relationality and the whole exists as an endless and continuous manifestation of agape. . . . *I relate, therefore I exist*.⁵⁵

Another theologian who crossed a number of the boundaries was Henry Major, Principal of Ripon College, a Church of England theological college in the liberal tradition. For Major, "the divine suffering is voluntary—prompted by love. If God did not create He would not suffer. Yet love moves him to create."⁵⁶ Geoffrey Studdert Kennedy was a student of Major's at

---

49. Brierley, "Introducing the Early English Passibilists," 218.
50. Brierley, "Introducing the Early English Passibilists."
51. Brierley, "Commemorating C.E. Rolt," 351.
52. Rolt, *The World's Redemption*.
53. Brierley, "Commemorating C.E. Rolt," 353.
54. Rolt, *The World's Redemption*, 16.
55. Nicolaidis, "Relational Nature," 106.
56. Henry Major, "A Modern View of the Incarnation," unpublished paper, quoted in Brierley, "Introducing the Early English Passibilists," 226.

Ripon Hall,[57] and was clear that Major's lectures in the philosophy of religion had influenced both his life and his theology.[58]

Passibilism was much assisted by the Kenotic Christology of P.T. Forsyth in which God was understood to have emptied God of divine characteristics in order to become incarnate in Jesus, and Kenotic Christology, as well as Passibilism, informed the Panentheism of John Robinson and Norman Pittenger:[59] a theological stream that makes God's suffering inevitable. By the end of Chapter 7 we shall find that we have reinterpreted Kenotic Christology as a self-emptying of humanity and not just of the divine.

More recently, John Austin Baker has suggested that God's suffering is an inevitable consequence of the doctrine of the incarnation, which itself implies that "the heart of what it means to be God cannot be such things as immortality or infallibility or cosmic power." [60]

> God bares himself to suffering . . . by creating, God makes himself vulnerable. For the very values which he most cherishes, and for which he intends his creation to be the setting, all depend on freedom; and in the process of learning to share these values, to achieve this freedom, his creatures misunderstand and misuse his work with terrible consequences not only to each other, but, precisely because he loves, to himself as well.[61]

Tom Wright puts it a different way round: "The 'God' who has become human in Jesus is the God who, as he had always promised, was returning to claim his sovereignty over the whole world . . . and would do so by himself sharing the pain and suffering of his people."[62] Dietrich Bonhoeffer, while in prison in Tegel during 1944, not long before his execution, wrote that "the Bible directs [us] to the powerlessness and suffering of God; only a suffering God can help"; [63] and Jürgen Moltmann, who was present at the opening of the German concentration camps, writes of a "crucified God":[64] although he, like Whitehead, does not seem to want to evacuate God of

---

57. Parker, *A Seeker after Truths*, 25; Brierley, "Introducing the Early English Passibilists," 228.

58. Mozley, "Studdert Kennedy: Home life and early years of his ministry," 53.

59. Brierley, "Introducing the Early English Passibilists," 229–31.

60. Baker, ". . . Who is God and Lord of All," 8.

61. Baker, *The Foolishness of God*, 141–42.

62. Wright, *How God Became King*, 187.

63. Bonhoeffer, *Letters and Papers from Prison*, 164; *Widerstand und Ergehung*, 534: "*Die Bibel weist den Menschen an die Ohnmacht und des Leiden Gottes; nur der leidende Gott kann helfen.*"

64. Moltmann, *Das Dekreuzigte Gott*; *The Crucified God*.

all unchangingness. W.H. Vanstone has explored some of the pastoral and other consequences of God's vulnerability and suffering;[65] and Paul Fiddes has offered a wide-ranging study of "a God who suffers eminently and yet is still God, and a God who suffers universally and yet is present uniquely and decisively in the sufferings of Christ," with "God's suffering in one instance of history affecting his suffering in all others."[66] Fiddes identifies a Platonic philosophical framework as a problem when it comes to discussion of God's suffering: for only if God suffers change, and only if change is God's nature, can God be free to be in need[67]—and Fiddes is right to suggest that the more we contemplate the cross as God's death, the more we find God's impassibility impossible. For Fiddes, God suffers and remains God.[68] For process theology, there is a danger, as Fiddes sees it, that the two poles of God—the consequent and primordial poles—remain divided,[69] so that, in the end, God does not suffer. Fiddes wants to say that God is "vital in his own victory over death, and relevant to an adult and yet broken world";[70] and he suggests that a Trinitarian understanding of God might be better able to preserve both the suffering and the transcendence than a dipolar God.[71] What is certainly required is a robust Christology in which Jesus Christ is both fully human and fully God. As David Brown suggests, God's "experience of the world would remain radically different from ours unless he has somehow entered into the human condition. In virtue of having done so, he can then come alongside the sufferer, and offer grace from the inside."[72] No ontology could ground an understanding of such a coming alongside. An actology, on the other hand, can understand the changing patterns of action that constitute Jesus, and in particular his suffering and death, as changing patterns of action that constitute God. There is no need of a kenosis, a self-emptying, here. There might be more to be said about God than we might be able to say about Jesus, but Jesus' action in changing patterns *is* God's action in changing patterns: the changing patterns of action of a human being who shares them with the creator and with the Holy Spirit in a Trinity entirely defined by action in changing patterns.

---

65. Vanstone, *Love's Endeavour, Love's Expense*.
66. Fiddes, *The Creative Suffering of God*, 3, 12.
67. Fiddes, *The Creative Suffering of God*, 3.
68. Fiddes, *The Creative Suffering of God*, 110.
69. Fiddes, *The Creative Suffering of God*, 126.
70. Fiddes, *The Creative Suffering of God*, 206.
71. Fiddes, *The Creative Suffering of God*, 131.
72. Brown, *Divine Humanity*, 208.

CONCLUSION

The "Baroque grandeurs of process theology"[73] are certainly splendid, and they take us some way towards an appropriate framework within which to understand God and creation: but process philosophy is not adequate to express God's suffering because it retains a "primordial pole" in God, and it is not obvious that God's "superject" can enable that primordial pole to be completely involved in suffering. If God is both consequent and creative, and if God is Action and changing patterns of action, then there is at least the possibility that we might be able to understand God as love, as utterly involved in every instance of human suffering, and as intimately involved in every instance of God's own suffering.

The Action and changing patterns of action that are God give birth to patterns of action, and those inevitably give birth to evil patterns, and thus to suffering, making suffering inevitable. There is no other way. And the deepest suffering is God's because God is love.[74]

---

73. Polkinghorne, *Science and Creation*, 83.
74. 1 John 4:8, 16.

Chapter 5

Beginning with Jesus of Nazareth

Thesis: Theology can begin anywhere, and particularly anywhere within the Trinity. An actological approach might usefully begin with the action in patterns that constitute Jesus of Nazareth.

INTRODUCTION

There are many places from which to set out on a theological journey. Within our new paradigm we can discuss Jesus as changing patterns of action, and the New Testament as the revelation of the patterns of action that define him; we can discover ourselves and the universe as changing patterns of action; we can understand relationships between God, Jesus, the universe, and ourselves, as changing patterns of action; and we can start our apologetics in any one of these places. Where we start in any particular situation will of course depend on the agenda set by that situation: but it is at least worth considering some novel possibilities. For instance: using static categories suggests starting the doctrine of the Trinity with God the Creator, then going on to understand Jesus Christ, and then to the Spirit, or maybe beginning with the Creator, then discussing the Spirit, and finally mentioning Jesus Christ. But to employ dynamic categories suggests that we might begin with either Jesus or the Spirit, and then move on to the one whom Jesus called Father and we might call Mother, Father, or both. In the previous two chapters I set out from God the creator, understood as Action and as action in changing patterns. I shall now begin from a different place: from Jesus of Nazareth. This echoes N.T. Wright's proposal which is not that we know what the word "god" means, and manage somehow to fit Jesus into that. Instead I suggest that we think historically about a young Jew, possessed of a desperately risky, indeed apparently crazy, vocation, riding into Jerusalem in tears, denouncing the Temple, and dying on a Roman cross—and that we somehow allow our meaning for the word "god" to be recentred around that point.[1]

Jesus was a particular person, in a particular place, at a particular time: a Jew who lived in Galilee, occasionally travelled to surrounding territories, and finally travelled to Jerusalem to die.[2] An important reason for restarting our theological explorations with Jesus of Nazareth is that our understanding of physical reality, at both the microcosmic and the macrocosmic levels, is increasingly of action in changing patterns, whereas early Platonic influence and a Reformation distinction between the Kingdom of God and the Kingdom of this world have located Christian theology firmly within a "beings that change" ontology and God as Being and the source of being. As Oliver Davies puts it, what we now need is "a properly *doctrinal-referential* account of the 'world' as the place in which God became real for us in Jesus Christ and where he continues to be real for us as incarnate Word;"[3] and similarly Oliver Quick asks for

> a doctrine which enables us to think of the life of Jesus as God's act only because it is characteristic of God always and thus truly symbolic of His whole purpose in the world, and again to think of it as the supreme symbol both of God's nature and man's perfection only because here uniquely is the act of God.[4]

Jesus is action in changing patterns, we understand the world as action in changing patterns, and we can understand God as action in changing patterns and as Action and the source of action, so an actological approach that begins with Jesus of Nazareth could look like a useful way to satisfy the need for "a properly *doctrinal-referential* account of the 'world' as the place in which God became real for us in Jesus Christ and where he continues to be real for us as incarnate Word";[5] real for us as the action in changing patterns that constituted Jesus as he lived and worked around the Sea of Galilee, and then briefly in Jerusalem, and that constitutes Jesus of Nazareth

---

1. Wright, *The Challenge of Jesus*, 92. See also Wright, *The New Testament and the People of God*, xv.
2. Vermes, *Jesus the Jew*.
3. Davies et al., *Transformation Theology*, 11.
4. Quick, *The Gospel of Divine Action*, 110.
5. Davies et al., *Transformation Theology*, 11.

for us still. For Jesus is what he did and what he does. He preached and read the Scriptures in synagogues; he travelled; he taught about the coming of the Kingdom of God; he healed those who were ill or living with disabilities; he prayed; he trained disciples; and he ate with people of different social classes.[6] He was "a prophet mighty in deed and word."[7]

JESUS OUR GOD

Perhaps we shall go a little further than Wright, Davies, and Quick choose to go. Rather than recenter an existing meaning of "God" around Jesus we shall begin our definition of God with Jesus of Nazareth, we shall define "God" as "Jesus," and we shall then speak of "Jesus' Father" and of "the Spirit of Jesus":[8] a Spirit of Jesus whom we might identify with the risen Christ. This is no more one-sided than more traditional Trinitarian formulations which effectively begin with the Creator, for we have to begin somewhere, even if we then go on to speak of equality between three persons in one God: and there might be New Testament warrant for starting our definition of God with Jesus. Titus 2:13, 2 Peter 1:1 and John 20:28 all identify "Jesus Christ" with "God,"[9] a fact often noted but rarely allowed to influence Christological debate.[10] Similarly, in John 1:1, the difference between "God" and "the Word" is normally at the heart of interpretation, rather than the Gospel-writer's clear identification of them with each other.[11] "In the beginning was the Word, and the Word was with God, and the Word was God . . . and the Word became flesh and lived among us . . ."[12] Jesus is the Word and the Word is God and Jesus is God; and when Jesus said to Thomas, "Reach

---

6. Wright, *Jesus and the Victory of God*, 148–49.

7. Luke 24:19, NRSV: "deed and word." Wright, *Jesus and the Victory of God*, 168 erroneously translates as "word and deed," and then places sections about Jesus' teaching ministry before material on Jesus' "works": Wright, *Jesus and the Victory of God*, 171–96.

8. Acts 17:7; Philippians 1:19.

9. Titus 2:13 and 2 Peter 1:1, NRSV, permit of readings which do not make this identification, but Cullman, in *The Christology of the New Testament*, 313–14, persuasively argues that in the case of Titus 2:13 "'God' is not to be distinguished from 'Saviour Jesus Christ.'"

10. For instance, the designation of Jesus as "God" is tackled in the final substantive chapter in Cullmann, *The Christology of the New Testament*, 306–14, and is dealt with in the context of Jesus' designation as "Lord" rather than in its own right.

11. A somewhat speculative possibility is that Mark 1:1 once contained the designation of Jesus as "God" and that some scribes removed it and others changed it to various forms of "Son of God."

12. John 1:1–14, NRSV.

out your hand and put it in my side. Do not doubt but believe," Thomas answered him, "My Lord and my God!"[13] Also in the fourth gospel, Jesus saying "I am" is a clear reference to the "I am" spoken by God to Moses.[14] The letter to the Hebrews applies the words of Psalm 45 to Jesus: "Your throne, O God, is for ever and ever, and the righteous sceptre is the sceptre of your kingdom" ;[15] in the letter to the Romans Paul refers to the Messiah—who for him is Jesus—as "God, blessed for ever";[16] in the letter to Titus Jesus is called "our great God and Saviour";[17] and in the second letter of Peter Jesus is called "our God and Saviour."[18] A significant non-biblical witness to the early Christians' identification of Jesus as God is Pliny the Roman: "It was their habit on a fixed day to assemble before daylight and recite by turns a form of words to Christ as a god."[19]

For these early Christian communities, Jesus is God and God is Jesus. In the New Testament such an identification lives contentedly alongside other designations for Jesus, designations that relate Jesus to a God previously defined and worshipped: but in our day, when the idea of such another God has become such a problem, we might do well to return to this early definition of God: that Jesus is God and God is Jesus. Thus we shall worship as God someone who belongs to our world, someone who is one of us and one with us, someone known and yet not known. So when someone says: "What is God like?" I can say: "God is Jesus." And when someone says: "Who is Jesus?" I can say: "Jesus is God." Jesus is not simply a "parable of God,"[20] or a "sacrament of the encounter with God,"[21] as Edward Schillebeeckx suggests: although he is those. He is the changing patterns of action that is God. He is God.

Might the failure to treat the ancient identifications of Jesus with God as important be due to the fact that we have not possessed the conceptual equipment that would enable us to treat the identifications as determinative?

---

13. John 20:27–28, NRSV.

14. John 8:24; Exodus 3:14, NRSV. The Greek of John 8:24 is *hoti ego eimi*, so "Jesus said, 'I am,'" is a better translation than "Jesus said 'I am he.'" Barrett, in his *The Gospel According to St. John*, p. 342, suggests that Jesus is not here claiming an identity with God. Whether or not Jesus was making such an identification, the gospel writer was certainly making it.

15. Hebrews 1:8, NRSV.

16. Romans 9:5, NRSV.

17. Titus 2:13, NRSV.

18. 2 Peter 1:1, NRSV.

19. Pliny, quoted in Stevenson, *A New Eusebius*, 14.

20. Schillebeeckx, *Jesus*, 626.

21. Schillebeeckx, *Christ the Sacrament of the Encounter with God*.

Are we perhaps still too much under the influence of a Neoplatonic conceptual framework that regards Jesus as a human being and God as an unchanging Platonic "Form" and thus as incompatible with the human Jesus? However much we might attempt to discount the continuing influence of a Neoplatonic dualism, we might never actually escape from it until we have challenged it with an alternative framework that prioritizes the dynamic and within which we would come to understand God as Action and as changing patterns of action, and Jesus as changing patterns of action, and their unity as a unity of changing patterns of action, and not as one of substance. Thus "The Father and I are one"[22] becomes a statement about the changing patterns of action that define both Jesus and his Father; and John 1:1 becomes a statement that God is the Word and the Word is God (the Word being the action that is God), and those New Testament passages that designate Jesus as God become the beginning of Christology, and no longer a disconnected and disconcerting appendix. "Whatever the Father does, the Son does likewise."[23] As Kathryn Tanner puts it:

> The acts of Jesus are . . . genuinely twofold in character, displaying both divinity and humanity as distinct features of the very same acts. Jesus' acts are one though twofold—not sometimes divine and sometimes human—and show a consistency of purpose and effect, because they are directed and shaped by the same one who is both divine and human . . .[24]

Such a new conceptual framework would, of course, have other effects on our interpretation of the New Testament, and particularly on the interpretation of such concepts as "grace," which would become unambiguously a pattern of action, a self-giving generosity, and no longer some sort of spiritual substance: but the major effect would clearly be to enable us to reunderstand the New Testament's Christology as one of identification between the patterns of action that constitute Jesus and the patterns of action that belong to God. Choosing this new conceptual framework might bring into question some important doctrinal words. For instance, "incarnation" used of Jesus suggests that an existing God, who was not flesh, became flesh. To identify Jesus with God is to see the patterns of action that we call "flesh," and in particular Jesus' flesh, as intrinsically God: as at the heart of what we mean by God, and not as something that might or might not have been true of God: so flesh and matter are now eternally sacred.[25] Yes, "the Word

---

22. John 10:30, NRSV.
23. John 5:19, NRSV.
24. Tanner, *Jesus, Humanity and the Trinity*, 49.
25. Leech, *The Social God*, 37.

became flesh"[26] at a point in time: but Jesus is eternally God, and God is Jesus. Similarly, in the context of our own history, we can say that Jesus is "God's Love Incarnate":[27] but Jesus is eternally God's Love. Love is a changing pattern of action intrinsic to the patterns of action that constitute God: and those patterns of action constitute Jesus.

And might not this reunderstanding be closer to the New Testament writers' intentions than are the centuries of substance-based interpretation from which their work has suffered? Might not this reunderstanding invite us to say with a meaning closer to that of Thomas: "My Lord and my God"?[28] Might not the Jesus-centered Trinity that these considerations offer to us have biblical warrant in the words "the grace of our Lord Jesus Christ, the love of God, and the fellowship of the Holy Spirit" to be found at the end of Paul's second letter to the Corinthians? And might this new understanding lead to a new Trinitarian formulation: Jesus our God; his Father our God; his Spirit our God? Such a formulation could be a focus of unity between sectarian religion, academic systematic theology (which could identify with it), the mainstream churches, and society at large, which could identify with a human God who did not require an alien metaphysic in order to be meaningful.

CHOOSING JESUS

To choose Jesus as our God will give to us a God with whom we can empathize, for in Jesus "we do not have a high priest who is unable to sympathize with our weaknesses":[29] rather, we have a God who shares our experience: of birth, commitment, exploration, God-talk, prayer, hope, friendship, love, betrayal, despair, confusion, loneliness, and forsakenness—and of being at the end of the world as we have known it. Jesus' apocalyptic convictions have parallels today in our fear of nuclear obliteration and ecological disaster, and in our sense that the world is changing. Jesus questioned his age's traditions as we question those of our own age; he employed ambiguity and irony in order to criticize systems that oppressed his fellow men and women; and his redefinition of the Jews' God, and his feeling of abandonment, bring him closer to our secular skepticism than we might at first have thought. Above all, Jesus changed. He was changed by the Gentile woman

---

26. John 1:14, NRSV.
27. Hick, *Christianity at the Centre*.
28. John 20:28, NRSV.
29. Hebrews 4:15, NRSV.

who wanted her daughter healed,[30] and this event might have been the trigger for Jesus recognizing that the Kingdom of God was for everyone, and not just for the Jews. In Matthew's Gospel, Jesus saw himself as "sent only to the lost sheep of the house of Israel,"[31] and he called his disciples to go "to the lost sheep of the house of Israel" and not "among the Gentiles";[32] but in Luke's Gospel he riles his local Nazareth audience by pointing out that

> there were many widows in Israel in the time of Elijah, when the heaven was shut up for three years and six months, and there was a severe famine over all the land; yet Elijah was sent to none of them except to a widow at Zarephath in Sidon. There were also many lepers in Israel in the time of the prophet Elisha, and none of them was cleansed except Naaman the Syrian.[33]

Whether these different emphases represent the interests of the different gospel writers, or different periods in Jesus' ministry, is difficult to say. Similarly, it is difficult to know the extent to which Jesus initially saw himself as a disciple of John the Baptist,[34] and therefore as calling Israel to a keeping of the Law even more rigorous than the Law itself demanded;[35] and the extent to which his recognition that the Kingdom of God is for unrepentant sinners[36] was a radical change.

Jesus changed: and if he is God then he is a changing God, and God changes. In a world that is changing fast, we need this God with change at his heart, and whose character is change. Not only does such a revised definition of God offer us a God more comprehensible in a secular age, but it also offers additional theological dividends: it identifies God with suffering humanity rather than leaving us to fit suffering and evil into an existing image of an all-powerful, righteous God—a difficult task, to say the least—and it relativizes religion, doctrine, interpretation of the Scriptures, and authority in general, because the choice of the individual person Jesus as the starting-point for a definition of God is essentially arbitrary—even if there are good reasons for making this choice, which there are—and your Jesus will not be my Jesus, however much we both seek to know the Jesus of history and to identify what we perceive to be the risen Christ with that Jesus.

---

30. Mark 7:24–30.
31. Matthew 15:24, NRSV.
32. Matthew 10:5, NRSV.
33. Luke 4:25–27, NRSV.
34. Mark 1:9.
35. Matthew 5:17–48.
36. Mark 2:15–16; Sanders, "Jesus and the Sinners," 5–36.

The secularization of our society has implications for the very heart of Christian believing, and especially for Christology and for Trinitarian theology. To go on as before, hoping to make a traditional Christology and a traditional Trinity meaningful in a secular society, is no longer an option; and to respond by abandoning Christological and Trinitarian language would be a sterile reaction that would impoverish us all. To develop a Jesus-centered Trinity is one viable option: an option implicitly chosen in relation to the discussion of "grace"—a changing pattern of action that constitutes Jesus—to be found in chapter 7 of *An Actology of the Given*.[37]

There is of course nothing definitive about starting with Jesus. It remains entirely legitimate to begin a theological exploration with either the Holy Spirit, or with the God whom Jesus called his Father, or with the same God, the Creator. Wherever we start, an action in patterns conceptual structure will lead us to the others.

But how are we to understand Jesus? We can understand Jesus only in terms of his activity, for that is all that we know about him, and that with little certainty. So for us Jesus is his activity, and the activity recorded in the gospels is Jesus. He can be nothing else, and nothing else can be him. Jesus is action in changing patterns.

However, none of this answers the question as to why we should choose *Jesus* as the starting point for our definition of God rather than some other arbitrary individual. The New Testament and the weight of Christian tradition, while those rarely speak in terms of the clear identification that we are discussing here, would lead us to choose Jesus rather than someone else as the beginning of our definition of God: but for each individual, appreciation of the New Testament and of the Christian tradition might emerge after choosing Jesus rather than before. Here generalization is impossible, of course. Each of us might choose Jesus for a wide range of different reasons: perhaps because it is a choice that we imbibed as children and have never had reason to question; perhaps because we have found ourselves members of a Christian community within which making that choice has seemed the obvious thing to do; or perhaps because we have seen something attractive in Jesus.

Whichever route we might have followed, there will often be points in time when the choice has come into question and has had to be remade; and if we have never made that choice, then there might come a point when we are faced with the decision as to whether to choose Jesus as our God— perhaps when we find ourselves praying, and we find ourselves praying to Jesus and wonder whether we should. The decision to choose Jesus as God

---

37. Torry, *An Actology of the Given*, 118–52.

will always be tentative and temporary, because the choice can always be unmade, or simply neglected. For all of us, the choosing of Jesus will be constantly a particular pattern of action—maybe one that continues in the background of our lives and is occasionally revisited, or one that constantly comes up for question and renewal in the context of other rapidly changing patterns of action. Always the decision will be different; and we shall always be choosing our own picture of who Jesus is: but that portrait will always to some extent be influenced by Jesus himself, as he is communicated through the patterns of action of the Church across the ages. And somewhere in the complex changing patterns of action that constitute our choosing will be the changing patterns of action that are those that constitute Jesus himself, however submerged they might sometimes be by multiple historical, cultural, personal, emotional and conceptual patterns of action.

A first reason for choosing Jesus as our God must be that so many millions of people have thus chosen him. In the past, such a choosing might have had quite a lot to do with a belief that Jesus was somehow intimately related to a prior God to whom allegiance had already been given, or whose existence was simply assumed. This might or might not be our reason today, as today we have more of an option of starting with Jesus, and then finding that the Father that he worshipped is God, and that the Spirit that he sent is God.

A second reason for choosing Jesus as our God might be the character of the Jesus we discover in the gospels, or perhaps the character that we imagine him to be. "He was a good man": not in a technical "sinless" sense,[38] but in the sense that we find in Jesus all that we value as worthwhile. His goodness might be described as selflessness, courage, and love: all particular patterns of action, with each example of each characteristic bound to the other examples of the same characteristic by family resemblance relationships. There are good reasons for attributing these characteristics to Jesus: and in particular for seeing Jesus as the embodiment of what the New Testament writers meant by the pattern of action that they called *charis*, "grace."[39]

THE HOUSE OF SIMON THE PHARISEE

One characteristic that Jesus did not possess was humility. Take as an example the story of the woman who anointed Jesus' feet while he was having a meal with a Pharisee.[40] Jesus preferred the discomfort of sparks flying to

---

38. Hebrews 4:15; 1 Peter 2:22.
39. Torry, *An Actology of the Given*, 118–52.
40. Luke 7:36–50.

the tedium of like-minded people uttering tired and well-rehearsed clichés; he had an adventurous mind, a mind that reveled in the unpredictable; he was a sensual being, and did not recoil from the unknown woman's touch and her highly erotic actions (or perhaps he did know her); he was able to understand this woman's feelings and needs and her boldness and gift of herself—and in general Jesus grasped quickly the deeper needs that people brought to him, and knew the deeper recesses of their fears: and to do this he must have been closely in touch with his own motivations, his own feelings, his own sexuality, and his own convictions. Jesus seems to have been at home amongst the deepest emotions, without anxiety, knowing that here was the way to the Kingdom of God. But the acceptance of people did not imply agreement, and Jesus could be highly critical, as he was of Simon the Pharisee's attitude towards the woman. He took no notice of Simon's status even though he was a guest in Simon's home, and it is a reasonable description of the event to describe Jesus as rude. His words to Simon reveal Jesus' own sense of hurt (he had correctly remembered that Simon had not welcomed him very well); he was hurt that Simon did not want to be physically or emotionally close to him: and he says all of this, probably in the presence of others. Jesus had no wish to hide the way that he felt, and he had no problem telling Simon what he thought of him. I hope they remained friends. Finally, Jesus assumed a colossal authority, and told the woman that she was forgiven: and to Simon this would have appeared both an arrogance and a blasphemy. Jesus was willing to take a most unorthodox initiative and to claim for himself an authority that not even the Pharisees would have granted to themselves, and by doing that he communicated acceptance to the woman and a deep understanding, and he offered to her a kind of peace that Simon's cerebral distance from her could never have offered, and that Simon would not have wished to offer. Whatever else we have discovered here about Jesus' mind, we have discovered that he did not possess humility: and thus to possess humility is not necessarily a Christian virtue, and to exercise it might distance us from the Jesus we claim to follow: although of course an objective assessment of our own personalities might still be a good idea, along with the kind of consideration of the needs of others that we find exercised by Jesus.

But did not Paul recommend that Christians should exercise the kind of humility that they found in Jesus? "In humility regard others as better than yourselves . . . Let the same mind be in you that was in Christ Jesus . . . being found in human form, he humbled himself, and became obedient to the point of death . . ."[41] Here Paul recommends a particular kind of

---

41. Philippians 2:3, 5, 8, NRSV. There is a mention of humility in Ephesians 4:2: a

humility, rather than the kind that Simon might have wished that Jesus had exercised. Jesus' humility was of a particular and extreme kind: a willingness to die. To be a Christian is to follow Jesus: the real Jesus; and it is in the patterns of action that constitute Jesus in the gospels that we find the Jesus whom we are called to follow.

Jesus' goodness or graciousness—grace—is all the more impressive because he did not exhibit humility. What he did exhibit was the ability to sit loose to wealth, ambition, and political power, a characteristic of his that gave rise to the temptation myths: a potent expression of some vital elements of Jesus' personality.[42] Jesus' decision to seek no gain for himself but only the Kingdom of God is at the center of what we call his "goodness," a goodness still enormously attractive in spite of, and perhaps because of, the fact that we live in a society driven by ambition, the drive to accumulate wealth, and the pursuit of power and advantage. In Jesus we see a model of the humanity that we long to be, and we therefore choose him as our God.

FOLLOWING JESUS

To find in Jesus a model of the humanity for which we long inevitably asks us to choose whether to follow him with a following that overlaps with our other followings: and perhaps one of the most important characteristics that recommended Jesus to his early followers, and that recommends him still, was and is his creativity. He created a new Law to replace the old—although he valued the old Law and regarded his Law as in continuity with it;[43] he established a new covenant;[44] and he intended his twelve apostles to be the kernel of a new Israel.[45] In the fourth gospel—which was probably intended more as a meditation on the meaning of Jesus than as a historical account—we discover reflection on Jesus' creativity. He was the one through whom the world was created;[46] he was the true bread, as opposed to the manna in the wilderness;[47] and he was the one who gave a new commandment.[48] Jesus created, and he creates still: a vital reason for choosing him as our God.

letter probably not by Paul himself; and in Colossians 2:23 Paul is critical of a distorted humility.
42. Luke 4:1–13.
43. Matthew 5:1–7:29.
44. Mark 14:24.
45. Mark 3:13–19.
46. John 1:3.
47. John 6:25–59.
48. John 13:34.

Jesus, like us, our world, and our cosmos, was an accident. I see no reason to believe that there was anything surprising about the process of evolution of our cosmos, planet, and species.[49] It is just that this is the planet that accidentally developed the conditions both for survival and for the development of self-reflective and freely-choosing patterns of action that we call persons. Other planets might have evolved in this or in different ways. Given the existence of action—or rather, given action—and given the possibility of patterns emerging and evolving, anything can happen.[50]

The process is accidental, and we are accidents; and if we are to choose a God who is meaningful, then that God must not only be one of us, but must also be accidental in the fullest sense of that word, even if in the end this characteristic does not exhaust what we choose to mean by "God." And just as each of us has to choose for ourselves how we define God, so each of us will inevitably choose the Jesus whom we follow, and we shall choose the patterns of action that we envisage him exhibiting and the patterns of action that he means to us today. And so the accidents of Jesus' life, and the accidents of our choosing, will compound the accidental nature of our following of Jesus, and the accidental nature of the Christian Faith and the Church today.

For instance, we must choose the manner of Jesus' birth. The circumstances of Jesus' birth will forever be hidden from us behind a conglomeration of narratives of indeterminate status.[51] Matthew's Gospel locates the birth in Bethlehem, but that might have been because the prophet Micah said that this is where the Messiah, the one who would rescue and vindicate Israel, would be born.[52] I might instead choose to locate Jesus' birth in Nazareth, where he grew up. As for his parentage, again we shall never know. Jesus' mother was Mary, but who was his father? The virgin birth stories[53] suggest that Jesus might have been illegitimate, so it seems reasonable to assume that he was conceived by Joseph before he married Mary, or that he had a different father whose name we shall never know. Joseph disappears from the gospel story fairly quickly, and as Jesus had brothers and sisters, and we hear of no other man in Mary's life, we have to assume that either Joseph died or left Mary several years after Jesus was born. I choose Joseph as Jesus' father, and honor him as such alongside Jesus' mother Mary.

---

49. Deane-Drummond, *Christ and Evolution*.
50. Davison, *Astrobiology and Christian Doctrine*.
51. Luke 1:1—2:20; Matthew 1:18—2:23.
52. Matthew 2:1; Micah 5:2.
53. Matthew 1:18–25; Luke 1:26–38; and possibly John 1:12–13 if the text is slightly amended.

What was the household like? Again, we must understand the accidental nature of it, and we must choose what we think it was like. If Joseph was a carpenter, then it might not have been poverty-stricken; and if Mary sang the Magnificat—"My soul magnifies the Lord, and my spirit rejoices in God my Saviour . . . He has brought down the powerful from their thrones, and lifted up the lowly; he has filled the hungry with good things, and sent the rich away empty"[54]—then there were distinctly revolutionary tendencies contributing to Jesus' upbringing.

Jesus was influenced by particular people, just as we are: not only by his mother, but also by John the Baptist, of whom he might have been an active follower: but precisely how we understand Jesus' relationship with John is up to us. The story that I choose is that Jesus was baptized by John, became one of his followers, and preached John's call to repentance: but that they then parted company, perhaps because Jesus enjoyed people, food and wine, and John frowned on all three;[55] but perhaps also because Jesus, like John, hoped for the coming of the Kingdom of God, a new community in which Israel would be free from its oppressors and in which there would no longer be evil, sickness, poverty, injustice or death, but hoped for a Kingdom that would include nations other than Israel[56] and that would come as a free gift from God,[57] whereas John thought a righteous life to be a precondition for entry into the Kingdom. John's disciples were a sect, a close-knit group of people who had turned away from their old life and begun a new life of righteousness, whereas Jesus' followers were an open and diverse group of poor and rich, unrighteous and righteous, socially unacceptable and socially acceptable, who sometimes responded to the offer of the Kingdom of God by changing their lifestyles, but who remained Jesus' friends if they did not.[58] For Jesus, the Kingdom of God was a gift to be enjoyed by everybody, whereas for John the Kingdom was for the dedicated few.[59]

Jesus' parents, John the Baptist, his close followers, and many others, would have formed his thinking and his behavior, and that thinking and that behavior became significant by accident and by a process of historical evolution. Jesus' message and actions, as interpreted and spread by his followers, happened to find a ready seed-bed in the cultures and groups oppressed by the Roman Empire, and then the more powerful became

54. Luke 1:47, 52–53, NRSV.
55. Mark 2:16; Matthew 11.16–19; Luke 7:13–35.
56. Mark 11:15–19.
57. Mark 4:26–34.
58. Mar 2:13–17; Luke 19:1–10.
59. Luke 15; Matthew 20:1–16; Luke 7:18–27.

interested, presumably because they wanted to control this movement that was influencing the powerless: and so the Christian religion became available to Constantine and the many others who have found in the Christian Church a cement with which to bind fragmenting societies.

Jesus, like us, was involved in particular social, political and religious movements of his time, and was crucified by the processes of justice of a relatively humane empire. He went where history led him, as well as where he chose to go: and Christian faith has similarly gone where history and politics have led, as well as where Jesus' followers have decided that the faith should spread.

Jesus was an animal, as each of us is; he possessed self-consciousness, a particular personality, and a particular sexuality, the character of which we cannot know; and he suffered the human condition in all its complexity. So did he sin?[60] We "sin" insofar as we corporately and individually do not live according to some pre-existing set of rules: but now that Jesus' Kingdom of God has relativized all such legal structures, there is no meaning to the concept of "sin," and to ask whether Jesus sinned has become a meaningless question. The question can no longer be asked in its traditional terms for another reason: We have chosen Jesus to be our God, so he is our primary authority in matters of conduct: so any definition of sin must be formulated in terms of Jesus' own changing patterns of action. To say that Jesus did not sin is to utter a tautology.

JESUS' KINGDOM OF GOD

As we read the gospels we discover a Jesus who confronted evil in whatever form he found it, whether in the possessed mind,[61] or in the religious and commercial worlds.[62] In his baptism by John we discover a Jesus who committed himself to new ways of life;[63] and in his going into the wilderness,[64] and in his times alone,[65] we find a Jesus struggling with a relationship with his God and Father, and we discover someone who teaches others to pray.[66]

---

60. Hebrews 4:15.
61. Mark 1:25.
62. Mark 11:15–17: the passage in which he turns the traders out of the temple.
63. Mark 1:9.
64. Mark 1:13.
65. Luke 11:1.
66. Luke 11:2.

In his healings,[67] and in his parables,[68] Jesus gives people hope for personal and social renewal; he declares people forgiven;[69] and in his prophecy[70] he gives people hope for an ending of this age and the beginning of a Kingdom of God in which there shall be peace and justice and an end to oppression. In Mark's Gospel we discover a Jesus who breaks his society's moral code for the sake of humanity;[71] and when he meets a Syro-Phoenician woman who challenges his racism, we find a Jesus who learns equality and social justice.[72] In the gospels, we find a Jesus who is "a friend of tax-collectors and sinners,"[73] that is, of unrepentant sinners;[74] and on the cross we find Jesus welcoming into paradise someone whose life he knows nothing about.[75] Jesus holds children up as an example to adults;[76] he declares that "many who are first will be last, and the last will be first";[77] and in his parable of the vineyard-workers who are paid the same for unequal work we find a commitment to economic equality founded on his God's equal love for every person.[78] Jesus judges hypocrisy and injustice severely;[79] he calls his followers to be perfect;[80] and he calls people to follow him.[81] His life is a scandal from one end to the other. He is human and vulnerable,[82] he contradicted himself,[83] and he clearly understood little of politics. His conviction that the Kingdom of God was coming very soon meant that his perspectives were always unbalanced. He was liberal and radical, and occasionally conservative, and there seems to have been little systematic about his thought or his action. He was an apocalyptic fanatic who got the details wrong, but he was a human and attractive fanatic with a sense of humor and an often

---

67. Mark 1:40–45; 8:23–24, amongst many such incidents.
68. Mark 4 and many other places.
69. Mark 2:1–12.
70. Luke 6:2–23, Mark 13, and so on.
71. Mark 2:23–27; 3:1–6.
72. Mark 7:24–30.
73. Matthew 11:19.
74. Sanders, "Jesus and the Sinners," 5–36.
75. Luke 23:43, NRSV.
76. Mark 10:15.
77. Matthew 19:30, NRSV.
78. Matthew 20:1–16.
79. Matthew 23.
80. Matthew 5:48.
81. Mark 1:16–20.
82. Mark 14:32–42.
83. Mark 13:30, 32.

biting wit[84] whose vision of the coming Kingdom of God was of a human community in which God, spoken of as a parent,[85] would reign for the benefit of the formerly deprived and for the establishment of justice and peace. The Kingdom was both a welcome and a warning.[86] It was a gift, a free gift, and that gift was already present and inviting a response—although it never insisted on one—and Jesus' open community of disciples was a "sacrament" of the coming Kingdom, a sign of its coming which itself contributed to the coming of the Kingdom, a Kingdom that was the perennial subject of Jesus' stories and the reason for his healings. The Kingdom of God offered "invitation ... welcome ... challenge ... and summons"[87]—all functioning as verbs: and so a judgement on contemporary practice, and particularly on the behavior of the privileged and wealthy, as well as an unconditional admission for everyone. It was Jesus' longing to see the Kingdom's coming, and his willingness to contribute towards its birth-pangs, that took him to Jerusalem and to his death.

In the Garden of Gethsemane we find Jesus struggling with his future suffering, with his task, and with his destiny;[88] we find him suffering betrayal and abandonment;[89] at his trials we find him suffering humiliation and injustice;[90] and on the cross he suffers excruciating pain, and he dies.[91] Here we have described Jesus in terms of action in patterns rather than in terms of his nature, his status, or his being. We have left to one side the kinds of questions about him that were asked during earlier Christian history. We have not troubled to ask about how Jesus' substance relates to God's substance. We have instead employed the conceptual structure, the actology, that we have developed, in order to describe Jesus as his action in changing patterns, for this is who he is, and it is what he is in relation to God, for these are the changing patterns of action that constitute God as well as the patterns of action that constitute Jesus.

Jesus' activity is complex, as is the activity that defines each one of us, and no single definition will encapsulate the diversity: but much of the activity recorded in the gospels could well be defined as "grace," as unconditional generosity: generosity with himself, with his attention, with his

---

84. Matthew 7:3; Luke 11:37–54: much depends on the tone of voice.
85. Luke 11:2
86. Wright, *Jesus and the Victory of God*, 243, 244–368.
87. Wright, *Jesus and the Victory of God*, 244–319.
88. Mark 14:32–42.
89. Mark 14:43–50.
90. Mark 14:51–15:20.
91. Mark 15:21–41.

prayer, with his time, with his forgiveness, with his acceptance . . . a grace especially visible in his love for unrepentant sinners.[92] If we live in a secular world in which there are no miracles, no virgin births, no metaphysics, and no spiritual battle between the occupants of heaven and hell, then in this secular world Jesus—the grace and Kingdom of God personified—can still be God for us. And if we live in a less secularized world then the same can be true.

We have chosen a particular happening to be our God: this particular person, Jesus, at that particular time in the world's history, at that particular place. Wolfhart Pannenberg has similarly focused his Christian theology around the particular historical event of Jesus, and particularly around his resurrection.[93] Timothy Jenkins expresses the same choice:

> The New Testament texts are very largely attempts to make sense of the resurrection event. . . . in Jesus, matter and history express fully God's will and purposes. . . . in the New Testament, Jesus is called . . . the Alpha and the Omega, the beginning and the end. And he is also called the Word, or Logos, which means the pattern or reason of things: how they come into being, what they are for, and how they will in the end add up.[94]

We have gone further than either Pannenberg or Jenkins by choosing Jesus to be our God, and to be the focus around which we shall integrate our life together. We seek connections and we invent "laws," but they are all provisional, all accidental, and all relative and chosen by a corporate process of reasoning; and tomorrow the connections will change. We choose to relate other accidental events to this one single accidental event, Jesus of Nazareth: the relationships are possible because the elements are all of a kind: all patterns of action, all accidental, and all meaningful because we too are accidents of an evolutionary process. Herein is a true liberation from any and every oppressive metaphysical structure, and it is Jesus whom we call our God who is our liberator.

THE JESUS WHOM WE CHOOSE

The Jesus whom we have chosen is "God with us"[95] in the sense that he travels with us through our experience of life, but also in the sense that he is

---

92. Matthew 11:19.
93. Galloway, *Wolfhart Pannenberg*, 35, 70.
94. Jenkins, *An Experiment in Providence*, 74–75.
95. Matthew 1:23, NRSV.

a judgement upon us: as was "God with us" when uttered by the prophet Isaiah eight centuries before the phrase was applied to Jesus' birth in Matthew's Gospel.[96] Jesus is a judgement on those parts of our individual activities and our corporate actions that lead to injustice and inhumanity. We are in the same position as the first disciples, and by choosing Jesus we experience a judgement that renews us and causes us to "turn round"[97] and to face the Kingdom of God that is about to break upon us and is already present. We can hold this hope without forcing ourselves to believe in some God other than Jesus, without convincing ourselves that a metaphysic is needed, and without ceasing to be secular human beings in a secularized society.

But let us be clear: the Jesus whom we have chosen has been constructed by us on the basis of the evidence: of evidence that we have chosen and interpreted. He is our God because we have decided that he shall be. We have chosen Jesus as our God for our own reasons, and we have thus chosen a Jesus who as well as being influenced by Jesus of Nazareth is also created in our own image. My Jesus is liberal and radical, with not too much of the latter. Your Jesus might be different. This is all inevitable. Jesus will be different in every different period of history, in every different place, and for every different individual: but as long as there is a family resemblance with the Jesus of the gospels, it is Jesus whom we are following, and it is Jesus whom we are worshipping as God. As long as the Jesus we construct is in touch with the gospels, and with the Jesus of other people, there is no great harm done if he is a little eccentric, for the process of dialogue with the gospels and with other Christians will continually inform the Jesus whom we worship, especially if we strip away the metaphysical and theistic trappings. After all, Jesus himself changed—for instance, by turning from a mission purely to the Jews to a mission more open to non-Jews, perhaps propelled in that direction by his meeting with the Syrophoenician woman[98]—so we should expect Jesus to be different for every individual, and to be different at different times for each of us. The truth about Jesus is the active network of dialectic between the many changing patterns of action related to Jesus today, so it is as we build relationships between many different relationships with Jesus that we know the truth about him, and that we know him: with truth here understood as a continuous truth-seeking process rather than as some kind of permanent possession. And so still today the Body of Christ is action in changing patterns, with the changing patterns constantly relating to relationships with Jesus across time and space and to the billions of

96. Isaiah 7:14.
97. Mark 1:4.
98. Mark 7:24–30.

individuals who have related to him: and this Body of Christ is the risen Christ—the action in changing patterns that constitute Jesus—living among us still. This is particularly true of the Eucharist: the action in patterns of Jesus taking bread and wine, giving thanks, breaking the bread, and sharing the bread and wine with his followers. As we fulfil these same but of course different actions today, so we relate to two millennia of Christians doing these actions, and to Jesus and his first followers doing them: and we know Jesus, because these patterns of action are who he is.[99] And it is the entire Jesus that we know, because, as Gustav Aulén reminds us, Jesus asked us to do the patterns of action that constitute the Eucharist "in remembrance of me,"[100] not merely in remembrance of his death.

> Because the eucharist is primarily an act, and because the church in doing this act fulfils the will of Christ, the eucharistic act becomes of necessity his action of sacrifice, and what is offered must then be what he himself offered,[101]

which was the whole of his life, from birth to death, through resurrection, to his continuing life with God and with us. As we break and share the bread we know the risen Christ, because these were his actions at the home on the Emmaus Road.[102] As Oliver Davies puts it, "the Eucharistic body of Mt. 26.26–9 [the account of the Last Supper] . . . mediates to us Christ's current or ascended embodiment liturgically and cosmically."[103] He goes on to point out that

> the bodies of those in need, in whom Christ is present to us, of Mt. 25.34–46, mediate the ascended body under the accent of its humanity and particularly . . . There is the presence of Christ among those "who are gathered in my name" of Mt. 18.20, and Christ's promised presence to his Church to "the end of the age" of Mt. 28.20. There are the mediations of Christ's presence in the Word as preached, and in the biblical text as received and performed. . . . however "mediated," the ascended body always remains directly active . . . pushing urgently and disruptively into the "everyday" of our ordinary lives.[104]

---

99. Robinson, *The Body*, 47, 57–58.
100. 1 Corinthians 15:24–25, NRSV
101. Aulén, *Eucharist and Sacrifice*, 40.
102. Luke 24:13–35.
103. Davies et al., *Transformation Theology*, 56.
104. Davies et al., *Transformation Theology*, 57.

Because all of this is so, we influence Jesus just as much as he influences us. It is in the turbulence and the controversy that we know and change Jesus: and this is at it should be, because we are the Body of Christ and so are the risen Christ. There will never be a fixed consensus about who Jesus is: the patterns of action change constantly, so there is always more to be said. So the task of the Church is to value the many different ways of understanding Jesus of Nazareth and the risen Christ, and to do the actions of the Eucharist, because this is Jesus' presence among us still, and because these changing patterns of action are the actions of God living a human life, they are God's symbolic activity[105]—changing patterns of action that constitute God—and they constitute us as the Church and as the risen Christ, with a responsibility to heal, promise, forgive, release, and reconcile in the world today. It is in doing these things that we shall know Jesus and that we shall be the risen Christ.

> The living Christ . . . cannot be encountered "representationally" by theology at all, cannot become part of any conceptual system. The reality of revelation, in its fundamentally causal character, comes to us rather through a primary attentiveness to sensibly embodied reality where revelation declares itself *as* a divinely causal disclosure; and also, as a consequence of this, as a demand on our practical willing: as a summons and a sending. It comes to us as new creation.[106]

Gustave Martelet asks us to go beyond "substance" language to understand the Eucharist, and suggests that the "body" language that Jesus used at the Last Supper can unite an understanding of the Eucharist with that of Jesus' resurrection body.[107] It is Jesus' risen body that is present as we do the actions of the Eucharist: a relationship all the more comprehensible on the basis of an understanding of the body as action in changing patterns.

A CONSTANT CHOOSING

By choosing Jesus, each of us becomes a member of a community, and rather than being simply my God or your God, Jesus will become our God, and we shall begin to construct the basis for a community of faith that has open boundaries because Jesus is one of us: a human being. The arguments

---

105. Brown, "God and Symbolic Action."
106. Davies et al., *Transformation Theology*, 168.
107. Martelet, *The Risen Christ and the Eucharistic World*, 157–79.

over precisely which Jesus we should worship will no doubt go on,[108] but each of us is to some extent related to Jesus of Nazareth, and your Jesus is thus related to my Jesus, and together we choose that Jesus shall be our God. Thus to choose Jesus as God is to put an end to private religion and to the division between secular and sacred, and to choose Jesus as our God is to tackle at its roots the process of secularization.

Having once chosen, we must not stop choosing, for we change, our world changes, and our interpretation of Jesus changes: so having chosen Jesus, we must immediately choose again. Christian faith can no longer be propositions permanently believed and believed to be permanent: rather, Christian faith is an activity that constantly involves us in choosing afresh. No longer can we be Christians: so Hans Küng's book titled *On Being a Christian*[109] might have been better titled *Doing Christianly*. Now we must "do Christianly": and as this process evolves for each of us, and for the corporate bodies to which we belong, the meaning of "God" will change, and the meaning of "Jesus" will change, and we shall change, and we might find ourselves ceasing to choose Jesus because his meaning, the meaning of "God," and what we mean to ourselves, can no longer be integrated into a single coherent pattern of activity: and at that point we might choose some other God. However, because Jesus is one of us, and is changing patterns of action that we experience, it is possible for what he means to us, and for what we and our world mean to us, to evolve together and to create a relationship constantly in motion but always connected though constantly connected in different ways. The constant choosing is like a dance,[110] with Jesus and ourselves in constant motion, moving together and moving apart, but together creating a pattern on the floor of history, which itself is action in changing patterns.

Throughout this section I have used "Jesus" rather than "Christ." We might choose to call Jesus "Christ," the anointed one: but it is Jesus whom we are invited to choose as our God, a God who was born, who lived, and who died. Our God has died: let nothing take any of the horror and difficulty away from this stark fact: by choosing Jesus as our God, we are choosing as our God someone who has died. We are invited to choose this enigmatic, apocalyptic, crucified man as our God, and to live with the consequences.

---

108. Schweitzer, *The Quest for the Historical Jesus*.
109. Küng, *On Being a Christian*.
110. The dance imagery is from the *Acts of St. John*, written after the New Testament.

Chapter 6

Grace in the Scriptures

Thesis: A particular changing pattern of action that constitutes Jesus and that constitutes God is "grace": a constant and generous giving.

INTRODUCTION[1]

In our discussion of Jesus we have understood him as action in changing patterns, but have had to use a proper noun—"Jesus"—to designate him. This inevitably communicates static and unitary connotations, which is rather the opposite of what we might wish to convey. We have the same problem with "grace," which means unconditional love. This can only be understood as action in patterns, but English grammar still requires us to use a noun to express it. So when here we use the word "grace," we shall have to try to leave to one side the connotations of being and unchangingness that nouns carry with them, and to understand by the word the activity of freely giving, of unconditional love: a changing pattern of action that we find in Jesus our God.

Theological formulation is always going to be difficult. To systematize, to create an orderly whole, is to deny the diversity of religious experience, and is to suggest that change can be kept within firm boundaries: but to leave everything disconnected is to deny both the connectedness of life and our relationships with one another and with the past. Recent English theology has seen much good spirituality, pastoral theology, biblical studies,

---

1. A discussion of "grace" similar to this can be found at Torry, *An Actology of the Given*, 118–52.

Church history, and liturgical studies, but not much about how we might understand God during the twenty-first century, about how we might relate Jesus the Christ to our world today, and about how we might do Christian theology and ethics in something like a systematic fashion. I recognize that systematic formulation is always partial, never assured, and always specific to its culture and its time, and that in the context of an actology any formulation will be local, tentative, and temporary, and with meanings that shift: but still we need to attempt temporary, local, and tentative formulation if the Christian tradition is to develop, and if as churches and as individuals we are to take the next steps on our pilgrimage. And we particularly need such formulation if we are to have something to react against, for where there is no thesis there will be no antithesis and no new synthesis.

GRACE, AND DEATH AND RESURRECTION

We have already asked how we might think about God in the light of a changed conceptual structure. God is Action, the source of all action, and action in changing patterns, so we ought to say something about some of these patterns of action, and in particular about two that are intimately connected: the action in patterns that we call "grace": an infinite self-giving love; and the action in patterns that is "death and resurrection." The intimate connection is well understood by Simone Weil:

> God created through love and for love. God did not create anything except love itself, and the means to love. He created love in all its forms. He created beings capable of love from all possible distances. Because no other could do it, he himself went to the greatest possible distance, the infinite distance. This infinite distance between God and God, this supreme tearing apart, this agony beyond all others, this marvel of love, is the crucifixion. ... This tearing apart, over which supreme love places the bond of supreme union, echoes perpetually across the universe in the midst of the silence, like two notes, separate yet melting into one, like pure and heart-rending harmony.[2]

Jesus died, and was raised to new life; and we too, through baptism, are buried with Jesus and raised to life with him, both now and in the future.[3] Later on I shall explore this pattern as the heart of Christian living: but the

---

2. Weil, *Waiting on God*, 82–83.
3. Romans 6:3–11; 8:11.

pattern of action to which I shall return here as an example of a changing pattern of action that belongs to the definition of God is "grace."

"Grace" has been a vital pivot of Christian thought and action through two thousand years; it is a pattern of action and not a substance, so it will find new life as a concept within the framework that I have suggested; and grace is a fertile concept for the future evolution of the Christian tradition, of Christian theology, and of Christian ethics.

But "grace" is a noun, and it has often been understood to refer to something substantial, something that can be possessed, even if the substance is not like other physical substances. But I take "grace" to denote activity: to be generous, self-giving activity, activity aimed at the knowing and the benefit of the other. It would be better if the word were a verb, but as it is not we shall have to make do with the noun and constantly remind ourselves that we are discussing action: a pattern of action that we see in the life of Jesus—a life which we might define as "grace"—a pattern of action that constantly changes but that retains a family likeness with the grace that is Jesus and with the grace that is God: a grace that we might legitimately use as a definition of God. As John Barclay suggests when discussing Paul's employment of *charis*, "grace": Paul uses *charis* "for God's act of beneficence toward the world in Christ . . . or that of Christ himself."[4]

Jesus, the Grace of God

Was Jesus' religion a religion of grace? Was his life a life characterized by grace in the sense in which I have defined it? A possibility that we cannot now ignore is that we cannot be sure how much of what we find in the gospels is what Jesus said and did and how much of it is what early Christians said that he said and did but in fact he didn't. We are now more aware of the gospels as the literary creations of their authors, and we are aware that the authors had concerns of their own, molds into which they pressed the words that came to them through the Church's oral tradition. For our purposes we need to note that in relation to Jesus' death and resurrection, Mark's Gospel offers a message of vulnerable generosity, whereas Matthew's Gospel contains one of sheer power that might tend to negate the "gift" nature of the gospel: but as long as we are aware of each author's concerns, we shall be able to decide for ourselves how much of what we find in the gospels is what Jesus said, how much is what early Christians said, and how much it matters. The distinction between what Jesus said and did and what early Christians said he said and did does not seem to have been one in which

4. Barclay, *Paul and the Gift*, 577.

early Christians were particularly interested. They believed the Spirit of Jesus to be present in the Church, leading them into new truth, so it was perfectly legitimate to tell a parable in which the main character was Jesus:[5] for didn't Jesus himself tell parables?

And how much does it in fact matter to us whether the words and actions were those of Jesus, or whether they reflect the change that Jesus brought about in the lives of early Christians? In either case we are in touch with the roots of the Christian tradition, and we can ask whether there is anything distinctive about that tradition, and in particular whether grace, an unconditional love, is a central component.

Take the parables as an example. Are they Jesus' words, or are they constructed by early Christians or by the gospel-writer to express their own theological convictions? Take as an example the parable of the workers in the vineyard in Matthew's Gospel chapter 20, in which workers who had worked for different lengths of time in the vineyard were all given the same pay.[6] John Drury suggests that the parables tell us a great deal more about the gospel-writers than they do about Jesus, and that in this parable the gospel-writer's message is that God's welcome of Gentiles into the Kingdom of God is not unjust to the Jews, for they will receive their agreed reward.[7] Joachim Jeremias, on the other hand, suggests that the parable is Jesus' own vindication of his welcome to sinners.[8] Which interpretation is the right one? And how do we tell? The form of the parable in the gospel is the gospel-writer's, but to what extent are the sentiments expressed in the parable those of Jesus?—and does it matter whether the recorded words are those of Jesus or those of his followers? All we can be certain of is that the words of the parable are influenced by Jesus, by the gospel-writer, and by other early Christians: but that is sufficient for our purposes, for what I need to know from the parable is whether in the early Christian tradition God's love is an active and unconditional generosity—in short, whether it is grace—and in this parable God's love is active and generous. In the parable itself we do not find expressed a universal love, as there are people who are not workers in the vineyard, and only those who have put in at least an hour's work are paid: but it is as universal as the parable can make it, and we are therefore justified in finding in this parable an active, generous, and universal love of God.

5. Mark 12:1–12 is a likely candidate.

6. Matthew 20:1–16.

7. Drury, *The Parables in the Gospels*, 93: "The divine favouring of the Christians is not unjust to the Jews. They, who have worked in God's vineyard longer, also get their agreed reward and so have nothing to resent."

8. Jeremias, *The Parables of Jesus*, 132.

Is this unconditional and active generosity in any sense new? For there is certainly a great deal in the gospels that is not new.

In the Hebrew Scriptures, the Christians' Old Testament, we find plenty of reliance on the unmerited grace of God: "I shall heal my people's apostasy; I shall love them freely, for my anger is turned away from them."[9] God's choice of Israel was not because of any virtue on its part, but was an act of unmerited love:

> It was not because you were more numerous than any other nation that the Lord cared for you and chose you, for you were the smallest of all nations; it was because the Lord loved you . . .[10]

The covenant between God and Israel was a gift of God, and so was the Torah, the Law, which itself looked forward to a new Law:

> For this is the covenant I shall establish with the Israelites after those days, says the Lord: I shall set my law within them, writing it on their hearts; I shall be their God and they will be my people. No longer need they teach one another, neighbour or brother, to know the Lord; all of them, high and low alike, will know me, says the Lord, for I shall forgive their wrongdoing, and their sin I shall call to mind no more.[11]

The Old Testament assumes a relationship between God and Israel established by God's unconditional love, which is why it doesn't always mention it. The relationship must be maintained by obedience, but its birth is an act of grace; and this loving God is always ready to receive back the repentant sinner, whether the sinner should be an individual or a nation. The "waiting Father" in the parable of the Prodigal Son would have been entirely familiar as an image of God to Jews of Jesus' time.[12]

Similarly, the new age for which Jesus hoped would not have been new to his hearers, and neither would the resurrection of the dead have been, although Jesus' disciples' experience after his death might have been a new departure. Jesus' followers hoped for the dawn of a new age in which Israel would be renewed and in which the Gentiles would be welcome: but none of this was new, as the prophets had held such a hope:

---

9. Hosea 14:4.
10. Deuteronomy 7:7, 8, NRSV.
11. Jeremiah 31:33, 34, NRSV.
12. Luke 15:11–32; Thielicke, *The Waiting Father*, 29: "The ultimate theme of this story is not the prodigal son, but the Father who finds us. The ultimate theme is not the failures of men, but the faithfulness of God."

> Arise, shine, Jerusalem, for your light has come;
> and over you the glory of the Lord has dawned.
> Though darkness covers the earth
> and dark night the nations,
> on you the Lord shines
> and over you his glory will appear;
> nations will journey towards your light
> and kings to your radiance.[13]

So there was nothing new about Jesus' attitude to God's covenant with Israel, to the unmerited love of God, or to the promise of the Kingdom of God. Was Jesus' attitude to the Jewish Law new? Probably not. The disputes over the meaning of the Law in which Jesus participated were within the mainstream of such debate in the Judaism of the time, and the existence of such disputes implies that the participants agreed that the Law was an integral part of God's covenant with Israel.[14]

Jesus made flour out of grain on the Sabbath,[15] thus breaking the commandment about not working on the Sabbath; and he healed a man on the Sabbath:[16] two things which other Jews who sought the deeper rather than the surface meaning of the Law might have done. Whether or not Jesus was intentionally criticizing those parts of the Law that maintained Judaism's firm boundaries against the Gentiles we don't know, but it is unlikely that by themselves these instances of Jesus' breaking of the Law would have been regarded as a complete innovation. What might be different is the consistency of an attitude that sees God as grace, as unconditional generosity, and therefore the Sabbath as God's gift, and so to be filled with grace, with unconditional generosity. Because the Kingdom of God was so close—close enough to be already present[17]—no Jewish law could be of absolute validity. The Law—even the most important parts of it—was "fulfilled" and "abolished":[18] that is, its task was completed, and now a new era was dawning, in which mercy and justice would be a natural way of life for God's people, and in which grace would replace law as the determinant of people's relationships with each other and with God.

Just as there is nothing radically new about Jesus' attitudes towards the Covenant and the Law, so his ideas about repentance were not new. If

---

13. Isaiah 60:1–3.
14. Sanders, *Jesus and Judaism*, 319.
15. Mark 2:23–27.
16. Mark 3:1–6.
17. Mark 1:15.
18. Matthew 5:17–18; Torry, "Two kinds of ambiguity."

"repentance" was part of Jesus' vocabulary—that is, if the parables of the lost coin, the lost sheep, and the prodigal son in Luke 15 are Jesus' words rather than Luke's exhortations to repentance—then there would have been nothing at all new about them, for the message of repentance was the message of John the Baptist whose follower at some time Jesus might have been. Similarly, a belief that the Gentiles would be drawn into the Kingdom of God was not new. If Jesus did not conduct or envisage a mission to the Gentiles—for he does seem to have thought that his mission and that of his disciples was only to Israel[19]—and yet recognized that the Gentiles were also to experience salvation,[20] then there would have been nothing original about such a position. So what was new?

One thing that was new was that Jesus ate with "sinners" and regarded them as unconditionally welcome in the Kingdom of God. We are indebted to E.P. Sanders for the clear distinction that we can now draw between "the common people" and the "sinners" or the "wicked" at the time of Jesus.[21] Very few in Jesus' time would have thought that the common people, who might not have kept all of the purity laws that the Pharisees and others worked hard to keep, were to be excluded from the salvation promised in the Covenant. In any case, purity rules were related to Temple attendance, and weren't particularly relevant if you lived in Galilee and could not get to the Temple without undertaking a substantial and difficult journey.[22] But "sinners," the unrepentant wicked, were another matter: and it was the sinners with whom Jesus ate. Jesus was "a glutton and a drinker, a friend of tax-collectors and sinners,"[23] and it was this, and not his occasional breaches of the Sabbath Law, that would have ensured that he was regarded as a social menace.

What seems to have been distinctive about Jesus is that he did not demand repentance from sinners, and did not reject them if they did not offer it.[24] No Jew would have objected to repentant Zacchaeus being in the Kingdom of God, nor to Jesus eating with him:[25] but for Jesus to eat with unrepentant sinners,[26] and thus to express a conviction that they too would

19. Matthew 10:5; 15:24.
20. Matthew 8:11–12.
21. Sanders, "Jesus and the Sinners," 5–36, 10.
22. Sanders, "Jesus and the Sinners," 13.
23. Matthew 11:19.
24. Sanders, "Jesus and the Sinners," 23–24: "Could it be that he offered them inclusion in the Kingdom *while they were still sinners* and *without* requiring repentance?" (Sanders" emphasis). Sanders clearly believes that Jesus did.
25. Luke 10:1–10.
26. Mark 2:15–16.

be included in the Kingdom of God, would have been as unpopular with the average Jew as with the self-appointed defenders of the Law's minutest points of detail. John the Baptist was the spokesman for repentance and for righteousness, so was it over the issue of whether or not unrepentant sinners were still within the Covenant that Jesus and John parted company?[27]

Sanders concludes that

> the novelty of Jesus' message was that he promised inclusion in the coming Kingdom to those who followed him, even if they did not make restitution and follow the normal procedures for gaining atonement.[28]

It is unlikely that Jesus' eating with sinners would have been invented by early Christians, who seem from the Acts of the Apostles and Paul's letters to have been deeply concerned about moral purity among Church members. Early Christians demanded repentance before either Jews or Gentiles could enter the new Covenant established by their Lord Jesus,[29] and in this respect they failed to be Jesus' followers. The early Church failed to comprehend a central point of Jesus' message—perhaps *the* central point—and ever since then the grace of God has come with conditions attached.

"Whoever does not accept the Kingdom of God like a child will never enter it."[30] If Jesus said this, then he was inviting a radical new attitude to the Covenant between Israel and God: the reception of the Kingdom as a gift, a gift that remains a gift, a constant giving, to be received without any sense that we have to achieve something in order to remain in the relationship that has been established by God's sheer generosity. The idea that the Covenant was a gift was not new, but the idea that nothing had to be achieved in order to remain in the Covenant was new, and the unconditional love of God at the center of Jesus' teaching, and at the center of his life, is what is distinctive about the gospel of Jesus: the gospel Jesus proclaimed, and the gospel about Jesus. Jesus' love of others was unconditional, and it remained unconditional: it was an active and life-changing love, and it looked forward

---

27. Matthew 21:32; 11:18; Sanders, "Jesus and the Sinners," 25: "John was the spokesman for repentance and for righteousness ordinarily understood; Jesus, equally convinced that the end was at hand, proclaimed the inclusion of the wicked."

28. Sanders, "Jesus and the Sinners," 27.

29. Matthew 5:20; 25:3; 18:15–17, and numerous passages in Luke and Acts. But the Matthaean passages and others might well have roots in Jesus' words. Might Jesus have come *slowly* to his conviction that the wicked were to be welcomed unconditionally? Might some of the gospel material have roots in his earlier convictions, which might have been closer to John the Baptist's? This would go a long way towards explaining the diversity of the gospel material.

30. Mark 10:15.

to a Kingdom of God in which "many who are first will be last, and the last first."[31]

Jesus had no quarrel with the Law, which he believed to be God's gift to Israel: but for him the new age was about to dawn, and in such circumstances all that mattered was a raw, unconditional love, and a welcome with no strings attached: which is not to say that Jesus did not make substantial, if not impossible, demands. He demanded that the rich man should give everything he had to the poor and then follow him;[32] he called on his followers to renounce themselves, and to lose their lives;[33] and he demanded perfection.[34] The Sermon on the Mount[35] is sufficiently packed with such teaching that we have to conclude that Jesus did in fact demand such perfection from his followers.

It is difficult for us to put ourselves inside the minds of Jesus and his followers. They belonged to an oppressed people, and they hoped for the imminent arrival of a Kingdom of God in which Israel would be released from oppression and would be the righteous judge of the nations. And it is in this context that apparently contradictory messages do in fact cohere:

- All of Israel would be released from oppression, including the wicked—so Jesus mixed with the wicked, for they too would be welcome in the Kingdom of God, which is a gift;
- This Kingdom of God will be a Kingdom of righteousness, so Jesus called his followers to be righteous, with a perfection greater than that of the Pharisees, so that they might begin to live now the life of the Kingdom of God.

Thus, far from the demand for righteousness being a contradiction of the grace of God, it is its essential accompaniment, revealing the character of the Kingdom of God that is the gift of God, which is the grace of God, the center of Jesus' gospel.

However much the early Christians philosophized or moralized the grace at the heart of the gospel, they could not destroy its influence entirely, and perhaps the point where its influence is most visible is the mission to the Gentiles. Of Jesus' own attitude to the Gentiles we cannot be sure, but that the Church welcomed Gentiles, at first requiring obedience to parts of the Law, and then requiring only "faith," is surely a consequence of Jesus'

31. Matthew 19:30.
32. Matthew 19:16–30.
33. Mark 8:23–24.
34. Matthew 5:48.
35. Matthew chs. 5—7.

life of grace, a life of unconditional welcome. As Sanders puts it: "The overwhelming impression is that Jesus started a movement which came to see the Gentile mission as a logical extension of itself."[36]

Whether Jesus' declaring of all foods clean[37] is Jesus' own words, or the words of early Christians reflecting on the meaning of Jesus' life as they debated whether or not Gentile Christians should keep the Jewish food laws, we can recognize in this saying a Jesus committed to God's covenant with Israel and to the Law, but also a Jesus judging the Law on the basis of an all-important unconditionality. Thus Jesus opened up the traditional boundaries within the society of his time, and loosened the grip of those parts of the Law which in his view confined God's grace within tight boundaries. By doing this Jesus opened the way for a Church in which Gentiles would eventually be accepted without having to conform to the Law—although given our ineradicable desire for boundaries, the Church has never quite believed that God's love can be totally without conditions; and he opened the way for a Christian Faith in which grace—a continual, unconditional, active giving—might be the dynamic center, a Christian Faith that might have the capacity to be rediscovered in a secular age urgently in need of a theology, a politics, and an ethics focused on unconditional generosity. As Mike Higton sums up Rowan Williams' expression of the Christian good news: God's love

> is utterly gracious, utterly gratuitous love . . . God's universal love active in the world in the life, death, and resurrection of Jesus of Nazareth . . . Jesus' impact—the impress which his life, death and resurrection made on those around him, and on those to whom they proclaimed him . . . was experienced . . . as divine action.[38]

Over the course of Christian history, "grace" has often ceased to be action, and has been turned into a substance, a possession, something that is given and then retained.[39] It is not that. Grace is action: it is generous self-giving—and its definition is to be found in the life, death, and risen life of Jesus, a life by definition "perfect" if this Jesus is our God, for the one whom we worship as God is the definition of perfection. The same statement can be made in a negative fashion by saying that Jesus is "without sin."[40]. Of course he is: for if Jesus is our God, then Jesus is the definition of sinlessness. It is not that

---

36. Sanders, *Jesus and Judaism*, 220.
37. Mark 7:15.
38. Higton, *Difficult Gospel*, 5, 12–13.
39. Torry, *Actology*, 130–48.
40. Hebrews 4:15, NRSV.

there is some a priori definition of sinlessness to which he conforms: it is rather that his activity, throughout his life, is the definition of sinlessness.

The gospels' witness to Jesus

This is the Jesus who is our God, and God is this Jesus: this is the activity that he is, the activity that we worship by following him, and the activity to which the New Testament bears witness: but not necessarily in the most straightforward fashion.

The stories of Jesus' birth are probably parables. The early Christians were followers of Jesus in many ways: through their proclamation of the coming Kingdom of God, through their prayer to Jesus' Father, through their healing of the sick, and in their telling of stories to express their deepest truths. This means that the first chapter of Luke's Gospel is about Jesus' relationship with John the Baptist, and is a statement that Jesus is greater than John; and in Luke 2:1–7, Jesus is born in Bethlehem in order to fulfil the prophecy in Micah 5:2 and symbolize the fact that he belongs to the tribe of Judah and can thus be the promised King—which is not to say that there was not a census or that Jesus was not born in Bethlehem: there might have been, and he might have been.

The story of the shepherds[41] is a parable of Jesus' meaning for the poorest, and the story of the astrologers from the East[42] is a parable of his meaning for the wealthy and powerful, and for all the nations and not just Israel. The story of Jesus' birth to a virgin mother, which neither Mark's Gospel nor Paul's letters seem to know anything about, and which would not only be biologically impossible, but, more importantly, destructive of Jesus' humanity, is a parable of Jesus' "sonship," of his unique relationship to his Father and his God. The genealogies in the gospels[43] lead to or from Joseph, and thus to a descendent of David, and the earliest Christians would have experienced no conflict between the genealogies and the parabolic birth stories. Later, of course, when the birth stories were taken as historical fact, the genealogies were altered to say that Joseph was Mary's husband, or was thought to be Jesus' father—which is a pity, because Joseph might have been Jesus' father and, if he was, ought to be honored as such. This leaves modern Christians with something of a problem, as it leaves us with a difficult choice: either to believe that Jesus did not have a virgin birth and to regard the gospel accounts as parables, or to believe that Jesus did have a

---

41. Luke 2:8–20.
42. Matthew 2:1–12.
43. Matthew 1:1–16 and Luke 3:23–38.

virgin birth and therefore to compromise his humanity and the reconciliation that his humanity and divinity achieves. This author believes that the doctrine of the incarnation is non-negotiable for Christians, and so while believing that it is perfectly possible for Jesus to have had a virgin birth—for "what is impossible for mortals is possible for God"[44]—he hopes that it did not happen and that Joseph was Jesus' father.

The flight into Egypt[45] is a story about Jesus' fulfilment of prophecy, and in this case of the prophecy that "out of Egypt I have called my son";[46] and the slaughter of the innocent children might indeed have happened, but the gospel account is again a statement that Jesus is the fulfilment of prophecy, for in Jeremiah's prophecy[47] we find Rachel weeping for her children.

Throughout Christian history Mary has been revered as the mother of Jesus, and if we worship Jesus as God then we too shall revere Mary as the mother of God. And equally we might choose to revere Joseph as the father of God if we decide that he was Jesus' biological father. The early titles of Jesus are equally of interest because they reveal people's estimation of him and how he thought about himself.

Jesus called himself "Son of Man":

> "But so that you may know that the Son of Man has authority on earth to forgive sins"—he said to the paralytic—"I say to you, stand up, take your mat and go to your home."[48]

He was referring to himself, but using a term from Jewish apocalyptic literature, and thus injecting a note of ambiguity about his role.[49] In the Book of Daniel is pictured "one like a Son of Man, and he came to the Ancient of Days."[50] Jesus refers to this prophecy in his own apocalyptic words: "Then they will see 'The Son of Man coming in the clouds,'"[51] and he uses the same words at his trial:[52] a use that the High Priest interpreted as blasphemous. Jesus might well have seen himself as the one who was to represent Israel before God, and as the one to bring in God's Kingdom—and he might not have been sure: hence the ambiguity. So we find ourselves worshipping someone

---

44. Luke 18:27, NRSV.
45. Matthew 2:13–15.
46. Hosea 11:1, NRSV.
47. Jeremiah 31:15.
48. Mark 2:10, NRSV.
49. Mark 2:10, 28; 8:31, 38; 9:12; 13:36; 14:62.
50. Daniel 7:13–14, NRSV.
51. Mark 13:26, NRSV.
52. Mark 14:62.

aware of his task and yet not sure of it, and if we are Christians and followers of Jesus then this should be our pattern of action too: commitment to an enormous task, and an element of doubt concerning our place within it.[53]

When Jesus said "Who do people say that the Son of Man is?" Peter responded, "You are the Messiah, the Son of the Living God."[54]. These mean the same. The Messiah is the Rescuer, the Savior, the expected King; and in the Psalms the King of Israel is referred to thus: "You are my Son, today I have begotten you."[55] Later speculation turned "Son of God" into a metaphysical being and disconnected the title from that of "Messiah", but to Jesus and to his first followers they meant the same: that Jesus was the one sent by God to bring justice and peace to Israel and to all the nations. The titles were not ontological: they were and still are actological. They express the changing patterns of action that constituted Jesus and that constitute him still: and if we worship Jesus as our God then this is the one we worship: the one who brings justice and peace, reconciliation and renewal, then and now and in the future.

These various titles—and there are others—are all very understandable. They express the people's hopes and Jesus' understanding of his task. We might choose to use them, and in doing so we might try to understand what they meant then and what they might mean for us today; or we might do as Jesus did, and as the early Christians did: we might seek out for our own time some appropriate titles for Jesus. The rehabilitation of "God" as a title for Jesus might be a good place to start. It is an ancient title, as we have seen; it gives us a human God (whatever else we might go on to say about God), and thus a God for a secular and nonmetaphysical age; and it calls us to worship and to follow someone who knew himself called to a task and who pursued it, through doubt, suffering, and death, and whose task now and always extends to kingship in the Kingdom of God in which "the whole world process receives its structure and meaning."[56] In the action in changing patterns of Jesus' life, suffering, death, and resurrection, Jesus embodied the changing patterns of action of God returning to Jerusalem for both judgement and rescue:[57] action in changing patterns that we are

---

53. Geza Vermes confidently asserts that Jesus' use of "Son of Man" bore no relation to Daniel 7:13, but that that connection was made by his later followers and thus found its way into the gospels (Vermes, *Jesus the Jew*, 161). As Jesus might have been aware of Daniel 7:13 it might be best to retain an element of doubt, as we do here.

54. Matthew 16:13–16, NRSV.

55. Psalm 2:7, NRSV.

56. Pannenberg, *Jesus God and Man*, 396.

57. Wright, *Jesus and the Victory of God*, 652–53; Torry, *Mark's Gospel*.

invited to embody in our own individual and social lives—that is, in who we are because in what we do.[58]

And at the heart of all of it is grace: an unconditional generosity, represented by the feeding of the hungry,[59] the healing of the sick,[60] the stories about welcome,[61] and the mixing with all manner of people across multiple social boundaries:[62] all foretastes of a Kingdom of God that would come as a gift to all nations and in which all would be welcome. This is the pattern of action that defines who God is and who Jesus is, and that therefore defines the relationship between Jesus and God.

Paul's gospel: Saved by grace, or saved by faith?

What of the Apostle Paul? Was his gospel a gospel of grace?

The most important fact about Paul is that he was converted from the strict Judaism of the Pharisees to a comparatively new sect, and that he experienced his conversion as a call to take this new religion to the Gentiles. His formative years as a Christian were spent in Damascus and Antioch, that is, among Gentiles; and the polarities characteristic of conversion experiences, combined with the needs of a Church progressively more Gentile, resulted in a distinctive theology from which Christians will never escape.

But is it a theology of grace? However radical Paul's conversion might have been, he remained a Jew, his thoughtforms remained Jewish, and his convictions slowly returned from a radical rejection of the Law to a more positive evaluation of it. In an early letter he spoke of the Law as of no consequence,[63] but by the time he wrote the Letter to the Romans he had come to regard the Law as God-given and as good.[64] This is an understandable transition for someone converted to Christ and then having to come to terms with his own past, with the relationship between Jews and Gentiles in the Church, and with the relationship of God's choice of Israel to God's choice of Jesus Christ.

Clearly a key experience in Paul's spiritual pilgrimage was a dispute with Peter at Antioch, recorded in the Letter to the Galatians. There was already a difference of view within Judaism as to whether it was right to share

---

58. Wright, *Jesus and the Victory of God*, 660.
59. Mark 6:30–44.
60. Mark 1:29–45.
61. Luke 15.
62. Luke 19:1–10; John 3:1–21; Luke 7:36–50.
63. Galatians 3:25.
64. Romans 7:22.

table-fellowship with God-fearing Gentiles. Peter had been eating with Gentiles at Antioch, but when some Jerusalem Christians visited the city he ceased to do so. His motives for abandoning table-fellowship with Gentiles were probably admirable: he did not want to disturb the consciences of visiting Jewish Christians (and later on, Paul wrote to the Church in Rome about respecting weak consciences:[65] maybe he had learnt something from the Antioch event). But at the time, as far as Paul was concerned, Peter's action was a betrayal of the gospel. Peter would not have disagreed with Paul that justification was by faith (for the Book of Genesis says that Abraham was justified by faith), or that salvation was a free gift: but he seems not to have agreed that a justification by faith common to both Jews and Gentiles was more important than the traditional distinctions resulting from God's gift of a distinctive Law to the Jews.

Paul does not record that Peter agreed with him, so we can assume that Paul lost the argument at Antioch: but that does not mean that the event had no impact on him, for it clearly had an enormous effect upon him, and probably focused for him the radical difference between faith in Christ and the Covenant offered by God to Israel. The event at Antioch might have been the point at which the boundaries of the Covenant were redefined for Paul—to include Gentiles as well as Jews—and at which the conditions for remaining in the Covenant were equally redefined: faith in Christ rather than the keeping of the Law.[66]

What was not redefined in this process was the importance of grace. Grace, for Paul as for Jesus, was a given of Judaism.[67] Certainly there was a new channel for the grace of God: Jesus Christ: but God's gracious character was the same when he gave the Old Covenant and the Law as when he gave Christ and the new Covenant. Paul says nothing particularly new about grace because the questions that the young churches were posing for him did not require him to do so. What Paul was interested in was who was in the new Covenant established by God's grace. In the Letter to the Romans Paul is clear that "if it is by grace, then it does not rest on deeds, or grace would cease to be grace."[68] The boundaries of the Covenant have opened up to include those who have entered by faith and thus have experienced grace: ". . . now that we have been justified through faith, we are at peace

---

65. Romans 14.
66. Dunn, *Jesus, Paul and the Law*, 122.
67. Barclay, *Paul and the Gift*, 6.
68. Romans 11:6, NRSV.

with God through our Lord Jesus Christ, who has given us access to that grace in which we now live."[69]

In the eleventh chapter of the Letter to the Romans, a discussion of the relationship between Jews and Gentiles in God's purposes does not mention "Jesus" or "Christ" at all. The discussion is simply not interested in the source or the nature of the grace that the chosen people have received. What interests Paul is where the boundary lies: and his conversion and subsequent experience of the Church had led him to the belief that there was now a larger chosen people, established by God's grace, and including all those with faith in Christ, a faith witnessed to in a baptism that brought both Jews and Gentiles into the same community. This faith was one that Abraham had exercised, and was thus a means of maintaining membership of the chosen people older than the keeping of the Mosaic Law.[70]

Paul was not against the Law as such: he regarded it as God's gift. The parts of the Law to which the converted Paul did take exception were those parts that excluded Gentiles from the Covenant: circumcision, the Sabbath laws, laws regarding table fellowship, and so on: but even here Paul continued to obey the Law,[71] because he was a Jew as well as a Christian. To declare that Paul was anti-Law because pro-grace is to read him with Reformation spectacles on. Paul held a number of basic convictions:[72] that salvation is by faith in Christ; that Jews and Gentiles are equal in the Church; and that the Law is from God. His ethical views remained essentially those of the Law, and he knew the Law to be God-given. This gave him continuing problems as to the Law's current status: but he was quite clear that Jews and Gentiles alike entered the Abrahamic Covenant through faith in Christ, and that the keeping of the Law had nothing to do with access to salvation: a salvation established by the grace of God. For Paul, Christ was the central focus, so any part of the Law that diminished the importance of faith in Christ as a means of entering the Covenant was to be abandoned—or, as Paul later saw, valued as a gift to Israel alone, a gift secondary in importance to the gift of salvation through Jesus' death and resurrection.

There certainly is judgment by works in Paul's letters,[73] but punishment related to not doing God's will does not appear to deny salvation to

---

69. Romans 5:1–2, NRSV; Barclay, *Paul and the Gift*, 6.

70. Galatians 3.

71. Acts 16.

72. Sanders, *Paul, the Law and the Jewish People*, 14.

73. Romans 2:12–16; 2 Corinthians 5:8–10; 1 Corinthians 3:10–15; 1 Corinthians 11:29–32.

the sinner. Both in Paul's letters,[74] and in the Letter to the Hebrews,[75] right behavior maintains the Christian in the Covenant, and wrong behavior risks putting the believer outside it: but just as the Jews believed that final salvation was possible for the Gentiles, so Paul believed that final salvation was available to Christians who had put themselves outside the Covenant by their behavior.

Perhaps the most important question that we need to address here is whether Paul's gospel is a gospel of grace or the rather worse news that admission to the Kingdom of God requires the keeping of a new law, for neither in Paul's letters, nor in the other New Testament documents of the early Church, do we find Jesus' radical welcome of unrepentant sinners as full members of the Covenant: a radical welcome represented by Jesus' table-fellowship with "the sinners" and rather less evident in Paul's churches and letters. What we do find is a new corporate identity regarding itself as living at the end of time and awaiting Christ's return[76]—a corporate identity entered by faith and baptism, with membership maintained by a continuing faith and by righteousness. In the Letter to the Philippians, Paul writes this:

> So you, too, my friends, must be obedient, as always; . . . You must work out your own salvation in fear and trembling; for it is God who works in you, inspiring both the will and the deed, for his own chosen purpose.[77]

For Paul, salvation is not solely by God's grace: it is by our faith and our good deeds as well as by grace. We must certainly try to understand the roots of Paul's theology—was he encouraging righteousness among Gentile Christians so that Jewish Christians would be content to abandon their last ties with Judaism and join a predominantly Gentile Church?—but that does not entail agreement with his solution to a difficult pastoral problem. He has substituted a faith commitment for those parts of the Law that distinguished Jews from Gentiles, and has thus turned "faith" into a work of a new Law: which is not surprising considering Paul's deep Jewish roots. Paul has constructed a new exclusivism based on God's choice of Jesus Christ rather than on God's election of Israel, and the mechanism for remaining within the new Covenant is "faith in Christ" rather than a keeping of the Law, a faith that Paul thought Abraham had exercised[78] and which was thus an

---

74. Romans 11:22; 1 Corinthians 6:9–10; Galatians 5:21.
75. Hebrews 10:32–39.
76. Paul's later letters envisaged something of a delay in this final event's coming.
77. Philippians 2:12–13.
78. Genesis 15:6; Galatians 3:6.

older means of including people in the covenant than was the keeping of the Mosaic Law. The Christian community as a whole is kept within the Abrahamic Covenant by its faith and its behavior, and the individual is maintained within the Covenant community by her or his faith and behavior. It might be that such a theological framework was essential for the survival of a Jewish reform movement as it adapted itself to welcome Gentiles and eventually became a predominantly Gentile sect: but Paul's solution is still a betrayal of Jesus' radical grace: which leads us to wonder whether he knew about Jesus' welcome of the sinners. It might be true, as John Barclay suggests, that

> both in content and character, the Christ-event shatters every human paradigm of congruity and connection: it grounds a life that is "not in accord with human norms" . . . [Galatians] 1:11 . . . not beholden to schemata or value derived from human history or culture:[79]

but that does not mean that Paul's theology was entirely characterized by the grace represented by the Christ-event. It is surely significant that "grace" does not appear in the index of E.P. Sanders' *Paul, the Law, and the Jewish People*. Was it inevitable that grace should have been submerged by the early Church's need for boundaries in order to survive?—for "grace" as a central theological concept is not likely to be a very effective way of maintaining the boundaries required by an exclusive corporate identity: in fact, it would tend to demolish them. Perhaps it was simply not possible for the churches that Paul founded to remember the radical grace at the center of Jesus' faith and practice: but that is not to say that there are no elements of that radical grace to be found in Paul's churches.

"There is no such thing as Jew and Greek, slave and free, male and female; for you are all one in Christ Jesus."[80] Equality between Jews and Gentiles appears to have become a reality in the early Church. They ate together, they married each other, and they regarded themselves as of equal status: for they were all of them baptized into Christ. To us this is a commonplace, but in the first century it was a colossal achievement. It was not new for Gentiles to become Jews, and it was not new for Gentiles and Jews to regard themselves as heirs of a common salvation on the basis of differing entry criteria: but for there to be equality of salvation, equality of entry criterion, and equality of status within the Covenant people, was an achievement that we might properly describe as an act of grace—an act of grace which gave birth to a community of grace. Paul's active objection to those works of the

---

79. Barclay, *Paul and the Gift*, 387.
80. Galatians 3:28, NRSV.

Law that marked Jews off as privileged was probably the determining factor, but the theological underpinning of the equality practiced and experienced by Christians was "faith in Christ." In the second chapter of the Letter to the Romans it is Judaism that teaches salvation by grace alone (by God's choice of the Jews) and Paul who teaches salvation by one's own achievements: but he writes this because he wants the Church in Rome to continue to contain Jews and Gentiles, both of whom are recipients of God's grace—and it is this equality between Jews and Gentiles that appears to override every other theological consideration. Francis Watson is right to ask: "Can a Paul who devotes his energies to the creation and maintaining of sectarian groups hostile to all non-members, and specially to the Jewish community from which in fact they derived, still be seen as the bearer of a message with profound universal significance?"[81] The answer can in principle be "yes" if we recognize that much of what Paul says in his letters is intended to maintain the young Church's existence and integrity, and if we understand the equality between Jews and Gentiles in the Church as a pointer to an equal salvation for all.

Much of what Paul wrote in his letters was intended to minimize conflict within the Church by giving practical expression to a fundamental equality: for instance, the language of "the body of Christ" was designed to persuade rich Corinthians to share their food with poorer Christians.[82] The abolition of boundaries between male and female, slave and free, Jew and Gentile, rich and poor,[83] was an obsession for Paul, although clearly we cannot expect him to have been entirely consistent, considering the strong social pressures towards inequality with which he would have had to cope.

Just as Jews rarely discussed but always assumed God's gracious choice of Israel, so Paul assumed (and comparatively rarely mentioned) God's gracious choice of Jesus Christ and of all who are "in Christ" by faith and baptism. But the grace-foundation of Paul's religion did have at least one important practical effect: that is, the dismantling of boundaries within the community. Paul might not have been able to envisage a Covenant community totally without boundaries, but the "faith" that Abraham exercised offered to Paul a route from his own history to a Covenant community that would at least include the Gentiles to whom he had been sent by his conversion—an inclusion which has made it possible for us to keep alive the idea of a universal grace and the accompanying idea of a universal Covenant people.

81. Watson, *Paul, Judaism and the Gentiles*, 181.
82. In the case of 1 Corinthians 11:17–34, equality between rich and poor.
83. Galatians 3:28.

Paul's inclusion of the Gentiles, along with Jesus' inclusion of the "sinners," point unremittingly forward to the destruction of all boundaries—but not yet. Paul's replacement of the ritual boundary of Sabbath, circumcision, and food laws with a "faith" boundary sets us a question that has troubled Christians throughout the centuries: If salvation is by grace alone, then isn't our response irrelevant?—and do we not therefore remove all human responsibility? But if faith is a requirement, then have we not denied the grace of God?

There are clues to a possible approach to a solution to this dilemma in Paul's letters themselves. In *From Adam to Christ*,[84] Morna Hooker suggests that the phrase *pisteōs Christou*, in such passages as Romans 3:22 and Galatians 2:16, generally translated "faith in Christ," is a simple genitive and might be better translated "faith of Christ,"[85] and so referring not to our faith in Christ but to Christ's faith or faithfulness. "If Paul appeals to his converts to be obedient on the basis of Christ's obedience (Philippians 2:8, 12), is it not likely that their faith also will be dependent on his?"[86] Christ's faith leads to our faith through our participation in him, and the righteousness that rests on faith rather than on works of the Law might be best understood as a righteousness that rests on Jesus' faith rather than on ours. Thus the antithesis that Paul offers is between works of the Law and the work of Christ, including Christ's faith, a faith that gives birth to our faith.

As we might expect, the evidence for Hooker's assertion is somewhat ambiguous:[87] and it might be that when Paul used a simple genitive—"the faith of Christ"—he was himself indulging in a little purposeful ambiguity, and was leaving his readers to decide whether he meant "Christ's faith" or "our faith in Christ."[88] But if we agree with Morna Hooker—and I think that I do—then no longer need faith and grace be pitted against one another, for the faith is primarily Jesus Christ's faith, and it is the generous activity of

---

84. Hooker, *From Adam to Christ*.

85. Romans 3:22 and Galatians 2:16: *dia pisteōs Jesou Christou*; Galatians 2:16 and Galatians 3:22: *pisteōs Christou*.

86. Hooker, *From Adam to Christ*, 168: *pisteōs Christou*.

87. It all turns on whether a simple genitive can mean "in" as well as "of." In Mark 11:22, the most natural translation of *Egete pistin Theou* in the context would be "Have faith in God": but "Have the faith of God" would be an interesting alternative. In 2 Corinthians 10:5, the most natural translation of *tēn hupakoēn tou Christou* in the context is "obedience to Christ," and not "Christ's obedience [to God]." In 2 Thessalonians 2:13, *pistei alētheia* is generally translated "faith in truth," but it could also mean "truthful faith." In James 2:1, *tēn pistin tou kuriou hēmōn Jesou Christou* could mean either "faith in our Lord Jesus Christ" or "faith like that of our Lord Jesus Christ."

88. Torry, "Two Kinds of Ambiguity."

God. The "grace of our Lord Jesus Christ"[89] is the grace exercised by Jesus Christ, as well as the grace which is Jesus Christ, a grace from which flows the faithfulness of Jesus Christ and from which flows our faith.

It seems to me that Paul's gospel is in fact a gospel of grace, and that we can agree with C.K. Barrett that in Paul's letters grace

> is not a love that God is almost obliged to entertain for those who, on their side, keep their part of the covenant; it is love for the undeserving, indeed for the covenant-breakers . . . Galatians 2:21 ("I do not make void the grace of God; for if righteousness comes through the Law, then Christ died for nothing") . . . It appears at once that Law is contrasted with grace as a means of obtaining righteousness.[90]

Yes, there are moralistic passages in Paul's letters—because he remained a Jew and he wanted his churches to survive and to grow and to exhibit that equality that a gospel of grace implied: but such moralizing is incidental to the foundation of grace underlying Paul's theology, a grace more basic than the faith that is Christ's faith and that is itself an act of grace.

CONCLUSION

James Moffatt wrote *Grace in the New Testament* in 1931, but the more recent scholarship on which I have based this chapter's discussion of Paul has thoroughly borne out Moffatt's thesis

> that the mission of the Lord Jesus was a mission of grace, that the apostle Paul's message or what he called his "gospel" presupposes this more seriously than some have been prepared to admit, and that a fair appreciation of the affinities and indebtedness of Christianity to its environment leaves the historical student impressed by the creative energy of the new faith mentally and morally.[91]

Is there any faith needed for salvation that is not Christ's but ours? Paul might not have been able to answer that question unambiguously, and his letters do contain passages that suggest salvation by works—and they certainly suggest firm boundaries around the Covenant people, although not necessarily around the people destined for final salvation: another question

---

89. Romans 16:20; 1 Corinthians 16:23.
90. Barrett, *Paul*, 88–89.
91. Moffatt, *Grace in the New Testament*, xii.

about which Paul might not have been able to respond unambiguously. Paul's gospel was not unambiguously a gospel of grace, but it pointed in that direction: that is, in the direction of a gospel of unconditional, active generosity, a direction sometimes submerged by Paul himself and certainly somewhat submerged during the following centuries.

It would be difficult to better Peter Groves' summary of grace as it is understood in the Jewish and Christian scriptures.

> The grace of God, in scripture, is over and over again the loving kindness of God towards those whom he has chosen to favour. This is seen in his relentless mercy towards his errant children and his unfailing love in the face of the faithless and loveless behaviour of those whom he has created. In this sense, the word "grace" describes what God is like, and what God is like is self-giving love. . . . So the grace of God characterizes all that we can say about God's revelation of himself in Jesus Christ: this is what God is like. This is the God whose revelation is witnessed by the texts that we call scripture or the Bible, and proclaimed in word and deed by the Christian Church. To say, however, that grace can tell us about the nature of God is not to suggest that it is merely an attribute or a description. Love is not an attribute of God in the way that speed is an attribute of cheetahs. Love is what God is, something active and dynamic, and so grace is never simply a characteristic.[92]

If love is "active and dynamic", and if love is "what God is", then an actological theology is clearly required.

---

92. Groves, *Grace*, 3.

Chapter 7

Grace after the New Testament

Thesis: After the New Testament, "grace" became less a changing pattern of action and more a substance that Christians could possess.

INTRODUCTION

Paul does talk about the grace that God has "given" him[1] as well as using "grace" to express the character of a God who constantly gives, so it should come as no surprise that after the New Testament period grace came to be regarded more as something substantial, as a possession of the Christian, and less as a pattern of action. "Grace" came to mean an endowment, given by the Holy Spirit, rather than the active generosity of God in Jesus Christ.

THE SLIDE TOWARDS "GRACE" AS THE POSSESSION OF A SUBSTANCE

The process of change, already latent in Paul's letters, is clearly visible in the Letter of James ("the grace he gives . . ."[2]), and when T.F. Torrance surveys the second century literature of the Didache, the First Letter of Clement, the Epistles of Ignatius, the Epistle of Polycarp, the Epistle of Barnabas, the Shepherd of Hermas, and the Second Letter of Clement, he finds a firm trend towards the pre-New Testament use of the word *charis*, in which it

---

1. For instance, Romans 12:3.
2. James 4:6.

means a character trait that a person possesses.[3] In the hands of these early theologians, a gospel of God's grace gave way to a call to active discipleship and a handing-down of revealed truth, a call and a handing-down aided by a "grace" given to the believer by the Spirit. The gospel thus became a "new Law," and "grace" an enabling power given by the Holy Spirit to enable us to keep this new Law: a "grace" given to the Church as a possession and bestowed by the Bishop at baptism and ordination.

There might in fact be something of a spectrum of usage from grace as changing patterns of action to grace as something given, but Torrance is right to note a shift from "grace" as the generous activity of God to "grace" as a spiritual substance bestowed by God on the Church. Torrance thinks that the real problem is that "grace" had become disconnected from the life and work of Jesus Christ and had been given to the Holy Spirit to bestow:[4] but the major difference is that "grace" has become less dynamic and more static, less a generous activity and more the bestowal of a characteristic that enables us to be faithful Christians.

If we are looking for reasons for the transition of the meaning of "grace" from God's generous activity to an endowment given to the elect, then we shall probably find them in the social situation of the early Christians. Particularly in urban contexts, the Christian Church was one religious institution among others, so the maintenance of boundaries was clearly an important consideration. It was probably inevitable that Christians would come to be defined by specific confessions of faith, by the exercise of faith, and by thinking that they had received something from God that non-Christians had not received; and what better term than "grace" to denote this "something": for to commandeer "grace" for this task meant that it could no longer express a generous activity that might tend to dissolve the social boundaries necessary to the Church's survival in a complex society.

Of the most prominent theologians of the early years of the Church, the third-century Origen recovered some of the active sense of "grace" but made it conditional on our response;[5] Tertullian used the term in a variety of ways, and generally in such a way as to deny us the exercise of free will in relation to God's grace;[6] and the fifth-century Augustine reacted against

---

3. Torrance, *The Doctrine of Grace in the Apostolic Fathers*, 133: "The great presupposition of the Christian life [for the Fathers] was not a deed of decisive significance that cut across human life and set it on a wholly new basis grounded upon the self-giving of God. What took absolute precedence was God's call to a new life in obedience to revealed truth. Grace, as far as it was grasped, was subsidiary to that."

4. Torrance, *The Doctrine of Grace in the Apostolic Fathers*, v.

5. Drewery, *Origen and the Doctrine of Grace*, 64.

6. Williams, *The Grace of God*, 16. Williams quotes Tertullian, *De an.* 21: ". . . divine

Pelagius to give us a concept of grace that made free will a difficult concept but that retained the nature of grace as a gift.

For Augustine, the primary theological fact was the "Fall," the first sin of Adam that implicates all of us in sin and in guilt for sin. The grace exercised towards those whom God has chosen to save is of a character that Paul would have recognized: it is an unconditional, active generosity, although also an endowment leading to a sanctified life. It is not surprising that Pelagius accused Augustine of introducing the pagan concept of "fate" when Augustine wrote passages such as this: "We must not doubt that human wills are incapable of withstanding the will of God in such a way as to prevent Him from doing what He wishes to do."[7] As far as Augustine was concerned, "grace" is irresistible, and its apparent arbitrariness is unquestionable. Whether the grace leads to faith, baptism, and membership of the Church, or to salvation sealed by a grace of final perseverance (and he didn't think that everybody who was given the first kind was necessarily given the second), grace appears to be for some and not for others. Augustine certainly claimed to believe in the freedom of the will, but himself demolished the claim by saying that God creates some who will will salvation and some who will not; and by saying that "eternal life is the wages owing to the merit of righteousness"[8] he made it clear that righteous deeds were the result of God's irresistible grace in the Christian. Such a theological position, which preserved the unconditionality of grace by making its exercise somewhat arbitrary, was no doubt a result of Augustine's sense of his own worthlessness: but its uncompromising character was the result of the dispute with Pelagius.

Pelagius was a Briton who in Rome, Carthage, and Palestine proclaimed a gospel of grace, but one that refused Augustine's conclusion that God's grace rendered the human will impotent. A major reason for Pelagius saying what he said was that the Church was not in very good shape. Much of its activity had become conventional, and he feared that Augustine had too readily accepted the sinful world to which we belong. The Roman Empire was collapsing as Pelagius and Augustine wrote their treatises, and in the midst of such social crises reform movements sometimes catch on because people need to feel their own dignity and that they have the ability to change their own lives and their world. Augustine was a member of the Roman establishment by education and experience, and it is not surprising

---

grace, which is assuredly mightier than nature, having in subjection to itself within us the faculty of free will."

7. *De corr. et grat.*, xii, 38, quoted in Williams, *The Grace of God*, 26–27.

8. *Ep.* cxciv, 20, quoted in Williams, *The Grace of God*, 41.

that he formulated a theology that offered spiritual security to the elect and effectively left the secular world to fall apart without interference from a robust Christian ethic: but Pelagius was from the fringe of the Empire and brought with him a Christianity used to a more hostile context and thus one more dependent on the action of the Christian than on the invisible action of God.

It is a pity that Augustine and Pelagius never met to hammer out their differences, for if they had done then they might have discovered that they were both attempting to give expression to a mystery, and that it was possible to live with ambiguity—something that Pelagius was better at doing than Augustine was. It is also a pity that Pelagius was not well served by his associates, one of whom, Caelestius, turned Pelagius's legitimate concern with morality into a systematic theology, thus doing for Pelagius what Augustine had done for himself. Neither was Augustine well served by those on his side, particularly by Jerome, who branded Pelagius a heretic and rejected all attempts at reconciliation, apparently on the grounds that Pelagius believed that by God's grace some people might have remained sinless.

A Synod in 415 CE in Jerusalem agreed with Pelagius that Paul's "In my labours I have outdone them all—not I, indeed, but the grace of God working with me"[9] implied that if we strive to be righteous then God gives the possibility of being so. A subsequent Synod in Palestine heard Pelagius repudiate a caricature of his position (to the pleasure of Augustine and the displeasure of Jerome), and in Rome Pope Zosimus decided in favor of Pelagius. Pelagius was firmly opposed to Augustine's predestinarianism, but had not publicly questioned Augustine's orthodoxy. Augustine's allies, however, had fueled the controversy in Rome, and Zosimus's verdict had gone to Pelagius because he appeared more concerned with the peace and unity of the Church than did Augustine. But Augustine had not given up, and he asked the Emperor to intervene. A Synod at Carthage condemned Pelagius's views, and Zosimus caved in and excommunicated Pelagius and Caelestius for transgressing the central tenets of the Christian Faith. Thus a Christian ethicist for whom love was the highest category, and who believed in both God's grace and the freedom of the will, was condemned as a heretic.

Pelagius's concern to give equal weight to passages of Scripture that appeared to contradict each other (those about grace in Paul's letters, and Jesus' parables of the Good Samaritan and the Sheep and the Goats, which assume that we can choose to act righteously) lost out to Augustine's God who gives the ability to act righteously or chooses not to give that ability. Pelagius, being concerned about what it meant to be a Christian disciple,

---

9. 1 Corinthians 15:10.

could not accept that God's grace is an irresistible power that leaves no room for human freedom—and I have to agree with him. What is so tragic is that the Synod in Carthage found in favor of an Augustine who could so caricature his opponent's position as to say that Pelagius "under the pretence of defending the freedom of the will, disputes the grace of God and endeavours to overthrow the foundation of the Christian faith."[10] In the end, the dispute comes down to different emphases (no doubt the result of differing personal experiences) polarizing themselves against each other, so that in the end Augustine could not see any of his own position in that of Pelagius.

What is required now is a thorough rehabilitation of Pelagius, the theologian who spoke of God's grace of creation, God's grace of revelation, and God's grace of redemption. In Augustine's theology "grace" became a somewhat impersonal and irresistible power—a power perhaps modelled on that of the Roman Emperor, and a power that Augustine wanted to see exercised in and by the Church, and it ceased to be the personal activity of a creative and saving God seeking a relationship of love with the created order. "Grace," which should have been understood as a generous, self-giving activity, had become an arbitrary, irresistible power.

The dispute did not need to have been so vicious, and it did not need to have happened at all, for it is possible to conceive of events having multiple causes rather than single causes. Augustine's conversion was an exercise of God's grace, but it was also the result of co-operation on Augustine's part. In J.R. Lucas's view, "St. Augustine had been right to ascribe the credit not to himself but to God, wrong to say that he himself had had no say in whether he would do God's will or not. Pelagius was right to stress man's freedom, wrong to convert autonomy into autarky, and freedom into pride."[11]

After Augustine, Cassian suggested that "when God sees us incline towards willing the good, he runs to meet us, directs and strengthens us."[12] This grace is "co-operant," that is, a matter of a relationship between God and humanity; and the thirteenth century Franciscans, and especially Duns Scotus, declared all grace to be co-operant. But the urge to tidy things up did not go away, and Anselm of Canterbury offered to the Church of the twelfth century a tidy theology of the atonement. He managed to avoid making the devil the payee of Christ's ransom, but he got quite close to doing that by declaring God to be subject to a universal justice that it was his duty to uphold. Because we have sinned, there must be some righting of the balance, and this was achieved through Jesus offering himself. Anselm and his

---

10. Quoted in Rees, *Pelagius*, 15.
11. Lucas, "Pelagius and St. Augustine," 73.
12. *Coll.* xiiii, 11, quoted in Williams, *The Grace of God*, 49.

modern-day commentator Colin Gunton think that this is an example of grace, for God is not here a judge, and there is no compulsion on Jesus to go to his death:[13] but this is still not the grace that Jesus exercised during his ministry, for it demands that accounts be settled, that someone puts things right. And it is not the justification of which Paul speaks—a counting of the sinner as righteous when the sinner is not righteous. Paul found a complete generosity difficult, and there are roots of Anselm's atonement doctrine in Paul's ideas about Jesus' death: but Anselm has tried to make a logical system out of ideas culled from Paul's letters—letters that were never intended to be systematic theological treatises—and he thus wandered even further from Jesus' total generosity than did Paul.

Why is it that we find it so hard to believe that God's welcome of us is without condition? Why did Anselm feel the need to demand that justice be satisfied? The metaphors of "justice" and "satisfaction" might have been helpful at the time if they gave to people who for some reason could not grasp an absolute generosity at least a glimpse of it: but they are metaphors, and if they now cloud our vision of the glory of an unconditional grace then we must abandon them and find some new way to express our theology of grace.

Augustine and Anselm might have done us a favor that Pelagius and Duns Scotus could not do, for to recognize and express ambiguity is not necessarily an effective way of keeping alive a vital element of the Christian tradition. However much we might question the details of Augustine's scheme, he did believe that grace is God's grace, and that God is gracious towards sinners. And it is Augustine whom Aquinas and Catholic theologians followed, and Augustine whom Luther and Protestant theologians followed.

Thomas Aquinas found the rediscovered philosophy of Aristotle useful as a framework for expressing Christian Faith, and within a framework that understood reality as to some extent dynamic[14] he sought to understand grace. He distinguished between two kinds: actual grace (the movement of the soul by God), and habitual grace (a grace infused into the soul). Actual grace was not too far from the grace of the New Testament, but habitual grace was rather a long way from it. Aquinas's theology was largely determinative for Roman Catholic theology until earlier this century, and it still possesses enormous influence, as does his understanding of grace.

---

13. Gunton, *The Actuality of Atonement*, 92. Gunton quotes Anselm, *Cur Deus Homo*, II, xviii: "Therefore, since he himself (Jesus Christ) is God, the Son of God, he offered himself for his own honour to himself, as he did to the Father and the Holy Spirit."

14. Torry, *Actology*, 70–76.

Luther preferred to think of our wills as passive in relation to God's grace, thus returning to a scheme closer to Augustine's, and the debate between Augustine and Pelagius re-emerged as one within early Lutheranism between Luther and Melanchthon: but this time without quite as much damaging polarization. What appears to have been common ground between Luther and his associates was the centrality of "faith," which unfortunately became a new work of a new law and the primary cause of Protestantism losing touch with grace, and thus losing touch with a gracious God, the search for whom had been the cause of Luther's Reformation. The centrality that Calvin ascribed to grace had an effect similar to Augustine's reaction against Pelagius, as it left Calvin with a sovereign God who was generous to some but not to others.[15]

In England, the Reformation took a different turn again, and turned grace into the kind of "substance" that the early Church Fathers and Aquinas would have recognized. The Collects of the Book of Common Prayer pray to a God "who has given unto us thy servants grace . . ." as if grace is a medicine given by God to members of the Church of England. The priest and poet George Herbert might have understood something of the nature of unconditional grace when he wrote poems about God's love,[16] but the Book of Common Prayer did not, and neither did the thirty-nine articles, which followed Augustine's and Calvin's ideas on predestination to "life everlasting" or "the sentence of God's predestination."[17]

---

15. MacCulloch, *A History of Christianity*, 604–44.
16. cf. George Herbert's poem, "Love bade me welcome":
    Love bade me welcome: yet my soul drew back,
    Guiltie of dust and sinne.
    But quick-ey'd Love, observing me grow slack
    From my first entrance in,
    Drew nearer to me, sweetly questioning,
    If I lack'd any thing.
    A guest, I answer'd, worthy to be here:
    Love said, You shall be he.
    I the unkinde, ungratefull? Ah my deare,
    I cannot look on thee.
    Love took my hand, and smiling did reply,
    Who made the eyes but I?
    Truth Lord, but I have marr'd them: let my shame
    Go where it doth deserve.
    And know you not, sayes Love, who bore the blame?
    My deare, then I will serve.
    You must sit down, sayes Love, and taste my meat:
    So I did sit and eat.
    (from Herbert, *The Poems of George Herbert*).
17. Article 17.

Modern Protestant thought is so diverse that it is difficult to give the category a definition, and the diversity is nowhere greater than in the tradition's treatment of grace. Kant's concern for autonomy and responsibility[18] would have been recognized by Augustine as what he was attacking in Pelagius's theology; and Schleiermacher located the roots of faith so firmly in human experience, and particularly in our feeling of dependence,[19] that he was in danger of turning the story of God's generosity into one purely about ourselves. Bultmann, following Paul, knows that grace is God's gracious action, but he is clear that a decision is a requirement, and his language is so ambiguous that it is far from clear where grace occurs, if at all;[20] and whilst Karl Barth is clear that "the reality of Jesus Christ" is that "God is this Man and this Man is God . . . there can be no question of understanding *how* the condescension of God acts."[21] Here is a radical grace that is pure gift, but without any "economy" of an ability to respond.

Amongst modern Roman Catholic theologians, Hans Küng is the nearest to Protestant thought when he describes grace as "the free personal favour of God, as His powerful and sovereign act."[22] He criticized Barth for not recognizing that grace is a personal relationship established by God, but Küng himself wrote that grace "has been given through the Holy Spirit in the Church,"[23] making it sound like an endowment rather than a continuous activity. And far from objecting to the Roman Catholic habit of dividing up grace into different kinds of grace, he approves of it.

Charles Journet, in *The Meaning of Grace*,[24] describes five "states of grace," without any recognition that a "state of grace" might be a contradiction in terms; James Burtchaell defines grace as being "favorable in complete priority to another person's behavior,"[25] but then abandons his discussion of God's grace universally active for one about the Church's ritual; Edward Yarnold[26] has attempted to relate actual and habitual grace by noting that God's active grace changes us so that our behavior changes—but he still feels it necessary to divide the "first gift" of creation from the "second gift" of grace,

---

18. Kant, *Critique of Practical Reason*; *What is Enlightenment?*

19. Schleiermacher, *The Christian Faith*, 16; Sykes, *Friedrich Schleiermacher*, 26–30.

20. Bultmann, *Essays Philosophical and Theological*, 133; *Faith and Understanding*, 265; *Kerygma and Myth*, 44; Roberts, *Rudolf Bultmann's Theology*, 105, 119; Torry, "Two Kinds of Ambiguity," 26.

21. Barth, *Church Dogmatics*, I (2), 31, 34.

22. Küng, *Justification*, 203.

23. Küng, *Justification*, 200.

24. Journet, *The Meaning of Grace*.

25. Burtchaell, *Living with Grace*, 21.

26. Yarnold, *The Second Gift*.

not realizing that creation is the activity of God's grace. Karl Rahner, in *Grace in Freedom*,[27] expresses the opinion that there is no point in discussing the causality of our actions, yet goes on to describe grace as God himself setting our freedom free from its refusal of God's self-communication. On Roman Catholic theologians such as Richard Cole[28] Teilhard de Chardin's optimistic evolutionary scheme[29] has had an impact—an influence that has enabled Cole to recognize grace as a universal activity operating in the secular world as well as in the sacred: but he still manages to confuse "grace" and "Spirit," and because he doesn't grapple with the use of "grace" in the New Testament, he writes of an "order of grace" in which, whether we like it or not, our wills recognize the universal kingship of Christ.

It is not entirely the fault of the theologians whom I have discussed that they have wandered such a long way from the grace that we see in Jesus' life. Paul grasped something of the character of this grace when he experienced a call to take the gospel to the Gentiles and had to work out how Jews and Gentiles might be equally "in Christ": but his solution of "justification by faith" lost Jesus' unconditionality, even if at the time it might have been an emphasis essential to maintaining the Church's unity and self-identity, and even if the faith concerned might have been Jesus' faith in which we participate.

And so it has always been. The Church needs boundaries, and grace crosses boundaries, so grace has been compromised throughout the Church's history. And in the personal sphere, we have moral needs, and Pelagius's reaction to Augustine was inevitable and healthy. As John Oman puts it: "How is the personality which alike gives meaning to morality and value to religion to be preserved if not by . . . setting our religious dependence and our moral independence in antagonism?"[30] The Catholic compromise is an Augustinian Church with Pelagian members, and the Protestant compromise a Pelagian Church with Augustinian members. Oman tries to integrate religious dependence with moral independence by locating them both in a personal relationship with God, but this is at the cost of dividing morality and religion: an impossible division to maintain.

Is it simply that we cannot reconcile grace and freedom because we are trying to be too literalist about language that is essentially metaphorical? Colin Gunton thinks so, believing that because we have not understood the

---

27. Rahner, *Grace in Freedom*.

28. Cole, *Universal Grace*.

29. Deane-Drummond, *Christ and Evolution*, 37; Teilhard de Chardin, *The Phenomenon of Man*.

30. Oman, *Grace and Personality*.

metaphorical status of theological language we have moved the center of attention from Jesus Christ to the believer's response, simply because that is what we can speak about. Perhaps this is why Paul ended up emphasizing "faith" at the cost of a genuine grace. Gunton[31] recognizes that Wittgenstein's philosophical work on the nature of language has dissolved the absolute distinction between the metaphorical and the literal, and he urges us to treasure our metaphors, in science as much as in theology. It is true that metaphors like "victory," "justice," "sacrifice," and so on, were attempts to speak of a grace that cannot be pinned down by language: but the problem is that Gunton has not told us how to discriminate between valid metaphors and invalid ones. On what basis might we decide whether or not to use Augustine's predestinarian language? And when we speak of the freedom of the will, is that a metaphor? Unfortunately, the problem that Augustine and Pelagius faced of reconciling the freedom of the will with the sovereignty of God will not go away that easily, for to appeal to metaphor does not make self-contradiction a valid use of language.

Perhaps we can sidestep the problem by recognizing that Jesus' contexts and ours are very different. It was all very well for Jesus to live a life characterized by grace, and to eat with the wicked, but he didn't have a Church to keep in one piece, he didn't have a society to keep moral, and he didn't have to square morality and religion with each other—for as far as he was concerned the world as he knew it was about to end and a whole new order of existence was to be inaugurated.

If grace is the predominant characteristic of Jesus' ministry, the focus of Paul's theology (even if he did not always recognize this), and the primary definition of God's activity in relation to the universe and to every human being, then there are some problems that we must solve, problems with which, as we have seen, Christians have grappled for two thousand years: and an appeal to metaphor is not sufficient to resolve the dilemma.

So how are we to reconcile God's decisions with our free will?[32] How are we to reconcile morality with grace? How are we to reconcile a deciding God with a suffering humanity? How are we to conceive of God's activity in a secular world? And perhaps more importantly than all of these questions: How are we to speak about God and about grace in a world in which philosophy has asked so many questions about the nature of language that we fear that we cannot speak about our own existence, let alone about the grace of God?

---

31. Gunton, *The Actuality of Atonement*, 17–19.

32. For a discussion of the "paradox of grace" in relation to ourselves and to Jesus, see Baillie, *God was in Christ*.

JESUS: THE GRACE OF GOD

I hope to return to such questions: but for the moment I have shown that grace is self-giving activity, that grace is the character of Jesus' activity, that grace was at the heart of Paul's Christian faith, that grace has been the focus of theological debate since the early Church, that grace has often slid from being changing patterns of action that constitute God to being a substance of some kind that God grants to believers, and that grace has been constantly lost and rediscovered as the distinctively Christian center of Christian doctrine.

In the worlds in which we live we shall never experience or exercise grace in its pure form, for our generosity shrivels in the absence of response, our motives are mixed, and human institutions need to defend themselves if they are to retain their integrity: but this makes it all the more necessary to pursue the notion of grace, and to speak clearly of grace even though we know that we shall never in this life meet it in its pure form: because if we do not speak of such a grace then we shall be less able to reform our theology, our ethics, and our institutions in conformity with a grace that is the character of the God who is the absolute grace for which we seek.

The philosophical scaffolding that I have constructed gives us a means for expressing this center of Christian faith, a means whereby, possibly for the first time, grace can be spoken of as grace, as self-giving activity, and a means whereby God can be spoken of in terms of the activity that is self-giving love.

Are we now ready to understand the relationship between Jesus and God?

Who is Jesus? Jesus is what he does: When John heard in prison what the Messiah was doing, he sent word by his disciples to say to him, "Are you the one who is to come, or are we to wait for another?" Jesus answered them, "Go and tell John what you hear and see: the blind receive their sight, the lame walk, the lepers are cleansed, the deaf hear, the dead are raised, and the poor have good news brought to them. And blessed is anyone who takes no offence at me."[33]

When a man from whom Jesus had cast out demons asked to go with him,

> Jesus sent him away, saying, "Return to your home, and declare how much God has done for you." So he went away, proclaiming throughout the city how much Jesus had done for him.[34]

---

33. Matthew 11:2-6, NRSV.
34. Luke 8:39, NRSV.

As Tom Wright puts it:

> If Luke was not trying to tell us that what Jesus was doing God was doing—and vice versa—then the sentence has no meaning . . . all three synoptic gospels are clear: in telling the story of Jesus they are consciously telling the story of how Israel's God came back to his people . . .[35]

Jesus does God. If reality is action, then this is the highest possible Christology. God is Action—the source of all action—and God is those particular patterns of action that God freely chooses. If Jesus' patterns of action are those patterns, and Jesus' patterns of action change as God's patterns of action change, then Jesus is God: for we are action in changing patterns.

So how to describe Jesus? Jesus is both God and a human being. Jesus is changing patterns of action that are uniquely God-patterned, and Jesus is changing patterns of action that are human patterns of action: that is, they have family resemblances to the patterns of action that constitute ourselves.

But this leaves open a question: Are the changing patterns of action that constitute Jesus uniquely those that constitute God because God has chosen that that will be the case, or are Jesus' patterns of action those that have evolved through human history and have become Jesus, and God has then decided that those patterns of action will constitute God? Karl Barth opts for the former interpretation, but interestingly leaves open the possibility of the latter.

> We have here no universal deity capable of being reached conceptually, but this concrete deity—real and recognisable in the descent grounded in that sequence and peculiar to the existence of Jesus Christ. . . . It is when we look at Jesus Christ that we know decisively that God's deity does not exclude, but includes His *humanity*. . . . *God* wants in His freedom actually not to be without man but *with* him and in the same freedom not against him but *for* him . . . In this divinely free volition and election, in this sovereign decision . . . God is *human*. His free affirmation of man, His free concern for him, His free substitution for him—this is God's humanity. . . . In the mirror of this humanity of Jesus Christ the humanity of God enclosed in His deity reveals itself.[36]

Here we are asking about causality, which requires a notion of time, which in turn requires an understanding that time is changing patterns of action.

---

35. Wright, *How God Became King*, 100–101.
36. Barth, *The Humanity of God*, 45–46, 48–49.

There is no particular problem with this, because there is no reason to think that God does not relate to time: but still we have not answered our question. The question is unanswerable. The changing patterns of action that constitute Jesus as he was born, grew up, taught, healed, suffered, and died, and that constitute Jesus still as we and all creation experience the changing patterns of action that continue to constitute Jesus as the risen Christ, are also changing patterns of action that constitute God: and all of it continues to change, and all of it is action.

Underlying the unanswerable question is the question as to whether God is causally active in the world. The fact that we have ascribed action in changing patterns to God, to the universe, to the microcosmos, and to humanity, suggests that those that constitute God are as much members of causal chains as are any other changing patterns of action.[37]

> God works and reveals himself *causally* in the real affairs and to the sensibly embodied lives of human beings today in space and time, with real, life-changing effects. . . . this causality will show itself to be not a mere efficient causality which operates entirely *from within* the causal dynamic order like any natural causality. It is rather a *divine* causality whose origin is not temporal or finite, but infinite; yet whose effects are no less dynamic, no less empirical, no less real for human embodied life today than any natural causality, however "infinite" these "effects" may *also* be for the eternal redemption of human beings beyond this life, and for God's reconciliation of the whole world to himself.[38]

So were the changing patterns of action that constituted and still constitute Jesus God's choosing to be a human being among us, or were they evolved through human history and God subsequently chose them? Perhaps we don't have to choose. Either way, Jesus chose to do as he did. In neither case is Jesus' humanity in any way dissolved. In both cases Jesus is uniquely God actively and causally involved in the world, living a human life, and suffering a human death. As Arthur Peacocke and Ann Pederson put it:

> The diverse meanings written into the many levels of creation coalesce like rays of light with an intensity that so illuminates for us the purposes of God that we are better able to interpret God's meanings, communicated in his creative activity over a wider range of human experience of nature and history.[39]

---

37. Davies et al., *Transformation Theology*, 77.
38. Davies et al., *Transformation Theology*, 68.
39. Peacocke and Pederson, *The Music of Creation*, 39.

"In the beginning was the Word, and the Word was with God, and the Word was God."⁴⁰ Any interpretation of this passage must take account of both the difference between "the Word" and "God," and the complex identification between them: "the Word was with the God, and the Word was God," with perhaps the loss of the definite article in the second of those clauses implying that *theos* should be translated "divine" rather than "God." One ancient conceptual structure that enabled an identity to be established between two entities at the same time as a difference between them was maintained was Aristotle's distinction between "substance" (which unites the two entities) and "form" (which distinguishes between them). This was possible for Aristotle, but is hardly possible in a world in which the physical sciences cannot conceptualize such a distinction.⁴¹ And if we abandon the substance/form distinction, and thus find ourselves failing to identify Jesus with God, might this be because we are still too much under the influence of a Neoplatonic conceptual framework that regards Jesus as a human being and God as an unchanging Platonic "Form" or "Idea," making them incompatible with each other? A conceptual structure that prioritizes the dynamic would enable us to understand God as Action and as action in changing patterns; the Creator, whom Jesus called "Father", as action in changing patterns; Jesus as action in changing patterns; the unity between Jesus and God as a unity of changing patterns of action, not one of substance; the unity between the Father and God as similarly one of patterned action; and the "Word" as changing patterns of action, as a verb and not as a noun, with every pattern of action changing in relation to and along with every other: as Jean Racine put it in the words that became the text for Gabriel Fauré's *Cantique de Jean Racine*: "Verbe égal au Très-Haut,"⁴² "Word/Verb, one with the highest." God

---

40. *En arché én ho Logos, kai ho Logos én pros ton Theov, kai Theos én ho Logos*: John 1:1.

41. MacKinnon is right to suggest that translating "substance" language into the language of "events" cannot offer us a complete translation (MacKinnon, "'Substance' in Christology—a cross-bench view," 287), but the same could be said the other way round: that the translation of events language into substance terms cannot be complete either. Both "action" and "substance" are clearly paradigms: models with which we attempt to communicate with each other about our experience. So I cannot agree with MacKinnon when he states that to ask about Jesus Christ's relation to the Father is necessarily to ask about ontology in the sense of "substance," for the answer could easily be about action, thus suggesting that MacKinnon is correct when he writes that "substance" language is not necessarily integral to Christian theology but is indeed a "useful but unnecessary alliance between philosophy and theology" (MacKinnon, "'Substance' in Christology," 288).

42. https://en.wikipedia.org/wiki/Cantique_de_Jean_Racine.

in Christ is a drama that is a polyphony,⁴³ which is why "narrating the divine drama is an integral part of setting out a theological epistemology."⁴⁴

The difference between Jesus and the Father thus becomes a difference between patterns of action at one level ("I am not alone because the Father is with me"⁴⁵) while the unity becomes a unity of pattern at another level ("the Father and I are one"⁴⁶). Just as we become one when we work together, when our actions are united in a single cause, so Jesus and the Father are one in their changing patterns of action, in their working together. The mission that they both share, the *missio Dei*, the mission of God, *constitutes* their unity, and is now our mission as well: and so Jesus asks for his followers that "they may all be one. As you, Father, are in me and I am in you."⁴⁷ It might be objected that by uniting Jesus and God in this way we are fashioning God in Jesus' image rather than asserting the transcendence of God and Jesus' unity with that transcendent God. Not at all. A God understood as the source of all action, that is, as Action, and also as changing patterns of action freely chosen, and Jesus understood as constituted by the same changing patterns of action, loses none of the mystery of God and none of the transcendence. What it does achieve is unity between Jesus and God at the same time as retaining God's transcendence.

So now John 1:1 is a statement that God is the Word and the Word is God (the Word being action in changing patterns that constitute God),⁴⁸ and we can more easily think ourselves into the Apostle Thomas's mind when he sees Jesus and says, "My Lord and my God."⁴⁹ The Last Supper, the entry into Jerusalem, the temple incident, and every incident of Jesus' life, are the Kingdom of God among us. They are not simply a signpost to it: they are it. These are Jesus' changing patterns of action, so they are God's, so they are God living in our midst, and we are at one with Jesus and his Father as we share in their changing patterns of action.

"And the Word became flesh,"⁵⁰ that is, a material being, "and lived among us"⁵¹—which is action: the changing patterns of action that constitute

43. Peacocke and Pederson, *The Music of Creation*, 42.
44. Ayres, "(Mis)Adventures in Trinitarian Ontology," 142.
45. John 16:32, NRSV: *kai ouk eimi monos, hoti ho Pater met' emou estin.*
46. John 10:30, NRSV: *ego kai ho Pater hen esmen.*
47. John 17:21, NRSV: "that all [of them] might be one, as you, Father, are in me and I in you, so that they might be in us": *hina pantes hen ōsin, kathōs su, pater, en emoi kagō en soi, hina kai autoi en hēmin ōsin*
48. Wright, *The Challenge of Jesus*, 90–93.
49. John 20:28, NRSV, *egō kai ho Pater hen esmen*;
50. John 1:14, NRSV: *Kai ho logos sarx egeneto.*
51. John 1:14, NRSV: *kai eskēnōsen en hēmin.*

the whole of Jesus' life: his birth, his childhood, his adulthood, his death, his resurrection, his living among us still as his changing patterns of action are lived by the Church and by anyone who follows him. And all of this is eternally God, and it is eternally action in changing patterns entangled with infinitely many other changing patterns of action. As N.T. Wright puts it,

> For the earliest Christians, to speak of Jesus' resurrection was to speak of something that, however (in our sense) earth-shattering, however much it drew together things earthly and heavenly, was still an "earthly" event, and needed to be exactly that. It had earthly consequences: an empty tomb, footprints by the shore, and, at Emmaus, a loaf broken . . .[52]

Jesus is his action in patterns: so at the last supper, the taking, thanking, breaking, and sharing of the bread are Jesus, and they are God—which means that when we do these things, we are the body of Christ, and we are God—at least to that extent. Jesus is truly present, because he is what he does. And it is this Jesus's changing patterns of action that reveal God: his "deed and word,"[53] not his "word and deed": so it is his healings, his welcomings, and his forgivings, that are the revelation of God[54]—yes, and also his words, because those too are action in changing patterns that change us: but the primary revelation is the deeds that are the changing pattern of action that define Jesus and that are his revelation of God; and the primary deed has to be Jesus' resurrection from the dead.

THE RISEN CHRIST

Christmas is two festivals at once: a celebration of Jesus' birth, and the feast of the incarnation: that is, of God living a human life. In our parish churches we tend to concentrate on the former, which is to the detriment of the latter, because a virgin birth is incompatible with a normal human life. This is not to say that a virgin birth is in any sense impossible: clearly anything is possible for God, who is Action and the source of all action: but if a genuine human life is what is required then that does rather rule out birth to a virgin. But perhaps we should leave Christmas as it is, and instead regard Good Friday as the Feast of the Incarnation: for it is in Jesus' death that God's living of a human life is focused: in God suffering and dying a terrible human death. And perhaps this should lead us to ask about Jesus' resurrection, and

---

52. Wright, *The Resurrection of the Son of God*, 736–37.
53. Luke 24:19, NRSV: *en ergō kai logō*.
54. Mark 2.

the narratives of the empty tomb. If the empty tomb had never occurred, or if Jesus' body had been stolen and had rotted elsewhere, then would Jesus not be more one of us than if his earthly body had disappeared as the risen Christ came to birth? But there is of course nothing impossible about the events "on the third day"[55] as they are recorded in the gospels: the offering of peace in the context of terror, the breaking of bread, the sharing of a meal, the sending out to preach and to heal:[56] these are the activities of Jesus and thus of the risen Christ. Any other elements of the experience apart from these activities are closed to us and irrelevant to the theology that we are constructing, as in fact they always have been. This is no great loss compared to the hope that is communicated by the activity that the Apostles experienced, that Christians through two thousand years have experienced, and that we experience still. There is no ontological connection between Jesus, the risen Christ of the Apostles, and our world, for there is no longer a publicly-owned metaphysic that would enable us to posit such a connection: but that does not mean that a theology of the risen Christ is no longer possible. The connection between Jesus' activity, the activity experienced by the Apostles, and our activity, is a positive and potent connection that meshes completely with the Christian hope that we have chosen: for we have chosen Jesus as our God, Jesus is his changing patterns of action, God is a verb, and we are the risen Christ as we participate in this activity: and these elements constitute an appropriate and necessary kernel of any tentative, local, and temporary systematic theology that might be offered to an age in which action is understood and being rather less so.

This is what God does, and this is what Jesus does, so Jesus is God: and wherever we discover the risen Christ, we shall never understand him, but we shall rather participate in a constantly-renewed activity in which the risen Christ heals and proclaims and offers hope for a City of God.

Such a new conceptual framework would, of course, have other effects on our interpretation of the New Testament, and particularly, as we have seen, on the interpretation of such concepts as "grace," which becomes unambiguously a pattern of action, a self-giving generosity, and no longer some sort of spiritual substance: but the major effect would clearly be to enable us to reunderstand the New Testament's Christology as one of identification between the changing patterns of action that constitute Jesus and those that constitute God.[57]

---

55. 1 Corinthians 15:4, NRSV.
56. John 20:21; Luke 24:30; John 21:12–14; Matthew 28:16–20.
57. Malcolm Torry, "'Logic' and 'Action,'" 97–98.

The resurrection narratives[58] all express patterns of action to be found in Jesus, and in the Church, and in the risen Christ wherever he is to be found, so we can understand Jesus' resurrection as changing patterns of action bearing family resemblances to patterns of action during his ministry. This is especially true of the echoes of the last supper at the house at Emmaus.[59] Wherever those changing patterns of action are to be found, there is the risen Christ. These patterns function as Kantian categories in our minds as we recognize patterns of action with family resemblances to other patterns of action. And these patterns are God's patterns of action: which is the meaning of the Ascension: "Since, then, we have a great high priest who has passed through the heavens, Jesus, the Son of God, let us hold fast to our confession."[60]

What was it that those early disciples of Jesus experienced during the days following the first Easter Day? Clearly an event both unique and transformational. As John Austin Baker argues, "the intensity with which the first Christians looked for the dénouement of history in their own lifetime testifies to the reality of the resurrection which they inevitably understood as raising the curtain on the final scene."[61] They experienced Jesus—they were sure of that: but in several of the accounts it took a while to recognize him. One way of understanding this is to see Jesus' resurrection body as the kind of "spiritual body" that Paul says will be ours when we are raised from death:[62] an essential transformation because "flesh and blood cannot inherit the Kingdom of God, nor does the perishable inherit the imperishable."[63] As the first letter of Peter puts it, Jesus "was put to death in the flesh, but made alive in the Spirit."[64] The risen Christ was the same and not the same as the Jesus who walked in Galilee. What was indubitably the same was that the action in changing patterns that constitute the risen Christ bear family resemblances with the still changing patterns of action of Jesus of Nazareth. This person was and still is God living a human life: but now it is the human life that will be ours.

We might choose to discover the risen Christ in the Church or amongst the poor, or in the activity of the Eucharist, but wherever we find him we shall not understand him, but rather we shall participate in a constantly

---

58. Mark 16:1–8; Luke 24; Matthew 28; John 19 and 20.
59. Luke 24:13–35.
60. Hebrews 4:14, NRSV.
61. Baker, *The Foolishness of God*, 281.
62. 1 Corinthians 15:44, NRSV; Robinson, *On Being the Church in the World*, 38–42.
63. 1 Corinthians 15:50, NRSV; Winter, "The key to the mystery," 18.
64. 1 Peter 3:18, NRSV.

renewed activity in which the risen Christ heals and proclaims and offers hope for a City of God.

The risen Christ, once chosen, becomes the standpoint from which to view our experience, from which to evaluate our activity, from which to judge the Church, and from which to offer what description we can of the City of God: for it is as legitimate to take the risen Christ as a criterion for evaluating discourse of all kinds as it is to evaluate discourse about the risen Christ in terms of historical or scientific discourse. But although we might choose to evaluate everything else in relation to the risen Christ, the complex event of the risen Christ changes as we change, as our world changes, and as the coming City of God changes, and we must constantly make new decisions about where to identify the activity that is the risen Christ; and at the point that each decision is made, it must be abandoned and made again: and if the Church and its Eucharist are to continue to be the location of the risen Christ, and to be sacraments of the Kingdom of God, then they too must be constantly reformed.

For both the Acts of the Apostles and Paul "God raised Jesus."[65] Jesus is the Word made flesh and so is both God and with God:[66] Jesus is himself God, and it is the God whom he called "Father" who raised him from the dead. There are no contradictions here. Jesus is constituted by changing patterns of action that constitute both God and a human life; the Father is constituted by changing patterns of action that constitute God; and the bond between Jesus and his Father is changing patterns of action that constitute God the Holy Spirit. But perhaps precisely how and by whom Jesus was raised from death is of less significance than the fact that he is risen, and that it is our responsibility to discover the risen Christ, and to be that activity that is the risen Christ.

If we were able to return to the days following Jesus' death, what would we experience? We don't know. Perhaps it doesn't matter. And how should we describe what happened? Not in terms of beings, of substances, of human and divine natures, or in terms of ontological metaphysics: but rather in terms of action in changing patterns—in terms of an actology that describes in terms of verbs, of the dynamic, of action in changing patterns, and above all in terms of an absolute generosity of giving: in terms of grace. Jesus is risen—or perhaps rather, Jesus rises—and the changing patterns of action that he is are still changing patterns of action that we experience as grace, that continue to change the world, and that are changing patterns of action that constitute God. An action in changing patterns actology has enabled

---

65. Acts 2:24, 32; 3:15, 26; 4:10; 10:40; 13:30, 37; Romans 10:9; 1 Corinthians 6:14.
66. John 1:1, 14.

us to tell a narrative about Jesus' resurrection that is scriptural, comprehensible, and integrated with the way that we and the universe work. If this had been the only achievement of our actology then the exercise would have been worth it for that alone.

A THEOLOGY OF GRACE

There have been many attempts at theologies centered on the concept of grace, and a particularly seminal one is Donald Baillie's *God was in Christ*: but his God is still a Being distant from the activity that we have called "grace," for Baillie defines God as "the One who at the same time makes absolute demands upon us and offers freely to give us all that he demands."[67] What is now required, if grace is to be the beating heart of a Christian theology applicable to today's world, is a wholesale transformation of theological language into categories of activity and diversity, that has as one element of that diversity a speaking of God in terms of grace, and that identifies God as active (rather than present) wherever we see grace in action: in the creation of the cosmos, in relationships, and above all in Jesus Christ. To approach theology in any other way is to make God responsible for human suffering. Today, we can worship a suffering and powerless God, but not one who can act to abolish suffering and yet chooses not do so. To say that God is powerful and chooses not to exercise his power, because to exercise it would be to deprive us of free will, is not a legitimate response, for any action that is God's changing patterns of action will interfere with our free will to some extent, and an action of God to prevent suffering is not something to which we would be likely to object. But God does not so act, so the only terms that I can use of God are "powerless" and "grace." If we were to remove the comforters' speeches and the ending from the book of Job, then that ancient text would exemplify such a theology. It was clearly written by someone who knew that theological questions do not have easy answers. A rather more recent book that breathes the same air is Paul Tillich's *The Shaking of the Foundations*:

> Grace strikes us when we are in great pain and restlessness. It strikes us when we walk through the dark valley of a meaningless and empty life. . . . It strikes us when, year after year, the longed-for perfection of life does not appear, when the old compulsions reign within us as they have for decades, when despair destroys all joy and courage. Sometimes at that moment a wave of light breaks into our darkness, and it is as though a voice were

---

67. Baillie, *God was in Christ*, 121.

saying: "You are accepted. *You are accepted* . . ." If that happens to us, then we experience grace.⁶⁸

Tillich has in this sermon captured the essence of the God who comes to us, a God who is grace, a God accepting, a God who is the accepting: who accepts the suffering, the questioning, the guilt, and the anger, and who loves and gives when we do not know how to pray, when we do not want to pray, when we are not interested in God or in other people or in ourselves or in our world, a God whose giving of God is endless and whose accepting of what we give is endless and transforming. As Richard Rohr puts it in the context of his understanding of Jesus as the "Universal Christ,"

> Faith at its essential core is *accepting that you are accepted!* We cannot deeply know ourselves without also knowing the One who made us, and we cannot fully accept ourselves without accepting God's radical acceptance of every part of us. And God's impossible acceptance of ourselves is easier to grasp if we first recognize it in the perfect unity of the human Jesus with the divine Christ. Start with Jesus, continue with yourself, and finally expand to everything else. As John says, "From this fullness (*pleroma*) we have all received, grace upon grace" (1:16), or "*grace responding to grace gracefully*" might be an even more accurate translation. To end in grace you must somehow start with grace, and then it is grace all the way through.⁶⁹

To worship such a God is not to answer questions about the origin of evil, about children who die in pain and terror, or about nuclear weapons, starvation, war, or the innate corruption of human beings and their institutions: for such questions cannot be answered, and the anger that we feel is rightly directed at the God who is the action in changing patterns that is the accepting of all of it. However, to worship a God characterized by grace can stimulate a wide variety of gracious human action in response to those questions.

> To believe in God means to live our life as a gift from God and to look upon everything that happens in it as a manifestation of this gift . . . a true and full encounter with our neighbor requires that we first experience the gratuitousness of God's love . . . The experience of the gratuitousness of God's love . . . gives human becoming its full meaning.⁷⁰

---

68. Tillich, *The Shaking of the Foundations*, 163–65.
69. Rohr, *The Universal Christ*, 29.
70. Gutiérrez, *We Drink from our Own Wells*, 110–12.

Julian of Norwich (a woman, despite her name) lived in the fourteenth century and recorded a series of visions that are still valued by many Christians and by many who are not Christians—especially by those of us who value female imagery of God alongside a more frequent male imagery: for she writes: "As truly as God is our father, so just as truly is he our mother . . ."; and she writes of "the strength and goodness of [God's] fatherhood, the wisdom of [God's] motherhood."[71] Julian calls Jesus "our mother . . . who is all love, bears us into joy and endless living,"[72] and she employs the word "courtesy" to denote what we are calling "grace":

> In tender courtesy [Jesus] gives us the Blessed Sacrament, the most treasured food of life . . . As by his courtesy God forgives our sins when we repent, even so he wills that we should forgive our sin, and so give up our senseless worrying and faithless fear.[73]

We might find Paul Tillich's and Julian's passages on grace useful as we construct our own theologies of grace, and then revise them over and over again. What we build is accepted and transformed and given back; and we are accepted, however twisted our personalities, however bad we are at reflecting in our lives the grace-filled pattern of action that is Jesus' life, or the grace-filled activity of the God we see at work in the created order and in the people around us.

The difficult part is keeping alive a theology with grace at its heart. We can easily find elements that deny the activity of grace; and our minds can quickly turn to the response to grace, which in the New Testament is termed "faith." We have been brought up to believe in a work ethic so the faith response quickly demands our attention and we lose sight of the primacy of grace.

Paul, although so conscious of God's gracious approach to him, could not make up his mind when writing the Letter to the Romans whether he was "justified by faith" or saved by "God's act of grace."[74] Perhaps he was simply finding it difficult to believe that God's love is unearned and free, and deep in his mind was the conviction that just as the Jews were expected to continue to earn God's love by works of the Law, so Christians had to earn it by a new work: faith. Similarly, the gospel writers cannot resist the temptation to write that it is by the act of faith of the one healed that the healing has

---

71. Julian of Norwich, *Enfolded in Love*, 35.
72. Julian of Norwich, *Enfolded in Love*, 36.
73. Julian of Norwich, *Enfolded in Love*, 36, 46.
74. Romans 5:1, 15, NRSV.

taken place: they cannot cope with the idea that there might be a truly free gift, that there might be grace, that Jesus might have healed people simply because they needed to be healed, and because the Kingdom of God was coming as a gift, undeserved, unearned.[75]

So whether or not our definition of God is centered on Jesus, whether or not we find traditional theological language helpful, we are invited to center our theology on grace, to receive the gift freely offered, and to reflect in our own lives the pattern of action of a God who is gracious activity.

The case for a gospel of grace might have been overstated, but perhaps just at the moment it needs to be, as it has ranged against it some still-dominant ancient ontological philosophies, the work ethic, and institutional boundaries. Without the gospel of grace there is no acceptance and no forgiveness, there is no reconciliation, and there is no God who comes, suffers, loves, and transfigures the created order into the community of grace for which we hope.

We have followed a discussion about beginning our theology with Jesus with an exploration of the centrality of grace to Christian theology, and particularly to our understanding of Jesus. So are we really here thinking about action in changing patterns? If God is always characterized by grace, and if Jesus always exemplifies the particular changing pattern of action that we call grace, then is there not something unchanging in God? Yes and no.

There are passages in the New Testament that suggest an unchangeableness in God. For instance, in the letter of James: "Every generous act of giving, with every perfect gift, is from above, coming down from the Father of lights, with whom there is no variation or shadow due to change."[76] The following sentence provides the context: "In fulfilment of his own purpose he gave us birth by the word of truth, so that we would become a kind of first fruits of his creatures."[77] So here the unchangeableness relates to God's purpose for the Church: so here we have a pattern of action in God, and a changing one at that, for as the world changes, and as the Church changes, so God's actions must change if the purpose is to be fulfilled. There is no static and unchangeable God here.

In the letter to the Hebrews we find a similar idea:

> When God made a promise to Abraham, because he had no one greater by whom to swear, he swore by himself, saying, "I will

---

75. Luke 17:11–19. Here is where the addition by the gospel writer is at its clearest, as the statement that the man's faith has healed him is tacked on after a totally different point has been made about only the Samaritan returning to give thanks.

76. James 1:17, NRSV.

77. James 1:18, NRSV.

> surely bless you and multiply you." And thus Abraham, having patiently endured, obtained the promise. Human beings, of course, swear by someone greater than themselves, and an oath given as confirmation puts an end to all dispute. In the same way, when God desired to show even more clearly to the heirs of the promise the unchangeable character of his purpose, he guaranteed it by an oath, so that through two unchangeable things, in which it is impossible that God would prove false, we who have taken refuge might be strongly encouraged to seize the hope set before us. We have this hope, a sure and steadfast anchor of the soul, a hope that enters the inner shrine behind the curtain, where Jesus, a forerunner on our behalf, has entered, having become a high priest for ever according to the order of Melchizedek.[78]

God has made a promise, and God has sworn an oath—both patterns of action—and these have set a trajectory. The promise and the oath might not change, but if they are to be fulfilled in the context of a changing world and a changing Church then God must be active and the patterns of action must change. Again, there is no static or unchanging God here: but there is a God who is faithful to his oath and his promise,[79] and that faithfulness is an enduring and changing pattern of action.

Further on in the letter to the Hebrews we find this: "Jesus Christ is the same yesterday and today and for ever."[80] There is a pastoral context to this statement. Previous to this statement the writer has been discussing the kind of behavior required of the Church, and then he or she[81] turns to the question of false teaching:

> Remember your leaders, those who spoke the word of God to you; consider the outcome of their way of life, and imitate their faith. Jesus Christ is the same yesterday and today and for ever. Do not be carried away by all kinds of strange teachings . . .[82]

The letter's readers are being offered an example of appropriate behavior to follow, and also an example of teaching faithful to the Christian gospel. There are boundaries around what should be taught as the Christian Faith,

---

78. Hebrews 6:13–20.

79. 1 Corinthians 1:9; 10:13; 2 Corinthians 1:18.

80. Hebrews 13:8.

81. I am grateful to the Rev'd Andrew Stevens, Vicar of St. Nicholas's, Plumstead, for suggesting the possibility that the Letter to the Hebrews was written by a woman.

82. Hebrews 13:7–9.

and there are ideas outside those boundaries which the writer goes on to discuss. Jesus is being offered to them as the permanent authority for appropriate behavior, and as the authority for right teaching: always the same Jesus. The historical Jesus never changes in the same way that the totality of the changing patterns of action in the past never change: but of course the Jesus that the Church knows changes constantly as we change and as the world around us changes. Jesus will always be the primary authority for behavior and doctrine for Christians, but our interpretation of Jesus has always changed, changes still, and will always change, and the risen Christ is changing patterns of action at work in a world that is changing patterns of action. Jesus was changing patterns of action, and he always will be changing patterns of action. And at the same time "Jesus Christ is the same yesterday, today and for ever."[83]

There is no unchangeableness in God, but there is faithfulness, and what we might call constancy. There are "family resemblance" relationships between the patterns of action that we find in God's relationships with the created order, humanity, Israel, and the Church: but there is nothing the same; there is nothing unchanging. Always there is changing patterns of action.

A HUMAN AND RECONCILING GOD

> Let the same mind be in you that was in Christ Jesus,
> who, though he was in the form of God,
>   did not regard equality with God
>   as something to be exploited,
> but emptied himself,
>   taking the form of a slave,
>   being born in human likeness.
> And being found in human form,
>   he humbled himself
>   and became obedient to the point of death—
>   even death on a cross.
> Therefore God also highly exalted him
>   and gave him the name
>   that is above every name,
> so that at the name of Jesus
>   every knee should bend,
>   in heaven and on earth and under the earth,

---

83. Hebrews 13:8.

>   and every tongue should confess
>   that Jesus Christ is Lord,
>   to the glory of God the Father.[84]

The straightforward interpretation is that Jesus was a divine being before becoming human,[85] and that in order to become human he underwent a variety of self-emptyings—"kenosis of omnipotence . . . kenosis of simple eternity . . . kenosis of omniscience . . . kenosis of causal status":[86] that is, a divine being accepted the constraints of time, chose not to know everything, and submitted to normal causalities: and then he reascended to heaven, suggesting a brief visit of a divine being to our planet. But what happens if we begin with Jesus not just as the human face of God[87] but as God?—with a God whose normal mode of being is to be human and for whom the highest reality and the highest glory is humanity, as opposed to a God whose essential nature is non-human and for whom the non-material is the truly real? If our God is human, then, and only then, are we really created in the image of God, and then, and only then, do we worship a God whom we can begin to know, and whose nature we can and do share. Perhaps we should interpret the whole of the hymn as a song in praise of Jesus' humanity. The Book of Genesis declares all of us to be created "in the image of God,"[88] and Jesus "being in the form of God" can thus be taken as an expression of his humanity, not of his divinity. Jesus did indeed make himself a servant,[89] humble himself, and die on a cross; and he was experienced as risen and was worshipped as Lord in his risen humanity—not in his divinity.

It has to be this way if ever there is to be relationship between God and humanity. If we cannot become God, then God has to become one of us: and God is now forever human, and God is eternally the atonement between God and ourselves. But let us not avoid the complexity of that: for if the changing patterns of action that constitute Jesus are the changing patterns of action that constitute God, and vice versa, then God is emotional, in despair, and violent,[90] and knows the experience of crucifixion, death, and resurrection.

In this brief theology that I am writing, Jesus is the very being of God, the very love of God, the very grace of God, and it is this Jesus who empties

---

84. Philippians 2:5–11, NRSV.
85. Ramsey, *From Gore to Temple*, 30–43.
86. Polkinghorne, "Kenotic Creation and Divine Action," 102–4.
87. Robinson, *The Human Face of God*.
88. Genesis 1:26, NRSV.
89. Mark 10:45.
90. Mark 14:32–37; John 11:35; 2:15.

himself, giving himself to us utterly, even to the point of death at our hands. God freely empties God of the human life that is God's crowning joy, and it was no easier for God to die than for any of us: the doubt and the dereliction were real. This is God's "self-emptying," and it is *God's* self-emptying. Out of love for us, God empties God of the physical and limited life in which God found love, friendship, and joy, enabling us to relate to the God who is human, the God who is a person. This is why Jesus' death is experienced by us as atonement, as salvation.

For us, now, today, God is Jesus and Jesus is God, and the God whom we worship is human. If we take Jesus as our God then we shall find ourselves worshipping his Spirit as God and his Father as our Father or Mother: but never again shall we worship a God who is unchanging, who is distant from physical, active, historical humanity, because physical, active, historical humanity is God's action in changing patterns.

When Jesus said to Thomas, "Reach out your hand and put it in my side. Do not doubt but believe," Thomas answered him, "My Lord and my God!"[91] Thomas saw in the changing pattern of action standing in front of him the changing pattern of action that is God. As Rowan Williams puts it:

> If he is translucent to God in all he does and is . . . He is God; in infancy, in death, in eating and drinking, in healing and preaching . . . This is the Lord, God in flesh. God made known in history, God fearing, struggling and suffering; the only God we know or can know, the glory of God in the face of Christ, love and healing in human hands and eyes.[92]

It is the whole of Jesus' human life that is the Word of God: not just some particular events, and not just part of Jesus. It is the human Jesus who is the Word of God.[93]

---

91. John 20:27–28, NRSV.
92. Williams, *Open to Judgement*, 70.
93. Higton, *Difficult Gospel*, 30.

Chapter 8

The City of God

Thesis: The Kingdom of God that we find present in Jesus, and for the completion of which he hoped, remains that changing pattern of action that we continue to find in Jesus Christ and for which we continue to hope: now probably better termed "City of God" than "Kingdom of God."

INTRODUCTION

Jesus believed that the Kingdom of God would arrive very soon, that it would put an end to history, and that it was so close that it was already present: "The Kingdom of God is among you."[1] It is Jesus who is among them. It is he who is the Kingdom of God. Jesus is his activity, so this activity is the Kingdom of God. And this is the Kingdom of God that we continue to find in Jesus Christ, we continue to find active in the world around us, and we continue to hope for as the City of God.

THE KINGDOM OF GOD, THE CITY OF GOD

Jesus' healing of others was and is the Kingdom of God; Jesus' welcoming of others was and is the Kingdom of God; and Jesus' telling of parables is the Kingdom of God, for the telling is the Kingdom and the parables are about the Kingdom, about the action in changing patterns that constitutes the

---

1. Mark 1:15, NRSV; 13:24–31; Luke 9:27; 11:23; 21:17.

Kingdom. Thus the parable of the sower[2] is about the growing of the corn; the parable of the mustard seed is about growth from a tiny seed and birds building their nests in the tree;[3] the misnamed parable of the prodigal son is about the Father waiting; and that is followed by parables of the shepherd searching and celebrating, and the woman searching and celebrating.[4] This action in changing patterns is the Kingdom of God. And the parable of the treasure in the field—"The kingdom of heaven is like treasure hidden in a field, which someone found and hid; then in his joy he goes and sells all that he has and buys that field"[5]—is probably better understood as representing a Kingdom of God that finds us rather than as representing us finding the Kingdom: or perhaps the ambiguity is intended, as it is elsewhere in Jesus' sayings, and the Kingdom and ourselves find each other.[6]

A Kingdom in the future? Jesus clearly believed so, and expected the righteous to "inherit the Kingdom prepared for [them] from the foundation of the world."[7] Jesus believed that there would be signs of the Kingdom's coming: "From the fig tree learn its lesson: as soon as its branch becomes tender and puts forth its leaves, you know that summer is near. So also, when you see these things taking place, you know that it is near, at the very gates";[8] and he believed that its coming would be soon: "Truly I tell you, this generation will not pass away until all these things have taken place."[9]

Jesus encouraged people to seek signs of the Kingdom's coming, and was angry when he did not find them where he expected to do so.[10] He believed that already the poor were blessed with the Kingdom,[11] for the Kingdom of God was so close that the time before its coming was a split-second that counted for nothing; and the closeness of the Kingdom meant that nothing else was of any importance, not even his own family.[12] For the same reason, the Law, which Jesus respected, had to become a sign of the Kingdom of God's coming: so work could be done on the Sabbath if it

---

2. Mark 4:1–9.
3. Mark 4:30–31.
4. Luke 15; Thielicke, *The Waiting Father*.
5. Matthew 13:44, NRSV.
6. Matthew 5:17; Torry, "Two Kinds of Ambiguity."
7. Matthew 25:34, NRSV.
8. Mark 13:28, NRSV.
9. Mark 13:30, NRSV.
10. Mark 11:12–14.
11. Luke 6:20–23.
12. Mark 3:31–35.

promised the Kingdom of God.[13] Already the Law, including the important parts of it, were "fulfilled":[14] that is, its task was completed, and now a new era was dawning in which mercy and justice would be a natural way of life for God's people.

Jesus was an apocalyptic prophet, and his expectations and his language were those of an apocalyptic prophet: "You will see the Son of Man seated at the right hand of power and coming with the clouds of heaven."[15] Such prophets tend to offer predictions about the future, as Jesus did:[16] but Jesus also believed the Kingdom to be among us:[17] that is, he knew that his activity already was the Kingdom of God. And so his healing of the sick, his feeding of the crowds, and his parables about a community that seeks out those who are not members rather than excluding them, were acted parables of the Kingdom's presence.[18] And similarly, wherever today there are those changing patterns of action, there is the Kingdom of God; and wherever in the future there is that pattern of activity—in an apocalyptic future, in a new order of things, or in more of the same—there is the Kingdom of God, for there is Jesus' changing pattern of activity still "among us."[19] So wherever we can identify a changing pattern of activity like Jesus' pattern of activity, then there is the Kingdom of God.

There will always be diverse views about how to understand the Kingdom of God: Is it primarily a future cataclysmic event bringing in a wholly new order of reality, or is it a present reality, a new quality of life now? The differences between these positions matter, and we must not minimize them: but unfortunately we shall not know until it happens, and in the meantime what matters is that the Kingdom of God is among us in Jesus and in the risen Christ, that is, that the pattern of action that is Jesus is alive and active, giving birth to a Kingdom of God that bears the character of that activity. And what unites the different futures of the Kingdom of God is this changing pattern of action. Whether Jesus returns in a recognizably personal way with apocalyptic accompaniments,[20] or returns as his Spirit ("I am with you always"[21]) is far less important than the character of both of these comings:

13. Mark 2:23–3:6.
14. Mark 5:17, NRSV.
15. Mark 14:62, NRSV.
16. Mark 13.
17. Luke 17:21.
18. Mark 1:21–34; 6:30–44; Luke 15.
19. Luke 21:17, NRSV.
20. 1 Thessalonians 4.
21. Matthew 28:20, NRSV.

they are both patterns of action that bear family resemblances to the pattern of action that is Jesus of Nazareth: both of them are Jesus come again.

And so those who hold different views about the coming of the Kingdom of God share what matters: the conviction that the Kingdom of God is Jesus' changing patterns of action present now and in the future, raising us to new life, to a life renewed by the changing patterns of action that constitute Jesus. Jesus returns, and Jesus shall return—but as to the manner of his coming we don't know, and we never shall know until he comes.

What we do know is that however the Kingdom of God comes it is preceded by suffering. Paul says:

> I consider that the sufferings of this present time are not worth comparing with the glory about to be revealed to us. For the creation waits with eager longing for the revealing of the children of God; for the creation was subjected to futility, not of its own will but by the will of the one who subjected it, in hope that the creation itself will be set free from its bondage to decay and will obtain the freedom of the glory of the children of God. We know that the whole creation has been groaning in labour pains until now; and not only the creation, but we ourselves, who have the first fruits of the spirit, groan inwardly while we wait for adoption, the redemption of our bodies.[22]

If Jesus' sufferings were the labor pains of a new age, and those of the early Christians were too—for Paul says: "I am now rejoicing in my sufferings for your sake, and in my flesh I am completing what is lacking in Christ's afflictions for the sake of his body, that is, the church"[23]—then the passage in Romans 8 above declares this world's sufferings to be the labor pains of a new age. Paul hoped for a renewed created order in which we would be clothed with "spiritual bodies,"[24] "spiritual" in the sense that they will be shaped by Jesus' Spirit, by Jesus' pattern of action, and "bodies" in the sense that we shall be our changing patterns of action, as our bodies are now—and so this future Kingdom, this new order, will be Jesus come again (though clearly not "in the same way"[25]), for the spiritual bodies will be his changing patterns of action as well as ours.

The Father whom Jesus worshipped, the Father to whom he prayed and whom he trusted,[26] is the guarantor of this new age as far as Jesus was

---

22. Romans 8:18–23, NRSV.
23. Colossians 1:24, NRSV.
24. 1 Corinthians 15:44, NRSV.
25. Acts 1:11, NRSV.
26. Matthew 6:9–13; 7:7–11.

concerned. Thus, if we follow Jesus, we too shall look to the Creator, to Jesus' Father and Mother and our Father and Mother, for the coming of the Kingdom of God, and we shall pray for that Kingdom's coming.[27] And the creation and its renewal are "in Jesus" or "by Jesus,"[28] for he is the generous creativity that characterizes the universe and that characterizes the Kingdom of God that is coming to birth by his Spirit. Thus it is God—Jesus, his Spirit, and his Father—who through their love for one another, and by their creative longing for new life, give birth to new patterns of action that will be both God and humanity, patterns that are the activity that are Jesus, our God, and that already infiltrate and will transform the universe: hence Raimon Panikkar's concept of an all-encompassing "christophany" which

> constitutes the deepest interiority of all of us, the abyss in which, in each one of us, there is a meeting between the finite and the infinite, the material and spiritual, the cosmic and the divine.[29]

Jesus is God come to us, reigning already, being the King, that is, doing what the King does. Jesus is about the Kingdom of God, which is the renewal of all things—or better, the renewal of all patterns of action; the repatterning of action. The Kingdom of God is changing patterns of action, the patterns of action that are God's patterns of action, now and not yet, and already lived in Jesus: so in Jesus' life and death, and particularly in his resurrection, patterns of action that belong to the Kingdom that is still to come are active already in our own time. We discover Jesus' patterns of action in the New Testament: grace, forgiveness, nonviolent revolution to bring in the Kingdom of God, and a radical welcome and transformation of the whole created order in the Kingdom of God.[30]

We can live the Kingdom of God now by following Jesus and living now these changing patterns of action. "If anyone is in Christ, there is a new creation."[31] It is not just the person who is in Christ who lives in a new creation: for one person to be in Christ means that their changing patterns of action are those of the new creation, and those patterns of action affect every other pattern of action, so there is a new creation: that is, the patterns of action that constitute the Kingdom of God are happening today. Repentance is a shifting from one pattern to another: from non-Kingdom

---

27. Matthew 6:10.
28. Colossians 1:16.
29. Panikkar, *Christophany*, 189.
30. Romans 8:18–25.
31. Corinthians 5:17, NRSV: *ei tis en Christō, kainē ktisis.*

to Kingdom. It's the changing pattern of action that matters, not a particular time or situation or place.

So now there is hope. "May the God of hope fill you with all joy and peace in believing, so that you may abound in hope by the power of the Holy Spirit."[32] God hopes. There is no fulfilment or completion, not yet, but God hopes, and we hope.

Jesus' feeding of the five thousand is the action in patterns of the Kingdom of God; and there is a triangular action-constituted relationship between the Kingdom of God, the feeding of the five thousand, and the Eucharist. It is not only the Church that can live the Kingdom of God: our cities can too: and perhaps "city of God" is today a better way of expressing what Jesus meant by "Kingdom of God" than for us to continue to use his own phrase of "Kingdom of God" for it. "Kingdom" speaks of uniformity rather than diversity, and of the static rather than the dynamic, so it is unlikely to be an appropriate vehicle for our hope for a community in which the variety of human culture is both retained and transfigured, and in which nothing is decided but all is changing, all constantly evolving into new patterns of justice, new relationships, and new fulfilments, and conversely in the present age into new patterns of injustice, broken relationships, and destruction. To speak of a city, on the other hand, is to speak first of diversity and of the dynamic, and only then of sameness and the static: so "City of God" might be a better expression for the community for which we hope. The fulfilment of our hope is not just God, understood as a being in whom we sink and disappear; not just heaven, where we are bodiless, emotionless, and alone; not just a Kingdom, where God is in charge: but a city, a community, where God is with us as one of us. God has created us free, and God is free: and our hope is for a city in which the changing patterns of action that constitute who we are form a symphony of changing patterns of action in which we remain both free and immersed: a circumstance that requires that the pattern of action that we call grace will be ubiquitous and will constantly relate to every other changing pattern of action.

While "City of God" might express this hope better than "Kingdom of God" might now express it, the city as an image is not unambiguous, just as the Kingdom is not, for the city is the place where the greatest evils have been perpetrated as well as where the greatest cultural achievements have been found. The Bible might begin with a garden and end with a city, but the story of an attempt to build a tower that would reach to the heavens, an enterprise with which God does not seem to have been able to cope, reveals a writer ill at ease with urban living and with its cosmopolitan character. The

---

32. Romans 15:13, NRSV.

writer, for whom God is to be found in the isolation of the desert wanderings, could only see the concept of the city as an expression of arrogance. We are still living with such a theological rejection of the city, and "God the shepherd" rather than "God the city-dweller" is still central to many people's idea of God. The idea of a God at home in the urban world is a strange one to many, and would certainly have appeared strange to the writer of the story of the tower of Babel.[33]

But Psalm 48 is totally different:

> Great is the Lord and greatly to be praised
>   in the city of our God.
> His holy mountain, beautiful in elevation,
>   is the joy of all the earth,
> Mount Zion, in the far north,
>   the city of the great King.
> Within its citadels God
>   has shown himself a sure defence.
> We ponder your steadfast love, O God,
>   in the midst of your temple.
> Your name, O God, like your praise,
>   reaches to the ends of the earth.
> Your right hand is filled with victory.
>   Let Mount Zion be glad,
> let the towns of Judah rejoice
>   because of your judgements.[34]

The city was not a secure place, and it could be a source of exclusivity: but to conceive of God as dwelling in the city as well as in the temple or in the desert, to see the city as God's creation and as God's concern: here is the beginning of a theology of the city that might be of use to us in our cities as we seek a theology for a secular society, a theology full of activity and diversity.

The prophet Jeremiah had little time for those who believed themselves to be safe in Jerusalem, but he was not against city-dwelling. He wrote to the exiles in Babylonia:

> Thus says the Lord of hosts, the God of Israel, to all the exiles whom I have sent into exile from Jerusalem to Babylon: Build houses and live in them; plant gardens and eat what they produce. . . . seek the welfare of the city where I have sent you into

---

33. Genesis 11:1–9.
34. Psalm 48, NRSV.

exile, and pray to the Lord on its behalf, for in its welfare you will find your welfare.³⁵

The city might be a foreign city, a place of exile, a temporary place of residence, but it is still a place to be made beautiful, and a place in which to find God. Our own cities are not the celestial city, and often they are places of destruction and grief,³⁶ but they are still to be served and prayed for, for God is there. The city is the focus of the glory of humanity and of its corruption, it is the place of security and of destruction, it is the place of God's presence and the place of God's wrath, it is the place of promise and the place of disappointed promise. This same ambiguity is to be found in the gospels. The city of Jerusalem was the place of revelation,³⁷ of wrath,³⁸ and of betrayal and trial,³⁹ and Jesus experienced Jerusalem as the focus of a tradition that he valued, and as the place of the deepest corruption of that tradition. Luke's Gospel in particular⁴⁰ makes clear Jesus' conscious decision to go to Jerusalem, and his sorrow that its great promise had not been fulfilled:

> As he came near and saw the city, he wept over it, saying, "If you, even you, had only recognized on this day the things that make for peace! But now they are hidden from your eyes. Indeed, the days will come upon you, when your enemies will set up ramparts around you and surround you, and hem you in on every side. They will crush you to the ground, you and your children within you, and they will not leave within you one stone upon another; because you did not recognize the time of your visitation from God."⁴¹

The city was for Jesus a sign of the Kingdom of God for which he hoped, yet it was not that Kingdom, and it was to reject the one person in whom that Kingdom's life was truly lived. But the city to which Jesus came to experience the deepest pain and the death of humanity was the city in which his renewed humanity was experienced, and it is the city in which Luke locates the birth of the Christian Church.⁴² Luke's Gospel leads towards Jerusalem,

---

35. Jeremiah 9:4–8, NRSV
36. Lamentations 2.
37. Mark 11:1–11.
38. Mark 11:15–18.
39. Mark 14:10–11, 43–65.
40. Luke 9:51.
41. Luke 19:41–44, NRSV.
42. Acts 2.

and his Acts of the Apostles leads from Jerusalem to the rest of the world. It was in the cities that churches were first founded, and Paul's letters are witness to those churches' early battles with the conflicting ideologies, gods, and value-systems of the Greek and Asian cities in which they were set. For Paul, the city was where spiritual and temporal power lay. It was to Jerusalem that he went for approval of his mission,[43] it was to the Church in Rome that he addressed his defense of the gospel,[44] and it was to Rome that he appealed for justice.[45]

The Book of Revelation sums up most of the ideas surrounding the use of the word "city" in both the Old and New Testaments. "Babylon,"[46] which probably means Rome, is the focus of evil and of God's wrath, and Jerusalem is the image used to speak of God's coming Kingdom:

> Then I saw a new heaven and a new earth; for the first heaven and the first earth had passed away, and the sea was no more. And I saw the holy city, the new Jerusalem, coming down out of heaven from God, prepared as a bride adorned for her husband. And I heard a loud voice from the throne saying,
>
>> "See, the home of God is among mortals.
>> He will dwell with them;
>> they will be his peoples,
>> and God himself will be with them; . . ."[47]

Thus, in the New Testament, as in the Old, the city is an ambiguous image, carrying a diversity of meanings. The city is the place of promise and the place of death; the place of conflict between spiritual powers, and the place of ultimate peace.

In the Old and New Testaments we find city-words used of God and God-words used of the city, and it is difficult to separate the two halves of the "theological circle," for God and the city and the People of God are more closely identified with each other than they are in our normal theological languages. Jeremiah uses God-words of the city, and Revelation uses city-words of God, and in Psalm 48 the city and God are so closely identified that the two "semicircles" have collapsed into a single point.

Just as the word "kingdom" resonated in Jesus' time, so "city" resonates in ours, which enables us to see the city in which we live as the raw material

---

43. Acts 15:1–35.
44. Romans.
45. Acts 25:10.
46. Revelation 18.
47. Revelation 21:1–3.

for the City for which we hope and as a signpost towards it. For Jesus, the City for which he hoped meant that Jerusalem was an object of grief, yet it was that Jerusalem and its law and history that gave to Jesus the raw material for the City of which he spoke. Thus Jesus completes the circle, using God-words of the city, and city (or kingdom) words of God. Jesus, along with the Old and New Testament writers, encourages us to use city-words of God and God-words of the city: to create a theology of the city to nourish us as we journey towards the celestial city. As the cry of the cities in which we live is heard, the gospel of the City of God must be the Church's response—a response at once active and contemplative; and the theological circle must be completed by city-words—such as "powerless," "poverty," and "work"—used to speak of the God who himself experiences poverty, hope, and frustration.

Just as Jesus represented the Kingdom of God in his actions and in his parables, so we can represent the City of God in similar ways. Just as Jesus garnered words from his own situation, so we can garner words from our experience of the city—"co-creation," "destruction," "frustration," "concrete," "accepting"—with which to create a language to speak of Jesus our God, a God for the city who with us hopes for a City into which our cities will be transformed. Insofar as we identify Jesus as our definition of God, we shall discover a God for the city, for Jesus knows what it is to be alone, as the city-dweller often does; Jesus knows what it is to be secular and godless; Jesus practiced reconciliation, as the city does; Jesus has a history as has the city; and Jesus is alienated from us just as we are from each other. Each of us, in the context of our own city, must create a city-theology with which to speak of Jesus and of Jesus' hope, and in so doing we shall discover an active hope of our own, and we shall begin to turn our cities into signposts to the City of God. The Christian, like Jesus, must go to the heart of the city to experience with our God the deeper degrees of freedom and of slavery, of death and of new life, of hope, community, and joy: for the city is the God-like place—it accepts the poor, it is angry at evil and injustice, it is the place of emotion, pain, history, careful building, and freedom, and above all the place of diversity: but the city is also the place of alienation, decay, prejudice, fear, destruction, and injustice. We are created in the image of God, that is, in the image of Jesus and of his freedom, so if the urban world is to hope for the coming of the City of God, then we, like Jesus, must enter the heart of the city, where we shall find a little of the death and resurrection that Jesus experienced in the city.

"The city" is thus an appropriate expression for our hope, but we must not stop there as if we had achieved something: for if the nature of God is diversity and action, and if we are people of different characteristics, then our hope will be many-faceted, and we shall need a plethora of words and actions with which to describe the city: preferably words like "city," which contain within them the concepts of diversity and action: for our hope is for a community of infinite and increasing diversity, and exhibiting the action in changing patterns that we might call grace. In the community for which we hope, each person will be in constantly changing relationships with every other person, and in a web of harmonious diversity which, far from decreasing our freedom, is the route to true personhood. The city is ideal if it contains an infinite variety of persons in an infinite diversity of relations with each other, if the action in changing patterns that we find in the city is the action in changing patterns that we find in God and that we call grace, and if the whole is suffused with the transformative action in changing patterns that we find in Jesus' resurrection. As Dennis Nineham puts it:

> One day God would judge this world and bring this age to an end, transforming whatever in it was capable of being transformed, and transferring it to the conditions of his realm. But meanwhile, so long as this world lasted, anyone in it who represented God's realm and its values must look for misunderstanding and persecution from the evil powers and the human beings under their sway. . . . The true servant of God would not be disconcerted by such suffering, but would realize that in some mysterious way it was a means by which the redemptive purpose of God for this world was carried out.[48]

The city imagery that we have employed leads to hope for permanent evolution into ever greater diversity, and we are offered at least the possibility of conceptualizing redemption and justice for the victims of Auschwitz: for is this not the plumbline against which any and every theology must now be judged? If our present complex history is to be gathered up whole into some greater evolutionary diversity, then the evil, the suffering, and the death, will also be gathered up, as will be matter, personality, and relationships, in all of their historical diversity: and the evolution will go on again, driven by the "within" of matter, now transfigured in ways that we cannot yet conceive: for all that we can experience is the complexity that the evolutionary process has currently reached.[49] This conception, leading on from our "city" imagery and Teilhard de Chardin's suggestions, contains echoes of the resurrection of the body, and it is not difficult to see in Jesus' resurrection, in all of its diversity, a foreshadowing of the new evolution towards new complexity for which we might choose to hope.

---

48. Nineham, *Saint Mark*, 228.
49. Teilhard de Chardin, *The Phenomenon of Man*; Torry, *Actology*, 131–49.

But this way of thinking about Christian hope does not in any way "solve" the problem of evil. Just as the nail holes were still present in Christ's risen body, so the evil of Auschwitz, and of every violent and inhumane act, every sinful act, and every natural disaster, before and since, remains evil: and it is clearly important to retain the diversity between good and evil, for the diversity is never lost even if it is transfigured. It is to do the greatest indignity imaginable to those who have suffered pain, torture, and violent death, to call evil good, for it can never be that: and if the persistence of evil through the transformations of patterns of action requires us to offer a definition of God in terms of evil, then so be it: for in the midst of other definitions of God, a definition centered on a shadow-side would be to make God our God in a way in which no other definition ever could.

The City of God is a gift that comes to us, a gift to some extent already present if we can see in Jesus' life, death, and resurrection the pattern of its life, and if we can see in our world patterns of action coherent with Jesus' activity: if we see people brought to wholeness, if we see injustice condemned, if we see hope revive, if we see the unacceptable accepted, and if we see forgiveness freely offered and received. The characteristic of the City of God least like those of our own cities is the characteristic of "grace," of freely-given, accepting community: and it is this tendency for which we must seek if we are to go in search of signs of the City's coming. For it is this characteristic of the City of God in which our hope resides, a hope beyond hope, for there is little reason to hope in a world ever more dangerous. It is only a City that can accept and transform everything that can be any kind of hope for us, and just such a City is promised to us if we can see in Jesus' resurrection the pattern of activity of the accepting and forgiving City of God.

Jesus told us that we had to lose our lives in order to find them,[50] and we find this to be true in practice: it is as our action in changing patterns enters the diversity of action in changing patterns that constitutes our world that we glimpse signs of the City's coming—but we are legitimately concerned about our personal destiny: Is death the end? In one obvious sense it is not, for our actions affect our world and thus live on; and if we are our actions, then we live on. But our hope reaches beyond this distributed immortality and towards a renewal promised in Jesus' resurrection, a renewal towards a community in which the diverse activity that has been ourselves is gathered together and transformed into a coherent new glorious activity, making harmony with other transfigured personalities in the City in which there is no weeping nor suffering nor death.[51] It is not for rest that we hope,

50. Mark 8:35.
51. Revelation 21:4.

nor for disembodied souls, but for spiritual bodies:[52] for rejuvenated action in changing patterns, with those patterns bearing a family resemblance to those that we have been, are, and shall be. It might be that a crisis in the created order will lead to a catharsis and new patterns of diverse actions foreshadowed by the glimpses that the Apostles and we have experienced of the risen Christ, to a City of God in which we are ourselves, truly ourselves: but still there will be no "last things," for if the City of God is of the character of a God who is diversity and action, then there will be no destination: there will be a community diverse and active, a City of God.

But still there is no ultimate division between the city of this world and the City of God. If their patterns of action bear family resemblances with those that constitute God, then individuals, families, communities, cities, states, and international communities, can be godly, and of the character of the City of God. Our cities—their buildings, institutions, individuals, and everything else about them—can be spiritual events if their patterns of action bear a family resemblance to God's patterns of action. A secular city is simply one in which these connections are not recognized. One of the Church's tasks is therefore to enable that recognition: to bring to consciousness the family resemblances between the patterns of action that constitute the city and those that constitute God. Religious institutions are where that recognition is focused in the activity of worship; civic institutions are patterns of action connected with those that constitute individuals, families, communities, and other institutions; and if religious institutions wish to bring to consciousness the godly patterns of action in civic institutions, and to facilitate the birth of new godly patterns of action within them, then they will create new mediating institutions through which the religious and civic patterns of action can influence each other. And the Church must ensure that its own patterns of action are godly[53]—which requires an open Eucharist: an equal participation of all in the changing pattern of action that promises a Kingdom of God in which all will participate; and in order to facilitate the Christianization of the city and its institutions we shall need to build the action in changing patterns that constitutes mediating institutions: institutions that relate to both religious institutions and secular institutions and thus enable them to relate to each other.[54]

There is no permanence here. Cities are evolving complex patterns of action, as is the City of God. The City of God might be a "lasting" city, as

---

52. 2 Corinthians 5:1–5.
53. Torry, *Managing God's Business*; *Managing Religion*.
54. Torry, *Mediating Institutions*; "On Building a New Christendom."

opposed to the "not lasting"[55] cities that we know today: but that does not mean that it will lack action or change. So if our cities are to promise the city that is to come—a city in which the patterns of action will be godly patterns of action—then they will need to be communities in which change can occur, and they will need the flexible and lived-in spaces that will enable that to happen. The apparently static will need to become consciously dynamic. Indeterminacy will be required.[56]

Whatever the future holds, we shall find the Kingdom of God, the City of God, in the interstices, in the relationships between Jesus and the poor, in the judgment, healing, and truth-telling of Jesus, and in the suffering and rising again of Jesus, as we experience those patterns of action today. And as we seek the City of God, we shall ourselves mold it, and we shall join in its often turbulent and painful development, for if our hope is for something dynamic, then what we hope for is action in changing patterns, and not some final arrival at something forever the same.

Now that the City of God has been founded by the life, death, and resurrection of Jesus, it grows continuously: and because the founding is eternally present to God, and because God comes in freedom, the City was growing before Jesus was born. The City was growing when Abraham set off into the desert, when Moses led Israel out of slavery, when Isaiah spoke of God's suffering servant, and when John the Baptist called people to repent.[57] And the City is still growing: through patterns of action that reflect the patterns of action that constitute the City of God. This is God's action and it is our action; and it is both a hoping for the City and a building of it, for although we cannot bring the City to its completion, we can help to establish the conditions for its growth, and we can help to make it grow—on condition that what we help to grow is of the character of the City of God that we find in Jesus' changing patterns of action. And so, for instance, the City that we build must be one in which "many who are first will be last, and the last will be first."[58] And if we do not evolve our cities in the direction of the City of God for which we hope, then we might find that our cities and the City of God become so distanced from each other in character that City of God language becomes no more useful than the language of the Kingdom of God.

---

55. Hebrews 13:14, NRSV: *ou gar echomen hōde menousan polin, alla tén mellousan epizētoumen.*

56. Philip Sheldrake, address to Sion College, Lambeth Palace, 23rd June 2011

57. Genesis 12:1–9; Exodus 12:21–42; Isaiah 52:13–53:12; Mark 1:1–13.

58. Mark 10:31

While we wait for the completion of the City of God, the Church's responsibility is to model that City: to discover and mirror the action in changing patterns that we find in Jesus and that constitute his Kingdom of God and the City of God for which we hope. We shall find those patterns in both the Church and the world around us, so we shall need a Church in constant touch with our changing society: for only in that way shall we be able to represent the City of God in the city of this world. And the Church's responsibility is to pray, perhaps like this:

> God of action and diversity,
> may you be worshipped.
> Your city come
> on earth.
> Give us today the bread of tomorrow.
> Forgive us our sin, rigidity, and uniformity
> as we forgive the sin, rigidity, and uniformity of others.
> Lead us not into isolation
> but deliver us from finality.
> For the City, the diversity, and the evolution are yours,
> now and for ever.
> Let it be so.

Chapter 9

An actological Trinity

Thesis: God is radically diverse—one, three, and beyond.

INTRODUCTION

If we are created "in the image of God,"[1] and if we are highly diverse, then God is better described as diverse than as unitary. The vast diversity of human beings are created "in the image of God."[2] This can only mean that "the image of God" is radically diverse, suggesting a radically diverse God—at least if "the image of God" is to mean anything.

A DIVERSE GOD

But how far should we take language about the diversity of God? We scapegoat, we are violent, and so on, and if we are in God's image then God does these things too: so—as we have asked already—God is not good? No, God is not good, and God is good. There is evil in the heart of God, which is why there is hope for the reconciliation of all things, that is, for "atonement": for an atonement in which God takes all of the abuse, evil, and scapegoating into the action in changing patterns that constitute God by God's choice, and in which God absorbs and transfigures them, using them as raw material for a reconciliation and transfiguration within God that will be an explosion of changing patterns of action that will transform every changing pattern of action into the City of God.

---

1. Genesis 1:27, NRSV.

2. I am grateful to Sue Faulkner, in a presentation at an Archbishop's Examination in Theology seminar on the 17th June 2016, for this insight.

If God is also Action, the source of all action, and the origin of myriad patterns of action (however those patterns might be changed and supplemented by patterns of action that emerge in the diverse and active cosmos), then we have to recognize both radical diversity and diverse changing patterns of action in God and in God's relationships with the cosmos and with ourselves. There might be "one God," but that God will be diverse and will be experienced and interpreted in multiple and changing ways, and those multiple experiences and interpretations will be grounded in the diversity of changing patterns of action that we call God.

And because every evil action is transfigured, the suffering too is transfigured: but because every action, across what we call time, is affected by every other, the suffering never goes away—it is transfigured, but it affects forever every action and every pattern of action: so however transfigured it might all become, every example of evil will always be a pattern of action that God absorbs, and all of the patterns of action that constitute the universe and ourselves will be patterns of action that God transforms, and that will continually change the patterns of action that constitute who God is. None of it will ever cease to belong to the diversity that is God.

But can that be correct? If diversity is a characteristic of reality, and if God is transcendent, then should we not say that God is beyond diversity? It is this insight that leads to the idea of God's "simplicity," which is an important element in the Christian tradition, and by implication ought to be part of our Christian apologetics.[3] For Stephen Holmes, the heart of the definition of divine simplicity is that God does just one thing, that is, to be God.[4] Here the definition of what "one" means is crucial. "One" can mean "one individual" or "one Trinity," and in relation to God it means "one Trinity." "Simplicity" also means that there is no change in God: that is, that God's personal nature is unchanging; for changing would imply diversity.[5] What it does not mean is that God cannot act, for instance, in creation. God can act as long as the act is in God and belongs to God's definition. This implies that the "forms" on which creation is modelled are in God, and are not separable, thus preserving God's simplicity.[6]

Holmes makes a good case for retaining the doctrine of God's simplicity (because of what it says about God) and an equally good case for suggesting that problems that people have with the idea often stem from a Platonic framework which defines God in such a way that much that Holmes wants

---

3. Holmes, "'Something Much too Plain to Say'", 137–54.
4. Holmes, "'Something Much too Plain to Say'", 139.
5. Holmes, "'Something Much too Plain to Say'", 147.
6. Holmes, "'Something Much too Plain to Say'", 152.

to find within the definition of God ends up outside it, meaning that when we try to reinclude it we end up with a non-simple God.

With a conceptual framework based on action in changing patterns, God is defined in terms of action: Action, the source of all action, and the myriad changing patterns of action that by God's choice constitute God: and all of this is included in the definition of God, and all of it is God. So God's suffering, God's action, God being changed by us and by the universe, the relationships within the Trinity, God's creativity: it is all God and it is all within God's simplicity, thus maintaining the simplicity throughout, as Holmes would wish us to do. What we might call "Holmesian simplicity" encompasses a radical diversity.

For the Christian, God is Trinity, so is intrinsically diverse: and just as God the creator is diverse, so is Jesus, and so is the Holy Spirit. There is no single Jesus, there are many Jesuses, and all are related to the Jesus who walked and talked in Galilee two thousand years ago. Jesus was diverse, and Jesus has been diverse ever since, so the Jesus of history is diverse, for he constantly changed: and because he changes still, the Christ of faith is diverse across time and space, and between one person and another, so nowhere is there to be discovered a fixed point from which to evaluate any particular Christological or historical position. So for us, Jesus is known in the relationship between one Jesus and another, and between the Church—the Body of Christ if it exhibits his changing patterns of activity—and the risen Christ—known wherever today we discover Jesus' activity. We influence Jesus as much as he influences us; it is in the turbulence of controversy about Jesus that we know him, and not in some temporary scholarly consensus; and there is always more to be said. The diversity, action, and changing patterns of action, are endless.

The practical implication of all of this is that we can and should value many different formulations of the meaning of Jesus of Nazareth and of the risen Christ, and of the relationship between them; that the Eucharist is the center of the definition of the Church, for this is Jesus' activity continuing among us—a forward-looking activity in the doing of which we are Christ today; and that as healing, promising, forgiving, and releasing actions are done, so Jesus is still present and active.

In an increasingly diverse world, and in the context of a conceptual framework that understands reality as action in changing patterns, only an apologetics and a theology constituted by diversity, and expressed in terms of diversity, will enable the world to relate to God. The Christian tradition is diverse, understandings of Jesus are diverse, interpretations of the Bible are diverse, the Church is diverse, and theologies are diverse. This is all as it should be. Above all, God is diverse.

THE HOLY SPIRIT

Where we find patterns of action that are God's patterns of action, then there is the Holy Spirit. And so in the creation narrative, *ruach Elohim*, "a wind from God," or "a spirit of God," swept over the face of the waters.[7] This was God's patterned action, bringing patterned action out of the chaos of action represented by the sea. In the second creation narrative, when God made the first human being, "he breathed" life into him:[8] again, bringing action in patterns to birth. It is this that constitutes us in the "image"[9] of God: not in terms of an object with similarities to an object called God, but changing action in patterns given birth by the action in changing patterns that constitutes God.

The same Spirit was present in the prophets[10] and in the conception of Jesus;[11] and the same Spirit led Jesus into the wilderness[12] and empowered his ministry of proclamation, healing, and liberation.[13] The Spirit preceded Jesus and was given to him at his baptism,[14] and Jesus gave the Spirit to his disciples[15] to empower and teach them.[16] The Holy Spirit is the Spirit of Jesus, or the Spirit of Christ,[17] because these changing patterns of action are those that we find in Jesus as he is interpreted to us by the New Testament and by the Church. As R.M. Benson puts it:

> The righteousness of Christ is not imputed to the faithful as an external compensation for sin; but it is really transmitted to them as a germinant energy of holy life. . . . We are truly made the righteousness of God in Christ by this action of the Holy Ghost. We are called to rise up to its Divine energy, and act in subordination to the personal unction of this grace. . . . The nature of God is pure activity. To him the mere creation is nothing. It is but the symbol and the shrine of active powers which are more or less communicated to it by God's creative will.[18]

---

7. Genesis 1:2.
8. Genesis 2:7.
9. Genesis 1:27.
10. Ezekiel 2:2.
11. Luke 1:35.
12. Luke 4:1.
13. Luke 4:18.
14. Luke 3:22.
15. John 16:7; 20:22
16. John 14:26; 15:26; Acts 2:4.
17. Acts 16:7; Romans 8:9.
18. Benson, *The Final Passover*, volume II, 49, 53.

We find no systematic "patterns of action" metaphysic in Benson: but this passage provides a clue as to the more systematic theology that he might have written if he had been able to work with a more systematic actology.

Were the actions of Jesus' apostles on the day of Pentecost after Jesus' resurrection their own actions or were they those of the Holy Spirit?[19] Their confident proclamation in a variety of languages was what they were doing, and it was what the Holy Spirit was doing. There is no need to distinguish. The changing patterns of action were the Spirit's changing patterns of action and they were the apostles' changing patterns of action. We are never isolated individuals. The changing patterns of action that constitute who we are are constantly enmeshed with other changing patterns of action, and in this case the enmeshing was with the changing patterns of action that were those of the Holy Spirit at work among them and among their hearers. This might be difficult to understand within a "being" metaphysic, but within an "action" actology it is perfectly comprehensible.

There are places in the New Testament where the Holy Spirit is called "the Spirit of Jesus," or "the Spirit of Jesus Christ."[20] Wherever we find a changing pattern of action like that of Jesus, there is the Spirit of Jesus. The pattern will never be quite the same, and all we can hope for is a "family likeness": but where we discover prayer, the confronting of evil, commitment to new ways of life, struggle with ultimate questions, hope-giving story-telling, forgiveness, prophecy, the pursuit of peace and justice, the breaking of laws for the sake of humanity, the learning of equality and social justice, the welcoming of unrepentant sinners, the overturning of the social order, the pursuit of economic equality, the call to perfection, the suffering of humiliation and injustice, struggle with task and destiny, and the suffering of excruciating pain and of death—then there is the Spirit of Jesus. Where there is grace, there is Jesus. For if Jesus is his activity, then in this changing pattern of action he lives still: and this is an important part of what the early Christians express when they write of Jesus being present after his death as he goes with them on the road, teaches them, breaks bread with them,[21] speaks peace to them,[22] shares bread and fish with them,[23] calls

---

19. Acts 2:1–36.
20. Acts 16:7; Philippians 1:19; Romans 8:9, NRSV.
21. Luke 24:13–35.
22. John 20:19–23.
23. John 21:1–14.

them to love him and to follow him,[24] and sends them out to call others to follow him.[25]

There are, of course, a variety of ways of interpreting the resurrection narratives in the gospels. Are they accounts of historical events? Are they parables? Let us not minimize the difference between these two positions, nor pretend that no difference exists. It does. But what matters is the changing patterns of action that constitute Jesus. Jesus is his changing patterns of action, and the risen Christ is changing patterns of action that bear family resemblances to Jesus' changing patterns of action. It is this activity that is abroad in the world today, in the cosmos as a whole, and in each of us, bringing to birth a City of God defined by Jesus' pattern of action: and it is this that unites all those who say that Jesus is risen, whether they understand the resurrection narratives as parables or as the recording of events. Beside the reality of the action that is the risen Christ, nothing else matters very much. The differences over interpretation of the resurrection narratives are real and they matter, but their mattering is of a different order from the mattering of the risen Christ. We shall never know what happened that first Easter day—so let us agree on the presence of the risen Christ, that is, that Jesus' changing patterns of action, his grace, his forgiveness, his proclamation, his healing, is Jesus Christ, is present, is that which is most real, and is God.

John's Gospel sums up Jesus' activity as "love,"[26] and Paul's definition of love as patience, kindness, rejoicing in the truth, bearing all things, hoping all things, enduring all things, and so on,[27] is a description of changing patterns of action that we see in Jesus, and a pattern of action that we can still experience and still participate in. Wherever that pattern of action is, there is the Spirit of Jesus, and there is God—for "God is love."[28]

Similarly, where there is healing and prophecy, there are patterns of action identifiable as Jesus' patterns of action, so there too is the Spirit of Jesus and thus the Spirit of God.[29] Paul calls the Church "the body of Christ"[30] because the body is its activity, and if the Church's changing patterns of action are identifiable with Jesus' changing patterns of action then the Church is indeed the body of Christ, the activity that is the risen Christ, the activity that is the Spirit of Jesus—for the activity that is the Spirit of Jesus is the

24. John 21:15–19.
25. Matthew 20:16–20.
26. John 15:12–17, NRSV.
27. 1 Corinthians 13:4–7, NRSV.
28. 1 John 4:8, NRSV.
29. 1 Corinthians 12:4–11.
30. 1 Corinthians 12:27–31.

activity that is Jesus risen from the dead: for Jesus is his changing patterns of action and these patterns of action are dead no longer.

An issue that this and every theology needs to address is that of gender. Is the Spirit of Jesus male or female? What gender-language should we use? Jesus is clearly male, and so our God is male: but Jesus was entirely content to ascribe female attributes to himself:

> Jerusalem, Jerusalem, the city that kills the prophets and stones those who are sent to it! How often have I desired to gather your children together as a hen gathers her brood under her wings, and you were not willing! See, your house is left to you, desolate. For I tell you, you will not see me again until you say, "Blessed is the one who comes in the name of the Lord."[31]

The Spirit of Jesus is the activity that is the risen Christ, and that activity is diverse, and is as female as it is male, in the same way as the wisdom of God is female in the Book of Proverbs.[32] The activity is human activity, it bears a family resemblance to the activity that is Jesus, and it is as legitimate to call it female as it is to call it male. A similar issue will recur when we discuss the God whom Jesus worshipped as "Father."

JESUS' FATHER

Jesus' Father, the "Abba" whom Jesus addressed in the Garden of Gethsemane,[33] is the one whom he worshipped, sought, struggled with, and taught his followers to pray to.[34] So if Jesus is our God then we shall do as he did, and his God shall be our God too. This is the God whose City is to come, and who is judge of our actions and of our thoughts;[35] and this is the God whom Paul believed had raised Jesus from the dead.[36] This is the God whom Jesus found in the books that we call the Old Testament: a God of creation[37], of judgment (in most of the prophetic books), and of love and forgiveness.[38]

---

31. Matthew 23:37–39, NRSV.
32. Proverbs 8:1.
33. Mark 14:36.
34. Matthew 6:9.
35. Matthew 25:31–46.
36. 1 Corinthians 15:15.
37. Genesis 1:1.
38. Psalm 103.

Jesus lived in a patriarchal society, and "Father," in its intimate or its less intimate form, would have come more easily to him than "Mother" when he wanted to describe the God to whom he prayed and whose will he sought to fulfil: although Jesus would have known Hosea 11:1–4, which pictures God in terms of activity at least as appropriate to a mother as it is to a father, and Jesus might not have objected if it had been suggested to him that he should call his God "Mother." The society that we live in is different, and we might well choose to call Jesus' creating, loving, and forgiving God "Mother."

To worship Jesus as our God is to worship a Jew and is to worship a Jew's heavenly Father: and so we worship that God with Jews everywhere, and they with us. This creative, merciful God is the God of Islam, too—and so Jews, Muslims, and Christians, worship together this one God. In John's Gospel, Jesus says this: "I have other sheep that do not belong to this fold. I must bring them also, and they will listen to my voice. So there will be one flock, one shepherd."[39] This is our God Jesus' desire, and it is ours. His voice is the voice of grace, of welcome, and of acceptance, and where this voice is heard there is one fold and there shall be one fold. We shall of course disagree over what Jesus' words mean, and over the gospel-writer's words, and particularly as to whether Jesus shall be our "one shepherd": but we can share his hope for "one fold" in which the followers of a variety of religious traditions worship a creative, merciful God; and we can understand our differences as differences within a fundamental unity.

We follow our God Jesus, and therefore worship his Father, a loving Creator, a merciful God, the one who brings new life. The followers of Islam, in obedience to the Qur'an, worship a loving Creator, a merciful God, the one who brings new life. The Jews, in obedience to the Torah, the Law, worship a loving Creator, a merciful God, the one who brings new life. There is of course diversity of belief and practice within each religious tradition, and there is diversity between the traditions, particularly in relation to where revelation of God is to be found: but there is a unity of belief and practice within each faith tradition, and important levels of unity of belief and practice between them, and thus grounds of hope for healthy ferment as well as for peaceful coexistence between and within the world's faiths.

Does this God, this Father, this Mother, change? In the Garden of Gethsemane Jesus clearly thought it worth discussing with his Father whether it really was necessary for him to die;[40] and his Father is the same

---

39. John 10:16, NRSV.
40. Mark 14:32–42.

God who changed his mind when Abraham asked him to.[41] The writers of the Hebrew Scriptures were convinced of their God's faithfulness, and of his steadfast love for Israel:[42] but within that steadfastness we find plenty of changes of attitude towards Israel.[43] This God is Jesus' God, Jesus' Father, Jesus' Mother, not someone who doesn't change, but someone affected by us and by what happens to us, someone who continues to love us, and someone whose faithfulness requires change on the part of God.

And this God suffers—suffers with us, and suffers our unfaithfulness.[44] We worship Jesus, our suffering God; we worship his Father, a suffering God; and we worship the Spirit, a God intimate with us, a God who is the risen Christ, and who suffers still, with us, in us, and because of us. This God, far from begin unchanging and distant, suffers more than we can begin to describe, loves more deeply than we can begin to imagine, and changes more than we can possibly conceive.

This book has contained much—perhaps too much—about Jesus, for not everyone will choose him as their God, and sometimes I cannot do so. Does that leave us Godless? There are many who would say "No." For some, the problem with Jesus is that he is male, and thus defines a God who is too male; for some simply that he is a particular person, and particularity does not fit with the kind of God they wish to worship. And there are others who have been brought up in or converted to a different religion. We can converse about God and about religion, we inhabit similar cultural worlds, and maybe we have no need to speak of Jesus.

If this is how we feel, and we refuse or decline to choose Jesus as the definition of God, then we can still worship a God who is Action and the source of all action, and who is action in changing patterns. We can worship a God who is defined by the changing pattern of action that we call "grace": an unconditional love, an unconditional and constant giving. Where there is freely given love, there is God: and God is the activity of grace, and not some ethereal being who undertakes that activity.

GOD IS TRINITY

Understanding God as Trinity—as three—is not only a tradition of the Church, although it is that: it is born of our understanding and conviction

---

41. Genesis 18:22–33.
42. Psalm 103:8, 17.
43. Psalm 103:9.
44. Hosea 11:1–4, 8–9.

that reality is action in changing patterns, and it is born of our own experience of Christians.

As we explore the accounts of Jesus' life, as we worship him as God, and as we seek to live out in our own world the patterns of action that constitute who Jesus is, we find that we are not alone, and that Jesus' promise is true: "I am with you always, to the end of the age."[45] For God is free, is free to be human, and is free to be with us, to relate to us, as the "Spirit of Jesus,"[46] as the "Holy Spirit."

The patterns of action that constitute the God who is Action and the source of all action, the God who is Jesus, and the God who is the Holy Spirit, are the same God and they are three: three in fact, three in our experience, three in the experience of the Church for nearly two thousand years: three because God in freedom chooses to be three. God is a community, drawing us into the community of love that God already is; and God—the Father or Mother who is Creator, Jesus of Nazareth, and the Holy Spirit—is and are action in changing patterns: both shared changing patterns of action and distinctive changing patterns of action. As Geoff Crocker puts it in a commentary on the end of Paul's second letter to the Corinthians—"The grace of the Lord Jesus Christ, the love of God, and the communion of the Holy Spirit be with all of you"[47]—"God means love, Christ means grace, and the Holy Spirit means fellowship."[48] They are together and singly action in changing patterns.

But still God is one. God is a "person." Human persons are not things, they are not beings: they are changing patterns of action. The source and ground of those patterns of action is God, and God is also constituted by particular changing patterns of action, and if these exhibit family resemblances with the changing patterns of action that are ours as persons, then we can call God a person. So we can call God the Creator a person, and, in even more personal language, we can call him Father, for in this we follow Jesus, who called his God "Abba, Father."[49] Just as "creator" describes what God does, so "Father" describes a changing pattern of action, as does the "mother hen" imagery that Jesus used of himself.[50]

We can also call the Holy Spirit a person, because the Spirit shares the changing patterns of action that constitute the Creator; and we can certainly

---

45. Matthew 28:20, NRSV.
46. Acts 16:7; Philippians 1:19, NRSV.
47. 2 Corinthians 13:13, NRSV.
48. Crocker, *An Enlightened Philosophy*, 111.
49. Mark 14:36, NRSV: *Abba ho pater*.
50. Luke 13:34.

call Jesus a person: so God is three persons in ways possibly less requiring an appeal to analogy than is the case within a Being metaphysic. A trinitarian God is more potent than a unitarian one in terms of its social implications,[51] its religious possibilities, its survivability, its fit with an actology that might reflect the thought-forms of today and tomorrow, and its connection with the Church's sense of its continuity and identity and therefore with its ability to undertake genuinely Christian mission.

So there are three persons who are God: but it is also entirely legitimate to call God "a person": that is, to recognize the unity as well as the Trinity. Within God there are patterns of action that we might term "personal": patterns that nurture other patterns and enable them to change in new and more personal directions. But the definition of these changing patterns of action is themselves, not our word "personal," which refers to our patterns of action: patterns of action that emerge in the universe because the universe is a changing pattern of changing patterns of action that has emerged from the ferment that is God. So we are personal because God is, though the language of the personal is a changing pattern of action that has emerged from the patterns of action that we are.

We can become less than personal, as we change, and as we change each other, and as our patterns become less like those that emerge from God—although the meaning of personal, too, changes, as God is Action, and so the patterns that constitute God change as well. But what does not change is the affecting of every pattern of action by every other—and so the ferment and the patterns of action and the stillness that are God constantly change us and we change God, and so the personality of God changes our personalities, we change each other's, and we change God's. The definition of "person" includes the notions of change, the changing of others, and the being changed by others—so the patterns of action that are God and ourselves all change each other: and "person" changes its meaning, for the meaning is a changing pattern of action, and not a stillness: but it is a changing pattern and not chaos—for there is only chaos in God, for God is Action, which means that God is constituted by chaos—by unpatterned action—in ways in which we are not.

So: we are persons, and that means that we are divided, changing, diverse, and constituted by our relationships—so we are the other person, and they are us, thus giving the notion of "one flesh" a far broader application than that of marriage. Any unity is a process, and this goes for the unity between people as much as for the unity between anything else. So when we use the word "unity" we are in fact speaking about the unity of the cosmos.

---

51. Leech, *The Social God*, 6–10.

It is because of our diversity that we can address ourselves, we can relate to ourselves, and we can change ourselves—as we do. We are thus both object and subject, and we are the changing patterns of action that both unite and constitute the object and the subject that we are.[52]

One of the marks of the pattern of action that we call "personal" is self-consciousness: we affect our own patterns of action, and our senses and our minds "know" themselves—that is, there are loops in the connectedness between the patterns, just as there are in God, and maybe elsewhere in the universe. In the context of an ontology in which the human being is a being that changes, relating mind and consciousness to a human body subject to causal chains will always be a challenge:[53] but in the context of an actology there is no fundamental division in anything, and so no necessary division between what we call "mind" and what we call "matter", and indeed no fundamental division between the planet, the diverse life that lives on it, and human minds:[54] it is all a ferment of action, connected with the action that we call other persons; and it is all patterned with changing patterns that change each other.

So God is personal, and we are persons, and the relating is deep, going to the heart of God where the ferment gives birth to personal patterns of action, and where the ferment relates to the actions that we are, and it changes them. As persons we relate, knowing one another and knowing God, changing one another and changing God, a community of persons, together, changing all the time what it is to be a person.

So God is Jesus, Jesus' Spirit, and Jesus' Father: in one sense three Gods, but in a more important sense one God, for they share a pattern of activity, the pattern that we see in Jesus and find also in his Spirit and in the Father to whom he prayed. This is their family likeness: their pattern of action—and this is what they are, and this is what God is.

A Trinitarian God is an essential element in the Church's sense of its continuity and identity and thus in its ability to do apologetics. The Church needs the Trinity: for the purposes of pastoral care, because a diverse God is going to satisfy more religious needs than a more unitive one; and for the purposes of institutional survival. Diversity and change encourage survival in a changing context. The Marcionite religion of the second century, which abandoned the Old Testament and its God, abandoned law in favor of grace, and generally favored simplicity over complexity, and unity over diversity,

---

52. Derrida, *La Voix et le Phénomène*, 67–97, on Husserl's resistance to the notion that we address ourselves, and Derrida's insistence that we do.

53. Torrance, "Theism, Naturalism and Cognitive Science," 214–15.

54. Midgley, "Mind and Body," 195–96.

died out. And in terms of Christian theology's and the Church's connections with other disciplines and institutions, a God diverse and changing will be able to adapt as philosophical trends change, and will itself be able to offer new possibilities: so A.N. Whitehead's process philosophy,[55] Marxism, and secularization itself, all have roots in a divers and changing Christian tradition. And perhaps now the Church can offer God understood as changing patterns of action as the focus for new thought about an actology of action in patterns.

God is Trinity: that is, a community of activity:[56] a concept related to the Eastern churches' conception of God as a Trinity in relationship, a God for whom "being is communion."[57] The three persons of the Trinity—"three divine subjects"[58]—are patterns of action with family resemblances to each other, but with differences too: and it is in the relating together of God the Creator, Jesus, and the Holy Spirit, that God is constituted by complex changing patterns of action.[59]

The differences are important. Jesus is a human being, which neither the Creator nor the Spirit are—although using personal language of both can be highly appropriate, as we have discovered; and the Creator is the source of all Action, which the Spirit is not. They are all God, and together they are God: it is the relationships between them that constitute God. The Creator who is the source of all action, Jesus the human being, and the Spirit, severally and together constitute God's changing patterns of action as God relates to the world, to us, and to everything else. The relationships are changing patterns of action, so the Trinity is more than the sum of its parts, and there is a sense in which there are four: the Creator, Jesus, the Spirit, and their relationships with each other.

Or might the New Testament in fact be offering us a binitarian God? The fundamental relationship is that between Jesus and the Creator, whom he called Father. This is already a Trinity, because the Creator is changing patterns of action as well as being Action, the source of all action; Jesus is God living a human life, sharing the changing patterns of action that constitute God; and the relationships between Jesus and the Creator are of course changing patterns of action: the Holy Spirit, binding together the two persons of the Binity. This binity will be experienced by us as Trinity. The changing patterns of action binding together Jesus and the Father reach

55. Whitehead, *Process and Reality*.
56. Moltmann, *Der gekreuzigte Gott*, 264–67; *The Crucified God*, 276–78.
57. Zizioulas, *Being as Communion*.
58. Ware, "The Holy Trinity," 115.
59. Ware, "The Holy Trinity," 115.

out to us as well, and to the whole of creation—to the whole of God's continuing creativity—binding us together with one another, with the Creator, and with Jesus.

A somewhat different collapsing of the Trinity is offered by Geoffrey Lampe, for whom God is "Spirit," and for whom

> the concept of the inspiration and indwelling of man by God as Spirit is particularly helpful in enabling us to speak of God's continuing creative relationship towards human persons and of his active presence in Jesus as the central and focal point within this relationship.[60]

Here God is "Spirit," and "Spirit" is both the Holy Spirit and the constant inspiration of Jesus, so that "the work of God in Christ is continuous with, and part of, his creation of human spirits thorough personal communion with them."[61]

Whether we maintain a significant separation between the Creator, Jesus, and the Holy Spirit, assert a binitarian God of Jesus and the Creator united by the Spirit, or collapse the Creator, Jesus, and the Holy Spirit, into Spirit: the members of the Trinity are God, and thus share in each other's changing patterns of action. So, if Jesus' changing pattern of action is non-violent revolution to bring in the City of God, then this is God's pattern of action, it is the Holy Spirit's, and it is the Creator's: although of course it is a changing pattern of action, and it is different in relation to each of the three persons' different roles within the Trinity: Jesus the human being; the Creator, Action itself; and the Spirit, the bond between the two and active in the world today. All three persons live out a new order of peace and justice in the midst of the old order, all three bear the consequent suffering, and all three bear responsibility for the evil that the world, ourselves, and other people inflict. Jesus might have been thought to be sinless, but he is only that if we define "sinless" to permit violence, prejudice, insults, and the like. It would be better to say that there is evil in the heart of Jesus, evil in the heart of the Creator, and evil in the heart of the Holy Spirit: that the Trinity is as afflicted by evil as the rest of us, and inflicts evil, just as the rest of us do, and as the universe does as it evolves: and here there is perhaps no need to insist on any difference between sin and evil, for they are both a lack of the good, of righteousness, of justice, of wholeness, of wellbeing, and of peace. The fact that there is evil at the heart of the Trinity, that evil is intrinsic to God the Trinity, is a matter for hope: for that is where transfiguration is

---

60. Lampe, *God as Spirit*, 34.
61. Lampe, *God as Spirit*, 34.

possible: and as the evil is overcome in the heart of God, and in the midst of the changing patterns of action that constitute God the Trinity, so all evil will be drawn in and overcome: a foretaste of which we have seen in Jesus' crucifixion, as he absorbed the evil and returned none of it.

But perhaps none of Trinity, Binity, or Spirit, is quite right. Just as there are potentially many dimensions, and we only experience three of them, perhaps God is a radical, even infinite, diversity, of which we experience the Creator, Jesus, and the Holy Spirit, but of which myriad dimensions are invisible to us. In the circumstances in which we live on planet Earth we experience the action in changing patterns that constitutes Jesus, and the action in changing patterns that constitutes the Creator, and we experience them as overlapping, and so Jesus is to that extent God, and the Spirit is the action in changing patterns that binds them together.

Chapter 10

The Reconciling God

Thesis: In Jesus, God, the universe, and ourselves, are reconciled.

INTRODUCTION

Soteriology is the science of being saved: of salvation. But saved from what, and into what? Again, it is all action in changing patterns, for salvation implies that someone is doing some saving, and someone is being saved from something and into something. In the Hebrew Scriptures, salvation was from defeat into victory, from physical death into life, from social exclusion into social inclusion, and from exile back into the promised land. In the Christian Scriptures it is salvation from illness to health, and from sin to a new relationship with God. We shall find that an actological approach to the question of salvation coheres with reconciliation between God, the universe, and ourselves, achieved in Jesus Christ.

SALVATION

How might our new actology enable us to make sense of a doctrine of salvation? To begin that discussion we could select just one theory of atonement—that is, one way in which Christians have understood the process whereby we are put right with God—from the wide diversity available to us, and ask how we might understand that theory in the context of an understanding of reality as action in changing patterns. In Thomas Aquinas's

Summa Theologiae[1] we find a substitutionary theory of atonement in which God accepts Jesus' death, understood as a punishment for sin, in place of the punishment due to us: not because God could not forgive us in some other way, but because this is the way that God chose to do it.[2] This might be how Jesus saw it, when he described his offering of his life "as a ransom for many."[3] This is his pattern of action, so it is God's: God offers himself as a ransom to himself. Or maybe it is simply God choosing Jesus as a scapegoat, and maybe God does sacrifice his son, and maybe it is child abuse: for if we are made in the image of God, then there is abuse and scapegoating in the heart of God. Here we must make a choice: Either God is good, or there is evil in the heart of God. Or perhaps with God both are possible?—both good and evil are patterns of action intertwined in the heart of God? Or perhaps the lesson of the story about Abraham taking his son out to slaughter him, and being stopped by God's messenger from doing that, and the message of the crucifixion itself, is that scapegoating constituted by sacrifice is *not* God's will: that such sacrifice is simply murder.[4]

And there are other models, too: God's choice to forgive in response to repentance;[5] an exemplarist approach, in which Jesus' suffering provides us with "an example of obedience, humility, constancy, justice, and the other virtues displayed in the Passion, which are requisite for man's salvation";[6] a revelatory approach, in which the cross reveals God's love for us in such a way that we are "thereby stirred to love Him in return, and herein lies the perfection of human salvation";[7] "Christus Victor," with the emphasis on Jesus' resurrection as the event that defeats death;[8] and "recapitulation": an idea developed by Irenaeus from Paul's "Christ as second obedient Adam"

---

1. I am grateful to Barnaby Perkins, in a presentation at an Archbishop's Examination in Theology seminar held on the 17th June 2016, for this insight.

2. Aquinas, *Summa Theologiae*, III, 46, 2.

3. Mark 10:45, NRSV: *dounai tén psuchén autou Lutron anti pollōn*.

4. Genesis 22:1–19; Pattison, *A Short Course in Christian Doctrine*, 98.

5. Aquinas, *Summa Theologiae*, III, 84, 5. In Aquinas, repentance is understood in terms of the sacrament of penance

6. Aquinas, *Summa Theologiae*, III, 46, 3: *exemplum obedientiae, humilitatis, constantiae, iustitiae, et ceterarum virtutum in passione Christi ostensarum, quae sunt necessariae ad humanam salute.*

7. Aquinas, *Summa Theologiae*, III, 46, 3: *per hoc provocatur ad eum diligendum, in quo perfectio humanae salutis consistit.*

8. Aulén, *Christus Victor.*

theology.[9] [10] Each of these theories of atonement constitutes a pattern of action that establishes a relationship between the action and the changing patterns of action that constitute God, and the changing patterns of action that constitute ourselves. All of the many patterns of action that we call "theories of the atonement" can occur at the same time without contradiction, in the same way as each of us can relate to another person via a diversity of patterns of action: body language of different kinds, a diversity of words, and multiple thought-patterns. Similarly, the different patterns of action that we might describe as "God sends his Son," "God comes," "Jesus suffers," "God suffers," can exist together—or rather, can be in action together, providing us with a constantly changing and radically diverse relationship with God.

An actological understanding of God and of ourselves brings to prominence another soteriological possibility: Death is Jesus' pattern of action, and so it is now eternally God's pattern of action. Jesus is reconciled with God, we with Jesus through his death and ours, and therefore we with God. We are reconciled with God, and so we must in practice be reconciled.[11] Of particular interest here is that such a conceptualization can be understood within some of the more traditional theories of atonement, and in particular within a theory of the payment of a price. God experiencing death in Christ is God paying the ultimate price for achieving a reconciliation: for God's experience of God reconciles God with humanity and thus humanity with God. As Paul Janz puts it, the unity

> of *causal reconciliation* between *God and the world* which is accomplished in empirical history on the cross is . . . a unity achieved by the divinely *causal* act of redemption in the real world of human embodiment in space and time.[12]

It is not that God has demanded this experience of human suffering and death of someone else. God demands it of God, in order to be reconciled with human suffering and death. God is the scapegoat that God demands; God is the sacrifice that God demands.

As for other theories of atonement: God's obedience to a human death is an extreme example of obedience, inviting our response; because it is God's death, Jesus' death reveals God to us, and particularly God's reconciliation with humanity; Jesus' resurrection is the ultimate victory because it is victory over the death of God; and God recapitulates in God's own

---

9. Ireneaus, "Demonstration of the Apostolic Preaching"; Romans 5:12–21; 1 Corinthians 15:21–22.

10. Astley, *SCM Studyguide to Christian Doctrine*, 123–28.

11. 2 Corinthians 5:20: *katallagéte tō Theō*.

12. Davies et al., *Transformation Theology*, 82. Italics in the original.

experience the depths of human experience, drawing that experience into God and reconciling God and humanity with each other: a theory of atonement that in the context of an ontology requires that "the one redeeming should be of the same nature as the ones being redeemed,"[13] but that in the context of an actology requires that the changing patterns of action of the one redeeming should bear sufficient family likenesses to the changing patterns of action of those being redeemed.

We can view this from God's end or from ours. Through Christ, we have been reconciled to God: ". . . just as by the one man's disobedience the many were made sinners, so by the one man's obedience the many will be made righteous."[14] And so, for instance, we are saved through Jesus' perfect faith in God: we are "justified by the faith of Christ," and we now possess a righteousness that "comes through the faith of Christ"—passages often translated to say that the faith is ours, when it might not be: the simple genitives do appear to say that the faith that saves us is "the faith of Christ."[15] New patterns of action have reconciled humanity with God, because these are God's changing patterns of action. And also through Christ God has been reconciled to us: that is, the human life and death that Jesus has lived are God's life and death, reconciling God with humanity. In particular: the pattern of action that is Jesus' death is God's pattern of action and is therefore God's death, and these bear a family resemblance to the patterns of action that are our deaths. We share that experience: that experience is what we are, or what we shall be, and it is what God is.

There are no conditions attached to forgiveness. Jesus asked forgiveness for those who crucified him, and he pronounced forgiveness for people he had apparently never met before.[16] This is Jesus' pattern of action, so it is God's: so there can never be conditions attached to the act of forgiveness. How we understand the process of forgiveness and reconciliation is another matter: and here diversity is not only permissible, it is essential. There is no need to choose between the theories of atonement: we can choose the ones that seem to us coherent with the God we find in Jesus Christ and leave the rest—and so we might wish to leave to one side theories that can look remarkably like child abuse; and we might find helpful a theory centered on "grace," in which salvation understood as reconciliation with God

---

13. Davison, *Astrobiology and Christian Doctrine*, 315.

14. Romans 5:19, NRSV: *hōsper gar dia tēs parakoēs tou henos anthrōpou hamartōloi katestathēsan hoi polloi, outōs kai dia tēs hupakoēs tou henos dikaioi katastathēsontai hoi polloi.*

15. Galatians 2:16, *dia pisteōs Jēsou Christou*; Philippians 3:9, *dia pisteōs Christou.*

16. Mark 2:1–12; Luke 23:34.

is established by God's grace,[17] that is, by the free gift of Jesus and of his Spirit. There is nothing to be earned, nothing needing to be done. It is by Jesus' faith[18] that the bond is secured, that is, by Jesus' faith in God and by Jesus' faith in us. This bond is possible because our God is one of us, and by his birth he creates the bond between us,[19] by his life he is one with us,[20] and by his death and resurrection he is one with us in both death and resurrection.[21] Paul understood Jesus' death as creating unity between God and ourselves as a sacrificial transaction, because he was a Jew and believed that Jesus' Father had always demanded such sacrifice if sin was to be forgiven and a new relationship formed: but the prophets and the psalmist had not always believed that,[22] and we need not do so either. If Jesus is our God, then his death creates a bond between us and God because the one we worship as God has suffered pain and death and is therefore one of us and is at one with us. We are now at one, there is atonement, there is reconciliation, and nothing can ever part us from each other.

RECONCILIATION

In Jesus there is reconciled God, the universe, and the whole of humanity—for every action affects every other, and in Jesus the patterns of action that are God and the patterns that are the universe and ourselves meet in a single complex and changing pattern of action.

Yes, in God these actions meet, but in God those patterns that have been given birth by the relating of the patterns that are God, and yet are not themselves God, are in God as patterns being transformed. But in Jesus they belong, they are his: so in Jesus every changing pattern of action meets: the good and the evil, the love and the destruction, the fear and the joy—every changing pattern of action—of God, the universe, and humanity—and the suffering and the transformation. This is the reconciliation: not just the birth, just the death, or just the resurrection, but all of it, for all of it is Jesus, a changing bundle of changing patterns of action to which every other pattern relates and is thus reconciled, so that from now on no pattern of action is ever a stranger to any other. And this Jesus, relating to every changing pattern of action that is God (not just then, but through time, for

17. Romans 5:15–21.
18. Romans 5:1 and 3:22.
19. John 1:14–18.
20. Hebrews 4:14—5:10.
21. Romans 5:6–11.
22. Psalm 40:6; Psalm 51:16–17; Jeremiah 6:20 and 7:21–23.

the Spirit of God is the Spirit of Jesus and is the risen Christ), and relating to every pattern of action that is the universe and is humanity, is himself the reconciliation; and the reconciliation is God and is in God, and the reconciliation reconciles all things, that is, all actions and all patterns of action, so that nothing is ever a stranger to anything else, no action is ever a stranger to any other—and now, through this reconciliation, those evil patterns that were not in God now belong to God, to be transfigured as belonging to God, not as something separate from God—for there is an intimate community between Jesus and God, more intimate than we can imagine, for they are one in their changing patterns of action in a way in which no-one else is one with God through their patterns of action, and this oneness is the foundation for every unity and every reconciliation, for every action affects every other. This is a cosmic reality: and, more than that, it is a reality in God, and a reality for every pattern of action ever, as every changing pattern of action is now transfigured by being reconciled in Jesus, in his birth, life, death, and resurrection.

What is it about Jesus' death that makes it so significant for Christians? It is that this is the death of God, which binds God to our experience and reconciles us to each other. The action that is dying is now God's action as well as ours, and so there is no longer any barrier between God and ourselves, or between God and the universe, because death comes to us all. It is God who is incarnate in Jesus, so it is God who suffers and dies, so there is a perfect empathy. God knows from within the reality and costs of sin. Here is the ground of forgiveness, because it is based on a perfectly intimate understanding of the inevitability of sin, of not knowing God, of distance, of the effects of past generations, and of the constant choosing between evils. And God knows from within the fragility of human life—its pain, and its death: and all of it is reconciled within God's experience of it.

And the cross and the resurrection together are our healing because just as God experiences our death, so we shall experience resurrection because Jesus has already done so: the pattern that is resurrection now belongs to our world as well as to the world to come, the pattern that is new creation already belongs to us and transfuses this world and our history and the universe, and because every changing pattern of action affects every other changing pattern of action, this pattern of action is our pattern of action as well as God's pattern of action. Our dying and rising God is one of us, and this God's activity is ours and ours is God's. The ultimate in change, in action, already belongs to us, and shall belong to us—and if action is reality, if change is reality, then death and resurrection together is surely the most real reality that there can be: it is reality itself, and every reality shall from now on be measured against this reality.

But death is still with us, and injustice, betrayal, and suffering are still with us, so for now there is both death and resurrection, for God and for ourselves, and we travel together, knowing death after death and new life after new life: death, newness, death, newness, and through this process, and through the deaths of our bodies, through our deaths into the as yet unknown, our God goes with us.

When Jesus died, he believed that his death belonged to the birth-pangs of the new age, to the suffering that they believed must precede the Kingdom of God's coming. In this sense Jesus' death is "for us": not to buy God's forgiveness, or to take someone else's punishment (for grace is free, and for God knowingly to punish the innocent for the guilty would be immoral in the extreme), but as a self-giving action to bring in the Kingdom of God, and thus the most self-giving action that there can be, and thus the pinnacle of grace, a grace let loose in the world, and an action still for us, a changing pattern of action in which we cannot help being involved, a pattern of action that involves us in the grace that is God—a pattern of action that is the reconciliation between God and all humanity because it is the self-giving of God to a death that is our death. Precisely because Jesus intended his death to be a death for us, it is forever a death for us, even if we no longer identify entirely with the ideas of sacrifice whereby Jesus thought it to be a death for us.

So Jesus' death is our healing and our reconciliation with God, and Jesus' resurrection is our healing and our reconciliation with God, and the death and resurrection together are our healing and our reconciliation with God. And if someone asks: "What's so important about Jesus' death?" we say this: Jesus is the grace of God and is God, so his death is God's death, and God is with us in our deaths; Jesus' death was freely offered, it is the most self-giving activity there could be, and so God's grace now belongs to our world and is part of our life; Jesus' death and resurrection is the greatest change ever, and thus the deepest reality, against which all other reality is now to be measured; Jesus' resurrection is the universe's transformation already in our world, and because every action is related to every other action, this new life is already our new life and we already live the Kingdom of God. And Jesus' asking forgiveness for his killers is God's forgiveness, and such forgiveness, like all forgiveness, has always been free.[23] Jesus' forgiveness was freely available; and in the Benedictus[24] it is knowledge of existing forgiveness that is the route to salvation, not vice versa—and this forgiveness is Jesus' action and is God's action and thus it is Jesus, who is God.

23. Psalm 103.
24. Luke 1:77.

No story in changing words can catch the suffering of the death, the self-giving of the death, nor the meaning of the death, which changes constantly. And no story in changing words can capture the newness of resurrection: of Jesus' resurrection, or of ours. But we try to speak because these events define the greatest change ever, and thus the deepest reality ever, and they are changing patterns of action in our world, and they are the character of the change that shall be reality for us and for the universe that we inhabit.

God dies: this is the reconciliation. And this God is involved in our life, then and now, and the action that is God is moved by and moves the changing patterns of action that we are. In Jesus, uniquely related to the patterns of action that God is, God lives and dies and rises (and is the God who raises Jesus), and we are action in patterns, changed all the time by the action in patterns that is God, and the action in changing patterns that is Jesus, and thus we are reconciled—and are called to "be reconciled," that is, to be reconciled to the changing patterns of action that God is and that Jesus is, and to grasp the meaning of Jesus, that is, the influence of his action on every action. Every part of Jesus' life is bound up with every part of ours, and by this involvement we are "saved," that is, brought into relationship with the changing patterns of action that constitute God, and we are changed into his likeness so that we too might begin to live the life of the City of God.

HUMANITY IN THE LIGHT OF JESUS CHRIST

So what are we, we men and women? We are "co-creators": we create meanings and we shape our world.

> This created co-creator has emerged from within the natural evolutionary processes as a creature who can and must (if it is to survive) scan its world, collect data, and construct complex interpretations of the world and its experience of the world.[25]

And we are made in the image of God, although not in the sense that God is an object, a thing.[26] So what is true humanity? For us, true humanity is defined by Jesus, and to the extent that we fall short of it we are not human: although the following and the falling short might not always be easy to distinguish. The "falling short"[27] is a falling short of the glory of God, that is, of the humanity that is Jesus. But now we are "justified by grace as a

---

25. Hefner, *The Human Factor*, 277.
26. Marion, *Certitudes Négatives*, 77.
27. Romans 3:23, NRSV.

gift,"[28] and our new humanity is shaped by the Spirit as we begin to "live by the Spirit"[29] and exhibit the "fruit of the Spirit."[30]

As for us: we are our bodies, and our bodies die. We die. There is no continuing "soul," but there is resurrection of the dead, with a new and imperishable body[31] constituted by changing patterns of action with family resemblances to those that constitute who we are in this life: and it is those family resemblances that we might represent by the word "soul."[32] But there will be other family resemblances as well, and it is "in Christ" that we shall be made alive,[33] that is, according to the pattern of his activity: his grace, his judgment, his love, his forgiveness—both now (for already we "follow him" to some extent) and in the future.

As for the manner of the resurrection of the dead, it is a mystery—not in Paul's sense of a story that he can now tell,[34] but in the sense that we cannot know it. Jesus sometimes got things wrong, and he knew that there were things that he did not know[35]—and so with us: there are things that we cannot know, and there are things that we can only get wrong. But what we can say is this: To know someone's changing patterns of action is to know them; to know our own changing patterns of action is to know ourselves; to know God's changing patterns of action is to know God: so all who experience or who do the patterns of action that are God know God and are God. This means that the Church is divine to the extent that its pattern of action is Jesus' pattern of action, and the same goes for individuals, families, and societies of all kinds: insofar as they participate in Jesus' patterns of action (whether or not they have ever heard of Jesus of Nazareth) they know God, they love God, they are God, and they live already Jesus' risen life.

Whilst Jesus' first disciples experienced many "conversions" in his presence, the first Easter Day must count as a uniquely significant conversion.[36] How did that happen? Was it a psychological necessity for them to believe Jesus to be risen from the dead—for how else could they continue to believe that they had been following the eschatological prophet who was himself the announcement of the Kingdom of God and who believed that

---

28. Romans 3:24, NRSV.
29. Galatians 5:16.
30. Galatians 5:22–25.
31. 1 Corinthians 15:42–49.
32. Ward, "Human Nature and the Soul," 172.
33. 1 Corinthians 15:22.
34. 1 Corinthians 15:51.
35. Mark 13:30.
36. Schillebeeckx, *Jesus*, 379.

he would see the dawning of the new age? If the tomb was in fact empty (for whatever reason), it is easy to see how belief in Jesus' resurrection might have arisen, along with stories about appearances—what we might call parables of the resurrection. Or did something unique happen which could only be described as "Jesus' resurrection"?—a unique pattern of action, undefinable in terms of any other: for where we have nothing similar with which to compare an event, it is impossible to speak of that event except by employing analogy and narrative. Whatever choice we make about what happened, it is sufficient to know that the first Christians were radically changed by an event that does not admit of plain description, and that ever since then Christians have claimed to have been changed in an analogous manner. To follow the Jesus who was the person experienced as risen, and as the cause of such radically changed lives, is to worship a God who might be able to change our lives so that we can remain human and acquainted with hope in a fast-changing world.[37]

In many parts of the world (less so in Western Europe than elsewhere), and amongst many kinds of people (amongst the poor more than amongst the wealthy), Jesus remains a focus for new orientations and for new community.[38] In spite of our understanding of Jesus being weighed down with metaphysics about the unitary and the unchanging, discipleship of this carpenter still creates challenging religious experience, personal change, engagement with a changing world, revolutionary movements, and hope in the midst of tragedy. Jesus continues to offer the Kingdom of God as a gift in the midst of a society in which increasingly everything must be earned, and by so offering he relieves individuals and communities of the hopelessness of trying to secure change by relying on the current options, and he thus propels communities towards new possibilities. Still Jesus is a source of hope; still we can hope with him for the Kingdom of God; still we can seek with him a "Father" who will bring about the Kingdom, and a "Mother" who welcomes us into it; still we can with him look for an end to oppression; still we can seek from him wholeness and community—always constantly changing wholeness and community—and still we can know that our God has been through suffering and death and that when we go through these experiences our God is with us in them and we are not alone. This Jesus satisfies religious and emotional needs as he has always done, and by choosing him as our God, and abandoning all other gods (and Gods), Jesus can serve our intellectual, ethical, and political needs in ways in which he could not

---

37. Moltmann, *Theologie der Hoffnung*; *Theology of Hope*; Jessey, *Profiles in Hope*.
38. Sobrino, *Christology at the Crossroads*, 33; Gutierrez, *A Theology of Liberation*.

before; and he can satisfy emotional needs and religious needs unhampered by a meaningless God described in analogical and negative terms.

To be truly human in a more secular world does not require us to secularize the Christian Faith: that is, to evacuate it of God, who is Action and the source of all action; nor to evacuate it of a Jesus whom we identify with and who is God. What we require is not a secularized theology,[39] but a theology of the secular: not one that starts with a God formulated in traditional "Being" language,[40] but one with Jesus at its core: Jesus with whom we can relativize our secular culture on the basis of a religious man who lived in a religious culture and whom to follow means to criticize the very basis of the culture in which we live.

---

39. Robinson, *Honest to God*; Van Buren, *The Secular Meaning of the Gospel*; Gregor Smith, *Secular Christianity*, 186–89.

40. Mascall, *The Secularisation of Christianity*.

Chapter 11

An actological church

Thesis: The Church is the Church insofar as its changing patterns of action are changing patterns of action that constitute Jesus Christ.

INTRODUCTION

An actological conceptual framework concentrates our attention on action in changing patterns: that is, on *practice*. As Jan-Olav Henriksen puts it, "by reconstructing Christianity as a cluster of practices, we can articulate the distinct character of the Christian tradition by other means than merely the comparison of doctrine."[1] However, spoken words, the writing of text, and the reading of text, are as much action in changing patterns—as much "practices"—as are such events as the Eucharist; and texts are patterns that are crystallizations of practices. For Henriksen,

> Given that Christianity is a historical phenomenon that relates to the everyday practices of communities and individuals under quite different cultural and social circumstances, the way the Christian tradition (or Christian traditions) articulates itself through different practices cannot be determined by these practices alone. Although Christianity cannot be understood without these practices, these practices cannot be understood as *Christian* apart from their relationship to, and as an expression of, the Jesus story.[2]

---

1. Henriksen, *Christianity as Distinct Practices*, 4.
2. Henriksen, *Christianity as Distinct Practices*, 193. The original of this paragraph

The Church is Christian to the extent that its pattern of activity is Jesus' pattern of activity;[3] and within such an actological context we should expect diversity as well as action in changing patterns. As Rowan Williams puts it:

> If "church" is what happens when people encounter the Risen Jesus and commit themselves to sustaining and deepening that encounter in their encounter with each other, there is plenty of theological room for diversity of rhythm and style, so long as we have ways of identifying the same living Christ at the heart of every expression of Christian life in common.[4]

However, an actological understanding of the Church might go further than that, for within a conceptual framework within which reality is understood as action in changing patterns, and within which every changing pattern of action is entwined with every other to some extent, and is closely entangled with some of them, we cannot neatly separate "the Jesus story" and "practices." All of it is practices, and the only distinction that we might be able to draw is that a text is a crystallization of practices whereas every other practice is as much a practice as is any other. What we cannot do is extricate the action in changing patterns that is the story of Jesus, written in texts, read in texts, and spoken from institution to institution and from person to person. That story is as much enmeshed in other changing patterns of action as is every other practice.

As well as understanding the Church as its practices we should also expect to find a clear understanding of the change experienced and inspired by the Church. Patterns of action are always *changing* patterns of action. As Bruce Epperly puts it:

> The church as the dynamic body of Christ embraces novelty, whether spiritual, scientific, or cultural, in light of the creative wisdom of tradition and the ongoing life-changing presence of Jesus Christ. . . . faithfulness to God requires the church to affirm and critically embrace the dynamic interdependence of life in all its varied forms. Further, faithfulness to God involves openness to God's ongoing process of creative transformation, both within and beyond the church.[5]

In this chapter we shall study how some of the changing patterns of action that constitute the Church might be understood in an actological context.

---

is in italics.

3. Ramsey, *The Gospel and the Catholic Church*.
4. Williams, "foreword."
5. Epperly, *Process Theology*, 121.

THE EUCHARIST

At the center of the Church's activity, and thus at the center of the Church, is the Eucharist, "the Thanksgiving": the taking of bread and wine, giving thanks for them, the breaking and sharing of bread, and the pouring and sharing of wine—for that is Jesus' changing pattern of action,[6] it is God's changing pattern of action, and it is our changing pattern of action: it binds us to God and God to us. When Jesus said "This is my body," it is the action that he was referring to; and when we say "This is my body," it is the action that we are referring to: the taking, the giving thanks, the breaking, and the sharing. This is Jesus' four-fold pattern of action: the pattern of action of his whole life as well as of his last meal with his disciples, and so Jesus is truly present at the Church's Eucharist, present because this pattern of action is his pattern of action, and because action is presence. The Eucharist is "the presence of an active Christ, moving in love not only towards the Father but towards us."[7] The Eucharist is "God's action in the sacrament":[8] or rather, the Eucharist is a pattern of action that is the pattern of action that God is: and it is a pattern of action that is constant giving—it is an example of the pattern of action that we term "grace," an unconditional giving. The Eucharist is not in any sense the possession of the Church. It is constantly God's gift to the Church.

To the extent that everyone is welcome at the celebration of the Eucharist, the Church is grace and is thus the body of Christ. And surely, everyone must be welcome to participate, whatever their faith, whatever their age, whatever . . . If the Eucharist is to be an effectual sign of the coming of the City of God, a City that is a gift to us—a constant giving—then does not the Church have an obligation to ensure that nobody is excluded? Young children might not "understand" what is going on, but neither do the rest of us; and children too are followers of Jesus simply by sharing in the Eucharist: the changing pattern of action that is Jesus, and the pattern of action that is the Church. The gracious activity of God is never earned: it is simply offered and received.

BAPTISM

Similarly with baptism: although here the history is rather complex.

---

6. 1 Corinthians 11:23.
7. Rowan Williams, "foreword."
8. Polkinghorne, *Science and Providence*, 93.

Jesus was baptized[9] as a sign of repentance, and so are we, and by being baptized as Jesus was we identify ourselves with his baptism and with the rest of his life, death, and risen life. Early Christians were baptized as a sign of repentance and commitment,[10] so we are baptized as a sign of repentance and commitment, as we belong with them to the company of the followers of Jesus. Paul understood baptism as a baptism into Jesus' death[11]—for the burial under water is the same pattern of action, and is intended to be the same pattern of action, as the burial of the dead Jesus. And for Paul, coming out of the water is the same pattern of action, and is intended to be the same pattern of action, as Jesus' rising to new life. The baptized man or woman, by going under the water and coming out of it again, was, and is, identified with Jesus, identified as his follower, as living already his life, his pattern of activity—for it is through our related patterns of action that we identify with one another—which all rather suggests that at whatever age we baptize people, we ought to put them under the water and not sprinkle it over them.

By baptizing someone, we declare them to belong to the City of God, and we welcome them as Jesus welcomed people.[12] Baptism does not appear to have been a major activity in which Jesus participated,[13] and it might be something that he did in the early part of his ministry during which he was closely associated with John the Baptist, but not during later phases, perhaps because he came to believe in a radically open welcome into the Kingdom of God for repentant and unrepentant alike.[14]

The point made here does not rely on Jesus baptizing. Because we use baptism as a sign of welcome into the Kingdom of God, and because Jesus welcomed people by a variety of means (healing them, telling them parables, eating with them, and so on), we shall be followers of Jesus if we baptize whoever asks for baptism; and the Church will be the body of Christ if in all of its activities, including baptism and the Eucharist, its welcome is radically open. Similarly, wherever the Church exercises grace, judgement, healing . . . indeed, any of the patterns of action that Jesus exercised, and that the Spirit of Jesus exercises still today—then there is the Church, and there is Christ's body, and there is Jesus Christ, and there is God.

---

9. Mark 1:9.
10. Acts 2:38.
11. Romans 6:4, Colossians 2:12.
12. Matthew 11:9; Mark 19:14; Mark 5:21–43
13. John 3:22 is the only reference to Jesus baptizing.
14. Sanders, "Jesus and the Sinners," 10.

THE CHURCH AND ITS BIBLE

And where the Church tells stories to express its faith, there is Christ speaking still. This is true of the Church today, and it is true of the Church of the first century. So when the earliest Christians told stories about Jesus' birth[15] and about Jesus' risen life, they were following Jesus the story-teller, and their action was that of the Spirit of Jesus. To what extent the stories reflect events is as relevant as whether there really was a shepherd who left ninety-nine sheep to go and look for the one that had got lost.[16] Jesus said "I am the way, the truth and the life":[17] that is, his changing pattern of action is the truth. So if our changing patterns of action bear a family likeness to his, then we shall be the truth too, in the same way as the early Christians were the truth to the extent that their activity bore a family likeness to Jesus' activity.

The earliest Christians followed Jesus to the extent that their changing patterns of action were his changing patterns of action. The same is true for us today. We know and love God to the extent that our patterns of action cohere with his. Our patterns of action will not be identical to his, nor will they be identical to any other Christian's, but there will be family likenesses—which is, after all, all that we can ever achieve with any spoken word or other action. The Church is therefore the body of Christ and the risen Christ in the same sense as anything is anything else.

The Church is its changing patterns of action, and part of that activity is the reading of the Scriptures, both the Hebrew Scriptures and the gospels, letters, and other documents of the New Testament. Jesus read the Scriptures, so we do. He read his Scriptures (the Law, the prophets, and the psalms) and he loved them and criticized them: "You have read that it was said, 'An eye for an eye and a tooth for a tooth.'[18] But I say to you, Do not resist an evildoer. But if anyone strikes you on the right cheek, turn the other also . . .'"[19] So we too read the Scriptures and we criticize them, both the Old Testament and the New Testament. Jesus interpreted the Scriptures for his day: for instance, in Mark 7:6–8 he interprets a passage from Isaiah, "The people honours me with their lips, but their hearts are far from me . . ." [20] to apply to the Pharisees. So we too shall interpret our Scriptures for

---

15. Luke 1 and 2.
16. Luke 15:3–7.
17. John 14:6.
18. Exodus 21:24.
19. Matthew 5:38–39, NRSV.
20. Isaiah 29:13, NRSV.

our day, and by so doing we shall be followers of the Jesus who read, loved, criticized, and interpreted his Scriptures.

All of this is action in changing patterns. The written text is always pure pattern: the action in changing patterns of the author's writing in crystallized form; but the reading is always new changing patterns of action, and in that sense it is always a new sacrament—and in this context we might define a sacrament as changing patterns of action that constantly entangle with action in changing patterns that constitute both God and ourselves. It is in this sense that baptism and the Eucharist are sacraments; it is in this sense that reading and interpreting the Bible are sacraments;[21] and it is in this sense that the Church is a sacrament. As Avery Dulles puts it:

> The Church becomes Church insofar as the grace of Christ, operative within it, achieves historical tangibility through the actions of the Church as such. The Church becomes an actual event of grace when it appears most concretely as a sacrament— that is, in the actions of the Church as such whereby men are bound together in grace by a visible expression. The more widely and intensely the faithful participate in this corporate action of the Church, the more the Church achieves itself.[22]

If the Church is its changing patterns of action, then the Church's structures and its ministry will be their changing patterns of action. The Church as a whole is apostolic when it does what the Apostles did (although with action suited to our own times); and the ministry will be apostolic when it proclaims, heals, and unites, as the Apostles did. In 1 Timothy 3:1–13, bishops and deacons are people with particular tasks and particular ways of behaving, and that is what they must be today. The Church is an institution, and its actions are in patterns. Those patterns will be changing patterns, but they are patterns nonetheless. There is a certain order about it all, which is as it should be, as long as the ordering reflects the patterns of action of the City of God.

THE CHURCH'S MISSION

If the Church is changing patterns of action, then an essential pattern of action will be evangelism: the proclamation of the good news that the Kingdom of God is on its way, and is here in Jesus Christ. We do this not to invite individuals to save themselves, for this would be to deny Jesus' universal

---

21. Astley, *SCM Studyguide to Christian Doctrine*, 67.
22. Dulles, *Models of the Church*, 61–62.

acceptance of us, and it would be to ignore his insistence that we should lose our lives rather than attempt to gain them:[23] rather, we evangelize in order to enable people and institutions to live now in the light of the City that is to come, to rejoice in acceptance and renewal, to hear the invitation to go with Jesus now into his task (and thus into knowing God), and to hope for the City of God. Evangelism will consist of following Jesus, as individuals and as a Church; it will mean words about Jesus—that is, apologetics; and it will mean the sacraments: the Eucharist and baptism.

The Church is not the completed City of God, and it is not the only place where the City comes: but it should be a place where the City is coming, and it ought to give expression to its conviction that the City will come, that God will be with us and we with God in its changing patterns of action: and at the heart of those patterns of action will be the patterns that we call worship, for without such patterns there is no Church. Where the Church worships God joyfully, experimenting with soul-stirring music, it reflects the worship of the City of God, the worship that the writer of the Book of Revelation tried to describe;[24] where the Church worships God from the depths of its soul, using the beauty of ancient sonorous plainsong and the flow of color, the dazzle of candles, and the thunder of organs, it reflects the worship of the City of God. Where people pray in silence, contemplating, reflecting in their own hearts the silence, freedom, and longing of God, the worship of the City of God is made known in the world, and the City of God is coming. Where the Church welcomes the homeless man with the distant eyes and the angry conversation, it proclaims the welcoming City of God— as long as it keeps everyone else safe in the process. Where the Church welcomes social outcasts, it gives hope for the City of God that will be entered first by tax-gatherers and prostitutes, and only then by the religious.

And what else should the Church do, collectively and individually? How should it behave?

A Christian is someone who "follows Jesus," as the early Christians did.[25] So our changing patterns of action will be informed by his and by the changing patterns of action of his followers. Jesus was baptized by John and was thus probably his follower,[26] and Jesus' message was originally John's— a message of repentance:[27] but their ways parted, possibly over whether unrepentant sinners could enter the Kingdom of God, and Jesus' message

23. Mark 8:34–38.
24. Revelation.
25. Mark 1:16–20.
26. Mark 1:9.
27. Mark 1:15.

became more characterized by grace than by the call to repentance. So, just as Jesus' following of another was critical and provisional, so our following of Jesus shall be critical and provisional—and this will be a true following of Jesus. And just as Jesus remained passionately loyal to John,[28] so we shall remain passionately loyal to Jesus. So when we consider Jesus' words on marriage and divorce,[29] we shall be both loyal and critical, seeking to do in our day what Jesus was concerned to do in his (in terms of protecting economically vulnerable women); and at the same time we shall seek a radical perfection,[30] loving our enemies[31] and cleansing the patterns of action of the mind as well as the patterns of action of the body.[32] Thus we shall try, for ourselves, to keep his commandments. For instance, his demand that marriage should be a lifelong commitment might be hard to fulfil in today's world, but we shall follow him more easily if our marriages become constantly changing patterns of action, and signs of the mutuality and reconciliation for which we hope in the City of God. However permanent in intention, marriages die, particularly in an age when people tend to live longer than they did in Jesus' time, and when that happens forgiveness and starting again must be the way in which we follow Jesus, and neither condemnation nor prohibition would be appropriate. We shall not judge—and whenever we fail to keep his commandments, the risen Christ will forgive us, just as Jesus forgave the woman caught in adultery.[33] Whether we attempt to fashion the laws of a secular state according to Jesus' specific commandments must remain an open question: but that we should help to fashion a society that coheres with Jesus' changing patterns of action is surely the most important task imaginable. To take just one example: as the parable of the vineyard workers[34] suggests, we should seek a generous measure of economic equality as a signpost towards a City of God in which all of us will experience the immeasurable generosity of the grace of God.[35]

---

28. Matthew 11:9–10.
29. Matthew 5:31–32.
30. Matthew 5:48.
31. Matthew 5:44.
32. Matthew 5:28.
33. John 8:1–11.
34. Matthew 20.
35. Torry, *An Actology of the Given*.

ON BEING A CHRISTIAN: OR RATHER, ON DOING CHRISTIANLY

So the Church, as its individuals and collectively, should fashion itself and wider society according to Jesus' changing patterns of action. Similarly, our believing should share the character of his believing. It will therefore be trust, and it will be an act of the will, something that we choose to do. Jesus tells a woman: "Daughter, your faith has made you well; go in peace, and be healed of your disease."[36] Jesus exercised faith, he commended the faith exercised by others, and if we are his followers then we too shall exercise faith—but not as a means to our own salvation. When Paul says "we are justified by faith,"[37] he probably means that we are justified by Jesus' faith—for in Romans 3:21, "The righteousness of God has been disclosed and is attested by the law and the prophets, the righteousness of God through faith in Jesus Christ for all who believe," should probably read "through the faith of Jesus Christ." Paul believed that faith was essential to our salvation, but this was hardly consistent with his conviction that our justification, our being made right with God, is "by grace as a gift."[38] So for consistency we must read Paul as believing that our justification is by grace and is by Jesus' faith in us; and that our faith is an exercise of the will in response to Jesus' faith. It is a "gift of the Spirit,"[39] and not every Christian has it to any great extent, but faith is something that all of us practice to some extent as we follow the Jesus who exercised faith. It is something that some do superlatively—and it is one of the many changing patterns of action that we do because we follow Jesus who himself exercised faith in his Father.

Thus faith is a "work," that is, something that we do: and Jesus clearly expected his followers to do such things as visit prisoners,[40] for the prisoner is Jesus who was a prisoner. Jesus, who shares our humanity, shares in the prisoner's humanity which is his changing pattern of action: so to visit the prisoner is indeed to visit Jesus, and not to visit the prisoner is not to visit Jesus. Jesus clearly believed that our final destiny depends on our patterns of action. Of course it does—for we are our changing patterns of action, and to the extent that we live Jesus' changing pattern of action we live the City of God: and whatever our future, and whatever the future of the universe, what we do is forever what we are and forever determines what we and the

---

36. Mark 5:34, NRSV.
37. Romans 5:1, NRSV.
38. Romans 3:24, NRSV.
39. 1 Corinthians 12:9, NRSV.
40. Matthew 25.

universe shall be, that is, what its changing patterns of action will be, as every changing pattern of action affects every other across time and space.

But, as I have suggested, it is often far from easy to know precisely how we should behave: and the issue of the family is a particularly difficult example, for Jesus himself was ambiguous towards his family. He commands his followers to honor their fathers and mothers,[41] and he criticizes those who don't use their wealth to care for their parents: but when his mother and brothers came to the door he declared his listeners to be his mother and his brothers.[42] So our attitude too should be ambiguous. We must love and support our families, and at the same time we must know that in the City of God these bonds are not ultimate, and that no simple ethical code can encapsulate the complexity of a City of God that will reflect both in our own day and in the future the changing pattern of action that is Jesus our God.

The Church's unity will thus not be any simple agreement over what to believe, over how to believe, or over how to behave. Its unity is its unity in Christ and in the Spirit, that is, in the patterns of action that bear a family resemblance to each other and to the patterns of action that constitute Jesus: in healing, in proclamation of the City of God, in the breaking of bread, and in praying for the City of God's coming. It is a scandal if we don't do these things together, whatever the supposed reason for not doing them together, be it differences in belief or differences over the status of a system of Church government—for not to do these things together is actively to destroy the Church's unity, which is a unity of patterns of action. In Corinth during Paul's time the Church's worship had become a scandal because the Lord's Supper was not the sacrament of unity that it ought to have been. They were ignoring one another,[43] and thus were not "discerning the body":[44] that is, they were not recognizing that they were one body, called to do together what Jesus had asked them to do—to take bread and wine, to give thanks, to break the bread, and to share the bread and wine.[45] In the same way, if we do not do these things together then we also "eat and drink judgment against ourselves."[46] Conversely, if we do do these things together, then we shall be one body, and we shall become one body—diverse in belief and practice, but also at one, knowing one another, and knowing the God whom

---

41. Mark 7:9–13.
42. Mark 3:31–35.
43. 1 Corinthians 11:21.
44. 1 Corinthians 11:29, NRSV.
45. 1 Corinthians 11:23–26.
46. 1 Corinthians 11:29, NRSV.

we worship, Jesus Christ. It is together that we are the Church by following Jesus.

So what is required of the Church? Firstly, that it receives grace— God's generous and constant giving; that it welcomes the risen Christ's activity in the world; that it welcomes forgiveness and reconciliation from a secular world; and, in Paul Tillich's words, that it hears the words "you are accepted."[47] By so receiving grace the Church will become a parable of grace: of grace that is the changing pattern of action that is Jesus Christ and that changes the pattern of action that is the Church and therefore the patterns of action that constitute the world around us. The Church is more likely to hear and to receive grace if it remains diverse, for it is through diversity that new ideas, new relationships, and new structures arise, a process that will be essential if the Church is to evolve and survive in a fast-changing context. In this process grace is experienced, and the new insights and new actions that emerge will be experienced as the grace of God. This is particularly true of the interpretation of the Bible, for where a variety of interpretations is available then we shall experience relationship with God:

> It is only through the stories, however they may be further mediated to us, that we can encounter the events and . . . that we can find them salvific, remaking our "worlds," intertwining with our own personal stories in such a way that well-being with God is the outcome,[48]

a well-being that is a grace that will in turn characterize the Church that hears and constantly reinterprets the stories.

This part of the book might have been longer if Peter Selby had not already written much of what I would want to say in his book *BeLonging*:

> The form of belonging which is appropriate to the Church is in radical contrast to the form of belonging we regard as natural in the ordinary groupings to which we are accustomed. The reason for that contrast lies deep in the longing of God for the entire created order to be transformed into the harmony and beauty for which it was made. God's actions and desires therefore point in the direction of inclusion, of a special concern for the "outcast," those who are beyond the boundaries created by persons and societies.[49]

---

47. Tillich, *The Shaking of the Foundations*, 155–65.
48. Houlden, *Backward into Light*, 12.
49. Selby, *BeLonging*, 3.

Selby discusses race, class, women and men, and homosexuality, and notes in all of these contexts a tendency towards tribalism. He expresses his opinion, particularly in relation to infant baptism,[50] that exclusion can only be tolerated when the integrity of the Church is at risk. But what is that "integrity"? Surely, it is the Church's pattern of action as a parable of the grace of God: so what must be maintained is the Church's welcoming of the wicked, the openness of its boundaries, the equality of its members one with another: that is the Church's integrity. So only if others' ability to receive grace is being compromised should exclusion of any kind be contemplated—which does not mean that the wicked are to be excluded because they make some of us feel uncomfortable.

Selby does not deal with who should and who should not receive communion. I do not see how the Church can think of excluding anyone from communion: yet the Church of England, the Roman Catholic Church, and numerous evangelical free churches, do so by erecting ritual barriers (such as baptism, confirmation. or confession), membership requirements (such as moral behavior or frequent attendance), or an age barrier (twelve or thereabouts for confirmation, or seven in some dioceses for the admission of children to communion). What kind of apologetics is that? Did not Jesus share table-fellowship with the wicked? Is grace not at the center of his life and of his message? Did he not tell his followers to let the children come to him?[51] In this context it seems difficult to justify excluding anyone from the sacrament of grace. And similarly, it seems difficult to justify refusing to baptize a child brought to the Church for baptism, or the putting of barriers in the way of that baptism, for by so refusing we are proclaiming an ungracious God. Just as both the Lord's Supper and baptism united Jews and Gentiles in the early Church, so they unite believers, half-believers, and unbelievers, adults and children, black and white, poor and rich, women and men, homosexual and heterosexual, in the Church today. Is this "cheap grace"? Yes, it is: and it is more than that: it is free grace.

By creating an open Church we shall create a Church open to the secular world in which the Spirit of Christ is active, and the gospel of grace will be heard and proclaimed by the Church, and the world will hope for the City of God that is a symphony of gracious activity—and apologetics will be the action that is the Church, and that action will be apologetics.

We and our world are constituted by layer upon layer of changing patterns of action, from the micro- to the macrolevel, patterns of action described as cosmos, matter, life, mind, spirit, and God. How we are to define

---

50. Selby, *BeLonging*, 58.
51. Mark 10:14.

the activity that is God will elude us in the same way as a definition of God in terms of substance has eluded us: but we can at least make a beginning by saying that where we perceive the changing pattern of action that is grace, there we find Jesus, there we find the risen Christ, there we find God: a pattern of action inextricably bound up with the activity that we also call cosmos, matter, yourself, myself.

If action is the real, and action in changing patterns is reality, then we should expect the Church to change. We should also expect the Church to be faithful to the changing patterns of action that we find in Jesus as he is interpreted to us by the Scriptures and the Church, and to the changing patterns of action that constitute the Holy Spirit at work in the world. We shall therefore study the New Testament and the Church, and we shall attempt to hear the Spirit's activity in our world today, in order to understand changes that have taken place in Jesus and in the Holy Spirit's activity in the Church and in the world in the past, and changes that the Holy Spirit is bringing about today. We would expect changing patterns to emerge: and the Church will be faithful to God as we find God in Christ and in the Spirit if it aligns itself with those changing patterns of action and contributes to faithful changing of them.

To take an example: In the Jewish Scriptures, God leads Israel out of chauvinistic nationalism and into seeing itself as God's Servant for the sake of non-Jews.[52] In the New Testament, we find Jesus converted to a Gentile mission by a Syrophoenician woman,[53] and we find the Church being converted to the equality of Jews and Gentiles in the Church.[54] During the following centuries we have found the Church constantly going through this conversion: being led by the Holy Spirit again and again into the breaking down of boundaries between one group of people and another. We are in the throes of more of those conversions: to the full inclusion of women; to the full inclusion of people divorced and remarried; to the full inclusion of lesbian, gay, bisexual, and transgender people—and there will be more.

But are there lines that the Church should not cross in this boundary-crossing pattern of action? The question has to be: Were there boundaries that Jesus would not cross? Yes: in relation to self-righteousness, hypocrisy, inequality, and legalism.[55] Jesus reinforced boundaries between such behavior and the Kingdom of God, which means that we should as well. But that did not stop Jesus' life being characterized by grace, and it did not stop his

---

52. Isaiah 42:1–9.
53. Mark 7:24–30.
54. Acts 10:1–11:18; 15:1–35.
55. Matthew 6:1–8.

life being a scandal. He was human, he was uncertain,[56] and he contradicted himself,[57] but following his conversion to God's Kingdom of grace Jesus was an apocalyptic prophet.[58] He got the details wrong, but he was convinced that the Kingdom of God—a kingdom of justice and peace—was coming very soon, and that God would reign for the benefit of the poor. The Kingdom of God is a gift, God's activity is a pattern of action that we call "grace," and Jesus' own life was shot through with grace from beginning to end.

Just as Paul was converted to the Christian Faith by an encounter with the risen Christ,[59] so we, the Church, need to be constantly converted. We are action in changing patterns, so conversion is never a once and for all experience: it is a constant gift, as old convictions fall away and are replaced by new ways of connecting together our beliefs and experience. Sometimes we might have been hiding from ourselves the new thoughts that we have been having, and sometimes we have not been conscious of them: but when the crisis strikes, the new convictions seem obvious, and we wonder why we didn't see the connections before.

Clearly any changes and new changing patterns of action that the Church decides on need to be decided on a case by case basis after reflecting on Jesus' and the early Church's boundary-crossing behavior, and on the boundaries that they did not cross. In relation to one particular current uncertainty: Should the Church recognize same sex marriage? This is not a question with which Jesus and the early Church had to concern themselves: but their general boundary-crossing behavior, and the fact that the Church risks self-righteousness, legalism, and the perpetuation of inequality if it does not recognize same sex marriage, suggests that the balance must fall in the direction of recognizing same sex marriage. Granted, Jesus assumed that marriage would be between a man and woman: but in his own day he could have assumed nothing else. Jesus' words about marriage:

> they are no longer two, but one flesh. Therefore what God has joined together, let no one separate ... whoever divorces his wife, except for unchastity, and marries another commits adultery[60]

suggest that a same sex partnership that bears the hallmarks of a marriage should be regarded by all parties as lifelong: which rather suggests that the

---

56. Mark 14:32-42.
57. Mark 13:30, 32.
58. Schweitzer, *The Quest for the Historical Jesus*, 60-69.
59. Acts 9:1-19.
60. Matthew 19:1-9, NRSV.

Church should be positively encouraging same sex marriage and insisting on its lifelong character.[61]

"The Spirit/wind blows where it chooses":[62] so we need to listen carefully for the direction in which it is blowing, and for changes of direction. And then we need to choose, individually and together, how the Church should evolve in the light of the evolving risen Christ, in the light of the evolving City of God, and in the light of our evolving society.

ECUMENISM

Ever since Justin Martyr framed his apologetics in terms of Plato's distinction between the real world of unchanging Forms (Good, Beauty, Truth, etc.) and the less than real world of appearances in which change and diversity are the norm, and located God among the Forms and us among the world of appearances, and ever since Augustine did the same, the Church has lived with a God whose unity is about hierarchy and unchangeability, and thus with an understanding of its own unity in terms of adherence to a particular person or hierarchy, or in terms of some "substance," however "spiritual."[63] The consequences of such a philosophical framework are that we believe truth to be ultimately simple and unchangeable and thus open to permanent and definable agreement; morals to be similarly simple, unchangeable, and open to permanent agreement; and authority to be located in a simple hierarchy, whether it be "God-Church-Papacy" or "God-Bible-minister." We have therefore come to believe that Christian unity depends upon agreement about truth (which entails agreement about truths), and on agreement with individuals and institutions in a given hierarchy, and that lack of such agreement entails disunity. We have also come to believe that the action of the Church, and particularly the action of the Eucharist and the action of the Church's ministers, can only be done together if there is prior unity based upon agreement about truth and thus about truths.

The tragedy is that we shall never completely agree about truths, and shall never agree within any communion, let alone between communions: something that Richard Hooker knew and expressed in his *Laws of Ecclesiastical Polity* in the seventeenth century[64]—which means that we are begin-

---

61. Torry, *Mediating Institutions*, 174–79, 237–42.

62. John 3:8, NRSV: *to pneuma hopou thelei pnei*.

63. Barnard, *Justin Martyr*; Brown, *Augustine*, 96–98; Chadwick, *Augustine* 26–28; Plato, *The Last Days of Socrates*; *Republic*; Prior, *Unity and Development in Plato's Metaphysics*.

64. Hooker, *Laws of Ecclesiastical Polity*, I, xvi, 1: There are several kinds of law: "The

ning to despair of unity between Christians. The cooling of relationships during the past few years, and a feeling that relationships have gone into reverse, is to some extent due to growing diversity of belief within all of the churches, a diversity that is bound to increase rather than decrease, and a diversity that is problematic in the context of a Being ontology. An action in patterns actology leads in a different direction, and it is one that John Zizioulas has taken. For him, "being" is "communion": that is, being is relationships, although he still has in mind persons defined in traditional terms as subjects who act rather than in terms of action itself.[65] Zizioulas defines the Church, too, in terms of "communion": that is, in terms of relationships, which inspires us to ask how an action-based philosophical framework might help us to redefine the Church.

If Heraclitus had eclipsed Parmenides in the ancient world, and if Plato had followed Heraclitus's lead rather than Parmenides', then what would our view of reality be like now? How would we be thinking about God, ourselves, the universe, and the Church? Probably in terms of action and change rather than in terms of substance and the unchanging. And if we were now to take "action" seriously as the foundation of a philosophical framework and of a view of reality in which the dynamic takes priority over the static, then might we not be starting to think of the Church as a diverse community of action in changing patterns bound together by family likenesses between patterns of action: patterns related to Jesus' pattern of activity?[66] And might we not be thinking of God, the cosmos, humanity, and the Church, in terms of active and constantly changing relationships, with those relationships understood in terms of action in changing patterns, and so as both constantly changing and as exhibiting family relationships from one moment to the next? As John Zizioulas puts it,

> the way God is and the way the world exists as relational beings coincide and relate to each other through the fact that in

---

law which God with himself hath eternally set down to follow in his own works; the law which he hath made for his creatures to keep; the law of natural and necessary agents; the law which angels in heaven obey; the law whereunto by the light of reason men find themselves bound in that they are men; the law which they make by composition for multitudes and politic societies of men to be guided by; the law which belongeth unto each nation; the law that concerneth the fellowship of all; and lastly the law which God himself hath supernaturally revealed." Throughout the *Laws of Ecclesiastical Polity* we find a balance maintained between the Scriptures, the Church's interpretation of the Scriptures, and what we might call "reason," that is, what God has revealed to every mind and conscience.

65. Zizioulas, *Being as Communion*, 17.

66. On "family likenesses" as a means of speaking of connectedness see Ludwig Wittgenstein, *Philosophical Investigations*, part I, §§66, 67.

both God and the world nature acquires stability and duration only in and through . . . a movement of communion similar to that which characterizes personhood, namely specific identity emerging through relationships.[67]

If Zizioulas had had an actological framework to work with then might he not have given us a theology conceptualized in terms of action in changing patterns, and an ecclesiology in which the Church is the sum of its changing patterns of action and in which the Church's unity is the shifting connections between different changing patterns of action in different places and at different times, connections that might exhibit "family likenesses"? And might he not have given us an ecclesiology in which orthopraxy defines the Church rather than orthodoxy?

The action that defines the Church is the taking of bread and wine, the giving thanks, the breaking of the bread, and the sharing of the bread and the cup. The Church is where these things are done, not where there is agreement on what the meaning is, as if the "meaning" expressed in words is somehow more important than the actions themselves.[68] It is not that the Church is a subject that does these actions, but that these actions are the Church: and, in general, where there is a changing pattern of action bearing a family likeness with Jesus' patterns of action as we find them in the gospels—patterns of action that we might generally characterize as "grace": a generous self-giving—then there is the Church and there is the risen Christ, for Christ is his patterns of action; and if the Church does these actions then

---

67. Zizioulas, "Relational Ontology," 154–5.

68. There is some debate over precisely what Jesus did and said at his last supper with his disciples before he died: Matthew 26:17-30; Mark 14:12-31; Luke 22:7-38 (with textual variants); John 13; 1 Corinthians 11:23-26. See Jeremias, *The Eucharistic Words of Jesus*; Dix, *The Shape of the Liturgy*, 48: The last supper contained seven actions: 1. Jesus took bread; 2. he gave thanks over it; 3. he broke it; 4. he distributed it; 5. he took the cup; 6. he gave thanks over it; 7. and he gave it. "With absolute unanimity the liturgical tradition reproduces these same actions as four: 1) The offertory; bread and wine are taken and placed on the table together. 2) The prayer; the president gives thanks to God over bread and wine together. 3) The fraction; the bread is broken. 4) The communion; the bread and wine are distributed together" (Dix, *The Shape of the Liturgy*, 48). "If the whole Eucharist is essentially one action, the service must have a logical development as one whole, a thrust towards that particular action's fulfilment, and not merely a general purpose of edification. It must express clearly by the order and connection of its parts what the action is which it is about, and where the service as a whole is 'going'. It is this logical sequence of parts coherently fulfilling one complete action which I call the 'shape' of the Liturgy . . . for a corporate action there must be in the minds of all a common agreement at least on what the action *is* on which they are solemnly engaged together. Agreement on what it *means* is less absolutely necessary, even if very desirable" (Dix, *The Shape of the Liturgy*, 2).

the Church is Christ's body. This is the point made by John Robinson in his book *The Body*: a point that he would have been able to make more connectedly if he had been working with a philosophical framework more about action than about being.[69] So no longer is the risen Christ an individual person, but is rather a corporate entity, a corporate Christ.[70]

Where these things are done, where grace and Eucharist are done, there is the Church, and there is unity with all other Christians: and, according to Paul, if we do not recognize "the Body"—that is, the changing patterns of action that are Christ creating the Church as a single body—then we are judged.[71] Jürgen Moltmann called the Church "one," "holy," and "apostolic" because it is those things in its action:[72] that is, where there is apostolic activity, there is the Church; and where there are changing patterns of action bearing family likenesses to the patterns of action that constitute the Church at different times and in different places, there is the unity that is the one catholic Church, and it is our task to recognize and celebrate that fact.

So where the churches act together, there is the unity of Christians, there is the means and the end: and anyone or any church that seeks to avoid this recognition by imposing its own belief-system as a criterion for recognition is failing to recognize Christ's Body and thus risks judgment. Thus where any Church recognizes the patterns of action that are the Eucharist, baptism, ministry,[73] grace, and so on, it recognizes the risen Christ and has no right to deny the validity of any body of people who do these things if their actions bear a family likeness to the changing patterns of action that constitute Jesus Christ. As Nicholas Wolterstorff has put it: to participate in the Eucharist "is to enter the sphere not just of divine presence but of divine action. God . . . is less a presence to be apprehended than an agent to be engaged."[74]

We shall never all believe the same, neither within our churches nor between them; but it is not by our beliefs that we shall be judged: it is by

---

69. Robinson, *The Body*, 47, 57–58: The Eucharist constitutes the "body," which is "the extension of the life and person of the incarnate Christ beyond His resurrection and ascension."

70. Moule, *The Origin of Christology*, 47–96.

71. 1 Corinthians 11:29.

72. Moltmann, *The Church in the Power of the Spirit*, 337–39. Moltmann might have expressed this insight more effectively if he had been using a conceptual framework *about* action rather than one into which action had to be fitted as a secondary matter.

73. On the question of ministry, it might be significant that the Church of England's *Alternative Service Book* ordinal defines the priest in terms of action rather than in terms of status, so there should be no difficulty involved in the Church of England recognizing the ministry of the Free Churches.

74. Wolterstorff, "Sacrament as Action, not Presence," 119.

our patterns of action, and by the validity that we ascribe to the patterns of action that constitute churches other than our own. If we wish to pursue the unity for which Christ prayed then we must do these things together: we must do grace, Eucharist, baptism, ministry, and so on, together. Maybe convergence of belief will follow and maybe it won't: that is of secondary importance. What matters is that together we become the risen Christ.

Just as God is constituted by Action, by action in changing patterns, and by relationships, so is the Church constituted by changing patterns of action and by relationships. "Church" is an action word, a verb: we "Church," or we "do the Church": an expression preferable to "do church."

MARY

There is no absolute God/human distinction, because we are made in the image of God: that is, we share changing patterns of action with God; and because Jesus shares in a unique way the changing patterns of action that constitute God, there is no longer a barrier between humanity and God. So should we ascribe any uniqueness to Jesus' mother Mary? It would be best not to do so: at least, none that would in any way compromise her humanity, just as it is essential never to compromise Jesus' humanity. Mary is as divine and as human as the rest of us. But there is of course a uniqueness, in that Mary was the mother of Jesus: the one whose changing patterns of action are uniquely those of God. For this we honor her and rightly call her *Theotokos*, Mother of God.

ANGELS

Angels are changing patterns of action. Whether they are bodily or not is beside the point. They emerged as the Israelites' God came to be understood as the "High God," and not simply as a tribal god. The other gods had to be found a place, so they became God's servants, the cherubim and seraphim.[75]

Might we be able to extend an understanding of reality as action in changing patterns, and therefore of layers of changing patterns of action, into a narrative about ranks of angels? And perhaps the Peruvian mountain gods to which Roman Catholics still make offerings belong in the realm of angels. If this is the particular pattern of action with which people can engage, then this is important for apologetics and therefore for theology.

---

75. Exodus 25:18–22.

Can we take the same approach in our multireligious world? A High God to which Jesus and the Spirit relate, to which the Qur'an relates, and so on? The alternative is competing gods, which means making choices, which opens the gates to a secular objectifying of gods as objects to choose between. Only keeping hold of God as Action, as the source of all action, and as not the possession of any particular religion, can rescue us from the secularization process.

Chapter 12

Doing Christianly

Thesis: To do Christianly is to echo in our lives the changing patterns of action that constituted and still constitute Jesus Christ.

INTRODUCTION

In the last chapter, in the context of a discussion of the Church as action in changing patterns, we broached the possibility of replacing a concept of being a Christian with one of doing Christianly: a verb qualified by an adverb, rather than the usual noun followed by a verb. In this chapter we pursue that discussion further by asking how an actology might contribute to an understanding of doing Christianly, and how that might inspire action in changing patterns.

DOING CHRISTIANLY

A further and essential consequence of an actions-in-patterns theology, and of the statement in the last chapter that where there are patterns of action bearing a family likeness with Jesus' patterns of action as we find them in the gospels—actions that we might generally characterize as "grace," a generous self-giving—then there is the Church and there is the risen Christ, is that no distinction can be drawn between orthodoxy and orthopraxy. No longer can a distinction be made between Christian theology and Christian ethics. Language and ideas are action in changing patterns of particular kinds, but in essence—or rather, "in action"—they are no different from any other individual and corporate activity of the Church. This means that any attempt to create a systematic theology that will be of service to the Church can make no distinction between theology and ethics, or between Christian action and Christian thought. A significant conclusion that we must therefore draw is that social and individual ethics will have to be integral to the theological project. We do Christianly, rather than are Christians; and doing Christianly is as important as believing Christianly.[1] We might even go as far as Paul Janz when he says that

> Christian dogmatics and Christian doctrine must be grounded foundationally in a "Christian ethics" . . . for two reasons. First, because the foundational question of all genuinely Christian ethics must always be nothing other than this: "What is the will of God?" And secondly . . . because it is Christian ethics which by its very definition *in* this foundational question can have as its only ultimate source of concern precisely the "*making real*" of the *righteousness* of God in the world today.[2]

Take the example of prayer, which is changing patterns of action in our minds, and sometimes is spoken words. A Christian prays, and the Church prays, as an expression of the incompleteness, as an expression of hope, and as an expression of the pain of our waiting for the City of God to come. Prayer gets to the very heart of God. There is no element of God not touched by our prayer, or by anything else. There is no mediator required because we and God are already intimately related to each other, but we experience Jesus as our mediator, particularly in relation to prayer, because he is changing patterns of action that are God's changing patterns of action: because he is God made flesh, the humanity of God. It might sometimes feel that prayer has no effect and that we might be doing nothing when we pray: but that is not true. Prayer, whether individual or corporate, is action in changing patterns in our minds; and where the intention is to relate to the action in patterns that are God, then that is what happens: and so God is changed by our prayers if God chooses to be; and God changes us as we pray if that is what God chooses and if it is what we choose. And because the patterns of action that we are affect changing patterns of action all around us, to pray is to change the universe as well as to change God. The future is open, and our prayers can change it.[3]

Jesus prayed because his perfectly human prayer reached into the heart of God, and if we are his followers then we too shall pray, and in particular

---

1. Davies et al., *Transformation Theology*, 151.
2. Davies et al., *Transformation Theology*, 108. Italics in the original.
3. Epperly, *Process Theology*, 36.

we shall pray the prayer that he taught us to pray.[4] What matters is to attend to God; to read the Bible; to pray—for by doing these things we shall open ourselves to God's changing patterns of action. We must wait on God: waiting is not passive—it is attentiveness, a scanning of the horizon, a pattern of action that reflects God's waiting for us.[5]

Commitment is what we do. We can "lose our faith" in the sense that the patterns in which action occurs in our minds might have changed: but it is up to us whether we continue to trust—that is, it is up to us how we commit ourselves and what we do. So it is up to us whether we continue to believe: for believing is something that we do, and so something that we can choose to do or choose not to do: and this pattern of action that we call believing relates to what is believed, which is, and must be, action in patterns: it is always events: "The eventual nature of Christianity arises from the fact that to be a Christian requires a belief in a singular event—the death and resurrection of Christ."[6]

In the context of an actology, "Christian practice" will be foundational, and in among the "eventual" nature of Christianity doctrine is just as much events as is any other doing Christianly. Doctrine, or teaching, is "communicative practice,"[7] and so is action in changing patterns, with an emphasis on the "changing." There are no certainties, because words change their meanings, and everything changes: so there are no doctrines that remain the same. A set of words might be the same as it has been for many years, but in new contexts those words will create new changing patterns of action as we read them and discuss them; they will stimulate new and different changing patterns of action in those who relate to them—new believing, new trusting, new committing, and generally new patterns of action—and we won't be able to control how the ancient words will influence patterns of action, either our own or other people's. We might be able to exercise some control over how we will be affected by the words in which doctrines are formulated, but not much: and we shall be able to exercise no control over how they will influence other people. There are no certainties, because God's speaking is "a sound of sheer silence,"[8] which is difficult to sort out from the cacophony of changing patterns of action to which we are constantly submitted. There are no certainties, and any supposed continuities are problematic as well, because words change their meanings, and everything

---

4. Matthew 6:9–13; Luke 11:2–4.
5. Luke 15:11–32; Thielicke, *The Waiting Father*.
6. Žižek, *Event*, 4.
7. Astley, *SCM Studyguide to Christian Doctrine*, 19.
8. 1 Kings 19:12, NRSV.

changes: so to believe in God is to choose to believe, over and over again, in every new circumstance: and because every new circumstance is a new set of patterns of action, in the context of which any apparent possessed certainties are immediately dissolved, and then the context immediately changes again, the believing will be a different changing pattern of action in every new moment. This means that any belief or trust must be a new act of commitment in every new circumstance.

As Søren Kierkegaard put it:

> Faith is precisely the contradiction between the infinite passion of the individual's inwardness and the objective uncertainty. If I am capable of grasping God objectively, I do not believe, but precisely because I cannot do this I must believe. If I wish to preserve myself in faith I must constantly be intent upon holding fast the objective uncertainty, so as to remain out upon the deep, over seventy thousand fathoms of water, still preserving my faith.[9]

But even that does not tell the whole truth, for we do not "preserve" an existing "faith." Everything is new in every new moment. There might be "family resemblance," but any faith in this new moment will be different from any faith in the past.

There are two ways in which we can choose not to believe afresh in each new moment. We can choose not to believe, not to trust, not to commit; or we can fail to do any new believing, new trusting, or new committing. A previous believing, trusting, or commitment, is precisely that: it is previous.

Jesus constantly changes because Jesus changes for us: so to follow Jesus is constantly to do new following: it is to take up new changing patterns of action that cohere with the patterns of action that constitute Jesus: and we find those patterns of action in the patterns of action that constitute the Church, and in the patterns of action that emerge as we read the New Testament—for the text, the signs, convey patternings from the past that shape new patterns of action today. We have no access to Jesus' times, to Jesus in Galilee or Jerusalem, or to the apostles, apart from the New Testament and the constant stream of changing patterns of action that constitute the Church throughout twenty centuries: but those are enough. We shall never trust or believe or act as Jesus did, and neither should we try: but we can do Christianly by allowing our own changing patterns of action to be molded in every moment by our reading of the New Testament, and by participating in the constantly changing life of the Church.

---

9. Kierkegaard, *Concluding Unscientific Postscript*, 182.

For instance: In Mark's Gospel, Jesus' pattern of action is one of non-violent revolution, the practice of a new world order over against both Rome and the Jewish authorities, and over against the violent insurgents of his day.[10] Jesus is already living the life of a new order, and he invites his followers to do the same. And if Jesus is God, then this is God's changing pattern of action too: and it must be ours. Ours will never be the same as Jesus' patterns of action, because we live in different times, and in any case Jesus' patterns of action change and so do ours: but we follow Jesus if our changing patterns of action bear family likenesses to Jesus' patterns of action. And so in the parable of the sheep and the goats Jesus declares righteous those who gave food to the hungry, gave drink to the thirsty, cared for the sick, gave clothing to the naked, and visited those in prison.[11] It was not "as if" the disciple does these things for Jesus: it is by doing these things that they are doing them for him.[12]

If God is changing patterns of action—if God the creator, Jesus, and the Holy Spirit, are patterns of action, as well being Action: the source of all action—then God will constantly influence the patterns of action that constitute ourselves and all of reality, and those patterns of action will constantly influence the patterns of action that are God. We here find ourselves with a rather Platonic understanding of our relationship with God, but with Action rather than Being as the universal in which we participate. There will never be certainty, in the sense that we shall never be aware of entirely settled patterns of action in our minds that we shall know to mirror reliably and permanently the patterns of action that constitute God: and even if that were to occur, then the patterns of action that are God would in that moment change, and we would again be seeking—as we constantly are. And we shall never in this life relate directly to the Action—action itself, and the source of all action—that constitutes God alone.

So can we commit ourselves to particular beliefs? We do in fact do so, one way or another. This is something that we do: there are such patterns of action in our minds—relatively settled patterns that constantly inform our actions, our relationships, and our ideas. Many of the changing patterns of action that constitute who we are and what we do are of this kind. But those patterns of action will be constantly tested by new patterns, and by new connections that come and go, and sometimes the most settled commitments will lose their anchors in our minds, and we shall experience conversion experiences: we shall change our minds—this is something that we do, and

---

10. Myers, *Binding the Strong Man*, 343.
11. Matthew 25:31–46.
12. Davies et al., *Transformation Theology*, 111.

it is what it says it is: we actively change the patterns of action that constitute our minds. And so, for instance, the Christian evangelical conversion experience of "new birth" is triggered by positive patterned action on our part when we "invite Jesus into our heart." New connections occur in the brain—that is, new patterns of action occur: and everything is different.[13]

It may be that a particular commitment has dissolved, but that others have survived for the time being, and on the basis of those we might make new commitments that might bear some resemblance to the commitments that we have abandoned. Whole societies can do this, and the Church can do it too. Again, certainty is impossible: but if the Holy Spirit is changing patterns of action that are God's changing patterns of action, then the Holy Spirit's changing patterns of action can bind us afresh into relationship with God, the Church, our society, one another, and ourselves: and that new binding will change a multitude of patterns of action, including God's.

I say here "we choose . . .": but how much control do we have over our beliefs, our commitments, our relationships, our ideas . . . ? Choosing is something that we do: it is changing patterns of action: it is a selecting of one idea rather than another, one action rather than another. There will be many changing patterns of action impinging on us, and how we choose might be a mystery to us: but we do choose. It is changing patterns of action that emerge from the changing patterns of action that constitute what we are. Choosing is something that we do. And so we choose whether to believe, what to believe, to what to commit ourselves; and then we might choose to change our minds about all of those. The choosing might be conscious or subconscious—that is, particular patterns of action in our minds might relate to those patterns of action that we call consciousness, or they might not. We might choose to drag mental processes into our consciousness, or we might not. But in any case we are choosing: we are selecting. This is what we do: it is a kind of pattern of action, and a particularly changeable one.

There are no disconnected patterns of action. Our believing, our trusting, our committing, our doing, our thinking, our relating, our praying . . . all of it is interconnected patterns of action. And all of it is connected to the patterns of action that constitute other people, and other people at other times; and all of it is connected with texts that shape our patterns of action; and all of it is connected to the patterns of action that are God active in the world—that is, to the Holy Spirit.

We can decide how conscious we become of all of this, and we can always decide what we will do. We can actively wait, we can expect, we can explore, we can experiment, we can commit, we can trust, we can believe:

---

13. James, *The Varieties of Religious Experience*; Sargent, *Battle for the Mind*.

and all of it will affect everything else. This is today's spirituality: to know that everything—or rather, every changing pattern of action—is of the character of a waterfall. There are no things. There are changing patterns of action. And the same is true of myself. So to know myself is to know that I am changing patterns of action, related to every other changing pattern of action; and to know myself in relation to God is to know that in Christ God shares the changing patterns of action that I am, and that I share the patterns of action that God is. This is for now a matter of hope—which is itself a changing pattern of action—and that hope is for a City of God in which we shall live the patterns of action that God is, just as Jesus did and still does.

Paul distinguishes between life "in the flesh" and life "in the spirit."[14] We might interpret Paul thus: "Flesh" is substance, material, being, the static: and life lived in this way leads to "death," to lifelessness, to the cessation of action. "The Spirit" is action in changing patterns: so to be in the Spirit is to have "life": is to share in God's changing patterns of action. Where our patterns of action bear family resemblances to God's patterns of action as we find them in Jesus' patterns of action as those are mediated to us by reading the New Testament and by participating in the Church, there God is at work, and to that extent our patterns of action are God's, and to the extent that our lives are "graced" we are "in Christ":[15] "These characteristics and deeds are ours only in so far as we become ourselves—new people—in relation to Christ, assumed by him."[16]

When we pray, our patterns of action bear a family resemblance to Jesus' praying, so God is at work in our praying; and when we heal, or forgive, or give, or live the life of the City of God, or proclaim the City of God's coming, then our patterns of action bear a family resemblance to Jesus' patterns of action. And particularly when we take bread and wine, give thanks, break the bread, and share the bread and wine, there our patterns of action bear a family resemblance to Jesus' changing patterns of action, the Kingdom of God is being lived, and Jesus is present—present because Jesus is constituted by his patterns of action.

These actions, along with baptism, assume belonging: which is itself a network of changing patterns of action—and so the assumption must be that to do Christianly we need to belong to the Church in an active manner. Belonging is action in patterns: it is not a state or a status. It does not belong to us. It is something that we constantly do or it does not exist. And it will generally be through belonging that we come to believe: one changing

---

14. Romans 8:5–9, NRSV.
15. 2 Corinthians 5:17, NRSV.
16. Tanner, *Jesus, Humanity and the Trinity*, 57.

pattern of action belongs to another, and the many changing patterns of action that impinge on us, and in which we participate, combine to create new patterns of action in our minds and in our activity. New paradigms—new patterns of action—make sense to us, and we experience conversion experiences, often many of them, and all triggering new ones. Above all, it is by belonging that we experience the resurrection, for it is by belonging that we belong to the body of Christ—to Christ still active in the world.

And just as God is Action that gives birth to constantly new changing patterns of action, when we give birth to patterns of action that bear family resemblances to God's ever new patterns of action, there God is at work, and there God is: for God is constituted by the changing patterns of action that ours might resemble. God is not Being or a being. God is not located. God is wherever Action gives birth to action, and wherever the patterns of action that constitute God are to be found—and then those patterns of action will change yet again, and we shall again need to do new things if our patterns of action are to continue to bear family resemblances to God's changing patterns of action. The patterns of action that constitute Jesus are uniquely those that constitute God, and we shall never be God in the same way: but to the extent that our changing patterns of action do resemble those of Jesus, and therefore those of God, and to the extent that they resemble those of the Holy Spirit active in the world, and therefore those of God, we become divine, we are divinized in a process in which "God's pattern serves as a map to show the connections between the Christian faith, the Christian life and Christian worship."[17] That process will never be complete, but by God's grace—by God at work in among the changing patterns of action that we are—both now and in the future we shall begin to share the character of God.

Jesus calls us to love God and to love our neighbor: To love God is to do as Paul suggests in his first letter to the Church in Corinth: we must be patient with God, kind to God, not envious or boastful or arrogant or rude. We must not insist on our own way, and must not be irritable or resentful. We must not rejoice in wrongdoing, but must rejoice in the truth. We must bear all things from God, believe all things, hope all things, and endure all things.[18] And according to the letter to the Colossians, we need to suffer with God:[19] to empathize with God, to share God's frustration, and to give all for God.

---

17. Stancliffe, *God's Pattern*, 13.
18. 1 Corinthians 13:4–7.
19. Colossians 1:24.

As for loving the neighbor: In his parable of the Good Samaritan,[20] Jesus is responding to a lawyer's question. In relation to the command "love your neighbour,"[21] the lawyer had asked: "who is my neighbour?"[22]—presumably meaning: who is it that I should help? Jesus then tells the parable, which is typically thought-provoking: not simply because two Jews refuse to help the man robbed and left lying by the road, and it was a hated Samaritan that helped him: but also because the parable answers a question different from the one asked. At the end, Jesus asked: "Which of these three, do you think, was a neighbour to the man who fell into the hands of the robbers?"[23]—not "Who was the person who was helped?" The obvious answer to Jesus' question was "The one who showed him mercy":[24] the lawyer chose not to use the word "Samaritan." Jesus then tells the lawyer to "go and do likewise":[25] that is, to take the hated Samaritan as his example, and to do as he did. And not only that: As the lawyer went away, he might have asked why Jesus had not answered his question, and might then have realized that he had: the "neighbor" was the Samaritan: so it was the Samaritan whom he needed to "love."

What Jesus had done in this parable was to turn "neighbor" into an active concept rather than a passive one. "Neighbor" is not something that someone is to me: it is something that we do. The concept has become a verb: "I neighbor . . ." Jesus neighbored, so those of us who follow him will neighbor as he did, and as the Samaritan did.

If Jesus is our God, then we shall do as God did, as God does, and as God will do. To undertake a task with someone is to know them, and to proclaim and enact the City of God along with Jesus will be to know him. This will never be simple, for we cannot be certain of his words, actions, or character—although there is only a difference of degree between the knowing of Jesus and the knowing of our closest companions; and we live in a different culture and thus cannot say and do as he did, for the same patterns of action, if carried out, would have different effects, and therefore would not be the same patterns of action; and the same words, if they could be said, would be received differently and therefore would not be the same words.

---

20. Luke 10:30–37.
21. Luke 10:27, NRSV: *Agapéseis . . . ton plésion sou hōs seauton.*
22. Luke 10:29, NRSV: *Kai tis estin mou plésion?*
23. Luke 10:36, NRSV: *tis toutōn tōn triōn plésion dokei soi gegonenai tou empesontos eis tous lystas.*
24. Luke 10:37, NRSV: *Ho poiésas to eleos met' autou.*
25. Luke 10:37, NRSV: *Poreuou kai su poiei homoiōs.*

In any case, we might not agree with Jesus. He argued with his God and with his age's concepts of God; and we are thus his followers if we argue with our God, Jesus, and if we dispute over different interpretations of his words and actions. We are Christians in the midst of our most fundamental disagreements over what Jesus believed. However, we shall attempt to have a similar effect in our day to the one that he had in his. We shall heal with him, tell stories with him, gather groups with him, and pray with him. We shall hope with him, and we shall begin to take on his character, the character of the City of God. With Jesus, we shall exercise freedom in relation to the law, constantly asking whether the law (be it religious tradition, moral consensus, canon law, or statute law) oppresses or liberates. And we shall be particularly careful in relation to so-called economic laws because what seems to offer freedom to individuals can enable the oppression of large groups of people. With Jesus we shall prophesy on the basis of the City that is to come, and with Jesus we shall declare all institutions to be provisional, and we shall confront every authority with radical alternatives. With Jesus, we shall repent—change our minds—and we shall seek symbols of that repentance; though these symbols might not be baptism, which to him was an expression of new commitment to doing God's will, and for us ought to be a sacrament of grace.

It is not so much belief that is required—although it is—but action. As Jesus formed a model of the City of God out of his disciples, so the Church and every human institution must be made into such models. As Jesus went to the most dangerous places and wept over the failure of the city to embody the City of God,[26] so we must go to the places where decisions and action are hardest, and we must weep, and then undertake risky activity. We, like Jesus, must provoke reaction, and we are under judgement if we do not. We must provoke reaction in the Church as well, and here responsible disobedience will be an expression of love for the institution, and acquiescence will be a failure of love.

It is not so much belief that is required (for Jesus' beliefs were sometimes wrong, and always closely related to the social and religious conditions of his time); it is actions that are needed. Actions "travel" more easily between one culture and another. The difficulty over our doing Jesus' actions is not so much the cultural gap, but the fact that we do not wish to do them. It is much easier to believe things that Jesus believed: but it might also be wrong to do so, wrong because such beliefs do not, in our cultural context, point towards the City of God.

---

26. Luke 13:31–35.

Trust is a different matter, for trust is about action, and is what is often meant by the New Testament Greek word *pistis* that is often translated as "faith."[27] Trusting and hoping are related to action and are to be practiced by Jesus' followers. To call Jesus our God is to place our trust in him, which is the basic predisposition that leads to specific actions based on his changing patterns of action.

Patterns of action are what form the steps of the dance of time, and history is a complex of discreet and related patterns of action in which nothing is stable and in which all is in process, and there is no identifiable stable process but only changing patterns of action. We follow Jesus as we undertake the task with him in the midst of this constantly shifting history: knowing the outcast, healing the sick, telling stories of the City of God, sharing a meal with friends, expressing anger, weeping with the bereaved, and weeping over the city. This is the way to follow Jesus, and the way to know him, for to follow and to know are one and the same.

All this must be done by us as individuals; and it must be done by the many corporate bodies to which we belong: by our residential communities, our workplaces, the organizations to which we belong, and our churches: for the City of God is a corporate reality, and our actions must be corporate, just as those of Jesus and his disciples were. If we follow Jesus, then we shall be willing to lose our individual selves in order to find our corporate selves and the City of God. Jesus will be our authority in our economics and in our politics, as well as in our individual moral dilemmas; and the Church as a body, even at the risk of being wrong, must dare to act as a corporate body: must act to change our society in the direction of the City of God.

Our following must have about it a global dimension, and not just a local one. The whole created order, and the whole human race, must be the domain of our action in relation to Jesus' action. We shall undertake our action in changing patterns on a small scale, among the groups to which we belong: but we must keep half an eye on the wider horizon, for "here we have no lasting city, but we are looking for the city that is to come."[28]

In every aspect of our life in which Jesus is one of us, we shall follow him. We shall be born, we shall teach, we shall heal, and we shall be free in relation to the law. We shall accept and reconcile; we shall die with him, and we shall rise with him—our activity will create new activity, and we shall be transformed and reborn in ways that we cannot now imagine. We shall argue with him, and we shall know that in no action can we truly follow him, for the City of God is not yet.

27. Matthew 9:22, NRSV.
28. Hebrews 13:14.

Thus a circle is inaugurated, Jesus being one of us, and us following Jesus; or perhaps it is best to view it as a spiral, for it has a direction: the City of God. In particular, we follow Jesus by losing ourselves for the sake of the City of God,[29] and—for we cannot help it—we follow him into death, as individuals and as a human race. Jesus invites us to go with him into death, hoping for the City of God. This we shall be more reluctant to do: but there have been many martyrs, and there will be more. In whatever way death comes to us we shall be following Jesus into it, and we shall know that he is there, that our God is dead, whatever else God might be. Jesus invites us to go now into losing our lives, for that is the only way to find them. We must go with him through betrayal and to the trial, and we must experience injustice; we must go with him into Gethsemane, and experience our whole society's confusion and despair, and the abyss of meaninglessness that has descended on a culture that has lost its metaphysics: and we must consciously join the rest of the world on Golgotha, and experience abandonment, even by the human God whom we thought that we had begun to know and to follow.

We shall then follow Jesus into a risen life: but this is not in our hands; and the world will follow Jesus into risen life, and that is not in our hands either. What such raising to new life might mean must be the object of a complete agnosticism; and, in any case, concern with an individual resurrection might or might not be to follow Jesus, for he did not seem to be so concerned, and to be overconcerned with our own resurrection is not to follow his constant demand that we must be prepared to lose our lives.[30]

If we are to do Christianly then we shall want to move the world towards the City of God, and we might have some temporary but obviously changing understandings of what we might be able to do to achieve that: but in a context composed entirely of changing patterns of action, creating the change that we intend is always going to be difficult, if not impossible. As Clemens Sedmak suggests, prerequisites will be an "understanding of the overall ontological order . . . understanding of motion that transforms A into B . . . a clear vision together with a flexible plan . . . a strong personal commitment."[31]

Because everything about society is changing patterns of action, we need to understand society in that way if we are to change it. So, for instance, instead of understanding poverty as a state, we need to understand it as changing patterns of action, and release from poverty not as another

---

29. Mark 8:34–38.
30. Matthew 16:26.
31. Sedmak, "The Logic of Change," 35.

state, but as different changing patterns of action. With such an understanding, poverty is the patterns of action that prevent a family from climbing out of social disadvantage and into social advantage;[32] and release from poverty becomes new patterns of action that enable families to climb out of social disadvantage and into social advantage. It will always be patterns of action. Our taking action in the world is patterns of action; our reflection on that activity is patterns of action; and then there will be yet more patterns of action in the world, and so on. For that is what God does, and it is what God is; it is what Jesus does, and it is what Jesus did and does; and it is what we do, and what we are.

But how are we to bind together our action in changing patterns, our changing society, and Jesus the grace of God? The practical translation of that question becomes: What social policies will enable our society to move towards the City of God, to change constantly, and to reflect the centrality of unconditional gift that we find in Jesus and in the Christian tradition?

We might take an example from the Hebrew Scriptures. At the heart of Israel's relationship with God is a covenant: a bond of mutual commitment, the details of which have been worked out afresh in each generation. The Law gives substance to this relationship. And so, for instance, every fifty years the land has to be returned to its original occupants.[33] This generates patterned change; it reduces land monopoly, thus increasing the diversity and therefore the efficiency of farming methods; and it reduces inequality, thus increasing economic efficiency.[34] There is almost no talk of rights in the Hebrew Scriptures,[35] but there is plenty about mutual responsibility: of the individual to society, of society to the individual, of the individual and of society to God, and of God to the individual and to society.

Jesus' Kingdom of God would see an end to poverty, and the feasting and the healing were acted parables of his expectation. He condemned wealth not as evil in itself, but as a potential hindrance to making radical decisions and to hearing God's promise of a new order;[36] and, in particular, the carrier of the good news was told to travel light for the sake of the Kingdom, for the Kingdom's coming places a question-mark against everything in this present age. No social grouping was deified by Jesus. He was ambivalent towards his own family, called on his followers to "hate" their natural

---

32. Lister, *Poverty*, 4–7, 145–46, 178–83; Dean and Platt, *Social Advantage and Disadvantage*.

33. Leviticus 25.

34. Lipsey and Chrystal, *Economics*, 413; Desai and Palermo, "Some Effects of Basic Income on Economic Variables."

35. Proverbs 31:5, 8–9.

36. Mealand, *Poverty and Expectation in the Gospels*.

families,[37] and in general did not regard the family as an absolute commitment. Allegiance to a coming community must not be compromised by allegiance to a social unit of the present age.[38]

Jesus told a parable in which those who worked in the vineyard for only an hour were paid the same as those who had worked all day: the point being that God's generosity has nothing to do with how hard we have worked or how religious we are. The movement that emerged after the first Easter Day was constituted largely by the poor, who were attracted by the promise of a Kingdom in which there would be no more poverty. Jesus' teachings and the circumstances of these first Christians reinforced each other,[39] and the seeds were sown of a servant Church offering to the world a vision of a new kind of community in which all boundaries between different groups of people would be abolished.[40] Christian history has tended to lose this early emphasis on the corporate nature of the Church and of the social order,[41] but there have always been Christians intent on bringing Christian faith to bear on the society of their day.

During the last century William Temple was notorious for his forays into social policy: often very public, sometimes naïve, but always evidence of a concern to bring the Christian tradition to bear on God's world. He insisted that every human institution, including democracy, must be grounded in Christian principles, and that no area of human life is outside the Church's concerns. Economic questions are as important to the Christian as are those of personal morality, and economic laws—including that of supply and demand—are as susceptible to a Christian's criticism as are society's other ethical norms. Temple offered a list of Christian social principles as a contribution to social policy: the sacredness of personality; fellow-membership; the duty of service; the power of sacrifice.[42] We might wish to add unconditional gift, diversity, and social change. Whether we agree with Temple's list or not,[43] I do not see how we can escape our responsibility

---

37. Mark 3:31–35; Luke 14:26. The Greek *misei* should be translated "he/she hates."

38. Matthew 12:46–50; Luke 14:26.

39. Matthew 20:1–16; Theissen, *The First Followers of Jesus*. I doubt whether Jesus had a Basic Income—an unconditional income for every individual—in mind when he told this parable, but it remains a parable that inspires those of us who argue for a tax and benefits system that might better reflect the character of God's grace.

40. Galatians 3:28.

41. Dowley, *Towards the Recovery of a Lost Bequest*.

42. Temple, *Personal Religion and the Life of Fellowship*, 59–68; *Christianity and Social Order*.

43. On "middle axioms" see Temple, *The Archbishop of York's Conference*, 15. On the history of Christian social thought in this country between the wars, see Oliver,

to shape a society that shares something of the character of the Kingdom of God. The Church must always be society's conscience, and occasionally its humble judge if that fails; and the Church is likely to be guided by such insights as the following:

- The world is God's. The wealth of the created order is freely given, to be gratefully received, and treasured.
- We are co-creators with God. Wealth is earned as well as given.
- Every individual is precious, and ought to be brought to a responsible maturity in which he or she can express their God-given capacity to create and to share their freedom.
- We are all equally loved and valued by God, we are equally his children, we are equally citizens of God's world, and we are equally recipients of the promise of the Kingdom of God.
- Human society is precious, and ought to be brought to a responsible maturity in which its members find both security and freedom and a sense of belonging to one another.
- In society there ought to be variety without division, freedom without anarchy, and order without oppression.

Any such list is bound to be contentious, but whatever list or definition we provisionally choose, we must ensure that the Church's life reflects in some way the character of the Kingdom of God that is coming, a Kingdom characterized by grace, and a Kingdom constituted by action in changing patterns: so the list of "principles" will constantly change.

William Temple, William Beveridge, and R.H. Tawney, were friends, and some such principles as those that Temple enunciated lay behind the Beveridge Report of 1942 which stated that "a revolutionary moment in the world's history is a time for revolutions, not for patching."[44] Both the plan and its implementation were in fact more of a patching up than a revolution, as have been all of the changes made since then to the UK's tax and benefits system. Unfortunately, society and the economy have changed immeasurably during the past eighty years, so it really is now time for a revolution. Given that social and economic change is unlikely to be slow in the near future, what is required is not a tax and benefits system that fits the current

---

The Church and Social Order. The Church of England's report, The Archbishop of Canterbury's Commission on Urban Priority Areas, *Faith in the City*, makes specific policy recommendations. For more recent reflection, see Brown et al., *Anglican Social Theology*.

44. Beveridge, *Social Insurance and Allied Services*, 6.

situation, but one that will fit any conceivable future configuration of the economy and of society. This suggests that the foundation level of the structure needs to be radically simple, which in turn suggests an unconditional income for every individual: a Basic Income.[45] Basic Income would be an activity of pure gift, unconditional, nonwithdrawable, and automatic. And it would contribute towards the creation of a society in which grace could more easily be exercised. People would have greater choice over their work patterns; and mixtures of employment, leisure, voluntary work, and "own-work" would develop more according to individual preferences than is possible today: they would be what people wanted to offer, and would therefore have more the character of grace than do people's current work patterns, which are often rigidly constrained by our tax and benefits structures and by employer demands. Similarly, people would form relationships and families because that is what they chose to do, and not because the tax and benefit rules forced them into particular rigid patterns of action; and they would no longer be prevented from forming relationships and families by regulations that made it advantageous to live apart. Families might sometimes break up because that is what people sometimes choose to do: and they would be able to do it because each individual would have greater economic and social freedom to change their patterns of action. All of this would reflect the Christian insights listed above, and it would give to everyone an income as an unconditional gift, and so would reflect in the economic sphere the grace of God in the theological.[46]

Jesus said, "You received without payment; give without payment."[47] If we ourselves are to be followers of Jesus, and we are to model the Kingdom of God in our own time, then our own actions must be of the character of a free gift: of grace. Other ethical values—such as William Temple's—might have their place: but the world changes, we change, and God changes, and the Kingdom of God is action in changing patterns: so no set of ethical values can be of permanent applicability. Seeking God's Kingdom and responding to its coming require constant initiative and risk, and it can all feel rather tiring, so I sympathize with Jesus' early followers, whose bewilderment and plain spiritual exhaustion are perfectly comprehensible. We might sometimes need temporary moral values to fall back on because they can save us from inventing new responses in every new situation in which the Kingdom of God demands our attention: but we must be aware that any "values" will always be second best. The gift of the Kingdom will always demand a

---

45. Torry, *Why we Need a Citizen's Basic Income*.
46. Torry, *Citizen's Basic Income*, 22–30.
47. Matthew 10:8.

constantly new giving: the changing patterns of action will change, and our response must be active and diverse and characterized by grace.

If, as we have suggested, Jesus' Kingdom of God must today be the City of God, and if we are to do Christianly, then we shall seek to change the cities in which we live into signposts towards the City of God. Choosing a Christian society will be our responsibility, and the character of that society will be grace. Jesus regarded the Kingdom of God as a gift; forgiveness and healing always came as free gifts; and if we are to create a Christian society, then that giving must be fundamental to every aspect of it.

There will always be possibilities open to us. The laws of economics might sometimes look like fixed givens, but they are not: they are human artefacts, and we can change them. We can change the ways in which institutions relate to each other; we can change our legal system; we can write for ourselves a new constitution; we can decide to decentralize some functions of government and to have others co-ordinated with other countries. It is up to us to choose. We can decide how information and money will behave, for they are both human inventions, and it is our responsibility to control them. We can decide how social policy should be constructed, and we can extend the "gift" characteristic of the UK's National Health Service and of its unconditional Child Benefit to other policy fields and to a Basic Income, an unconditional income for every individual.

Both individually and together, the task of the Christian, to whom much has been given, is to give much.[48] Whether we are deciding on an issue of personal ethics, or trying to transform our communities into something closer to the City of God, the task is to seek grace, ever greater diversity, constant openness to new changing patterns of action, and, above all, to create signposts towards Jesus' Kingdom of God. This is not a matter of principles or values, but of receiving and giving. What is required is constantly new enquiry into the character today of the risen Christ, and of the Kingdom of God, and an accompanying constant new choosing of what our own actions in changing patterns should become. It is the risen Christ and the Kingdom of God that must shape our own action in changing patterns, so that we come closer to the life of the Kingdom of God ourselves, and so that we can shape our society so that it becomes a sign of hope for the coming of God's Kingdom.

---

48. Luke 12:48.

Chapter 13

An Actological Bible

Thesis: The Bible is a crystallization of action in changing patterns that changes the action in changing patterns that constitutes who we are.

INTRODUCTION

The Bible is a text like any other text. It crystallizes the patterns of action of its writers, and the patterns of action that they and others experienced. As we read the text, which is signs, and therefore pure pattern, it contributes to the patterning of our own changing patterns of action. We are changed, by the text, by the changing patterns of actions of its authors, and by the changing patterns of action that patterned the activity of their writing. And so our patterns of action are changed by God's history with Israel, by Jesus, by the Apostles, and by the Holy Spirit: all action in patterns enmeshed with all of the many changing patterns of action that impinged on the writers' actions as they wrote the Bible's text.

READING THE BIBLE

We shall never untangle all of that. And neither shall we escape from the constant changing of the meanings of the text's words. The patterns that form our language, and that form its connections with everything else, constantly change, from time to time, and from place to place: and the same person reading the text in different circumstances will understand the text differently. It will always be our interpretation of the text, even if we read it alongside some interpretative person, text, or institution, that we might regard as authoritative. And this is how it should be for Christians. Jesus ransacked his Bible, our Old Testament, for material to enable him to proclaim the Kingdom of God's coming, not much caring what the material's context was, nor what it originally meant, nor how accurately he was quoting it.[1] The Bible was a tool to be used, not a law to be kept, or a book to be preserved from new interpretation. There were no absolutes, everything being relative to the coming Kingdom of God. The Kingdom of God was action in changing patterns, so that is how the Bible was to be treated: as action in changing patterns, with the text providing a pattern to be changed, and giving access to the action in patterns that gave birth to it, with the interpreter providing new action in changing patterns that developed the pattern to be found in the text and that communicated the action in patterns that gave birth to the text, all in the context of a long history of interpretation—of action in changing patterns—from the moment the text was written to the contemporary interpreter connecting the pattern of the text and the action in changing patterns of the interpretative tradition with the action in changing patterns of their own day and their own mind.

So does it matter whether the words recorded in the gospels were spoken by Jesus, or were mistakenly attributed to him, or were written as if the gospels were historical novels designed to represent how the gospel-writers evaluated Jesus and his message? Does it matter whether the events recorded at the ends of the four gospels happened, rather than being stories told by early Christians to represent their experience of Jesus' continuing presence with them? Does it matter whether Jesus had a virgin mother?

The question is irrelevant because we simply cannot know the combination of changing patterns of action that gave birth to the gospels: so we cannot know whether Mary was a virgin when Jesus was born,[2] whether Jesus ate fish after his death,[3] or whether Jesus spoke the words in the fourth gospel or the interpretation of the parable of the sower in the fourth chapter of Mark's Gospel. We might have our views on these things: but the patterns of action themselves are entirely lost to us.

What we do have is the text, hundreds of years of its interpretation, and the collaborative interpretative activity of the Church today. This is enough to be getting along with. As we read, as we study, and as we discuss, our patterns of action will be changed by the patterns of action that gave birth to the New Testament and to its interpretation across the centuries. So

---

1. Luke 4:18-30; Matthew 22:44.
2. Luke 1:34.
3. Luke 24:43.

we are in fact able to go right back to the very birth of the Christian Faith: to Jesus' birth, to Jesus life and teaching, to Jesus' death, to Jesus' resurrection: not in the sense that we can climb into a time machine and find out the detail of what happened when, but in the sense that all of that continues to pattern our changing patterns of action today.

To read the Bible is to do archaeology. We mine the text with our questions (known and unknown), and the "fossil record" that we call the Bible speaks to us and to our actions. We are moved by the gospel writers' actions crystallized in the text: and so we receive revelation. And the more different methods that we use to mine the text, the more we shall receive from it. Across the history of interpretation analogical interpretation, allegorical interpretation, redaction criticism (a study of the gospel-writers' editing tactics), form criticism (a study of literary forms), and other methods, have constantly thrown new light on the text.

We find plenty of ambiguity in the Bible: for instance, at the beginning of John's Gospel we find that the Word of God is both God and with God; and by "Do not think that I have come to abolish the law or the prophets; I have come not to abolish but to fulfil," did Jesus mean that he was giving a new law that would supersede the old, or that he had come to keep the Torah, the Jewish Law?[4] And by "Son of Man" did Jesus mean the heavenly figure who would rule in God's Kingdom?

> As I watched in the night visions,
> I saw one like a Son of Man
>   coming with the clouds of heaven.
> And he came to the Ancient One
>   and was presented before him.
> To him was given dominion
>   and glory and kingship,
> that all peoples, nations, and languages
>   should serve him;[5]

or did he simply mean himself?

> Then he began to teach them that the Son of Man must undergo great suffering, and be rejected by the elders, the chief priests, and the scribes, and be killed, and after three days rise again;[6]

---

4. John 1:1; Matthew 5:17; Torry, "Two Kinds of Ambiguity."

5. Daniel 7:13–14, NRSV, altered. The NRSV translation has "one like a human being," whereas the original Hebrew has "one like a Son of Man."

6. Mark 8:31, NRSV.

or did he employ ambiguity to force his hearers to make their own decisions as to whether he was the Son of Man who would rule in God's Kingdom?[7]

Do we need to "solve" any of this in any kind of final way? No. Ambiguity might be the right language to use—although it is probably better when we know that it is ambiguous. As the apostles discovered when asked to adjudicate complex issues relating to the relationship between Jews and Gentiles in the Church,[8] we can't get it right, but we have to say something, even if it isn't right. Our language is simply not adequate to the mystery of God: which is why language is often so ambiguous in relation to the most important doctrinal questions. To say or write ambiguous things is an important pattern of action, and it can be entirely appropriate. It communicates what unambiguous language could never communicate.

What matters is to read, to be changed by what we read, and to know that within the changing patterns of action in which our own patterns of action are gradually enmeshed, we meet God: for God is Action itself, and thus the source of all of the patterns of action that we encounter; God has lived a human life in Jesus, and Jesus' changing patterns of action give birth to the Kingdom of God and to the Church, within which we live, and within which we come to know the risen Christ. God, by the Holy Spirit, continues to relate the changing patterns of action that God chooses to be to the changing patterns of action that constitute ourselves, the Church, and the world; and we find in the text of the Bible a crystallization of the authors' patterns of action, and therefore of the changing patterns of action that are God living a human life in Jesus.

But there is always a risk to be taken, because revelation is always a command inviting our response. Just as we have chosen Jesus as our God, and just as we have chosen what interpretation of him to go with, so we must choose from among the literature that makes up the Church's Bible, and we must choose what to make of it, and then to act accordingly.

The Bible is a human record of human history and human opinion, and in dialogue with this record we shall create our own God and our own Church in the same way that the early Christians created their Trinitarian God and their Church. Just as they plundered their Bible, our Old Testament, for material to use and to interpret as they tried to understand what Jesus meant to them, so we must plunder the Old and New Testaments for material to enable us to worship and to follow Jesus. Just as they were selective, so we must be selective; and just as they discarded a great deal, so must we.

7. Torry, "Two Kinds of Ambiguity."
8. Acts 15:1–35.

To take an example: The genealogies at the beginnings of Matthew's Gospel and Luke's Gospel suggest that some early Christians believed Joseph to be Jesus' father,[9] and neither Mark's Gospel nor Paul's letters seem to know anything about a virgin birth. So what are we to do with the virgin birth stories contained in Matthew's and Luke's Gospels?[10] We can ignore them, or we can believe them, or we can positively decide that they are totally unhelpful, because in order to be one of us Jesus must have had an ordinary birth. I choose this latter course, while at the same time recognizing that it is not impossible that a virgin birth occurred, that God might have had a purpose in it being like that, and also that the narratives performed an original useful purpose as parables of Jesus being God's son.

Similarly, what are we do with the miracle stories? To understand why the early Christians retained the healing miracles and the feeding of the five thousand[11] is simple: because here were events that prefigured the Kingdom of God. It is possible that events like those recorded occurred, and if they did then Jesus would have intended them to be active parables, events that would enable his hearers to experience in their own time the Kingdom of God that was about to come in its fullness. We should not discard these stories but should retain them and continue to wonder what kind of events gave birth to this literature, for we have nothing modern with which to compare such stories and must therefore not be too quick to decide how they came to birth.

Similarly, the resurrection narratives—of the appearances and the empty tomb—are difficult to identify with because again we have no modern equivalents with which to compare them. We shall not discard them, but rather we shall choose which stories to take the most seriously—perhaps the shorter ending of Mark's Gospel as best conveying the terror of the life-changing event: but still the whole corpus of material must be pondered. The stories are only comprehensible in the context of the Jews' hope for the resurrection of the dead at the beginning of the new age. The disciples believed Jesus to be already risen, and their experiences confirmed them in this view. A conservative attitude towards the text is as rational as one that regards them as myths conveying a spiritual meaning—a concept that might not have been amenable to early Christians: but, as always, the choice as to how to interpret the stories is ours to make, and we shall best create a Church that reflects the character of the City of God if we retain an evolving diversity of interpretation.

9. Matthew 1:1–17; Luke 3:23–38.
10. Luke 1:26–38; Matthew 1:18–25.
11. Mark 2:1–12; Mark 6:30–44.

In the same way, decisions have to be made about Jesus' sayings in the gospels. Did he say those words? For instance, we might take a conservative attitude towards the material in the first three gospels, and regard the fourth gospel as a meditation on the meaning of Jesus by an unknown writer for an unknown Christian community: but other quite legitimate decisions could be made. And whatever decision we make about this, we can choose to employ fourth gospel material in our own portrayals of Jesus, or we can choose not to do so. This decision will largely depend on whether the reader believes that the fourth gospel sayings reflect what we understand from the first three gospels to have been Jesus' understanding of his mission and identity.

The letters in the New Testament are precisely that: letters; and we must take from them what we find helpful and interpret it for ourselves. And so, for instance, Paul quotes from a hymn in his letter to the Philippians,[12] and we might choose to interpret it as we did in Chapter 7. Each of us must choose our own interpretation of this passage, just as we must choose what interpretation to give to any biblical passage: and it might be, in this case as in others, that what at first seems like a radical departure from conservative interpretations is in fact nearer to the writer's original meaning than we might at first have imagined.

We might choose not only to abandon certain texts, but also to abandon some of those concepts that have appeared to Christians in the past to be essential to a Christian faith based on the Bible. One such concept is "faith." Paul says that we are "justified by faith,"[13] and that Abraham's faith was "reckoned to him as righteousness."[14] Has not Paul here replaced the old law by a new law? What of those who have no faith? What are we to say to the notion that faith leads to righteousness if Jesus regarded the Kingdom of God as a gift that elicited repentance and righteousness? Hasn't Paul got it the wrong way round? Hasn't he turned faith into a work? If we believe that he has, and that his Good News is not good news and is inconsistent with Jesus' Good News, then we might decide to abandon "faith" and replace it with "grace"[15]—a concept that Paul employs—and decide that the central concept of the Good News is "grace," that is, God's generous and unconditional giving, and that any attempt to gain God's favor, whether by works of the law or by faith, has no part to play in the gospel of Jesus.

---

12. Philippians 2:5–11.
13. Galatians 2:16; Romans 5:1, NRSV.
14. Galatians 3:6, NRSV.
15. Romans 3:24, NRSV.

Sometimes it will be the precise form of the biblical text that we shall have to choose before we get anywhere near to interpreting it. For instance: some manuscripts of the first verse of Mark's Gospel call Jesus "Son of God," and some do not. It is up to us whether we believe it to be more likely that this was in the original and that later scribes omitted it, or whether we believe that later scribes added it: or perhaps that the original text contained something entirely different—for instance, "God"—and that some scribes decided to omit that, and some changed it to "Son of God."

As for whole books that we decide to omit: it is possible to regard the Book of Revelation as incomprehensible and dangerous; and as it was the last book to make its way into the New Testament canon we might regard it as only ambiguously a member of it and therefore of less authority than other New Testament books: but we might also decide to take the book seriously, for it reflects an apocalyptic outlook not dissimilar to that of Jesus, and it might offer to us insights into Jesus' character—as the similarly apocalyptic chapter 13 in Mark's Gospel might—which are not to be discovered in other parts of the New Testament: but again, after each of us has sifted the evidence, and listened to others' opinions, what we do with the Book of Revelation is up to us.

Christians have always chosen how to use the New Testament and how to interpret it, and all we are asking here is that this process should be made conscious and deliberate. In the same way that we choose Jesus as our God, we must also choose which passages to use and how to use them: and the two choices will of course be connected with each other. The result will be action in changing patterns: a changing diversity of choices and interpretations, and never a settled consensus.

The Old Testament is in some ways as important as the New, for it is a collection of literature that Jesus knew and that early Christians knew, so study of it enables us to come to some understanding of their theology. Again, we must select what we find useful—as in fact Christians have always done. The songs in Isaiah about the servant of God[16] certainly affected the early Christians' view of Jesus, and might have influenced Jesus' own self-understanding; and many other passages are important background material for anyone trying to understand how Jesus might have thought about himself and his mission.[17] However, a great deal needs to be discarded, especially large parts of the historical books, unless we wish to keep them as a warning against the dangers inherent in tribal gods.

---

16. For instance, Isaiah 42:1–9; Isaiah 52:13–53:12
17. For instance, Psalms 2, 22.

In no sense is the Old Testament "the word of God," and in the New Testament only those words spoken by Jesus can in any sense be given that label, for we have chosen as our God Jesus of Nazareth, and there is no other God whose word the Bible can be. The books are witnesses to historical events and to other people's opinions, and they are of enormous value, but they are never to be given a status alongside that of Jesus himself, and certainly not one higher than his. So as with the New Testament, so with the Old, we must be prepared to discard some of the central concepts that give large parts of the literature their coherence; and, just as "faith" might need to be excised from Paul's theology—except as Jesus' faith in us,[18] and as the means that Paul employed to unite Jews and Gentiles in the one Church—so must "sacrifice" be excised from the Old Testament's theology and also from the theology of the New Testament. In particular, the story of Abraham taking his son Isaac up a mountain to sacrifice him has to be subjected to a radical critique,[19] for in its present form it is inhuman. No doubt in its original context it was virtuous propaganda, suggesting to the Israelites that God did not in fact require the sacrifice of children as the gods of surrounding nations did, and that an animal would do instead, for in the story God tells Abraham not to kill Isaac, and it is God who provides the ram for a sacrifice: but out of that context the story makes it look as if God approves of child slaughter, for did he not tell Abraham to sacrifice his son in the first place and only decided to stop the execution at the last minute? If there is any basis in history for this story, then the trauma inflicted on Isaac is unimaginable. The problem is compounded by the references to the story in the New Testament, in which Abraham's willingness to kill his son is applauded as a sign of his faith in God.[20] Not only is this story immoral, but the whole concept of sacrifice is morally ambiguous. It might be that under some circumstances it could be righteous to offer oneself in the place of another, but for someone to offer someone else, as Abraham offered Isaac, is beyond offensive. In the letter to the Hebrews, Jesus' death is likened to the offering of the Old Testament animal sacrifices,[21] and on such passages as these, and on the story of the killing by the vineyard tenants of the son sent by the owner to collect the rent,[22] has been constructed a theology of sacrifice that envisages God the Father offering his Son Jesus as a sacrifice so that we sinners might be forgiven our sins. To say that the idea is morally

---

18. Hooker, *From Adam to Christ*, 168.
19. Genesis 22:1–19.
20. Hebrews 11:17–19.
21. Hebrews 7:26–28.
22. Matthew 21:33–41.

obnoxious is to put it mildly. There is no need to continue to grapple with such ideas, nor to attempt to make them more palatable; they might have to be discarded and positively disowned. The only sacrifice that we can allow is self-sacrifice, and to speak of Jesus being prepared to sacrifice himself for the sake of the Kingdom of God's coming might be a legitimate description of his state of mind as he approached Jerusalem, and he might at that point have alluded to the song of the suffering servant in the book of the prophet Isaiah[23] when he said that "the Son of Man came not to be served but to serve, and to give his life a ransom for many,"[24] if he did say that;[25] but to speak of Jesus being sacrificed by another God is morally reprehensible. The biblical concept of sacrifice is an idea that might be largely responsible for the notion that young men "sacrificed themselves" by the million during the First and Second World Wars when in fact they were sent to their deaths by governments and armaments manufacturers. To be rid of the concept of sacrifice altogether might offer more long-term gains than attempting to keep and reinterpret it.

Having agreed that we are responsible for what we select and how we interpret it, let us not be too hasty to ignore passages simply because they are difficult. For instance: Jesus told a story about an unjust steward about to be dismissed who adjusted his master's debtors' bills downwards in order to make friends with them, and was commended by his master for his good sense.[26] What are we to make of this? It might be a parable telling us to prepare for the Kingdom of God's coming; or it might be a statement about the unimportance of the things of this world in comparison to those of the next. It could also be comedy, for reflection on the story reveals that every participant ends up morally compromised: the steward because he falsified the bills; the debtors because they participated in the fraud; and the master because he approved of it. Jesus' hearers would have listened and identified themselves with the master or the debtors, and would then have perceived their own morally ambiguous positions. There will be no end to the disputes about the meaning of this passage, which is why it is important to take it seriously and to invent our own interpretations of it.

Similarly, even if we jettison the virgin birth, the myths related to Jesus' birth should not be discarded, because here "myth" means a narrative conveying important truth that more literal accounts are unable to convey.

---

23. Isaiah 52:13—53:12.

24. Mark 10:45, NRSV.

25. The sentence does not appear in Luke's Gospel in the context in which it appears in Mark's and Matthew's Gospels, so it is possible that it is a Christian commentary on the meaning of Jesus' death rather than words of Jesus.

26. Luke 16:1–13.

For instance: the magi (often called "wise men" or "kings") from the East[27] were astrologers who offered to Jesus the tools of their trade after failing to discover him among the powerful of this world. Their gifts are the storyteller's way of saying that all wealth and spiritual power, and even death itself, are subject to Jesus' authority; and the magis' failure to return to Herod as he had told them to do is a way of saying that all human institutions and authorities are now relativized by this one child who is now our primary authority. If we seek a Biblical passage to encapsulate in story form our decision to choose Jesus as our God, then this could be it, for the magi (Gentiles) and the shepherds[28] (Jews) worshipped Jesus as their God, and the magi declared him to be their authority and to be more important to them than their wealth, their power, and their lives, and a more important authority than secular rulers. This was their choice: they chose to follow the star. In the same way, we choose to worship Jesus as our God, a human person like ourselves, and we offer to him our wealth, our power, and our very lives, and in his presence we know that never again can any secular power claim our absolute allegiance. We, like the magi, can choose to worship the child who went on to live a life like ours and to die between two criminals.[29]

The choosing among the literature of the Old and New Testaments that I am recommending, and our choosing of our own interpretations of it—better done as we converse with others about their choosing and their interpretations, for our religion is not a private affair—are a matter of simple honesty, for theology has always been a matter of choosing between options. Either we make our own choices, or we accept other people's, and it is better to make our own. We make our choices subconsciously or consciously, and it is better to make them consciously. Is it not better to be explicit about the most fundamental choices than to pretend that the foundations of our faith are somehow imposed in ways that we find it impossible to define or justify?

There are parts of the Old Testament that not even the most rigid fundamentalist takes any notice of, and few now make practical use of the passages about hell in the Old and New Testaments even if they say that they believe them in some literal way. All we are doing here is making conscious this process of selection and interpretation undertaken by every Christian, and we are taking upon ourselves the responsibility for choosing, both individually and together, which parts of the Old and New Testaments we are going to employ in order to create out of the hope that we have placed in Jesus a hope for the coming City of God: for out of the material offered by

---

27. Matthew 2:1–12.
28. Luke 2:8–20.
29. Mark 15:27.

the Bible we must construct a hope, a religion, an ethic, and a social justice, and it is up to us to decide how that should be done.

One way to read the Bible that might cohere well with the actological conceptual framework that we have developed might be to act it: to perform the stories, as we might do when we put on a passion play, or when we perform *Joseph and the Amazing Technicolor Dreamcoat*, or when during Holy Week we perform the liturgy that carries us through the actions of Jesus' triumphal entry into Jerusalem, his trial, his suffering, and his death. When we do these things, the text functions as a play: the changing patterns of action of those events are distilled into the text, and the text then repatterns our own changing patterns of action so that the events happen again in our midst: not as they did then, but as a changing pattern of action with a family likeness to the events of two thousand years ago. Or we can do this without putting on a play. We can become the characters in our own minds as we read the text or have it read to us: and by this means we come to know the people and the events that inspired the Bible's writers and that shaped the Bible's text. All of it is action in changing patterns: the original events; the transmission of oral tradition; the writing of the biblical books; and our reading of those books. The Bible demands an actological reading.

Chapter 14

An actology of religions

Thesis: An actology might be a more appropriate conceptual framework than an ontology for an exploration of relationships between different faiths.

INTRODUCTION

Our conceptual framework, characterized as it is both by action and patterns, can provide us with a useful way to understand the relationships between different religions: and if that were all that it could ever do then it would be worth developing it for that reason alone. John Drane has described our basic presupposition as "I move, therefore I am":[1] and those movements are in relatively predictable patterns that define our identity. Wherever action is not absolutely chaotic, there is a patterned action, the patterns change, there is pattern in the changing, and we arrive at a conceptual framework of layers of patterns of action: perhaps of "action and patterns" as much as of "action in patterns." In this context, God is the "still point,"[2] God is Action itself, and God is the creative source of changing patterns of action. This is a process theology that connects the "primordial" and "consequent" poles of Whitehead's God,[3] and it is the kind of theology that David Ray Griffin has evolved around the notion of "creativity"[4]—which, following Alfred North

---

1. Drane, *The McDonaldization of the Church*, 101.
2. Eliot, *Four Quartets*, 15.
3. Whitehead, *Process and Reality*, 488–89.
4. Griffin, *God and Religion in the Postmodern World*, 5. In chapter 2, Griffin posits a "direction" to the process, but the idea of creativity does not require this.

Whitehead, he understands as "ultimate reality";[5] and that Ronald Faber expresses when he writes of "the intercreativity between God and world and everything in the world"[6] and of the "creative dynamics of the mutual immanence of the experience of God and God's experience of the world."[7] Here everything is dynamic, and everything belongs with everything else; nothing is static, and there are no radical discontinuities; and our experience is constituted by changing patterns of action. On the basis of this conceptual framework we can study society, science, philosophy, and theology, and religious traditions can be related to each other and to a secular world.

RELATIONSHIPS BETWEEN RELIGIONS

We live in a diverse world and among a plurality of religions: a context that inevitably relativizes any particular religion to which we might be committed. If we had been born elsewhere, and in another time, we might have found ourselves committed to a different religion, which makes our existing commitment look and feel somewhat arbitrary and therefore fragile.

A variety of attempts have been made to conceptualize both the distinctiveness and the relationships between different religious traditions. David Tracy recommends an "analogical imagination" that recognizes "similarity-in-difference" and thus both pluralism and common criteria for truth.[8] John Hick also sets out from the fact of pluralism, records a growing recognition among Christians that not only must Christians respect followers of other faiths for their beliefs and practices, but that other religions are revelatory of God,[9] and he relates the different religions through the concept of a God understood as revealing in diverse ways.[10] Karl Rahner, on the other hand, relates different religions to each other via a set of theses[11] that retain Christianity's hegemony whilst allowing adherents of

---

5. Griffin, *Reenchantment without Supernaturalism*, 260–62.
6. Faber, *God as Poet of the World*, 315.
7. Faber, *Depths As Yet Unspoken*, 249.
8. Tracy, *The Analogical Imagination*, x, 408.
9. Hick, *God has Many Names*, vii.
10. Similarly, Knitter, in *No Other Name?* argues for a "theocentric Christology" (p.171) and a God understood as "defined in Jesus . . . not confined in Jesus" (p.204). In his *Jesus and the Other Names* it is "dialogue" that overcomes the finitude of our truth-claims, enabling us to "step beyond our limitations" (p.157). The consistent presupposition appears to be that there is a single God revealed differently in different religions and that through dialogue we press beyond our finitude and towards that God.
11. Rahner, "Christianity and Non-Christian Religions." The first thesis is: "Christianity understands itself as the absolute religion, intended for all men, which cannot

other faiths to be "anonymous Christians"[12] and their religions to contain "supernatural elements."[13] Alan Race[14] and Gavin D'Costa[15] discuss Hick's view ("pluralism") and Rahner's ("inclusivism"), along with "exclusivism" (a rejection of other religions' salvific meanings). As Race describes these categories, "exclusivism" "counts the revelation in Jesus Christ as the sole criterion by which all religions, including Christianity, can be understood and evaluated";[16] to be "inclusive" "is to believe that all non-Christian religious truth belongs ultimately to Christ and the way of discipleship which springs from him";[17] and for "pluralism" "there is not one, but a number of spheres of saving contact between God and man."[18] Each response is partial, unique, and incomplete, "but they are related to each other in that they represent different outwardly focused perceptions of the one ultimate divine reality."[19] D'Costa believes that Rahner's inclusivism reconciles the strengths of pluralism and exclusivism, because "this inclusivist position intelligibly reconciles and holds together the axioms of the universal salvific will of God and the axiom that salvation alone comes through God in Christ in his Church";[20] and Harold Wells' *Christic Center* also reconciles pluralism and a Christological focus by suggesting that "Jesus Christ, as bottom-line criterion and primary norm, does not constitute a principle for some eternally fixed set of theological truths. If he is the living Word and Wisdom of God he will constantly break through all our systems, and even our methods, however carefully thought out."[21] Race's preference is also for pluralism, which means

---

recognise any other religion beside itself as of equal light" (p. 291). The second thesis is: "Until the moment when the gospel really enters into the historical situation of an individual, a non-Christian religion . . . contains . . . supernatural elements arising out of the grace which is given to men as a gratuitous gift on account of Christ" (p. 293). The third thesis is: "Christianity does not simply confront the member of an extra-Christian religion as a mere non-Christian but as someone who can and must already be regarded in this or that respect as an anonymous Christian" (p. 300).

12. Rahner, "Christianity and Non-Christian Religions," 300.
13. Rahner, "Christianity and Non-Christian Religions," 293.
14. Race, *Christians and Religious Pluralism*.
15. D'Costa, *Theology and Religious Pluralism*.
16. Race, *Christians and Religious Pluralism*, 11.
17. Race, *Christians and Religious Pluralism*, 39.
18. Race, *Christians and Religious Pluralism*, 77.
19. Race, *Christians and Religious Pluralism*, 78.
20. D'Costa, *Theology and Religious Pluralism*, 111.
21. Wells, *The Christic Center*, 290.

that he chooses something like an "action" Christology in which "there is an equivalence between God and Jesus in terms of values and function."[22]

> Viewing Jesus in this way not only rescues Christianity from embarrassment in an age of radical historical consciousness; it also releases him to make his impact afresh in the dialogue, at the important level of religious experience.[23]

Pluralism and an "action" theology are thus, in Race's view, means to true dialogue between different faiths: but unfortunately they remain necessary rather than sufficient conditions for such dialogue, for if there are still radical discontinuities between different patterns of action and different language-games then no amount of "action" Christology, and no amount of pluralism, will enable dialogue to occur. This point is well made by Langdon Gilkey:

> No one doctrine in any system of symbols . . . can be abstracted out and be established as universal in all religions, a point of unity with other religious traditions . . . Nor . . . is there a philosophical way to transcend these particularities and achieve a universal standpoint, a standpoint above and so neutral to the fundamental differences between religions.[24]

The "one ultimate divine reality" of Race's definition of pluralism needs to find some kind of expression in patterns of action (constituted of patterns of action that include words spoken and written), otherwise there is only difference and no dialogue. Similarly, Gilkey's "ecumenical tolerance,"[25] and his requirement of "a series of manifestations [that] can coexist on the same level and with genuine validity,"[26] both require such patterns of action, and require that the patterns of action should include what we call the philosophical.

Rowan Williams recommends Raymundo Panikkar's retention of the radical diversity between different faiths. "In warning us away from the lust for religious Grand Theory . . . [Panikkar] does an exceptional service to authentic engagement between traditions in their particularity, in a way not to be found among programmatic relativists."[27] And DiNoia recommends that we make only "hypothetical" statements about other religions, because

---

22. D'Costa, *Theology and Religious Pluralism*, 129.
23. D'Costa, *Theology and Religious Pluralism*, 137.
24. Gilkey, "Plurality and its theological implications."
25. Gilkey, "Plurality and its theological implications," 44.
26. Gilkey, "Plurality and its theological implications," 49.
27. Williams, "Trinity and Pluralism," 14.

we cannot know other religions from within our own—although we can of course make use of those religions' own self-descriptions within our own tradition.[28] His theology of religions is inclusivist, like Rahner's,[29] but it recognizes more clearly the distinctiveness of each tradition, and it knows that only an "exploratory and hypothetical" approach is possible.[30] A more radical attempt to maintain the radical diversity of the religions is to be found in Mark Heim's *Salvations: Truth and Difference in Religions*,[31] where the presupposition that "salvation" means much the same in different religions is jettisoned.[32]

I contend that by doing theology on the basis of an "action and patterns" framework we have some hope of expressing both the genuine diversity of religions and the connections necessary if dialogue is to occur—that is, both the narratives and the metanarrative. A God understood as the spectrum between the dynamic and the static—as Action itself, as the still point, and as the creative source of patterns of action—can be both the particular God of each religious tradition (or rather, the Gods of each tradition, for there is often as much diversity within a religious tradition as there is between traditions), and the one God whom we all seek to know and serve. In this context, Jesus, who was and is a changing pattern of action, relates in a unique way to Action itself and to patterns of action that constitute God; and Race's view that pluralism and an "action" Christology belong together proves to be correct.

No "Being" conceptual framework can express both the changing discontinuities with which this situation presents us and the continuities that we need if dialogue is to be meaningful. On the other hand, an "action and patterns" approach to religious traditions recognizes that every religion is a changing pattern of action; that because patterns can relate to each other via the action that constitutes them, the different religions can relate to each other; that each religion constantly changes in relation to the others and so retains a distinctiveness (one always characterized by change); and that each religion can find echoes of itself in other traditions because there is a changing pattern of action that encompasses the others: we live in one world, in which every changing pattern of action affects every other, so there are no isolated patterns of action, and every part of every religion can in principle relate to every part of every other. The tentative conclusion that we can draw

---

28. DiNoia, *The Diversity of Religions*, 161.
29. DiNoia, *The Diversity of Religions*, 65–67.
30. DiNoia, *The Diversity of Religions*, 170.
31. Heim, *Salvations*.
32. Heim, *The Depth of the Riches*.

is that an actological conceptual framework would make the threefold "inclusivist," "exclusivist" and "pluralist" typology redundant, as it would reveal all three to be partial descriptions of a broader reality: that every religion is action in changing patterns relating to every other changing pattern of action.

Such a new conceptualization of reality, and in particular of religions, in terms of action and patterns, is important because it declares final resolutions or reconciliations to be impossible, it enables each religion to change and remain itself, it enables dialogue to be of the essence of religion, it enables every religion to relate to action beyond itself, and thus to know itself better, and it enables all of us to relate to a God understood as Action, and in particular as changing patterns of action that we might call "revelation." An "action in changing patterns" or "action and patterns" framework implies diversity and change, whereas Being does so only if Being itself is defined in terms of action and change; so an "action and patterns" framework offers us theological resources that a Being framework does not, and, most importantly for our purpose here, it enables religious traditions to be both truly distinctive and truly related.

RELIGIOUS TEXTS

To take an example: if the dynamic rather than the static is reality, then it is the reading of religious texts that constitutes the revelatory process: it is as we read that God is revealed. (To put this negatively: if nobody is reading, then the texts do not reveal and are not God's revelation.) Readings of the same text and of different texts relate to each other, and the action of reading falls into changing patterns: and these patterns of action reveal God. So, whilst there will be no final agreement between, for instance, Christians and Muslims—and, indeed, there must not be—through "Scriptural reasoning", that is, through reading each other's texts, we shall experience "polyphony in life,"[33] and God will be revealed as the God who is the creative source of all action and all changing patterns of action.

My task here is neither to address the particularities of faith traditions nor to explore the particularities of interfaith or interdenominational dialogue. My task is to ask whether, given that diversity and change characterize every faith and every dialogue, an "action in changing patterns" conceptual framework might help us to make sense both of the connections between

---

33. Cheetham, *Ways of Meeting and the Theology of Religions*, 200.

faith traditions (which tend to be ethical and religious) and the disconnections (which tend to be dogmatic, liturgical, and organizational).[34]

DIFFERENCES

In practical terms—and this is what matters—a religion is a complex network of action in changing patterns: actions, words (which are also changing patterns of action), images (which crystallize patterns of action, and are interpreted by them), institutions (which are changing patterns of action), and so on. Peripheral issues can sometimes look the same from one religion to another (the adherents of most religions pray): but when it comes to God's patterns of action, the different religions are radically different. In the Christian Faith, God is revealed in a person, Jesus: God living a human life. In Islam and in the Sikh religion, and to some extent in other religions, God is revealed through texts, which are not themselves patterns of action, but which crystallize patterns of action and pattern new changing patterns of action as the religions' adherents interpret them.

Different religions do in practice relate to each other, and the adherents of different religions relate to each other. The changing patterns of action that constitute the different religions thus intertwine, and the religions change each other.

But where is truth to be found? Truth, as we have discovered, is a changing pattern of action: it is an "uncovering."[35] In each of the religions there will be an uncovering: changing patterns of action as a religion's adherents and others relate to a religious tradition and are changed by it. Christians are likely to be most deeply changed by the Christian religion: their changing patterns of action will be more thoroughly intertwined than will be the Christian's with any other religion: so it is within the context of the Christian religion that most "uncovering" is likely to occur for the Christian, and within Islam most is likely to occur for the Muslim. The radical differences between the religions mean that any evaluation of one religion from a standpoint in another is bound to be superficial. For instance: someone whose mindset has been shaped within a text-based religion will find it difficult to engage with a person-based religion such as the Christian Faith, and in particular they will find a Christian's understanding of the Bible difficult to deal with: because for the Christian the Bible is a subsidiary authority in relation

---

34. I recognize that these terms belong to the Christian tradition and that different terms in different faith traditions have different connotations and also that the terms have different meanings within different Christian denominations.

35. Torry, *An Actological Metaphysic*, 113–17.

to Jesus, who is a primary authority. The same will be true the other way around. Someone committed to Jesus as God living a human life will find it difficult to identify with a religion in which the primary authority is a text: unless, of course, a Christian regards the Bible as their primary authority rather than Jesus, in which case a closer identification with Islam might be possible. I as a Christian might be able to start to explain how knowing God in Christ through reading the Bible, belonging to the Church, and seeking the Holy Spirit's action in the world, is an "embedding," an "uncovering," a getting to know the truth; and a Muslim might be able to start to explain how knowing God through the Qur'an is an embedding, an uncovering, a getting to know the truth: but my knowledge of the truth can only ever be partly available to the Muslim, and the Muslim's can only ever be partly available to me, making judgments about the relative values of our different processes of knowing the truth rather difficult to form. If the religions were things to be examined, then judgements might be easier to form: but they are not. Religions are changing patterns of action, as are we ourselves. Perhaps the approach will therefore have to be to get to know adherents of different religions, and then to slowly come to understand their ways of knowing the truth while they come to know ours: and then we shall have to contend with the fact that every religion is constituted by members with vast arrays of different ways of knowing the truth, making faith communities hugely diverse and constantly changing patterns of action, leading to us being even more sure that we shall never understand a religion from the outside.

It is only by commitment, by belonging, by coming to believe—that is, by entangling the changing patterns of action that constitute who we are with the complex changing patterns of action that constitute our religion, along with its history, its people, its institutions, its texts, and much else—that we shall come to know the truth: that is, that embedding and uncovering will occur.

DIVERSITY

The diversity of human beings, human histories, and human cultures, makes it essential that religion should be diverse, for only a religion that coheres with my experience can be my religion, and someone else's experience might be very different and so require a different religion, or at least a substantially different iteration of the same religion—which of course would not be the same religion. We recognize this when we seek out liturgy in which we feel comfortable and avoid liturgy in which we don't; when we pray in particular ways and not in others; and when we belong to one religious institution and not another. But it is not only our characteristics as individuals in relationship that determine that religion is and ought to be diverse: it is also the diversity of God that requires diversity of religion. If God is best characterized by diversity, then the activity and language whereby individually and collectively we relate to God is going to be diverse, and indeed ought to be diverse: for only then will it be about God. This means that it is essential that there should be differing religious traditions, and that within each tradition there should be sub-traditions; and that it is essential that we retain the differences.

There are thus two tendencies that we must avoid: 1. The conflation of religious traditions, either now or eschatologically; and 2. Religious imperialism: the statement, explicitly or implicitly, that one tradition is necessarily superior to others.

First of all: what is vital is the retention of diversity—the incarnation in Christian Faith, the positive lack of one in Islam; Islam's book-centeredness, Christian Faith's Jesus-centeredness; the Jews' eschatological Messiah, the Christians' historical one; Hinduism's elaborate ritual, Protestant Christianity's sparse ritual; Buddhism's atheist inward journey, and other religions' theistic pilgrimage. It is the diversity that matters, not some supposed unity: and it is not only misconceived to create a framework into which the different religions can be filed in accordance with some preordained scheme—a scheme inevitably shaped to some considerable extent by one particular religious tradition—but it is also misconceived to write a "comparative religion," for to relate the details of one religion to the details of another is quite impossible, because the details belong only to subsets of a religion, and never to the religious tradition as a whole, and to relate the central concepts of one religion to those of another is to assume an a priori framework into which both of the religious traditions can be fitted: essentially a "super-religion" in the context of which religions can be evaluated. To study a religion is to do precisely that: to use its language, to join in its activity, and to evaluate it using a variety of disciplines—history, anthropology, psychology, sociology, a variety of philosophical frameworks—always remembering that we only ever see a small corner of any one religious tradition and that we cannot generalize from one part to any "whole." And then we must pass on to another religious tradition. There is no need to "compare" one religion with another in any kind of dispassionate fashion—which is not to say that one religious tradition cannot learn from another, for most definitely it can. An adherent of one religion can come to understand one corner of another by entering into its language, ritual, relationship with society, and institutional life—and the student will be changed. Similarly, representative groups of people from different traditions can hold dialogues with each other, and they and their traditions will be changed, and the diversity of their own traditions will increase. But there is no external framework of criteria that might enable those undertaking the dialogue to look together at their respective traditions and to evaluate them for some kind of adequacy or in relation to concepts from outside the religions themselves. There are religions, but there is no such thing as religion.

Secondly: For the adherents of one religion to claim superiority for their tradition over against some other is both impossible and misguided. It is impossible because it is difficult to see how there might be some set of criteria that might enable a comparison to be undertaken; and misguided because to attempt such imperialism is to aim at reduced diversity among the world's religions and is thus to deny the character of the God who is diversity, action, and change. It is as we pursue diversity, both between traditions and within them, in terms of the variety of religious experience, spirituality, theology, institutional structure, texts, styles of ministry, types of relationship with the rest of the world, and so on, that our traditions come to know the God who is diversity.

This is not to say that commitment and rationality are not possible, for they are. Diversity requires commitment, but of a tentative kind. There is no religion without commitment of the self to the language and activity of the chosen tradition. To remain outside is to be unreligious, not to participate in the language game is not to understand it, and not to join in the ritual is to be impoverished, for it is as we seek out and interiorize religious experience and activity that the diversity of our individual experience increases, and we mature as we build relationships between old experience and new. Such commitment does not prevent us from exploring other traditions: and it is a sign of hope when Quakers experience Anglican worship and Anglicans experience Friends' meetings, or when a Roman Catholic attends an Anglican church and an Anglican a Roman Catholic one. However, for diversity to be maintained, joining in across the boundaries of different religions means less tight a hold on one's own religion, which reduces the diversity of religions, and for that reason alone should be avoided, unless there is some good reason on a particular occasion: for instance, to take part in an organized event that expresses an area's faith communities' solidarity in the face of some threat to one of them.

Any commitment to a religion that is not our own must be real, and a genuine commitment, but at the same time it must be tentative, because religion is diverse, we change, and religious traditions change, and to choose to leave one religion and join another must always be a possibility. Our commitments must be capable of change, for it is in the dialogue between positions that new possibilities become visible to us, so the dialogue must go on within us as well as around us.

What is important for any religious tradition is that the diversity should be maintained, for only diversity within a tradition can create the kind of dialectic required to move the tradition on in new situations, only diversity can serve the vastly different personalities of adherents to the tradition, and only diversity can give to the tradition a character that reflects the character of God. Individuals and groups must be able to move within the possibilities offered by a tradition and those offered by other traditions so as to keep alive the tradition with a vibrancy born of potentially infinite variety. This does not mean that the tradition will not have boundaries, but simply that the boundaries will constantly change, and that the boundaries will always be fluid and permeable and somewhat undefined so as not to restrict the organic tradition's ability to adapt to new circumstances and to serve its adherents and the world around it.

Chapter 15

Conclusions

Thesis: All that is—the cosmos, humanity, philosophy, metaphysics, theology—can be understood as action in changing patterns.

INTRODUCTION

The purpose of this brief chapter is to chart the actological journey that we have taken now that the sixth volume in the "Actological Explorations"—*An Actological Theology*—has been published. Without apology I shall begin by repeating the summary of the first five volumes offered in the concluding chapter of *An Actological Metaphysic*.

THE FIRST FOUR BOOKS IN THE "ACTOLOGICAL EXPLORATIONS" SERIES

In *Actology: Action, Change and Diversity in the Western Philosophical Tradition*, we have traced a thin actological stream from the presocratic Greek philosophers Parmenides and Heraclitus, through Plato, Aristotle, Aquinas, Hegel, Marx, Blondel, Bergson, Teilhard de Chardin, and Whitehead and the process philosophers, to Wittgenstein, Boys Smith, and Studdert Kennedy. To repeat the conclusions that we have been able to draw: We find among the writings of early Greek philosophers and Aquinas the building blocks for an action-in-patterns metaphysic; in Hegel and Marx an understanding of history as action in patterns (especially if we go on to understand dialectic as itself a changing pattern); in Blondel, we find that reality, including being, can be understood in terms of action; we find that if we remove his remaining rigidities, then Bergson can offer us an understanding of space and time as action in patterns; we find that although he did not get this far himself, Teilhard de Chardin invites us to contemplate God, the cosmos, and everything else, in terms of action in patterns; we find that Whitehead and the other process theologians invite a more consistent treatment of reality than they achieved, and also invite an understanding of God in terms of Action; in Studdert Kennedy we find a suffering God active in the midst of the world's suffering; in Wittgenstein we find an understanding of language in terms of action in patterns connected to other action in patterns; and we find that John Boys Smith invites an understanding of changing patterns of changing language, and changing patterns of other action in patterns too.[1]

In the subsequent *Actological Readings in Continental Philosophy*, we have read a number of continental philosophers on the basis that reality is action in changing patterns, both to understand what their philosophies might look like in that context, and to ask what their philosophies might have to offer to an actology. We have concluded that the philosophies of Kant, Husserl, Heidegger, Levinas, Deleuze, Gadamer, Merleau-Ponty, Bachelard, Foucault, and Serres, reveal not only the ubiquity of change and diversity, but also the absence of anything else. Apart from those inconsistent aspects of the philosophies that hanker after permanence and repetition, such as Nietzsche's will to power and eternal return, and Heidegger's "Being", all we can find is change and diversity. There is no solid ground on which to stand in order to evaluate changing and diverse reality. We find that verbs would often be more appropriate than the nouns that some of these philosophers have employed, and that an actology would be far more appropriate than an ontology as the basis for an understanding of these philosophies.

An Actology of the Given[2] represents a different approach. Instead of studying a number of philosophers to see what their philosophies look like through an actological lens, and asking what their philosophies might offer to the construction of an actology, *An Actology of the Given* studies a "giving" pattern of action on the basis of reality understood as action in changing patterns, and seeks out philosophers, anthropologists, and biblical texts, that might shed light on "giving." We find that reciprocity is ubiquitous; that the pure gift is a limit that is never reached; and that an actology concentrates attention on the act of giving rather than on the object given.[3]

1. Torry, *Actology*, 210–18.
2. Torry, *An Actology of the Given*.
3. Torry, *An Actology of the Given*, 192–95.

Mark's Gospel: An Actological Reading is what it says it is: a reading of Mark's Gospel on the basis that reality is action in changing patterns. We find in Mark's Gospel ubiquitous action in changing patterns, and a Jesus who is changing patterns of action that constitute God, and who is the servant of God who suffers death, is revealed to be the "one like a son of man," and is the one who receives authority to rule in the Kingdom of God.[4] However, *Mark's Gospel: An Actological Reading* is by no means the only book in the "Actological Explorations" series to offer some theology. All of them do; and in the fifth book in the series, *An Actological Metaphysic*, we have frequently found ourselves doing theology: that is, writing about God.

AN ACTOLOGICAL METAPHYSIC

In the fifth book in the "Actological Explorations" series we have taken an approach similar to that of *An Actology of the Given*, but rather than just one concept—"giving"—we have selected a variety of cosmological and metaphysical concepts and asked how we might understand them in an actological context.

We have divided the cosmological material into two parts. The first part is organized rather like *Actology: Action, change, and diversity in the Western philosophical tradition* and *Actological Readings in Continental Philosophy*: that is, we have studied a number of philosophers' cosmological speculations. Hesiod, Anaximander, Heraclitus, Lucretius, and Serres, offer us a chaos out of which temporary order emerges; for Leibniz, reality is relationships and so is active orderings; for Deleuze, difference and change are necessary to the evolution of reality; and for Whitehead, everything is process, with temporary orderings within the action. No consistent cosmology or metaphysic has emerged, which is as we would expect. Chaoses are all different, and orderings are all different, so any "laws" are contingent, temporary, and local. None of our philosophers have described their take on the reality of the universe as "action in changing patterns" or "changing patterns of action," but they could have done. We follow the philosophical explorations with cosmological insights from the natural sciences, particularly in relation to such concepts as universe, waves, particles, and natural laws. We find that an actological understanding of reality enables us to comprehend scientific developments rather more coherently than might be possible within an ontological framework.

The following two chapters study a range of metaphysical concepts. For instance, when we study events, causality, and substance, we find arbitrary

---

4. Torry, *Mark's Gospel*, 274.

boundaries around the changing patterns of action that constitute them; and we find that an actology sheds light on such concepts as event, substance, causality, perception, knowledge, truth, reason, logic, and universals. *An Actological Metaphysic* then gives two chapters to single concepts, time and space, both of which are understood as changing patterns within action. The final two chapters in the book tackle life and society, with a particular emphasis on the human person: again understood through an actological lens. As we would expect, we find action, change, and diversity everywhere, and an actology to be an appropriate context within which to explore the realities of time, space, life, society, and all of the other cosmological and metaphysical concepts that we have studied.

AN ACTOLOGICAL THEOLOGY

This present volume, the sixth in the "Actological Explorations" series, does for theology what the fifth volume has done for metaphysics: that is, it explores theology—and mainly Christian theology—on the basis that reality is action in changing patterns. Again we find ubiquitous action, change, and diversity, and nothing static or unitary has been found, resulting in a necessarily discursive and somewhat unsystematic theology. As Henri Bergson puts it, God "has nothing of the already made; he is unceasing life, action, freedom."[5]

The first two chapters have set the stage by exploring connections between philosophy, apologetics, and theology, and the following chapters have discussed a range of theological concepts through an actological lens: God; a suffering God; Jesus; grace; the City of God; the Trinity; a reconciling God; the Church; being a Christian—or rather, doing Christianly; the Bible; and relationships between different religions. Throughout, we have found an actology to be a fruitful basis on which to create a tentative, temporary, and local theology: that being the only kind possible once we understand reality as action in changing patterns.

CONTINUING TO EXPLORE

Models are "speculative instruments and heuristic constructions that systematize relevant aspects of a given context,"[6] and any model, whether in the physical sciences or in theology, is open to disruption. We have attempted

---

5. Bergson, *Creative Evolution*, 262; Carr, *The Philosophy of Change*, 160.
6. Sedmak, "Disruptions," 140.

a little disruption of a "Being, beings, rest, the unchanging, the static, and the unitary" model, and have explored the possibility of a model based on Action, action, change, movement, the dynamic, and diversity.

Throughout the "Actological Explorations" series I have occasionally reiterated the point that an "Action" narrative should be regarded as an alternative to, as complementary to, a "Being" narrative. Are we now in a position to decide that one of those narratives might be more in tune with the characteristics of the world in which we live? As our world is changing, might an actology characterized by change, movement, action, the dynamic, and Action, be the best way to go? Might an actology be a useful framework within which to continue to work on metaphysics, theology, and much more? There will never be proof of anything: but we can ask about persuasive explanation. It seems to me that in the fields of history, philosophy, metaphysics, economics, cosmology, language, the natural sciences, and theology, an actology about change, the dynamic, action, movement, and Action, would be closer to the issues than a metaphysic about being, the static, rest, the unchanging, and Being.

We have made a start. We have surveyed some of the Western philosophical tradition for insights that might assist us as we create an "action in changing patterns" actology; we have begun to create Christian theology and apologetics on that basis; and we have started to add a little detail to elements of a larger project. That larger project now needs to be carried out.

But that will never be the only project required, because both philosophy and theology must constantly maintain an experimental attitude. The possibilities are endless. Previous tradition might sometimes limit the diversity available, because some new ideas might flourish and develop in the current context, and some might not; and some ideas might not pass the "Auschwitz test" if they somehow deny the reality of evil, or do not recognize the irony and tragedy inherent in human activity: but this sifting process will still leave a far broader range of possibilities to pursue than we would ever be able to turn into new metaphysics and then work out the consequences. An actology, like an ontology, is one possibility among many, and as many of the options as possible must be explored.

Philosophy and theology are contingent, shaped by experiment, politics, personal preferences, other disciplines, and so on, and the process needs constantly to be offered new raw materials and new possibilities of relationships so that the many-faceted dialogue that constitutes both philosophy and theology can take on constantly new patterns and create constantly new possibilities. It is as misconceived to plan the outcome in theology as in any other sphere, for irony and tragedy are bound to result. Far better to work for infinite variety and to wait for new patterns to emerge as we participate in the evolution of the disciplines.

In particular, no longer can we create a systematic theology that will serve the Church's internal theological debate and its mission in the same way that Thomas Aquinas did for his own time and the centuries following: but this does not mean that we cannot attempt tentative, local, and temporary systematic theologies in the plural to serve a variety of needs experienced by a variety of people, Christians and otherwise. We shall do it by following a method similar to that of the current project: seeking an alternative conceptual framework, testing it in various ways for coherence with human experience, and then building a theology on that basis, constantly relating it to previous theological constructions.

Throughout I have not asked my readers to forget all that they know: simply to lay on one side, as far as possible, two presuppositions: that the unchanging is the real, and that the changing is the unreal; and then to experiment with a framework based on action, and to begin to build on it a new cathedral of the mind. All I have been able to achieve in this series of books is an outline of that framework, some testing of it, and a brief glimpse of what the new cathedral might look like.

So now God is Action and changing patterns of action, the universe is changing patterns of action, and we are changing patterns of action. Thus the Trinity is the action that is the Creator, Jesus, and the Spirit, and the "economic" and "imminent" Trinities (the Trinity as we experience it, and the Trinity as it is) are one and the same; Jesus is his changing patterns of action (which is rather what the resurrection narratives have suggested all along); God relates to everything and everything to God; language is changing patterns of action and it changes all other reality, that is, all other changing patterns of action, and all other changing patterns of action change language, making God and the world analogous realities.

This is a new agenda, and its exploration will be the work of many lifetimes. As we explore, a new cathedral of the mind will rise on the foundations that we have laid, and we shall study it, redesign it, rebuild it—and finally see it fall into decay. Then other minds will need to study the universe and their own worlds and start yet another new cathedral of the mind.

In relation to contemporary philosophy, theology should not be afraid. We must go forwards, taking on board all that both ancient and contemporary philosophy have to offer, and understand God, ourselves, and everything else, in the light of our particular understanding of reality—but always knowing that our actology remains just one conceptual framework out of many possibilities: one story among many.

What I am proposing is a tentative, local, and temporary paradigm shift. The changes that we can identify in science, the ways in which we understand society, the action in changing patterns stream that I have explored in Western philosophy, the changes taking place in theology: all of this and more demand a whole new way of seeing the world, the universe, God, and ourselves.[7] It is time not just for an adjustment, for a shift. We need a genuine discontinuity: to jump tracks, from a Being track to an Action track, from a unitary track to a diversity track, from an unchanging track to a change track, and so on. It is not just different ideas that we need: it is a different conceptual framework. And then we shall need to abandon that one and seek another, and another, and another.

This book, like the other five books in the series, is an invitation to conversions: to an actology of action in changing patterns; to Jesus as our God; to grace as a focal changing pattern of action . . . But not only to those ideas. If the book is an invitation to changing patterns of action, then every reader will contribute new experiences and new ideas: new theologies, new metaphysics, new understandings of God, Jesus, the world, and ourselves.

It is of course entirely appropriate that this sixth volume is either the final member of the "Actological Explorations" series or it is not.

---

7. Kuhn, *The Structure of Scientific Revolutions*.

Bibliography

Biblical passages in Greek are transliterated from Η ΚΑΙΝΗ ΔΙΑΘΗΚΗ, 2nd edition (London: The British and Foreign Bible Society, 1958), and English translations are taken from *The New Revised Standard Version, Anglicized edition* (Oxford: Oxford University Press, 1995)

Allen, Diogenes. *Christian Belief in a Postmodern World*. Louisville, Kentucky: Westminster/John Knox, 1989.
———. "Faith and the Recognition of God's Activity." In *Divine Action: Studies Inspired by the Philosophical Theology of Austin Farrer*, edited by Brian Hebblethwaite and Edward Henderson, 197–210. Edinburgh: T. & T. Clark, 1990.
Alpha International. "Welcome to Alpha." https://alpha.org/.
Alston, William. "How to Think about Divine Action." In *Divine Action: Studies Inspired by the Philosophical Theology of Austin Farrer*, edited by Brian Hebblethwaite and Edward Henderson, 51–70. Edinburgh: T. & T. Clark, 1990.
Aquinas, Thomas. *Summa Theologiae*. With a translation by Fathers of the English Dominican Province. http://dhspriory.org/thomas/summa/FP.html.
Archbishop of Canterbury's Commission on Urban Priority Areas. *Faith in the City: A Call for Action by Church and Nation*. London: Church House, 1985.
Astley, Jeff. *SCM Studyguide to Christian Doctrine*. London: SCM, 2010.
Atwell, Robert (Ed.). *Celebrating the Seasons*. Norwich: Canterbury Press, 1999.
Augustine. *City of God*. Translated by Henry Bettenson. Harmondsworth: Penguin, 1972.
———. *Confessions*. Translated by R.S. Pine-Coffin. Harmondsworth: Penguin, 1972.
———. *De Haeresibus*, §88. In *Sancti Aurelii Augustini, Hipponensis episcopi, Opera omnia*. Volume 42, edited by J.P. Migne. Paris: Venit apud J.-P. Migne editorem, 1861. https://earlychurchtexts.com/main/augustine/augustine_on_pelagianism.shtml. English translation, Beresford James Kidd, *Documents Illustrative of the History of the Church*, Vol. 2, 313–461 AD. London: SPCK, 1923. https://earlychurchtexts.com/public/augustine_on_pelagianism.htm.
———. *Earlier Writings*. Translated by J.H.S. Burleigh. Library of Christian Classics, vol.6. Philadelphia: Westminster, 1953.
———. *Of True Religion*. In Augustine, *Earlier Writings*, vol. 6, edited and translated by J.H.S. Burleigh, 218–83. Louisville: Westminster John Knox, 2006. First published in 1953.
Aulén, Gustaf. *Christus Victor: An Historical Study of the Three Main Types of the Idea of the Atonement*. New edition. London: SPCK, 1970.

———. *Eucharist and Sacrifice*. Edinburgh: Oliver and Boyd, 1958.
Ayer, A.J. *Language, Truth and Logic*. London: Victor Gollancz, 1946. First published in 1936.
Ayres, Lewis. "(Mis)Adventures in Trinitarian Ontology." In *The Trinity and an Entangled World: Relationality in Physical Science and Theology*, edited by John Polkinghorne, 130–45. Grand Rapids, Michigan: William B. Eerdmans, 2010.
Baillie, D.M. *God was in Christ*. London: Faber and Faber, 1948.
Baker, John Austin. *The Foolishness of God*. Glasgow: Fount/Collins, 1979.
———. ". . . Who is God and Lord of All." *Church Times*, 24 December 1993.
Barclay, John M.G. *Paul and the Gift*. Grand Rapids, MI: Eerdmans, 2015.
Barnard, L.W. *Justin Martyr*. Cambridge: Cambridge University Press, 1976.
Barrett, C.K. *The Gospel According to St. John*. London: SPCK, 1978.
———. *Paul*. London and New York: Continuum, 1994.
Barth, Karl. *Anselm: Fides Quaerens Intellectum*. Pittsburgh: Pickwick, 1975.
———. *Church Dogmatics*. Volume I, "The Doctrine of the Word of God." Part 2. Translated by G.T. Thomson and Harold Knight. Edinburgh: T & T Clark, 1956.
———. *The Humanity of God*. Translated by John Newton Thomas and Thomas Wieser. London and Glasgow: Collins/Fontana, 1967.
Bartholomew, David J. *God, Chance and Purpose: Can God have it Both Ways?* Cambridge: Cambridge University Press, 2008.
Benson, R.M.. *The Final Passover*. Volume II. London: Longmans, Green and Co., 1895.
Berdyaev, Nicholas. *The Beginning and the End*. Westport, Connecticut: Greenwood, 1976.
Bevans, Stephen. *John Oman and his Doctrine of God*. Cambridge: Cambridge University Press, 1992.
Beveridge, William. *Social Insurance and Allied Services*. Cmd. 6404. London: His Majesty's Stationery Office, 1942.
Blondel, Maurice. *L'Action*. Paris: Quadrige/Presses Universitaires de France, 1993. First published in 1893.
———. *Action*. Translated by Oliva Blanchette from *L'Action*. Notre Dame, Indiana: University of Notre Dame Press, 1984.
———. "The Letter on Apologetics." Translated by Illtyd Trethowan from *Lettre sur les Exigences de la Pensée Contemporaine en Matière d'Apologétique et sur la Méthode de la Philosophie dans l'Étude du Problème Religieux*. In *The Letter on Apologetics and History and Dogma*, translated by Alexander Dru and Illtyd Trethowan. London: Harvill, 1964.
———. *Lettre sur les Exigences de la Pensée Contemporaine en Matière d'Apologétique et sur la Méthode de la Philosophie dans l'Étude du Problème Religieux*. In *Les Premiers Écrits de Maurice Blondel*, 5–95. Paris: Presses Universitaires de France, 1956. First published in 1896.
Bonhoeffer, Dietrich. *Act and Being*. Translated by H. Martin Rumscheidt. Minneapolis: Fortress, 2009
———. *Letters and Papers from Prison*. Edited by Eberhard Bethge; translated by Reginald Fuller. London: SCM, 1953.
———. *Widerstand und Ergebung: Briefe and Aufzeichnung aus der Haft*. Gütersloh: Chr. Kaiser Verlag, 1998.
Bosch, David J. *Transforming Mission: Paradigm Shifts in Theology of Mission*. Maryknoll, New York: Orbis, 1991.

Brierley, Michael. "Commemorating C.E. Rolt (1881-1918)." *Theology* 121 (5) (2018) 348–56.
———. "Introducing the Early English Passibilists." *Journal of the History of Modern Theology* 8 (2001) 218–33.
Brown, David. *Divine Humanity: Kenosis Explored and Defended*. London: SCM, 2011.
———. "God and Symbolic Action." In *Divine Action: Studies Inspired by the Philosophical Theology of Austin Farrer*, edited by Brian Hebblethwaite and Edward Henderson, 103–22. Edinburgh: T. & T. Clark, 1990.
Brown, Malcolm, with Jonathan Chaplin, John Hughes, Anna Rowlands and Alan Suggate. *Anglican Social Theology*. London: Church House, 2014.
Brown, Peter. *Augustine: A Biography*. London: Faber and Faber, 1967.
Buber, Martin. *I and Thou*. Second edition. Translated by Ronald Gregor Smith. Edinburgh: T. & T. Clark, 1958.
Bultmann, Rudolf. *Essays Philosophical and Theological*. London: SCM, 1955.
———. *Existence and Faith*. London: Hodder, 1961.
———. *Faith and Understanding*. London: SCM, 1969.
———. *Kerygma and Myth*, volume I. Edited by H.W. Bartsch. London: SPCK, 1953.
Bunyan, John. *The Pilgrim's Progress*. Oxford: Oxford University Press, 1984.
Burrell, David B. *Aquinas: God and Action*. London: Routledge and Kegan Paul, 1979.
———. "Divine Practical Knowing." In *Divine Action: Studies Inspired by the Philosophical Theology of Austin Farrer*, edited by Brian Hebblethwaite and Edward Henderson, 93–102. Edinburgh: T. & T. Clark, 1990.
Burtchaell, James. *Living with Grace*. London: Sheed and Ward, 1973.
Butterfield, Herbert. *Christianity and History*. London: G. Bell and Sons, 1950.
Byrne, David. *God and Realism*. Aldershot: Ashgate, 2003.
Camus, Albert. *L'Homme Révolté*. Paris: Gallimard, 1951.
Caputo, John D. *The Weakness of God: A Theology of the Event*. Bloomington: Indiana University Press, 2006.
Cartwright, Nancy. *The Dappled World: A Study of the Boundaries of Science*. Cambridge: Cambridge University Press, 1999.
Chadwick, Henry. *Augustine*. Oxford: Oxford University Press, 1986.
Cheetham, David. *Ways of Meeting and the Theology of Religions*. Aldershot: Ashgate, 2003.
Cheetham, Richard. "Bishop Richard writes." *Noticeboard*. London: Diocese of Southwark, April 2018, 8.
Clement. "Protrepticus." In *Exhortation to the Greeks*, translated by G.W. Butterworth. Loeb Classical Library, vol. 92. Cambridge, MA: Harvard University Press, 2014.
Cobb, John. *The Structure of Christian Existence*. London: Lutterworth, 1968.
Cole, Richard G. *Universal Grace: Myth or Reality?* New York: Orbis, 1977.
Conrad, Richard. "Moments and Themes in the History of Apologetics." In *Imaginative Apologetics*, edited by Andrew Davison, 126–41. London: SCM, 2011.
Cooper, John W. *Panentheism: The Other God of the Philosophers*. Nottingham: Apollos/Inter-Varsity, 2007.
Copleston, F.C. *Aquinas*. Harmondsworth: Penguin, 1955.
Cowdell, Scott. *Atheist Priest? Don Cupitt and Christianity*. London: SCM, 1988.
Cranfield, C.E.B. *The Gospel According to Mark*. Cambridge: Cambridge University Press, 1959.

Crocker, Geoff. *An Enlightened Philosophy: Can an Atheist Believe Anything?* Ropley: O-Books, 2010.
Cullmann, Oscar. *The Christology of the New Testament.* 2nd edition. London: SCM, 1963.
Cupitt, Don. *The Long-Legged Fly: A Theology of Language and Desire.* London: SCM, 1987.
———. *The Sea of Faith.* London: British Broadcasting Corporation, 1984.
———. *Taking Leave of God.* London: SCM, 1980.
Daniélou, Jean. *A History of Early Christian Doctrine before the Council of Nicea*, vol. II, *Gospel Message and Hellenistic Culture.* London: Darton, Longman and Todd, 1973.
Davies, Oliver, Paul D. Janz and Clemens Sedmak. *Transformation Theology: Church in the World.* London: T. & T. Clark, 2007.
Davison, Andrew. *Astrobiology and Christian Doctrine: Exploring the Implications of Life in the Universe.* Cambridge: Cambridge University Press, 2023.
———. "Christian Reason and Christian Community." In *Imaginative Apologetics*, edited by Andrew Davison, 12–28. London: SCM, 2011.
———. "Introduction." In *Imaginative Apologetics*, edited by Andrew Davison, xxv–xxviii. London: SCM, 2011.
D'Costa, Gavin. *Theology and Religious Pluralism: The Challenge of Other Religions.* Oxford: Basil Blackwell, 1986.
Dean, Hartley and Lucinda Platt. *Social Advantage and Disadvantage.* Oxford: Oxford University Press, 2016.
Deane-Drummond, Celia. *Christ and Evolution: Wonder and Wisdom.* London: SEM, 2009.
Dembski, William A. *Being as Communion: A Metaphysics of Information.* Farnham: Ashgate, 2014.
Derrida, Jacques. *Marges de Philosophie.* Paris: Éditions de Minuit, 1972.
———. *Margins of Philosophy.* Translated by Alan Bass from *Marges de Philosophie.* Brighton: Harvester, 1982.
———. *La Voix et le Phénomène: Introduction au Problème du Signe dans la Phenomenology de Husserl.* Paris: Quadrige/Presse des Universitaires de France, 1993.
Desai, Meghnad and Ana Helena Palermo. "Some Effects of Basic Income on Economic Variables." In *The Palgrave International Handbook of Basic Income*, edited by Malcolm Torry, 91–110. Cham: Palgrave Macmillan, 2019.
Descartes, René. *Discourse on Method.* Harmondsworth: Penguin, 1960.
———. *Meditationes de Prima Philosophia.* http://www.wright.edu/~charles.taylor/descartes/medl.html. English translation by John Veitch, 1901: *Meditations.* http://www.wright.edu/~charles.taylor/descartes/mede.html.
DiNoia, J.A. *The Diversity of Religions: A Christian Perspective.* Washington DC: The Catholic University of America Press, 1992.
Dix, Gregory. *The Shape of the Liturgy.* London: Dacre Press, Adam and Charles Black, second edition, 1945.
Doctrine Commission of the General Synod of the Church of England. *Contemporary Doctrine Classics.* London: Church House, 2005.
Donovan, Vincent J. *Christianity Rediscovered: An Epistle from the Masai.* London: SCM, 1978.

Dowley, Roger. *Towards the Recovery of a Lost Bequest.* Liverpool: Evangelical Coalition on Urban Mission, 1986.
Drane, John. *The McDonaldization of the Church.* London: Darton, Longman and Todd, 2000.
Drewery, Benjamin. *Origen and the Doctrine of Grace.* London: Epworth, 1960.
Drury, John. *The Parables in the Gospels.* London: SPCK, 1985.
Dulles, Avery. *A History of Apologetics.* London: Hutchinson, 1971.
———. *Models of the Church.* Expanded edition. New York and London: Image Books/Doubleday, 2002.
Dunn, James D.G. *Jesus, Paul and the Law.* London: SPCK, 1990.
Eaton, Jeffrey. "Divine Action and Human Liberation." In *Divine Action: Studies Inspired by the Philosophical Theology of Austin Farrer,* edited by Brian Hebblethwaite and Edward Henderson, 211–29. Edinburgh: T. & T. Clark, 1990.
Eliot, T.S. *Four Quartets.* London: Faber and Faber, 1944.
English, Adam C. *The Possibility of Christian Philosophy: Maurice Blondel at the Intersection of Theology and Philosophy.* London: Routledge, 2007.
Epperly, Bruce G. *Process Theology: A Guide for the Perplexed.* London: T. & T. Clark/Continuum, 2011.
Evans, C.F. *Saint Luke.* London: SCM, 1990.
Faber, Roland. *Depths As Yet Unspoken: Whiteheadian Excursions in Mysticism, Multiplicity and Divinity.* Edited by Andrew M. Davis. Eugene, OR: Pickwick/Wipf and Stock, 2020.
———. *God as Poet of the World: Exploring Process Theologies.* Translated by Douglas W. Stott. Louisville and London: Westminster John Knox, 2004.
Fiddes, Paul. *The Creative Suffering of God.* Oxford: Clarendon, 1988.
Flew, Antony. "Divine Omnipotence and Human Freedom." In *New Essays in Philosophical Theology,* edited by Antony Flew and Alasdair MacIntyre, 144–69. London: SCM, 1955.
Ford, David. *Barth and God's Story.* Frankfurt am Main/Bern: Verlag Peter Lang, 1981.
Forsman, Rodger. "'Double Agency' and Identifying Reference to God." In *Divine Action: Studies Inspired by the Philosophical Theology of Austin Farrer,* edited by Brian Hebblethwaite and Edward Henderson, 123–42. Edinburgh: T. & T. Clark, 1990.
Galloway, Alan D. *Wolfhart Pannenberg.* London: Allen and Unwin, 1973.
Gibson, Arthur. *God and the Universe.* London: Routledge, 2000.
Gilkey, Langdon. "Plurality and its Theological Implications". In *The Myth of Christian Uniqueness,* edited by John Hick and Paul F. Knitter, 37–50. London: SCM, 1987.
Gilson, Etienne. *The Philosophy of St. Thomas Aquinas.* Translated by Edward Bullough. Cambridge: W. Heffer, 1929.
Gore, Charles. *The Incarnation of the Son of God: Being the Bampton Lectures 1891.* Eugene, Oregon: Wipf and Stock, no date; previously published in 1891 by Charles Scribner.
Graham, Billy. *Peace with God.* Milton Keynes: Word, 1986.
Grayling, A.C. "Metaphysics: Introduction." In *Philosophy: A Guide Through the Subject,* edited by A.C. Grayling, 183–84. Oxford: Oxford University Press, 1995.
Gregor Smith, Ronald. *Secular Christianity.* London: Collins, 1967.
Griffin, David Ray. *God and Religion in the Postmodern World.* New York: State University of New York Press, 1989.

———. *Reenchantment without Supernaturalism: A Process Philosophy of Religion*. Ithaca and London: Cornell University Press, 2001.
Groves, Peter. *Grace*. Norwich: Canterbury Press, 2012.
Gunton, Colin. *Act and Being: Towards a Theology of the Divine Attributes*. London: SCM, 2002.
———. *The Actuality of Atonement*. Edinburgh: T. & T. Clark, 1985.
Gutiérrez, Gustavo. *A Theology of Liberation*. London: SCM, 1974.
———. *We Drink from our Own Wells*. London: SCM, 2005.
Harris, James Rendel. "A Further Note on the Cretans." *The Expositor*, 7th series, 3 (4) (1907) 332–37.
Harris, James Rendel. "St. Paul and Epimenides." *The Expositor*, 8th series, 4 (4) (1912) 348–53.
Hart, David Bentley. *Tradition and Apocalypse: An Essay on the Future of Christian Belief*. Grand Rapids, Michigan: Baker Academic, 2022.
Hartshorne, Charles. *Creative Synthesis and Philosophic Method*. London: SCM, 1970.
———. *The Logic of Perfection and Other Essays in Neoclassical Metaphysics*. La Salle, Illinois: Open Court, 1962.
Haught, John F. *The Cosmic Vision of Teilhard de Chardin*. Maryknoll, New York: Orbis, 2021.
Hefner, Philip. *The Human Factor: Evolution, Culture, and Religion*. Minneapolis: Fortress, 1993.
Heidegger, Martin. *Being and Time*. Translated by John MacQuarrie and Edward Robinson. Oxford: Blackwell, 1962.
Heim, Mark. *The Depth of the Riches*. Grand Rapids: Eerdmans, 2001.
———. *Salvations: Truth and Difference in Religions*. Maryknoll, New York: Orbis, 1995.
Hemming, Laurence Paul. *Postmodernity's Transcending: Devaluing God*. London: SCM, 2005.
Henriksen, Jan-Olav. *Christianity as Distinct Practices: A Complicated Relationship*. London: T. & T. Clark, 2019.
Herbert, George. *The Poems of George Herbert*. Oxford: Oxford University Press, 1961.
Hick, John. *Arguments for the Existence of God*. Basingstoke: MacMillan, 1970.
———. *Christianity at the Centre*. London: SCM, 1968.
———. *God has Many Names: Britain's New Religious Pluralism*. London and Basingstoke: MacMillan, 1980.
Higton, Mike. *Christian Doctrine*. London. SCM, 2008.
———. *Difficult Gospel: The Theology of Rowan Williams*. London: SCM, 2004.
Hilary of Poitiers. *De Trinitate*. II. 2. In *Documenta Catholica Omnia*. http://www.documentacatholicaomnia.eu/04z/z_0315-0367__Hilarius_Pictaviensis__De_Trinitate_Libri_Duodecim__MLT.pdf.html. English translations from the *New Advent* website of Catholic resources, http://www.newadvent.org/fathers/330202.htm, and from *A Select Library of Nicene and Post-Nicene Fathers of the Christian Church*, series 2, vol. IX. Oxford: James Parker, 1899.
Holmes, Stephen. "'Something Much too Plain to Say': Towards a Defence of the Doctrine of Divine Simplicity." *Neue Zeitschrift für Systematische Theologie und Religionsphilosophie* 43 (2001) 137–54.
Hooker, Morna D. *From Adam to Christ*. Cambridge: Cambridge University Press, 1990.

Hooker, Richard. *Laws of Ecclesiastical Polity*. Volumes 1 to 4. London: Dent, 1925.
Houlden, J.L. *Backward into Light*. London: SCM, 1987
Hume, David. *Dialogues Concerning Natural Religion*. New York and London: Hafner, 1969.
Irenaeus. "Demonstration of the Apostolic Preaching." In *A New Eusebius: Documents Illustrative of the History of the Church to A.D. 337*, edited by J. Stevenson, 124–25. London: SPCK, 1960.
James, William. *The Varieties of Religious Experience: A Study in Human Nature*, reprinted in 2012, Oxford: Oxford University Press, 1902.
Jenkins, Timothy. *An Experiment in Providence*. London: SPCK, 2006.
Jenson, Robert W. *On Thinking the Human: Resolutions of Difficult Notions*. Grand Rapids, Michigan: William B. Eerdmans, 2003.
———. *Systematic Theology*. New York and Oxford: Oxford University Press, 2 volumes, 1997–1999.
Jeremias, Joachim. *The Eucharistic Words of Jesus*. London: SCM, 1966.
———. *The Parables of Jesus*. London: SCM, 1963.
Jessey, Cornelia. *Profiles in Hope*. Dublin: Veritas, 1978.
Journet, Charles. *The Meaning of Grace*. London: Geoffrey Chapman, 1960.
Julian of Norwich. *Enfolded in Love*. London: Darton, Longman and Todd, 1980.
Justin Martyr. "First and Second Apologies." In *The Apostolic Fathers with Justin Martyr and Irenaeus*, in *The Ante-Nicene Fathers*, edited by Cleveland Cox. Grand Rapids, Michigan: Eerdmans, 1977.
———. "Hortatory Address to the Greeks." In *The Apostolic Fathers with Justin Martyr and Irenaeus*, in *The Ante-Nicene Fathers*, edited by Cleveland Cox. Grand Rapids, Michigan: Eerdmans, 1977.
Kant, Immanuel. *Critique of Practical Reason*. Translated by T.K. Abbott. Amherst, NY: Prometheus, 1996.
———. *The Critique of Pure Reason*. Translated by J.M.D. Meiklejohn from *Kritik der Reinen Vernunft*. Project Gutenberg, http://onlinebooks.library.upenn.edu/webbin/gutbook/lookup?num=4280.
———. *What is Enlightenment?* 1784, Translated by Mary C. Smith. http://www.columbia.edu/acis/ets/CCREAD/etscc/kant.html.
Kee, Alistair. *The Roots of Christian Freedom: The Theology of John A.T. Robinson*. London: SPCK, 1988.
Keller, Catherine. *Face of the Deep: A Theology of Becoming*. London and New York: Routledge, 2003.
Kenny, Anthony. *The Five Ways*. London: Routledge and Kegan Paul, 1969.
Kerr, Fergus. *Theology after Wittgenstein*. Oxford: Basic Blackwell, 1986.
Kierkegaard, Søren. *Concluding Unscientific Postscript*. Translated by Hosard V. Hong and Edna H. Hong. Princeton: Princeton University Press, 1992.
Kim, Sebastian. *Theology in the Public Sphere: Public Theology as a Catalyst for Open Debate*. London: SCM, 2011.
King, Ursula. *Christ in All Things: Exploring Spirituality with Teilhard de Chardin*. London: SCM, 1997.
Knitter, Paul. *Jesus and the Other Names: Christian Mission and Global Responsibility*. Oxford: One World, 1996.
———. *No Other Name? A Critical Survey of Christian Attitudes toward the World Religions*. Maryknoll, New York: Orbis, 1985.

Krieger, David J. "Religion and the System of Meaning." In *Systems Theory and Theology*, edited by Markus Locker, 97–126. Eugene, Oregon: Pickwick, 2011.

Kuhn, Thomas S. *The Structure of Scientific Revolutions*. Chicago: Chicago University Press, 1962.

Küng, Hans. *Christianity: Its Essence and History*. Translated by John Bowden. London: SCM, 1995.

———. *Does God Exist? An Answer for Today*. Translated by Edward Quinn. London: Collins, 1980.

———. *Justification*. London: Burns and Oates, 1981.

———. *On Being a Christian*. London: Collins, 1978.

Lampe, Geoffrey. *God as Spirit*. Oxford: Oxford University Press, 1977.

Leech, Kenneth. *The Social God*. London: Sheldon, 1981.

Lewis, C.S. *The Lion, the Witch and the Wardrobe*. London: HarperCollins, 1998.

Liddell and Scott. *An Intermediate Greek-English Lexicon*. Oxford: Clarendon Press, 1889.

Lindars, Barnabas. *Jesus Son of Man: A Fresh Examination of the Son of Man Sayings in the Gospels*. London: SPCK, 1983.

Lipsey, Richard G. and K. Alec Chrystal. *Economics*. Tenth edition. Oxford: Oxford University Press.

Lister, Ruth. *Poverty*. Cambridge: Polity, 2004.

Lucas, J.R. "Pelagius and St. Augustine." *Journal of Theological Studies* N.S. 22 (1) (1971) 73–85.

Lyotard, Jean-François. *La Condition Postmoderne*. Paris: Les Éditions de Minuit, 1979.

MacCulloch, Diarmaid. *A History of Christianity*. London: Penguin, 2010.

MacKinnon, D.M. *The Borderlands of Theology: An Inaugural Lecture*. Cambridge: Cambridge University Press, 1961.

———. "'Substance' in Christology—a Cross-Bench View." In *Christ, Faith and History*, edited by S.W. Sykes and J.P Clayton, 279–300. Cambridge: Cambridge University Press, 1972.

Macleod, Alistair M. *Tillich: An Essay on the Role of Ontology in his Philosophical Theology*. London: George Allen and Unwin, 1973.

MacQuarrie, John. *An Existentialist Theology*. Harmondsworth: Penguin, 1963.

———. *The Humility of God*. London: SCM, 1978.

———. *Principles of Christian Theology*. London: SCM, 1966.

Marion, Jean-Luc. *Certitudes Négatives*. Paris: Bernard Grasset, 2010.

Martelet, Gustave. *The Risen Christ and the Eucharistic World*. Translated by René Hague. London: Collins, 1976.

Mascall, E.L. *The Secularisation of Christianity*. London: Darton, Longman and Todd, 1965.

Mayne, Michael. *The Enduring Melody*. London: Darton, Longman and Todd, 2006.

McGrath, Alister. *Bridge-building: Effective Christian Apologetics*. Leicester: Inter-Varsity, 1992.

———. *The Christian Theology Reader*. Third edition. Oxford: Blackwell, 2007.

———. *A Scientific Theology*: Volume 2, *Reality*. London: T. & T. Clark, 2006.

McLain, F. Michael. "Narrative Interpretation and the Problem of Double Agency." In *Divine Action: Studies Inspired by the Philosophical Theology of Austin Farrer*, edited by Brian Hebblethwaite and Edward Henderson, 143–72. Edinburgh: T. & T. Clark, 1990.

McLeish, Tom. *Faith and Wisdom in Science*. Oxford: Oxford University Press, 2014.
Mealand, David. *Poverty and Expectation in the Gospels*. London: SPCK, 1980.
Midgley, Mary. "Mind and Body: The End of Apartheid." In *Science, Consciousness and Ultimate Reality*, edited by David Lorimer, 173–96. Exeter: Imprint Academic, 2004.
Milbank, John. "An Apologia for Apologetics." In *Imaginative Apologetics*, edited by Andrew Davison, xiii–xxiii. London: SCM, 2011.
Moffatt, James. *Grace in the New Testament*. London: Hodder and Stoughton, 1931.
Moltmann, Jürgen. *The Church in the Power of the Spirit*. London: SCM, 1977.
———. *The Crucified God*. Translated by R.A. Wilson and John Bowden. London: SCM, 1974.
———. *Das Gekreuzigte Gott*. Munich: Chr. Kaiser, 1973.
———. *Theologie der Hoffnung*. Munich: Chr. Kaiser, 1964.
———. *Theology of Hope*. London: SCM, 1967.
Moscovici, Serge. "Toward a Theory of Conversion Behavior." In *Advances in Experimental Social Psychology*, vol. 13, edited by Leonard Berkowitz, 209–39. New York: Academic, 1980.
Moule, C.F.D. *The Origin of Christology*. Cambridge: Cambridge University Press, 1977.
Mozley, J.K. "Studdert Kennedy: Home Life and Early Years of his Ministry." In *G.A. Studdert Kennedy by his friends*, edited by J.K. Mozley, 13–83. London: Hodder and Stoughton, 1929.
Mullarkey, John. *Bergson and Philosophy*. Edinburgh: Edinburgh University Press, 1999.
Murdoch, Iris. *Metaphysics as a Guide to Morals*. Harmondsworth: Penguin, 1993.
Myers, Ched. *Binding the Strong Man: A Political Reading of Mark's Story of Jesus*. Maryknoll, NY: Orbis, 1988.
Newlands, George. *Theology of the Love of God*. London: Collins, 1980.
Newman, John Henry. *An Essay on the Development of Christian Doctrine*. Edited and with an introduction by J.M. Cameron. Harmondsworth: Penguin, 1974. First published in 1845.
Nicolaidis, Argyris. "Relational Nature." In *The Trinity and an Entangled World: Relationality in Physical Science and Theology*, edited by John Polkinghorne, 93–106. Grand Rapids, Michigan: William B. Eerdmans, 2010.
Niebuhr, Reinhold. *Christianity and Power Politics*. New York: Charles Scribner's Sons, 1940.
———. *Christian Realism and Political Problems*. London: Faber and Faber, 1954.
———. *The Godly and the Ungodly: Essays on the Religious and Secular Dimensions of Modern Life*. London: Faber and Faber, 1958.
———. *An Interpretation of Christian Ethics*. London: SCM, 1936.
———. *Moral Man and Immoral Society: A Study in Ethics and Politics*. New York: Charles Scribners' Sons, 1936.
Nineham, D.E. *Saint Mark*. Harmondsworth: Pelican, 1963.
Nowell-Smith, Patrick. "Miracles." In *New Essays in Philosophical Theology*, edited by Antony Flew and Alasdair MacIntyre, 243–53. London: SCM, 1955.
Oliver, John. *The Church and Social Order*. London: Mowbray, 1968.
Oliver, Simon. *Philosophy, God and Motion*. London and New York: Routledge, 2005.
Oman, John. *Grace and Personality*. Second edition. Cambridge: Cambridge University Press, 1919.

O'Murchu, Diarmuid. *Quantum Theology: Spiritual Implications of the New Physics.* New York: Crossroad, 2004.
Origen. *Contra Celsum.* Translated by Henry Chadwick. Second edition. Cambridge: Cambridge University Press, 1965. First published in 1953.
Otto, Rudolf. *The Idea of the Holy: An Inquiry into the Non-rational Factor in the idea of the Divine and its Relation to the Rational.* Translated by John W. Harvey. London: Oxford University Press, 1946.
Panikkar, Raimon. *Christophany: The Fullness of Man.* Maryknoll, NY: Orbis, 2004.
Pannenberg, Wolfhart. *Jesus God and Man.* London: SCM, 1968.
Parker, Linda. *A Seeker after Truths: The Life and Times of G.A. Studdert Kennedy ('Woodbine Willie') 1883–1929.* Solihull: Helion, 2018.
Pattison, George. *A Short Course in Christian Doctrine.* London: SCM, 2005.
Peacocke, Arthur and Ann Pederson. *The Music of Creation.* Minneapolis: Fortress, 2006.
Penner, Myron Bradley. *The End of Apologetics: Christian Witness in a Postmodern Context.* Grand Rapids, Michigan: Baker Academic, 2013.
Perkins, R.L. *Søren Kierkegaard.* London: Lutterworth, 1969.
Plato. *The Last Days of Socrates.* Harmondsworth: Penguin, 1959
Plato. *Phaedo.* In *Platonis Opera*, edited by John Burnet. Oxford: Oxford University Press, 1903. English translation from *Plato in Twelve Volumes*, vol. 1, translated by Harold North Fowler, introduction by W.R.M. Lamb. Cambridge, MA: Harvard University Press, and London: William Heinemann, 1966. www.perseus.tufts.edu/Texts/chunk_TOC.grk.html.
———. *Republic.* In *Platonis Opera*, edited by John Burnet. Oxford: Oxford University Press, 1903. English translation from *Plato in Twelve Volumes*, vols. 5 & 6, translated by Paul Shorey. Cambridge, MA: Harvard University Press, and London: William Heinemann Ltd., 1969. www.perseus.tufts.edu/Texts/chunk_TOC.grk.html.
Poland, Arlette. "If God *is* a Verb, then we are 'Human Becomings'". *Process Perspectives*, Fall 2007, 5.
Polkinghorne, John. "Kenotic Creation and Divine Action." In *The Work of Love: Creation as Kenosis*, edited by John Polkinghorne, 90–106. Grand Rapids, Michigan: Wm B. Eerdmans Publishing Company/London: SPCK, 2001.
——— *Science and Creation: The Search for Understanding.* Boston: New Science Library, 1989.
———. *Science and Providence: God's Interaction with the World.* London: SPCK, 1989.
Price, H.H. "Logical Positivism and Theology." *Philosophy* 10 (39) (1935) 313–31.
Prior, William J. *Unity and Development in Plato's Metaphysics.* London: Croom Helm, 1985.
Quick, Oliver. *The Gospel of Divine Action.* London: Nisbet, 1933.
Race, Alan. *Christians and Religious Pluralism: Patterns in the Christian Theology of Religions.* London: SCM, 1983.
Rahner, Karl. "Christianity and Non-Christian Religions." In Karl Rahner, *Theological Investigations*, vol. 5. Quoted in *Christianity and Plurality: Classic and Contemporary Readings*, edited by Richard J. Plantinga, 288–303. Oxford: Blackwell, 1999.
———. *Grace in Freedom.* London: Burns and Oates, 1969.
Ramsey, Arthur Michael. *From Gore to Temple: The Development of Anglican Theology between* Lux Mundi *and the Second World War 1889–1939.* London: Longmans, 1960.

———. *The Gospel and the Catholic Church*. London: Longmans, 1964. First published in 1936.
Ramsey, Ian T. *Models for Divine Activity*. London: SCM, 1973.
Rauschenbusch, Walter. *Christianity and the Social Crisis*. Louisville: Westminster/John Knox, 1923. First published in 1907.
———. *A Theology for the Social Gospel*. New York: Macmillan, 1917.
Reed, Bruce. *The Dynamics of Religion*. London: Darton, Longman and Todd, 1978.
Rees, B.R. *Pelagius: A Reluctant Heretic*. Woodbridge: Boydell, 1988.
Richardson, Alan. *Christian Apologetics*. London: SCM, 1947.
Ricoeur, Paul. *Du Texte à l'Action: Essais d'Herméneutique, II*. Paris: Éditions du Seuil, 1986.
———. *From Text to Action: Essays in Hermeneutics, II*. Translated by Kathleen Blamey from *Du Texte à l'Action: Essais d'Herméneutique, II*. London: Continuum, 2008.
Roberts, Robert Campbell. *Rudolf Bultmann's Theology*. London: SPCK, 1977.
Roberts, Tom Aerwyn. *History and Christian Apologetics*. London: SPCK, 1960.
Robinson, J.A.T. *The Body: A Study in Pauline Theology*. London: SCM, 1952.
———. *Honest to God*. London: SCM, 1963.
———. *The Human Face of God*. London: SCM, 1973.
———. *On Being the Church in the World*. London: SCM, 1960.
———. *Thou who Art: The Concept of the Personality of God*. New York and London: Continuum, 2006.
Rohr, Richard. *The Universal Christ*. London: SPCK, 2019.
Rolt, C.E. *The World's Redemption*. London: Longmans, Green and Co. 1913.
Sanders, E.P. *Jesus and Judaism*. London: SCM, 1985.
———. "Jesus and the Sinners." *Journal for the Study of the New Testament* 19 (1983) 5–36.
———. *Paul, the Law and the Jewish People*. Philadelphia: Fortress, 1983.
Sanneh, Lamin. *Translating the Message: The Missionary Impact on Culture*. Maryknoll, New York: Orbis, 1989.
Sargant, William. *Battle for the Mind: A Physiology of Conversion and Brain-washing*. London: Heinemann, 1976.
Saunders, Nicholas. *Divine Action and Modern Science*. Cambridge: Cambridge University Press, 2002.
Schillebeeckx, Edward. *Christ the Sacrament of the Encounter with God*. London and New York: Sheed and Ward, 1963.
———. *Jesus*. London: Collins, 1979.
Schleiermacher, F.D.E. *The Christian Faith*. Edinburgh: T. & T. Clark, 1928.
Schumacher, E.F. *Small is Beautiful: A Study of Economics as if People Mattered*. London: Abacus, 1974.
Schweitzer, Albert. *The Quest for the Historical Jesus*. London: SCM, 1981. First published in 1906.
Sedmak, Clemens. "Disruptions." In *Systems Theory and Theology: The Living Interplay Between Science and Religion*, edited by Markus Locker, 127–42. Eugene, Oregon: Pickwick, 2011.
———. "The Logic of Change: Three Perspectives and Lessons Learned." In *The Logics of Change: Poverty, Place, Identity, and Social Transforation Mechanisms*, edited by Elisabeth Kapferer, Andreas KIoch and Clemens Sedmak, 22–36. Newcastle: Cambridge Scholars, 2012.

Selby, Peter. *BeLonging*. London: SPCK, 1991.
Simon, Ulrich. *A Theology of Auschwitz*. London: SPCK, 1967.
Smith, John. *Select Discourses*. Cambridge: Cambridge University Press, 1859.
Sobrino, Jon. *Christology at the Crossroads*. London: SCM, 1978.
Sölle, Dorothee. *Christ the Representative*. Translated by David Lewis. London: SCM, 1967.
———. *Gott Denken: Einführung in die Theologie*. Stuttgart: Kreuz Verlag, 1990.
———. *Hinreise*. Stuttgart: Kreuz Verlag, 1977.
———. *The Inward Road and the Way Back*. Translated by David L. Scheidt. London: Darton, Longman and Todd, 1979.
———. *Leiden*. Stuttgart: Kreuz-Verlag, 1973.
———. *Stellvertretung*. Stuttgart: Kreuz Verlag, 1982. First published in 1965.
———. *Suffering*. Translated by E.R. Kalin. Philadelphia: Fortress, 1975.
———. *Thinking about God: An Introduction to Theology*. Translated by John Bowden. London: SCM, 1990.
Spufford, Francis. *Unapologetic*. London: Faber and Faber, 2012.
Stancliffe, David. *God's Pattern. Shaping our Worship, Ministry and Life*. London: SPCK, 2003.
Stevenson, J. (Ed.). *A New Eusebius*. London: SPCK, 1957.
Studdert Kennedy, Geoffrey. *The Hardest Part*. London and New York: Hodder and Stoughton, 1919.
———. *The Unutterable Beauty*. Fourteenth edition. London: Hodder and Stoughton, 1941.
Sykes, S.W. *Friedrich Schleiermacher*. London: Lutterworth, 1971.
Tanner, Kathryn. *Jesus, Humanity and the Trinity: A Brief Systematic Theology*. Minneapolis: Fortress, 2001.
Teilhard de Chardin, Pierre. *The Phenomenon of Man*. Translated from *Le Phénomène Humain* by Bernard Wall. London: Fontana / Collins, 1970. Subsequent editions were published under the title *The Human Phenomenon*.
Temple, William. *The Archbishop of York's Conference, Malvern 1941: The Life of the Church and the Order of Society*. London: Longmans, Green and Co., 1941.
———. *Christianity and Social Order*. London: Shepheard-Walwyn/SPCK, 1976. First published by Penguin in 1942.
———. *Personal Religion and the Life of Fellowship*. London: Longman, Green and Co., 1926.
Tertullian. *Against Marcion*. http://www.tertullian.org/anf/anf03/anf03-29.htm. Translated by Peter Holmes from *Adversus Marcionem*, book II, 1868, http://www.tertullian.org/articles/evans_marc/evans_marc_05book2.htm.
———. *On the Prescription of Heretics*. http://www.tertullian.org/latin/de_praescriptione_haereticorum.htm. Translated by Bindley, from *De Praescriptione Haereticorum*, 1914, http://www.tertullian.org/articles/bindley_test/bindley_test_07prae.htm.
TeSelle, Eugene. "Divine Action: The Doctrinal Tradition." In *Divine Action: Studies Inspired by the Philosophical Theology of Austin Farrer*, edited by Brian Hebblethwaite and Edward Henderson, 71–91. Edinburgh: T. & T. Clark, 1990.
Theissen, Gerd. *The First Followers of Jesus*. London: SCM, 1978.

Theodoret. "Apology." Quoted in Yannis Papadogiannakis, *Christianity and Hellenism in the Fifth Century Greek East: Theodoret's Apologetics Against the Greeks in Context*, 40. Cambridge, Massachusetts: Harvard University Press, 2012.

Thielicke, Helmut. *The Waiting Father*. Translated by J. Doberstein. San Francisco: Harper and Row, 1959.

Thomas, Owen. "Recent Thought on Divine Agency." In *Divine Action: Studies Inspired by the Philosophical Theology of Austin Farrer*, edited by Brian Hebblethwaite and Edward Henderson, 35–50. Edinburgh: T. & T. Clark, 1990.

Tillich, Paul. *The Courage to Be*. London: Collins, 1962.

———. *The Shaking of the Foundations*. Harmondsworth: Pelican, 1962.

Torrance, Alan. "Theism, Naturalism and Cognitive Science: Can the Academy Make Sense of Itself?" In *Science, Consciousness and Ultimate Reality*, edited by David Lorimer, 197–216. Exeter: Imprint Academic, 2004.

Torrance, T.F. *The Doctrine of Grace in the Apostolic Fathers*. Edinburgh: Oliver and Boyd, 1948.

Torry, Malcolm. *An Actological Metaphysic*. Eugene, OR: Resource/Wipf and Stock, 2023.

———. *Actological Readings in Continental Philosophy*. Eugene, OR: Resource/Wipf and Stock, 2023.

———. *Actology: Action, Change and Diversity in the Western Philosophical Tradition*. Eugene, OR: Resource/Wipf and Stock, 2020.

———. *An Actology of the Given*. Eugene, OR: Resource/Wipf and Stock, 2023.

———. *Citizen's Basic Income: A Christian Social Policy*. London: Darton, Longman and Todd, 2016.

———. *The Feasibility of Citizen's Income*. New York: Palgrave Macmillan, 2016.

———. "'Logic' and 'Action': Two New Readings of the New Testament." *Theology* 111 (860) (2008) 93–101.

———. *Managing God's Business: Religious and Faith-based Organizations and their Management*. Aldershot: Ashgate, 2005.

———. *Managing Religion: The Management of Christian Religious and Faith-based Organisations*. Two volumes, London: Palgrave Macmillan 2014.

———. *Mark's Gospel: An Actological Reading*. Eugene, OR: Resource/Wipf and Stock, 2022.

———. *Mediating Institutions: Creating Relationships Between Religion and an Urban World*. London: Palgrave Macmillan, 2016.

———. "On Building a New Christendom: Lessons from South London Parishes." *Theology* CXII (870) (2009) 435–43.

———. "On Completing the Apologetic Spectrum." *Theology* 103 (812) (2000) 108–15.

———. "A Place at the Table." *Church Times*, 3rd May 1991.

———. "Two Kinds of Ambiguity." *King's Theological Review* 3 (1) (1980) 24–28.

———. *Why we Need a Citizen's Basic Income: The Desirability, Feasibility and Implementation of an Unconditional Income*. Bristol: Policy, 2018.

Tracy, David. *The Analogical Imagination: Christian Theology and the Culture of Pluralism*. London: SCM, 1981.

Tracy, Thomas F.. "Narrative Theology and the Acts of God." In *Divine Action: Studies Inspired by the Philosophical Theology of Austin Farrer*, edited by Brian Hebblethwaite and Edward Henderson, 173–96. Edinburgh: T. & T. Clark, 1990.

Traherne, Thomas. *Centuries of Meditations*. I, 51–53. Quoted in *Celebrating the Seasons: Daily Spiritual Readings for the Christian Year*, edited by Robert Atwell, 316. Norwich: Canterbury Press, 1999.
Van Buren, Paul. *The Secular Meaning of the Gospel*. London: SCM, 1963.
Vanhoozer, Kevin J. "Once More into the Borderlands: The Way of Wisdom in Philosophy and Theology after the 'Turn to Drama.'" In *Transcending Boundaries in Philosophy and Theology: Reason, Meaning and Experience*, edited by Kevin J. Vanhoozer and Martin Warner, 31–54. Aldershot: Ashgate, 2007.
Vanhoozer, Kevin J. and Martin Warner. "Introduction." In *Transcending Boundaries in Philosophy and Theology: Reason, Meaning and Experience*, edited by Kevin J. Vanhoozer and Martin Warner, 1–13. Aldershot: Ashgate, 2007.
Vanstone, W.H. *Love's Endeavour, Love's Expense*. London: Darton, Longman and Todd, 1977.
Vermes, Geza. *Jesus the Jew: A Historian's Reading of the Gospels*. Third edition. London: SCM, 2001.
Vernon, Mark. *Science, Religion and the Meaning of Life*. Basingstoke: Palgrave Macmillan, 2007.
Von Balthasar, Hans Urs. *Martin Buber and Christianity: A Dialogue between Israel and the Church*. Translated by Alexander Dru. London: Harvill, 1961.
———. *Theodrama: Theological Dramatic Theory: IV: The Action*. Translated by Graham Harrison. San Francisco: Ignatius, 1994.
Ward, Keith. *The Concept of God*. Glasgow: Collins/Fount, 1977.
———. *The Evidence for God: The Case for the Existence of the Spiritual Dimension*. London: Darton, Longman and Todd, 2014.
———. *Holding Fast to God: A Reply to Don Cupitt*. London: SPCK, 1982.
———. "Human Nature and the Soul." In *Science, Consciousness and Ultimate Reality*, edited by David Lorimer, 161–72. Exeter: Imprint Academic, 2004.
———. "Plato and his Legacy." A Gresham College lecture. 22nd November 2007: http://www.gresham.ac.uk/lectures-and-events/plato-and-his-legacy.
Ware, Kallistos. "The Holy Trinity: Model for Personhood-in-Relation." In *The Trinity and an Entangled World: Relationality in Physical Science and Theology*, edited by John Polkinghorne, 107–29. Grand Rapids, Michigan: William B. Eerdmans, 2010.
Watson, Francis. *Paul, Judaism and the Gentiles*. Cambridge: Cambridge University Press, 1986.
Weil, Simone, *Waiting on God*. London: Fontana, 1959.
Wells, Harold. *The Christic Center: Life-giving and Liberating*. Maryknoll, New York: Orbis, 2004,
Whitehead, Alfred North. *Process and Reality*. New York: Macmillan, 1929.
———. *Process and Reality: Corrected Edition*. Edited by Ray Griffin and Donald W. Sherburne. New York: The Free Press, 1978.
Wigley, Stephen. *Balthasar's Trilogy*. London: Continuum, 2010.
Williams, N.P. *The Grace of God*. London: Longmans, Green and Co., 1930.
Williams, Rowan. "foreword." In *Mission-shaped Church: Church Planting and Fresh Expressions of Church in a Changing Context*, vii, London: Church House, 2004.
———. "Foreword." In *The Mystery of the Eucharist*, edited by Henry McAdoo and Kenneth Stevenson, viii–ix. Norwich: Canterbury Press, 1995.

———. *Open to Judgement*. London: Darton, Longman and Todd, 2002. First published in 1994.
———. "Trinity and Pluralism." In *Christian Uniqueness Reconsidered: The Myth of a Pluralistic Theology of Religions*, edited by Gavin D'Costa, 3–15. New York: Orbis, 1990.
Winter, David. "The Key to the Myste.'". *Church Times*, 27 April 2018, 18.
Wittgenstein, Ludwig. *Philosophische Untersuchungen / Philosophical Investigations*. The German text with a revised English translation, third edition. Translated by G.E.M. Anscombe. Oxford: Basil Blackwell, 2001. First published in 1953.
Wolterstorft, Nicholas. "Sacrament as Action, not Presence." In *Christ: The Sacramental Word*, edited by David Brown and Ann Loades, 103–22. London: SPCK, 1996.
Wright, N.T. *The Challenge of Jesus*. London: SPCK, 2000.
———. *Jesus and the Victory of God*. London: SPCK, 1996.
———. *The New Testament and the People of God*. London: SPCK, 1992.
———. *The Resurrection of the Son of God*. London: SPCK, 2003.
Wright, Tom. *How God Became King: Getting to the Heart of the Gospels*. London: SPCK, 2012.
Yarnold, Edward. *The Second Gift: A Study of Grace*. Slough: St. Paul, 1974.
Žižek, Slavoj. *Event: A Philosophical Journey Through a Concept*. Brooklyn and London: Melville House, 2014.
Zizioulas, John. *Being as Communion: Studies in Personhood and the Church*. London: Darton, Longman and Todd, 1985.
———. "Relational Ontology: Insights from Patristic Thought." In *The Trinity and an Entangled World: Relationality in Physical Science and Theology*, edited by John Polkinghorne, 146–56. Grand Rapids, Michigan: William B. Eerdmans, 2010.

Subject Index

acceptance, 44, 55–56, 86, 105, 108, 112, 124, 126, 141, 143, 159–61, 164, 175, 177, 188, 213, 217, 237, 253

accident, 66, 87, 107–8, 112

Action, viii–x, xiii, xv, 3, 25, 32, 38, 42, 45–53, 55–60, 63–67, 69–71, 74, 76, 88–89, 95–97, 100, 118, 150, 152–54, 182–83, 189–91, 193–94, 206, 225–26, 231, 234, 247, 255, 259–60, 267, 270–72

action, viii, xi, xiii, xv, 10, 18, 24–26, 28–29, 32–35, 37–38, 40, 42–61, 63–72, 74–78, 83, 86–91, 97, 100, 107, 114, 118–19, 126, 131, 142, 146, 150–56, 158–59, 171, 175–76, 178–80, 182–83, 186, 189–93, 198, 200–203, 206–7, 209, 211–12, 218–19, 221–28, 231, 236–37, 255, 258–60, 262, 264, 267–71

   in changing patterns, *see* changing patterns of action

Actological Explorations, ii, x–xi, xiii, xv–xvi, 10, 12, 26, 40–42, 49, 59, 266, 268–70, 272

actology, ii, x–xi, xiii–xvi, 1, 5, 12, 25–26, 37, 42–43, 45, 48–51, 53, 55–57, 60, 64–65, 69, 94, 96–97, 111, 118, 129, 138, 157–58, 185, 191–93, 196, 198–99, 207–8, 222–23, 227, 229, 254–55, 260, 266–72

Africa, 30

allegory, 15, 21, 246

Alpha Course, 21

ambiguity, 19, 55, 80, 82, 101, 128, 136, 142, 144, 146, 167, 173–74, 216, 246–47, 250–52

America, 81, 83

analogy, 2, 29, 39, 43, 48, 51, 53, 67, 70, 75, 77, 88, 90–91, 191, 205–6, 246, 256, 271

angel, 222, 225

anger, 89, 91, 121, 159, 167, 175, 213, 237

animal, 57, 78, 87, 109, 251

anthropology, ii, 263, 267

Antioch, 130–31

apocalyptic, 11, 101, 110, 116, 128, 168, 220, 250

apologetics, viii, xv–xvi, 1–45, 48, 50–51, 53, 96, 182–83, 192, 213, 218, 221, 225, 269–70

apostles, 37, 106, 130, 137, 153, 155, 178, 185, 212, 230, 244, 247

Arabic, 17

Aramaic, 10

art, 8, 48, 41–42, 77

ascension, 114, 156, 164, 224

atheism, 5, 15, 87, 263
Athens, 10, 29, 31, 37, 40
atom, 68
atonement, 43, 124, 164–65, 181, 200
    theories of, xv, 143–44, 196–200
Auschwitz, 85, 176–77, 270
authority, 5, 11, 15–17, 34, 83, 102, 105, 109, 128, 163, 221, 231, 236–37, 245, 250, 253, 261–62, 268

Babylon, 172, 174
baptism, 84, 108–9, 118, 132–35, 140–41, 184, 209–10, 212–13, 218, 224–25, 233, 236
Basic Income, ix–x, 239, 242–43
beauty, 32, 44, 65, 172–73, 213, 217, 221
becoming, 5, 11, 14, 23, 29, 31–33, 41, 45, 47, 52–53, 55–56, 58–59, 66, 71, 73, 76, 78, 93, 99–100, 114–15, 134, 140–41, 143, 150, 153, 155, 157, 159, 161–62, 164, 167, 179, 182, 191, 212, 214, 216–17, 225, 232–35, 239, 243, 254, 265
Being, i, viii–x, xiii, xv, 5, 15, 18–20, 28–29, 34, 37, 48–49, 51–52, 54, 57–58, 60–61, 64, 71, 75–76, 97, 118, 158, 191, 206, 222, 231, 234, 259–60, 267, 270, 272
being, ii, viii, x, xiii–xvi, 6, 17, 19–20, 30, 35, 37–38, 44, 46–52, 54–58, 60, 62, 64, 68, 71, 86, 97, 111–12, 117, 129, 142, 153, 157, 164, 170–71, 185, 189–90, 192–93, 215, 222, 224, 227, 231, 233–34, 238, 248, 267, 269–70
    see also human being
belief, 1, 3, 5–11, 14–15, 17, 23–24, 27, 31, 34, 43, 45, 51, 65, 69, 75, 78, 80, 85–86, 99, 103–4, 107, 113, 116, 120, 123, 125–28, 132–33, 140–42, 144, 147–49, 159–60, 165–68, 171–72, 187–88, 200, 202, 204–5, 210, 215–16, 218, 220–22, 224–25, 228–34, 236, 248, 250, 253, 256–57, 262
belonging, 21, 34, 66–67, 99–100, 116, 119, 125, 127, 141, 170, 182, 188, 200–202, 210, 217, 233–34, 237, 241, 256, 257, 259, 262–63
Bethlehem, 107, 127
Bible, xvi, 11, 16–17, 19, 23, 30, 37, 47, 62, 93, 138, 171, 183, 211–12, 217, 221, 229, 244–54, 261–62, 269
    see also Hebrew Scriptures; New Testament
biology, 29, 127–28
birth, 101, 111, 154–55, 161, 192, 200–202, 246
    narratives, 107, 113, 127, 211, 248, 252
    new, 15, 62, 232
    virgin, 107, 112, 127–28, 154, 248, 252
bisexuality, 219
bishop, 24, 84, 140, 212
body, 31, 33, 81, 114–15, 130, 155–56, 169, 176–77, 186, 192, 198, 204, 208–9, 214, 224, 236–37
    spiritual, 156
Body of Christ, 41, 85, 113–15, 135, 154, 183, 186, 208–11, 216, 224, 234
    see also Church
Book of Common Prayer, 145
boundaries, xv, 2, 13, 24, 29, 40, 42, 66, 92, 115, 117, 122, 126, 130–32, 134–37, 140, 147, 161–63, 217–220, 240, 264–65, 269

SUBJECT INDEX

Britain, 19, 22, 80

Cambridge Platonists, 18
  see also Platonism
Caribbean, the, 81
cathedral of the mind, 8-9, 12, 22,
    48-49, 271
  see also marquee
causality, ii, 17, 50-51, 60-61, 64, 78,
    113, 115, 143, 145, 147, 150-51,
    153, 164, 192, 198, 205, 268-69
change, ii, vii-vii, x-xi, xiii-xvi, 3-4,
    10, 19, 24-25, 32-33, 35-44,
    47-49, 51-53, 55, 57-58, 60,
    63-81, 83, 86, 88, 90, 94, 97-98,
    101-2, 112-13, 115-20, 139, 141,
    146, 150-51, 154, 157, 161-63,
    179, 182-83, 188-89, 191-93,
    201-3, 205, 208, 217, 219-22,
    228-32, 234, 236-45, 247, 250,
    255, 259-61, 263-72
changing patterns of action, viii-xi,
    xiii-xvi, 2-3, 5, 24-25, 38,
    41-53, 56-60, 62-80, 83, 85-91,
    94-97, 99-101, 103-4, 106-7,
    109-19, 129-30, 139-40, 149-
    71, 176-87, 189-235, 237-39,
    241-47, 250, 254-56, 258-62,
    266-72
chaos, 43-44, 50, 63, 66, 68-70, 184,
    191, 268
child, 54, 75, 84-86, 91, 103, 110, 124,
    128, 138, 154, 159, 169, 173, 187,
    209, 218, 241, 251, 253
  abuse, 197, 199
Child Benefit, 243
choice, 2-6, 14, 28-29, 35, 46, 51,
    53-54, 57-58, 74, 78-80, 82,
    86-88, 100-108, 112-16, 121,
    128-30, 133, 135, 142, 150-51,
    156-58, 176, 181, 183, 188-90,
    197, 199, 201, 205, 215, 221, 226,
    228-30, 232, 241-43, 247-50,
    253, 258, 264
Christian Faith, viii-ix, 1-3, 5, 6,
    8-11, 13, 15-19, 21-24, 27-28,
    30-32, 34-35, 38-40, 48, 53,
    59, 103, 107, 109, 116, 126, 137,
    142-46, 149, 162, 206-7, 220,
    234, 240, 246, 249, 256-58, 261,
    263
Christian gospel, see good news/
    gospel
Christian, viii, xvi, 13-15, 29, 31,
    34-35, 38, 51, 62, 99, 105-6,
    113-14, 116, 118-20, 124-36,
    139-42, 148, 154-56, 160, 163,
    169, 175, 183, 185, 188, 190,
    196, 201, 205, 208, 210-11, 213,
    215, 222, 224, 227-29, 232, 236,
    240, 243, 245, 247-50, 253, 256,
    260-62, 269, 270-71
  anonymous, 257
  apologetics, see apologetics
  believing, see Christian Faith
  doctrine, see doctrine
  philosophy, see philosophy,
    Christian
  scriptures, see New Testament
  theology, see theology, Christian
  tradition, see tradition, Christian
  see also doing Christianly
Christianity, see Christian Faith
Christmas, 85, 94, 154
Christology, 52, 98, 100, 103, 150,
    152, 155, 183, 256-59
  see also Kenotic Christology
Church, the, viii, xvi, 2-3, 7-8, 11-12,
    15-17, 23-24, 31-32, 38, 40-41,
    43, 45, 52-53, 58, 62, 65, 81, 83-
    84, 101, 104, 107, 109, 114-15,
    118-20, 124-26, 130-35,

(the Church continued)
  317–38, 140–43, 146–49, 154,
  156–57, 161–63, 169, 171,
  173–75, 178, 180, 183–84, 186,
  189–93, 204, 207–28, 230–34,
  236–37, 240–41, 245, 247–48,
  251, 257, 262, 269, 271
 catholic, 11, 224
 Fathers, 14–16, 145
 Roman Catholic, 11, 218
 see *also* Body of Christ
Church of England, vii, x, 92, 145,
  218, 224, 241, 264
circumcision, 132, 136
city, 16, 81, 89, 131, 149, 171–80, 187,
  213, 236–37
 secular, 178
City of God, xvi, 16, 81, 155, 157,
  166–81, 186–87, 194, 203,
  209–10, 212–16, 218, 221, 228,
  233, 235–43, 248, 253, 269
 see *also* Kingdom of God
class, social, 98, 218
co-creation, 175, 203, 241
commandment, 33, 80, 122, 214
 new, 62, 106
commitment, 4, 65, 101, 110, 129,
  133, 185, 210, 214, 229–32, 236,
  238–40, 256, 262, 264
communication, 1, 4–5, 9, 25, 27,
  36, 43, 53, 62, 104–5, 117, 147,
  151–52, 155, 184, 229, 245, 247
communion, 37, 54, 84–85, 190,
  193–94, 218, 221–23
community, 23–24, 34, 36, 41, 43,
  80, 82, 90, 99, 103, 108, 111,
  115, 132, 134–35, 161, 168, 171,
  175–79, 190, 192–93, 201, 205,
  207, 222, 237, 240, 243, 249, 262,
  264

complexity, 3, 5, 12, 28–30, 32, 34,
  41, 65, 69, 83, 87, 90, 104, 109,
  111, 140, 152, 157, 164, 176, 178,
  193–94, 200, 203, 209, 216, 237,
  247, 261–62
 Christian, 99, 103, 134, 249
conceptual structure, *see* structure,
  conceptual
contemplation, 23, 32, 44, 94, 175,
  213, 218
context, viii, xv–xvi, 3, 7, 12, 14,
  23–24, 36–38, 43, 48, 50, 52,
  55, 65, 77, 79, 92, 98, 101, 104,
  118, 125, 136, 140, 142, 148,
  155, 159, 161–62, 175, 183, 192,
  196, 199, 208, 212, 217–18, 222,
  227, 229–30, 236, 238, 245, 248,
  251–52, 255–56, 259, 261, 263,
  267–70
contingency, 2, 43, 67, 71, 268, 270
conversion, 3–5, 12, 15–16, 36, 130,
  132, 135, 143, 189, 204, 213,
  219–20, 231–32, 234, 253, 272
cosmological argument, 17, 64,
  268–70
cosmos, 3, 9, 51–52, 71, 77, 92, 107,
  158, 182, 186, 191, 218–19, 222,
  266–67
covenant, 121–24, 126, 131–34, 137,
  239
 new, 62, 106, 131
creation, 18, 34, 37, 45, 50–51, 56–59,
  62–63, 65–71, 73–75, 77, 79,
  87, 89–90, 93, 95, 106, 118, 138,
  143, 146–47, 151, 158, 160–61,
  163–64, 169–72, 175, 178,
  181–84, 188, 194, 203, 208, 217,
  237, 241, 255–56, 259–60
 new, 62, 106, 115, 169–70, 201

creativity, 55, 58, 77, 92, 106, 137, 143, 151, 170, 194, 208, 255–56, 259–60

Creator, 58, 65–72, 90, 94, 96, 98, 103, 152, 170, 183, 188, 190, 193–95, 203, 231, 241, 271
  see also Father, the; God

crucifixion, 21, 53–54, 90–91, 93–94, 97, 109–11, 116, 118, 163–64, 193, 195, 197–99, 201
  see also death

culture, 2–3, 5–6, 10–11, 16, 18–19, 22–24, 30, 35–36, 38–40, 42, 61, 69, 104, 108, 118, 134, 171, 189, 206–8, 235–36, 238, 262
  classical, 15–16

dark matter, 67, 70

death, 31, 41, 43, 53, 80, 86–87, 89, 91, 94, 105, 108, 111, 114, 118–19, 121, 126, 129, 132, 144, 151, 154, 156–57, 163–65, 170, 173–77, 179, 185, 196–203, 205, 210, 229, 233, 238, 245–46, 251–54, 268
  see also crucifixion

deconstruction, 41

definition, xvi, 4–5, 57, 75–76, 78, 91, 98–99, 101–3, 109, 111, 119, 126–27, 146, 148, 161, 175, 177, 182–83, 186, 189, 191, 219, 228, 241, 258

democracy, 81–83, 240

Didache, the, 139

différance, 7

disciple, 11, 41, 78, 98, 102, 108, 111, 113, 121, 123, 140, 142, 149, 156, 184, 204–5, 209, 223, 231, 236–37, 248, 257

disciplines, 2–4, 6, 9, 29, 32, 45, 49, 51, 193, 263, 270–71

discourse, 8, 11, 157
  see also narrative

diversity, ii, vii–viii, xi, xiii–xvi, 5, 7–10, 23–26, 32, 35, 37–38, 40–43, 48, 55, 65, 76, 79–80, 83, 90, 111, 117, 124, 146, 158, 171–72, 174–78, 180–83, 188, 192, 195–96, 198–99, 208, 217, 221–22, 239–40, 243, 248, 250, 258–60, 262–70, 272

divinity, 18, 23–24, 31, 41–43, 45, 50–51, 53, 60, 62, 75, 90–93, 100, 115, 126, 128, 150–53, 157, 159, 164, 170, 182, 184, 193, 198, 204, 224–25, 234, 257–58

doctrine, 2, 17, 21, 24, 31, 34, 36, 46–48, 50, 53, 56, 61, 81, 91, 93, 96–97, 100, 102, 128, 144, 149, 163, 182, 196, 207, 228–29, 247, 258

doing Christianly, 116, 215–21, 227–43, 269
  see also practice, Christian

double agency, 75

drama, 8, 41, 61–62, 71, 153

dynamic, the, ii, vii–viii, xi, xiii–xvi, 8–12, 35, 43, 48, 53–55, 57, 60, 69, 76–77, 96, 100, 126, 138, 1450, 144, 151–52, 157, 171, 179, 208, 222, 256, 259–60, 270

Earth, 66, 70, 89, 122, 128, 154–55, 163, 172, 180, 195
  new, 62, 174

earthquake, 62, 88, 90

economics/economy, 3–4, 50, 81–83, 110, 146, 185, 214, 236–37, 239–43, 270

ecumenism, 11, 221–25, 258

emotion, 6, 85, 90, 104–5, 164, 171, 175, 205–6

emperor, 142–43
Enlightenment, the, 11, 22, 34
entity, xvi, 3, 152, 224
epistle, 14, 139
equality, 82, 98, 110, 134–35, 137, 163, 185, 214, 218–20, 239
eschatology, 77, 204, 263
essence, 11, 18, 61, 66, 78, 159, 227
eternity, 15–16, 41, 43, 50, 52–53, 56, 58–59, 67, 71, 77, 92, 100–101, 141, 151, 154, 164, 179, 198, 222, 257, 267
ethics, 7, 18, 22–23, 36, 78, 82, 118–19, 125–26, 132, 137, 142, 147–49, 160–61, 205, 216, 227–28, 240, 242–43, 254, 261
Eucharist, 41, 43, 84–85, 114–15, 156–57, 171, 178, 183, 207, 209–10, 212–13, 221, 223–25
evangelical church/tradition, 22, 24, 218, 232
evangelism, 11, 23, 212–13
event, 11, 13, 19, 21–22, 34, 39, 49, 51, 57, 62, 75, 78, 85, 102, 105, 112, 131, 134, 143, 152, 154–57, 165, 168, 178, 186, 197, 203, 205, 207, 211–12, 217, 229, 245, 248, 251, 254, 264, 268–69
evil, 43–45, 73–81, 83, 86–88, 90–91, 95, 102, 108–9, 143, 159, 171, 174–77, 181–82, 185, 194–95, 197, 200–201, 211, 239, 270
evolution, 3, 20, 67, 71, 107–8, 112, 119, 147, 176, 180, 203, 268, 271
exclusivism, 133, 257, 260
exemplarism, 197
existence, 16–19, 23, 25, 32, 52, 55, 62, 64, 66–67, 92, 104, 107, 122, 135, 148, 150
existentialism, 19–20, 22

experience, viii, xiv–xv, 4–6, 9, 15–16, 18, 23, 35–36, 38, 40–44, 48, 52–54, 58, 62, 65, 67, 70, 75–79, 84–85, 87–88, 91, 94, 101, 112–13, 116–17, 121, 123, 126–27, 130–32, 135, 141, 143, 146–47, 149, 151–52, 155–57, 159, 164–65, 173, 175–76, 178–79, 182, 186, 190, 193, 195, 198–99, 201, 203–5, 208, 214, 217, 220, 228, 231–32, 234, 238, 244–45, 248, 256, 258, 260, 262, 264, 271–72

faith, 2, 8, 16–19, 27–29, 33–36, 39–40, 58, 64–65, 82, 109, 115, 121, 125, 130–37, 140–41, 145–48, 159–63, 183–84, 188–89, 199, 208–9, 211–12, 215, 219, 229–30, 234, 237, 249, 251, 253, 255–60, 264
  in Christ, 15, 58, 131–36, 215
  of Christ, 58, 136–37, 199
  see also Christian Faith; community
Fall, the, 43
family, 167, 178, 204, 216, 222, 239–240, 242
family likeness/resemblance, 41, 65, 75, 78, 104, 113, 119, 150, 156, 163, 169, 178, 185–87, 190, 192–93, 199, 204, 211, 216, 222–24, 227, 230–31, 233–34, 254
Father, the, 16, 33, 42–43, 81, 90, 96, 98, 100–101, 103–4, 109, 121, 127, 144, 152–53, 157, 161, 164–65, 167, 169–70, 187–90, 192–93, 200, 205, 209, 215, 251
  see also Creator; God
flesh, 2, 14, 98, 100–101, 153, 156–57, 165, 169, 191, 220, 228, 233
flux, see change

forgiveness, 54, 58, 74, 80, 85, 105, 110, 112, 115, 121, 128, 154, 160–61, 170, 177, 180, 183, 185–88, 197, 199–202, 204, 214, 217, 233, 243, 251
Form, *see* Platonism
form criticism, 246
form of God, *see* God, form of
fourth gospel, *see* John's Gospel *in the scripture index*
framework, conceptual/philosophical, viii–ix, 2, 4, 6–8, 12, 14–16, 20, 22–23, 35, 39–40, 42, 48, 51–52, 55, 65, 71, 80, 94–95, 100, 119, 134, 144, 152, 155, 182–83, 207–8, 221–24, 254–56, 259–60, 263–64, 268, 270–72
  see also structure, conceptual; system
France, 19
freedom, 22, 51, 54, 90, 93, 141–43, 147–48, 150, 169, 175–76, 179, 190, 213, 236, 241–42, 269
future, the, 20, 32, 36, 71, 79, 111, 118–19, 129, 167–69, 179, 204, 215–16, 228, 234, 241–42

Galilee, 97, 123, 156, 183, 230
Garden of Gethsemane, 111, 187–88
gender, 187, 219
genealogy, 127, 248
generosity, 78, 80, 87, 100, 111, 117, 119–22, 124, 126, 130, 136, 138–41, 143–46, 149, 155, 157, 161, 170, 214, 217, 223, 227, 240, 249
Gentiles, 10, 11, 13, 101–2
Germany, 19, 81, 93, 120–26, 130–36, 147, 218–19, 247, 251, 253
gift, ii, xiii, 19, 27, 32, 37, 47, 80, 86, 105, 108, 111, 119, 121–22, 124–25, 130–32, 134, 139–41, 145–46, 159–61, 177, 189, 200, 204–5, 209, 215, 220, 239–43, 249, 253, 257, 267
  see also grace
given, the, *see* gift
Gnosticism, 2, 87
God, *passim*
  form of, 163–64
  image of, 102, 121, 164, 175, 181, 197, 203, 225
  suffering of, vii, xvi, 44, 51, 57, 65, 73–95, 102, 154, 159, 161, 165, 183, 189, 194, 198, 200–201, 205, 267–69
  see also Creator; Father, the; Mother, the; Passibilism; Patripassionism
goodness, 18, 73–74, 78–79, 87–88, 90, 104, 106, 143, 160, 194, 200
good news/gospel, the, x, 14, 16, 29, 31, 39–40, 53, 81, 119, 124–26, 131, 140, 147, 149, 161, 174–75, 121, 218, 139, 249, 257
gospels, *see the scripture index*
grace, xvi, 23, 25, 41–43, 58, 75, 78–81, 86, 94, 100–101, 103–4, 106, 111–12, 117–49, 155, 157–61, 164, 170–71, 176–77, 184–86, 188–90, 192, 199–200, 202–4, 209–10, 212, 214–15, 217–20, 223–25, 227, 233–34, 236, 239–43, 249, 257, 269, 272
  see also gift
gravity, 68
Greece/Greek, 10–11, 14–15, 29–31, 46, 48, 59, 61, 99, 134, 174, 237, 240, 266, 273
guilt, 21, 141, 145, 159, 202

happening, 49, 54, 58–59, 65, 68, 88, 107, 112, 157, 159, 170, 186, 189, 204–5, 208, 214, 228, 245–46, 254

healing/health, 5, 58, 76–77, 87, 90, 98, 102, 110–11, 115, 121–22, 127, 130, 151, 154–55, 157, 160–61, 165–66, 168, 179, 183–84, 186, 196, 201–2, 210, 212, 215–16, 233, 236–37, 239, 243, 248

heaven, 54, 62, 66, 102, 112, 154, 156, 163–64, 167–68, 171, 174, 188, 222, 246

Hebrew Scriptures, xvi, 10–11, 54, 61, 121, 187, 189, 192, 196, 211, 239, 245, 247, 250–51, 253

see also Bible

hegemony, 11, 256

hell, 112, 253

Hellenism, see Greece/Greek

hermeneutics, 37, 39, 57, 61

see also interpretation

heterosexuality, 218

hierarchy, 221

High Priest, 101, 128, 156, 162

history, xiii–xv, 1, 3–4, 6–7, 12–25, 27, 29, 37, 39, 53–54, 61, 65, 81, 94, 97, 101–2, 104, 106, 108–9, 111–13, 116, 118, 126–28, 134–35, 137, 147, 150–51, 156–57, 163, 165–66, 175–76, 183, 186, 198, 201, 207, 209, 212, 237, 240–41, 244–47, 250–51, 257–58, 262–63, 266, 270

Holy Spirit, 41, 43, 52, 58, 62, 94, 101, 103, 139–40, 144, 146, 157, 171, 183–85, 190, 193–95, 219, 231–32, 234, 244, 247, 262

homosexuality, 218–19

hope, 6, 24, 44–45, 64, 76–77, 79–80, 82, 85–86, 89–90, 92, 101, 108, 110, 113, 121, 125, 128–29, 149, 155, 157, 161–62, 166, 169, 171, 173, 175–77, 179–81, 185, 188, 194, 205, 213–14, 218, 228, 233–34, 236, 243, 248, 253–54, 259, 264

human being, vii, 5, 43, 46, 57, 81, 94, 100, 105, 113, 115, 148, 150–52, 159, 162–64, 176, 184, 192–94, 246, 262

see also human nature; humanity

human nature, 79–80, 83

see also human being; humanity

humanity, 14, 19, 62, 87, 92–93, 100, 102, 106, 110, 114, 127–28, 143, 148, 150–51, 163–65, 170, 173, 185, 198–204, 215, 222, 225, 228, 266

see also human being; human nature

humility, 33, 104–6, 163–64, 197, 241

hymn, 164, 249

idealism, 18, 55, 82–83, 176

see also Platonism

identity, 52, 70, 75, 99, 133–34, 147, 152, 191–92, 223, 249, 255

illness, 98, 196

image of God, see God, image of

immanence, 43, 92, 256

incarnation, 2, 21, 32, 34, 41, 54, 56, 93, 97, 100–101, 128, 154, 201, 224, 263

inclusivism, 257, 259–60

India, 30

individual, ix, xi, 3–6, 16, 19, 25, 36, 82–83, 90, 102–3, 109, 113–14, 118, 121, 130, 134, 178, 182, 185, 204–5, 207, 212–13, 215, 221,

224, 228, 230, 236–43, 253, 257, 263–65
inequality, 135, 219–20, 239
injustice, 44, 108, 110–11, 113, 171, 175, 177, 185, 202, 238
inspiration, 133, 194, 208, 227, 254
institution, 5, 36, 65, 82, 149, 159, 161, 178, 192–93, 208, 212–13, 221, 236, 240, 243, 245, 253, 261–64
  religious, 5, 140, 178, 212, 263
interpretation, ix–x, 9, 15, 21, 28, 40, 56, 93, 98, 100–102, 108, 113, 116, 120, 128, 150–52, 155, 163–64, 182–84, 186, 203, 211–12, 217, 219, 222, 233, 236, 244–50, 252–53, 261
  see also hermeneutics
irony, 83, 101, 270
Islam, 188, 260–63
Israel, 13, 16, 61, 102, 106–8, 121–32, 135, 150, 163, 172, 179, 189, 219, 225, 239, 244, 251

Jerusalem, 31, 97, 111, 122, 129, 131, 142, 153, 172–75, 187, 230, 252, 254
  new, 62, 174
Jesus, *see the names index*
Jews, 10–11, 14, 37, 88, 97, 101–2, 113, 120–24, 126, 128, 130–35, 137–38, 147, 160, 188, 200, 218–19, 231, 235, 246–48, 251, 253, 263
  See also Hebrew Scriptures
Judaism, 10, 48, 122, 130–31, 133, 135
judgement, 45, 58, 76, 78, 89, 110–11, 113, 125–26, 129, 132, 144, 157, 172, 176, 179, 187, 204, 210, 214, 216, 224, 236, 241, 262

justice, 23, 37, 44, 56, 109–11, 113, 122, 129, 143–44, 148, 168, 171, 174, 176, 185, 194, 197, 220, 254
  see also social justice

Kenotic Christology, 93
  see also self-emptying
king, 127, 129, 170, 172
Kingdom of God, xvi, 3, 37, 40–41, 43, 45, 79–80, 85–86, 89–90, 97–99, 102, 105–6, 108–13, 120, 122–25, 127–30, 133, 153, 156–57, 161, 166–80, 202, 204–5, 210, 212–13, 219–20, 233, 239–43, 245–49, 252, 268
  see also City of God
Korea, 30

land, 102, 196, 239
language, 2, 7–8, 10–11, 19, 22, 25, 28–29, 33, 36, 39–40, 43, 46–47, 49, 51, 56, 58, 63–69, 71–72, 77, 88, 103, 115, 135, 146–48, 152, 158, 161, 174–75, 179, 181, 185, 187, 190–91, 193, 198, 206, 227, 244, 246–47, 258, 263–64, 267, 270–71
Law, the, 102, 106, 121–26, 130–37, 140, 160, 167–68, 188, 211, 239, 246
liberation, 23, 37–38, 54, 82, 112, 184, 236
life
  eternal, *see* eternity
  human, 60, 115, 140, 151, 154, 156–57, 165, 193, 199, 201, 240, 247, 261–62
  new, 62, 87, 108, 118–19, 140, 169–70, 175, 188, 202, 210, 238
  public/social, 5, 14, 81, 112, 117

(life continued)
    way of, 4, 23, 34, 44, 53, 82, 109, 122, 162, 168, 185
    see also Jesus *in the names index*
literature, 2–3, 13, 17, 31, 42, 61, 119, 128, 139, 246–48, 250–51, 253
liturgy, 7, 14, 114, 118, 223, 254, 261–62
    see also worship
logical positivism, 7, 29
Logos, see Word
love, 15–16, 25, 37, 43, 47, 54, 56, 58–59, 79, 82, 85–86, 90–95, 101, 104, 110, 112, 117–118, 120–22, 124–26, 137–38, 142–43, 145, 149, 159–61, 164–65, 170, 172, 186–87, 189–90, 197, 200, 204, 209, 211–12, 216, 234–36, 241

marquee, 9, 12, 48
    see also cathedral of the mind
marriage, 191, 214, 220
    same sex, 220
martyr, vii, 14, 30, 45, 221, 238
Marxism, 37, 193
Masai, the, 24
mathematics, 18, 49
meaning, 3–5, 11, 33, 36–39, 46, 50, 55, 58, 61, 64–65, 78, 97–98, 101, 103, 106–7, 109, 112, 116, 118, 122, 126–27, 129, 140, 147, 150–51, 156, 159, 174, 183, 191, 203, 223, 229, 235, 244, 248–49, 252, 257, 259, 261
men, 54, 101, 104, 107, 116, 121–22, 125, 146, 149, 203, 206, 210, 212–13, 218, 220, 235, 252–53
Messiah, 11, 14, 99, 107, 129, 149, 263
    see also Jesus *in the names index*
Messy Church, 34
metaphor, 144–48

metaphysics, ii, viii–ix, xi, xiv–xvi, 7–12, 35, 37–40, 42, 52, 55, 58, 60, 101, 112–13, 129, 155, 157, 185, 191, 205, 238, 266, 268–72
Middle Ages, 16
minister, 221
miracle, 70, 112, 248
missio Dei, 153
mission, 14, 23–24, 113, 123, 125–26, 137, 153, 174, 191, 212–14, 219, 249–50, 271
model, 3–4, 6, 64, 106, 143, 152, 180, 182, 197, 236, 242, 269–70
morality, see ethics
Mother, the, 43, 96, 165, 170, 188–90, 205
    see also Father, the; God
Mother of God, 225
motion, see movement
movement, vii, x–xi, xv, 10–11, 22, 35, 41–42, 47–48, 50, 54–55, 57, 60, 68, 71, 76–77, 81, 83, 109, 116, 126, 134, 144, 205, 223, 238, 240, 255, 270
music, 8, 15, 67–68, 213
mystery, 14, 19, 32, 52, 63, 70, 142, 153, 176, 204, 232, 247
mysticism, 44, 55

narrative, 9, 42, 61, 77, 107, 155–56, 158, 184, 186, 205, 225, 248, 252, 259, 270–71
    see also discourse
National Health Service, 243
Negative Way, the, 55
neighbor, 121, 159, 234–35
Neoplatonism, 15, 100, 152
    see also Platonism
New Testament, ix, xvi, 2, 11, 13–15, 24, 30, 58, 61, 65, 96, 98–101, 103–4, 112, 127, 133, 138–39,

SUBJECT INDEX

144, 147, 155, 160–61, 170, 174–75, 184–85, 193, 196, 211, 219, 230, 233, 237, 245, 249–51, 253
  see also Bible
non-dualism, xiv
non-reductionism, xiv
non-violence, 170, 194, 231
noumena, 50
noun, 3, 46–47, 117, 119, 152, 227, 267

obedience, 36, 105, 121, 125, 133, 136, 140, 163, 188, 197–99
object/objectivity, 6, 18–19, 31, 34, 45–47, 49, 54–55, 66–67, 70, 76, 78, 184, 192, 203, 226, 230, 238, 267
Old Testament, *see* Hebrew Scriptures
ontological argument, 16–17, 64
ontology, xvi, 5, 20, 48–50, 52, 55–57, 60, 94, 97, 129, 152, 155, 157, 161, 192, 199, 222, 238, 255, 267–68, 270
optimism, 79–81, 83, 147

panentheism, 60, 93
papacy, 221, 142
parable, 2, 99, 110, 120–21, 123, 127, 142, 166–68, 175, 186, 205, 205, 214, 217–18, 231, 235, 239–40, 245, 248, 252
paradigm, 4, 11, 34, 38, 49–50, 64, 96, 134, 152, 234
  shift, 4, 11, 23–24, 51, 64, 96, 234, 272
paralogie, 7
Passibilism, 91–94
  see also God, suffering; Patripassionism
passion play, 8, 254

Patripassionism, 90
  see also God, suffering; Passibilism
pattern, *see* changing patterns of action
Paul, *see* the names index
peace, 37, 89, 105, 110–11, 129, 131, 142, 155, 171, 173–74, 185, 188, 194, 215, 220
People of God, 174
personality, 85, 105, 106, 109, 147, 160, 176–77, 191, 240, 265
pessimism, 79, 83
Pharisees, 104–5, 123, 125, 130, 211
phenomena, 50, 71, 207
philosophy, xiii–xvi, 1–35, 39–42, 44, 46–51, 53, 55, 61, 66, 71, 81, 83, 93–94, 144, 148–49, 152, 161, 221–22, 224, 256, 258, 263, 266–72
  Christian, 27–28
  Continental, ii, x–xi, xiii, 12, 267
  Greek, 11, 15, 30–31, 48, 59, 61, 266
  process, 95, 193, 266
  Western, ii, viii–x, xiii, 12, 24, 42, 48, 50–51, 266, 270, 272
physical/physics, xiv, 3, 9, 29, 69–70, 97, 119, 152, 165, 196, 269
Platonism, vii, 7, 14–16, 18, 20, 30–31, 39, 48, 52, 94, 97, 100, 152, 182, 221, 231
  see also Cambridge Platonists; Neoplatonism
pluralism, viii, 23, 256–59
poetry, 8
politics, 3–5, 37, 80–83, 106, 109–10, 126, 205, 222, 237, 270
postmodernity, 22–23
poverty, 108, 175, 238–40

practice, 46, 61, 78, 84, 111, 134–35, 175, 177, 188, 198, 207–8, 215–16, 231, 237, 256, 261
  communicative, 229
  Christian, 229
  see also doing Christianly
prayer, 34, 44, 49, 101, 112, 127, 145, 185, 223, 228–29
predestination, 142, 145, 148
process philosophy, see philosophy, process
process theology, see theology, process
proof, 17–18, 27, 32, 36, 64, 270
prophecy, 13, 16, 98, 102, 107, 110, 113, 121, 127–28, 168, 172, 184–87, 200, 204, 211, 215, 220, 236, 246, 252
Protestantism, 11, 144–47, 263
psychology, 29, 204, 263

Qur'an, the, 11, 188, 226, 262

realism, 12, 81, 83
reality, ii, x–xi, xiii–xvi, 1–2, 5–6, 9–10, 12, 15–16, 23, 29, 35–37, 39–41, 44–45, 48, 50–51, 56, 58, 60–61, 64, 68, 70–71, 77, 80, 97, 115, 134, 144, 146, 150, 156, 164, 168, 182–83, 186, 190, 196, 201–3, 208, 219, 222, 225, 231, 237, 256–58, 260, 267–71
  ultimate, xiv, 256
reason, 1–3, 5, 7–9, 14, 17–18, 22–23, 28–29, 34, 42, 45–46, 53, 69, 82, 91, 97, 102–7, 109, 111–13, 140–41, 144, 146, 151, 167, 177, 205, 216–17, 222, 228, 255, 260, 264, 269
recapitulation, 197–98
reconciliation, xvi, 8, 50, 52, 60, 65, 86, 91, 115, 128–29, 142, 147–48, 151, 161, 163, 175, 181, 196–203, 214, 217, 237, 257, 260, 269
redaction criticism, 246
Reformation, the, 11, 97, 132, 145
regulative principle, 82–83
relation/relational/ relationship, ix, xi, 1, 4–6, 10, 16, 19, 22, 24, 26–29, 32, 34, 38–40, 43–44, 49–50, 52–54, 56, 60, 63–65, 70–71, 73–74, 76–78, 84, 87–92, 96, 104, 108–9, 111–13, 115–17, 119, 121–22, 124, 127, 130, 132, 140, 143, 146–49, 152, 157–58, 163–64, 171, 176, 179, 182–83, 188, 191, 193–94, 196, 198, 200, 203, 207, 217, 222–23, 225, 228, 231–33, 239, 242, 247, 255–56, 263–64, 268–71
relativism, 23, 82, 258
religion, xvi, 7–8, 10, 14–16, 18, 21, 27, 42, 44, 93, 101–2, 109, 116, 119, 130, 135, 147–48, 189, 192, 226, 253–64, 269
remembering, 75, 77, 134
repentance, 102, 108, 110, 112, 121–24, 133, 166, 170, 179, 185, 197, 210, 213–14, 236, 249
rest, viii, 35, 37, 64, 177, 270
resurrection, 16, 21, 39, 43, 45, 53, 112, 114–15, 118–19, 121, 126, 129, 132, 154, 156, 158, 164, 170, 175–77, 179, 185–86, 197–98, 200–205, 224, 229, 234, 238, 246, 248, 271
revelation, 11, 16–19, 22, 43, 47, 60, 62, 96, 115, 138, 143, 154, 173–74, 188, 213, 246–47, 257, 260
revolution, 108, 170, 194, 205, 231, 241
Rome, 14, 131, 135, 141–42, 174, 231

Sabbath, 122–23, 132, 136, 167
sacrament, 41, 99, 111, 157, 160, 209, 212–13, 216, 218, 236
sacrifice, 114, 148, 197–98, 200, 202, 240, 251–52
salvation, 13, 15, 61, 123, 131–37, 141, 165, 196–200, 202, 215, 257, 259
   see also reconciliation
satisfaction, 144
scapegoat, 181, 197–98
science, ix, xi, xv, 1–4, 7, 9, 17, 20–21, 27, 29, 34, 41–42, 45, 48, 50, 53, 64, 66–67, 71, 81, 148, 152, 157, 196, 208, 256, 268–70, 272
Second Vatican Council, 11
Second World War, 83, 252
secular age/society/world, xiv, 1, 4, 9, 17, 20, 34, 65, 101–3, 112, 116, 126, 129, 142, 147–48, 172, 175, 178, 206, 214, 217–18, 226, 253, 256
   see also city, secular
secularization, 103, 112, 116, 193, 206, 226
self-emptying, 93, 164–65
   see also Kenotic Christology
self-giving, 76, 78, 82, 91, 100, 118–19, 126, 143, 149, 155, 202–3, 223, 227
sermon, viii–ix, 8, 125, 159
service, 81, 85, 223, 240
silence, 33, 63, 118, 213, 229
simplicity, 31, 90, 182–83, 192
sin, 37, 73, 78–81, 86–88, 109, 121, 126, 141, 160, 180, 184, 194, 196–97, 200–201
   original, 79–80
sinlessness, 104, 126–27, 142, 194
sinners, 41, 121, 123, 133–34, 136, 144, 199, 251
   unrepentant, 102, 110, 112, 123–24, 133, 185, 213
slavery, 175, 179
social advantage/disadvantage, 239
social justice, 110, 185, 254
   see also justice
society, vii, 2, 5–6, 14, 17, 25, 37, 41, 79, 81–83, 101, 103, 106, 110, 113, 126, 140, 148, 172, 180, 188, 205, 214–15, 221, 232, 237–43, 256, 263, 269, 272
sociology, 1, 29, 263
Son of God, 33, 98, 129, 144, 154, 156, 250
Son of Man, 128–29, 168, 246–47, 252, 268
soteriology, see salvation
soul, 15, 18, 31, 33, 90, 108, 144–45, 162, 178, 204, 213
space, ii, x, 3, 49–51, 60, 66–67, 89, 113, 151, 183, 198, 216, 267, 269
spectrum, viii, 12, 45, 53, 63, 140, 259
stability, 68, 74, 79, 223
State, the, 13, 81–82
static, the, ii, vii–viii, xiii, 8–9, 12, 35, 37, 43, 46, 53, 56, 64, 68, 71, 78–79, 96, 117, 140, 161–62, 171, 179, 222, 233, 256, 259–60, 269–70
still point, 38, 42, 49, 68, 255, 259
stillness, 44–45, 63, 79, 191
structure, conceptual, viii, xv, 2–4, 7–10, 12, 19, 24, 32, 35–38, 40–41, 49, 103, 111–12, 118, 152
   see also framework; system
subject, 66, 76, 192–93, 222–23
substance, 24–25, 43, 46, 53–54, 66, 71, 78, 100–101, 111, 115, 119, 126, 139–40, 145, 149, 152, 155, 157, 219, 221–22, 233, 239, 262, 268–69

SUBJECT INDEX

substitution, 150, 197
suffering, vii, 14, 44–47, 53, 57, 60,
    76, 78, 84–95, 102, 109, 111, 129,
    148, 151, 158, 169, 176–77, 179,
    182, 185, 197–98, 200, 202–3,
    234, 246, 252, 254, 267
    see also God, suffering of
synod, 142–43
Syro-Phoenician woman, 110, 113,
    219
system, vii–ix, xi, xv–xvi, 4, 8–10, 12,
    15, 17, 22, 32, 38–40, 42, 48, 55,
    69, 71, 101, 110, 115, 117–18,
    142, 144, 155, 174, 185, 216, 224,
    228, 240–41, 243, 257–58, 269,
    271
    see also framework, conceptual/philosophical; structure, conceptual

table fellowship, 131–33, 218
tax collectors, 110, 123, 213
teleological argument, 17–18, 64
temple, 97, 109, 123, 153, 172
text, ii, 30, 33, 40, 77, 114, 152, 158,
    207–8, 212, 230, 244–50, 254,
    260–62
theology, ii, vii–ix, xi, xiv–xvi, 1, 3,
    8, 10, 12, 14–15, 18–20, 26–30,
    32–35, 37–42, 45–49, 50–55,
    57–58, 61–62, 64, 76–77, 81, 85,
    91, 93–96, 103, 115, 117, 126,
    130, 133–34, 137–38, 142–44,
    146, 148–49, 152, 155, 158,
    160–61, 164, 172, 175–76, 183,
    187, 197–98, 206, 223, 227–28,
    250–51, 253, 255–56, 258–59,
    264, 266, 268–72
    Christian, 7–9, 11, 13–14, 19–20,
        27–28, 30, 35, 37–38, 41, 46–48,
        55, 61, 97, 112, 118–19, 152, 158,
        161, 193, 227, 269–70, 205
    philosophical, 28
    process, viii–ix, 94–95, 255, 267
    secularized, 206
    systematic, *see* system
Theotokos, 225
thing, 6, 15, 18, 25, 38, 46, 52, 59–60,
    62–70, 74, 112, 190, 203, 233,
    262, 264
Thomism, *see* Aquinas, Thomas *in the
    names index*
thought-forms, 2–4, 6, 24, 30–31, 39,
    191
    see also worldview
time, ii, 3, 38, 40–41, 50–51, 53, 56,
    60, 63, 66–69, 77–78, 89, 92, 97,
    101–3, 112–13, 118, 133, 150–52,
    163–64, 167, 169–71, 182–83,
    198, 200, 216, 237, 244, 246, 248,
    256, 267, 269
Torah, the, *see* Law, the
tradition, 4, 41, 48, 61, 64–65, 83, 188,
    245, 256–61, 263–65
    Christian/Judaeo-Christian, 4–5,
        12, 14–25, 30, 35–37, 39–42,
        48–49, 59–61, 64–65, 77, 92, 98,
        101, 103, 109, 118–20, 126, 131,
        144, 161, 173, 182–83, 188–89,
        193, 198, 206–8, 222–23, 236,
        239–40, 245, 254, 259, 261
    philosophical, ii, viii–x, xiii–xiv,
        4, 10, 12, 30, 40, 42, 50, 55, 206,
        270
    see also evangelical tradition
tragedy, 77, 83, 85–86, 143, 205, 221,
    270
transcendence, vii, 7, 21, 43, 57, 60,
    64–65, 94, 153, 182, 258

SUBJECT INDEX

transfiguration, 45, 65, 78, 86–87, 89, 161, 171, 176–77, 181–82, 194, 201

transformation, 23, 43–45, 47, 57, 77–79, 86, 88, 156–60, 170, 175–77, 181–82, 200, 202, 208, 217, 237–38, 243

transgender, 219

translation, 11, 30, 33, 58–59, 61, 98–99, 136, 152, 159, 199, 237, 240, 246

Trinity, xi, xvi, 17, 43, 52, 56, 62, 94, 96, 98, 101, 103, 181–95, 247, 269, 271

trust, 35, 65, 169, 215, 229–30, 232, 237

truth, 2, 9, 13, 17, 22–23, 31–36, 62, 86, 113, 120, 127, 136, 140, 161, 179, 186, 211, 221, 230, 234, 252, 256–57, 261–62, 269

unchanging, the, ii, vii–viii, xiii, 3, 11, 16, 35, 37–38, 53, 56, 60–61, 64, 70–71, 73, 75, 78, 92, 94, 100, 117, 152, 161–63, 165, 182, 189, 205, 221–22, 270–72

unconditionality, ix–x, 111, 117, 120–26, 130, 138, 141, 144–45, 147, 189, 209, 239–40, 242–43, 249

unitarian, 191

unitary, the, ii, vii–viii, xiii, 3, 6, 8–9, 35, 37–38, 43, 65, 117, 181, 205, 269–70, 272

unity, 37, 42–43, 53, 55, 90, 100–101, 142, 147, 152–53, 159, 188, 191–92, 198, 200–201, 216, 221–25, 258, 263

universe, ii, xiv, 17, 20, 25, 32, 35, 41, 43–44, 50, 57, 59–60, 63, 66–70, 74, 76–79, 85, 87, 89, 91, 96, 118, 148, 151, 158, 170, 182–83, 191–92, 194, 196, 200–201, 203, 215–16, 222, 228, 268, 271–72
see also cosmos

urban world, vii, 140, 171–72, 175

utopia, 79–80, 83

values, 7–8, 55, 65, 81, 93, 104, 106, 115, 132, 134, 147, 160, 173–74, 176, 241–43, 258, 262

verb, 2–3, 25, 46–47, 56, 58–59, 111, 119, 152, 155, 157, 225, 227, 235, 267

victory, 14, 92, 94, 148, 172, 196–98

violence, 89, 164, 177, 181, 194, 231

virtue, 30, 44, 74, 105, 121, 197, 251

void, formless, 66

wave, 63, 68, 75, 158, 268

wealth, 106, 111, 127, 205, 216, 239, 241, 253

welcoming, 8, 41, 54, 58, 65, 84, 105, 110–11, 120–21, 123–26, 130, 133–34, 144–45, 154, 166, 170, 185, 188, 205, 209–10, 213, 217–18

women, 54, 77, 79, 101, 104–5, 110, 113, 160, 162, 167, 203, 210, 214–15, 218–20

Word, 2, 14–15, 30, 34, 41, 46, 97–98, 100, 112, 114, 152–53, 157, 165, 246, 257

work, x, 8, 10, 12, 20–21, 48–50, 52, 59, 71, 80–81, 92–93, 101, 110, 120, 133, 136, 140, 145, 148, 153, 160–61, 163, 167, 175, 185, 194, 215, 219, 223, 233–34, 242, 249, 270–71

world, xiv–xv, 2, 4, 7–20, 22–25, 32–35, 37–38, 40, 43, 47, 49, 51–54, 58–61, 64–65, 67, 69–71,

(world continued)
    74, 76, 78, 80–81, 86–88, 90–94,
    97, 99, 101–2, 106–7, 109, 112,
    115–16, 118–19, 126, 129,
    141–42, 147–49, 151–52, 155,
    157–59, 161–63, 166–67, 169,
    174–78, 180, 183, 186, 188–90,
    193–94, 198, 201–3, 205–6,
    213–14, 217–19, 221–23, 226,
    228, 231–32, 234, 238–42,
    247, 252–53, 255–56, 259, 262,
    264–65, 267, 270–72
    see also urban world
worldview, 1, 7, 14, 17, 22
    see also thought-forms
worship, 6, 33–34, 84–85, 99, 104,
    113, 116, 126–29, 158–59,
    164–65, 169, 178, 180, 187–90,
    200, 205, 213, 216–17, 234, 247,
    253, 264
    see also liturgy

Names Index

Abraham, 131–35, 161–62, 179, 189, 197, 249, 251
Allen, Diogenes, 23
Anselm, 16, 143–44
Aquinas, Thomas, 11, 17–18, 75, 144–45, 196, 266, 271
Aristotle, 9, 17–18, 31, 44, 144, 152, 166
Atkinson, David, vii, 39
Augustine, 15–16, 23, 80–83, 140–48, 221
Ayer, A.J., 7

Baillie, Donald, 158
Baker, John Austin, 93, 156
Balthasar, Hans Urs von, 61
Barclay, John, 119, 134
Barth, Karl, 22, 75, 146, 150
Benson, R.M., 184–85
Berdyaev, Nicholas, 54
Bergson, Henri, 55, 77, 92, 266–67, 269
Blondel, Maurice, 10, 18, 20, 26–29, 32, 40, 55, 58, 77, 266–67
Bonhoeffer, Dietrich, 43, 54, 93
Bosch, David, 23–24
Boys Smith, John, viii–ix, 266–67
Brierley, Michael, 92
Bultmann, Rudolf, 19–20, 22, 146
Burtchaell, James, 146

Butler, Bishop, 18

Caelestius, 142
Calvin, John, 145
Camus, Albert, 87
Clement, 15–16, 139
Cole, Richard, 147
Crocker, Geoff, 190
Cupitt, Don, 54–55

D'Costa, Gavin, 257
Davies, Oliver, 97–98, 114
Davison, Andrew, 29
Derrida, Jacques, xiii, 7, 77
Descartes, René, 32
DiNoia, J.A., 258–59
Donovan, Vincent, 24
Drury, John, 120
Dulles, Avery, 13, 16, 21, 212
Duns Scotus, 143–44

Epperly, Bruce, 87–88, 208
Eusebius, 16

Faber, Roland, 256
Fauré, Gabriel, 152
Fiddes, Paul, 94
Flew, Antony, 74
Forsyth, P.T., 93

NAMES INDEX

Gaudí, Antoni, 48
Gilkey, Langdon, 258
Goodbourn, David, 71
Graham, Billy, 21
Gunton, Colin, 56, 144, 147–48

Hart, David Bentley, 36
Harteshorne, Charles, 9
Haught, John, 71
Hegel, Friedrich, 44, 266
Heidegger, Martin, xiii, xv, 19–20, 267
Heim, Mark, 259
Heraclitus, 31, 48, 51, 55, 222, 266, 268
Herbert, George, 145
Hick, John, 256–57
Higton, Mike, 47, 126
Hilary of Poitiers, 33
Holmes, Stephen, 182–83
Hooker, Morna, 136
Hooker, Richard, 221
Hume, David, 18
Husserl, Edmund, xiii, 267

Janz, Paul, 60, 198, 228
Jenkins, Timothy, 112
Jenson, Robert, 43
Jeremias, Joachim, 120
Jesus, ii, xvi, 2, 11, 14–16, 19, 24, 31, 37, 40–48, 52, 56, 58, 60–63, 73, 78, 87, 90–94, 96–140, 142–44, 146–71, 173–77, 179–80, 183–220, 222–28, 230–40, 242–54, 256–58, 261–62, 268–69, 271–72
  Christ, 14, 24, 30, 47, 53, 94, 96–98, 101, 130–33, 135–40, 144, 146, 148, 150, 152, 158, 162–64, 166, 185–86, 190, 196, 199, 203, 207–8, 210, 212, 215, 217, 224, 227, 257
  of Nazareth, xvi, 77, 96–98, 112–13, 115–16, 126, 156, 169, 183, 190, 204, 251
John the Baptist, 102, 108, 123–24, 127, 179, 210
Joseph, 107–8, 127–28, 248, 254
Journet, Charles, 146
Julian of Norwich, 59, 160
Justin Martyr, vii, 14, 30, 221

Kant, Immanuel, 146, 156, 267
Kierkegaard, Søren, 18–19, 230
Kim, Sebastian, 30, 37
Küng, Hans, 11, 54, 116, 146

Levinas, Emmanuel, xiii, 267
Lewis, Charles Staples, 21
Lucas, J.R., 143
Luther, Martin, 81–82, 144–45

MacKinnon, Donald, 8, 152
Macleod, Alistair, 56
MacQuarrie, John, 20
Major, Henry, 92–93
Marcion, 2, 192
Marion, Jean-Luc, xiii
Marx, Karl, 37, 193, 266
Mary, 107–8, 127–28, 225, 245
McGrath, Alister, 22, 33
Melanchthon, 145
Milbank, John, 2, 29
Moffatt, James, 137
Moltmann, Jürgen, 93, 224
Moses, 30, 62, 99, 179

Newlands, George, x
Nicolaidis, Argyris, 92
Niebuhr, Reinhold, 81–83
Nineham, Dennis, 14, 78, 176

Oliver, Simon, x, 42

NAMES INDEX

Oman, John, 54, 147
O'Murchu, Diarmuid, 50
Origen, vi, 15–16, 140

Paley, William, 18
Panikkar, Raymundo, 170, 258
Pannenberg, Wolfhart, 112
Parmenides, 48, 51, 222, 266
Pascal, Blaise, 18
Pattison, George, 46–47, 53, 59–60
Paul, Apostle, 1–2, 10, 13, 29, 37,
    40–41, 75, 99, 101, 105–6, 119,
    124, 127, 130–39, 141–42, 144,
    146–49, 156–58, 160, 169, 174,
    186–87, 190, 197–98, 200, 204,
    210, 215–17, 220, 224, 233–34,
    248–49, 251
Peacocke, Arthur, 71, 151
Pederson, Ann, 71, 151
Pelagius, 80–83, 141–48
Penner, Myron Bradley, 34–35
Peter, Apostle, 129–31
Pittenger, Norman, 93
Plato, vii, 7, 14–16, 18, 20, 30–31, 39,
    44, 48, 51–52, 94, 97, 100, 152,
    182, 221–22, 231, 266
Polkinghorne, John, 67, 69, 74
Polycarp, 139

Quick, Oliver, 97–98

Race, Alan, 257–59
Rahner, Karl, 147, 256–57, 259
Ramsey, Michael, 33, 53
Rauschenbusch, Walter, 81–83
Richardson, Alan, 1, 39–40
Ricoeur, Paul, 60–61
Roberts, Tom, 21
Robinson, John, 52, 93, 224
Rolt, C.E., 92

Sanders, E.P., 123–24, 126, 134
Sanneh, Lamin, 11
Saunders, Nicholas, 50
Schillebeeckx, Edward, 99
Schleiermacher, Friedrich, 18, 75, 146
Schumacher, E.F., 80
Sedmak, Clemens, 238
Selby, Peter, 217–18
Simon, Ulrich, 85
Sölle, Dorothee, 54–55
Spufford, Francis, 34–35
Studdert Kennedy, Geoffrey, 20,
    91–92, 266–67

Tanner, Kathryn, 100
Tawney, R.H., 241
Teilhard de Chardin, Pierre, 20, 71,
    147, 176, 266–67
Temple, William, 240–42
Tertullian, 31, 90–91, 140
Theodoret, 16, 31
Thomas, Apostle, 98–99, 101, 153,
    165
Thomas, Owen, 75
Tillich, Paul, 55–56, 158–60, 217
Torrance, T.F., 139–40
Tracy, David, 256
Traherne, Thomas, 91

Vanhoozer, Kevin, 61
Vanstone, W.H., 94

Warner, Martin, 61
Watson, Francis, 135
Wells, Harold, 257
Whitehead, Alfred North, 9, 30, 77,
    93, 193, 255–56, 266–68
Williams, Rowan, 126, 165, 208, 258
Wittgenstein, Ludwig, 77, 148, 266–67

Wolterstorft, Nicholas, 224
Wright, N.T./Tom, 93, 96, 98, 150, 154

Zacchaeus, 123

Zeno, 31
Zizioulas, John, 54, 222–23

Scripture Index

GENESIS

1:1–2:3	71
1:1–3a	66
1:1	66, 187
1:2	184
1:26	164
1:27	181, 184
2:7	184
3:6	79
11:1–9	172
12:1–9	179
15:6	131, 133
18:22–33	189
22:1–19	197, 251

EXODUS

3:1–6	62
3:14	99
12:21–42	179
19:18	62
21:24	211
25:18–22	225

LEVITICUS

25	239

DEUTERONOMY

7:7–8	121

JOSHUA

8	89
24:10	61

1 SAMUEL

10:18	61
12:11	61

2 SAMUEL

12:7	61

1 KINGS

19:12	229

JOB

passim	158

PSALMS

2	250
2:7	129
2:10–12	89
22	250
40:6	200
45	99
48	172, 174
51:10	62

(Psalms continued)

51:16–17	200
81:7	61
103	187, 202
103:8	189
103:9	189
103:17	189
107:25	75
107:29	75

PROVERBS

8:1	187
31:5	239
31:8–9	239

ISAIAH

2:4	89
7:14	113
29:13	211
42:1–9	219, 250
43:19	62
45:7	89
52:13–53:12	179, 250, 252
60:1–3	122
65:17	62
66:22	62

JEREMIAH

6:20	200
7:21–23	200
9:4–8	172–74
31:15	128
31:33–34	121

LAMENTATIONS

2	173

EZEKIEL

2:2	184

DANIEL

7:13–14	128, 246
7:13	129

HOSEA

11:1–4	188, 189
11:1	128
11:8–9	189
14:4	121

MICAH

5:2	107, 127

MATTHEW

1:1–17	127, 248
1:18–2:23	107
1:18–25	107, 248
1:23	112–13
2:1–12	127, 253
2:1	107
2:13–15	128
5:1–7:29	106, 125
5:17–48	102
5:17–18	122
5:17	167, 246
5:20	124
5:28	214
5:31–32	214
5:38–39	211
5:44	214
5:48	110, 125, 214
6:1–8	219
6:9–13	169, 229
6:9	187
6:10	170
7:3	111
7:7–11	169
9:22	237
10:5	102, 123
10:8	242
11:2–6	149
11:9–10	214
11:9	210
11:16–19	108

11:18	124	2:15–16	102, 123
11:19	110, 112, 123	2:16	108
12:46–50	240	2:23–27	110, 122
13:44	167	2:28	128
15:24	102, 123	2:36–3:6	168
16:13–16	129	3:1–6	110, 122
16:26	238	3:13–19	106
18:15–17	124	3:31–35	167, 216, 240
19:1–9	220	4	110
19:14	210	4:1–9	167
19:16–30	125	4:13–20	245
19:30	110, 125	4:26–34	108
20:1–16	108, 110, 120, 214, 240	4:30–31	167
20:16–20	186	5:17	168
20:28	252	5:21–43	210
21:32	124	5:34	58, 215
21:33–41	251	6:30–44	130, 168, 248
22:44	245	7:6–8	211
23	110	7:9–13	216
23:37–39	187	7:15	126
25:3	124	7:24–30	102, 110, 113, 219
25:31–46	187, 215, 231	8:23–24	110, 125
25:34	167	8:27–9:1	78
26:17–30	223	8:31	128, 246
27:51–54	119	8:34–38	213, 238
28	156	8:35	177
28:16–20	155	8:38	128
28:19	11	9:12	128
28:20	168, 190	10:14	218
		10:15	110, 124
		10:31	179

MARK

		10:45	164, 197, 252
passim	14	10:52	58
1:1–13	179	11:1–11	173
1:1	98, 127, 249–50	11:12–14	167
1:4	113	11:15–19	108
1:9	102, 109, 210, 213	11:15–18	173
1:13	109	11:15–17	109
1:15	122, 166, 213	11:22	136
1:16–20	110, 213	12:1–12	120
1:21–34	168	13	110, 168, 250
1:25	109	13:24–31	166
1:27	62	13:28	167
1:29–45	130	13:30	110, 167, 204, 220
1:40–45	110	13:32	110, 220
2	154	13:36	128
2:1–12	110, 199, 248	14:10–11	173
2:10	128	14:12–31	223

(Mark continued)

14:24	106
14:32–42	110–11, 188, 220
14:32–37	164
14:36	187, 190
14:43–65	173
14:43–50	111
14:41	41
14:51–15:20	111
14:62	128, 168
15:1–39	119
15:21–41	111
15:27	253
16:1–8	156, 248
16:8	77

LUKE

passim	13, 124
1–2	211
1	127
1:1–2:20	107
1:26–38	107, 248
1:34	245
1:35	184
1:47	108
1:52–53	108
1:77	202
2:1–7	127
2:8–20	127, 253
3:22	184
3:23–38	127, 248
4:1–13	106
4:1	184
4:18–30	245
4:18	184
4:25–27	102
6:2–23	110
6:20–23	167
7:13–35	108
7:18–27	108
7:36–50	104, 130
8:39	149
9:27	166
9:51	173
10:1–10	123
10:27	235
10:29	235
10:30–37	235
10:36	235
10:37	235
11:1	109
11:2–4	229
11:2	109, 111
11:23	166
11:37–54	111
12:48	243
13:31–35	236
13:34	190
14:26	240
15	108, 123, 130, 167
15:3–7	211
15:11–32	121, 229
16:1–13	252
17:11–19	161
17:21	168
18:27	128
19:1–10	108, 130
19:41–44	173
21:17	166, 168
22:7–38	223
22:20	62
22:24–26	252
23:34	199
23:43	110
24	156
24:13–35	114, 156, 185
24:19	98, 154
24:30	155
24:43	245

JOHN

passim	ix, 2, 14, 99, 106, 245, 249
1:1–14	98, 153
1:1	98, 100, 152–53, 157, 246
1:3	106
1:12–13	107
1:14–18	200
1:14	101, 157
1:16	159
2:15	164
3:1–21	130
3:8	221
3:22	210
5:19	100

6:25–29	106	10:34–43	13
8:1–11	214	10:40	61, 157
8:24	99	13:30	61, 157
10:16	188	13:37	157
10:23	31	15:1–35	174, 219, 247
10:30	100, 153	16	132
11:35	164	16:7	184–85, 190
13:1	223	17:7	98
13:34	106	17:16–34	13, 37
14:6	211	17:19	62
14:26	184	17:24	59
15:12–17	186	17:28	129–30, 40
15:26	184	25:10	174
16:7	184	26:2–23	1
16:32	153		
17:21	153		
19–20	156		

ROMANS

passim	174
2:12–16	132
2:17–29	135
3:21	215
3:22	136, 200
3:23	203
3:24	204, 215, 249
5:1–2	132
5:1	160, 200, 215, 249
5:6–11	200
5:12–21	198
5:15–21	200
5:15	160
5:19	199
6:3–11	118
6:4	210
7:6	62
7:22	130
8:5–9	233
8:9	184–85
8:11	118
8:18–25	170
8:18–23	169
8:33	59
9:5	99
9:16	59
10:9	61, 157
11:6	131
11:22	133
12:3	139
14	131

20:19–29	79
20:19–23	185
20:21	155
20:22	184
20:27–28	99, 165
20:28	98, 101, 153
21:1–14	185
21:12–14	155
21:15–19	186

ACTS

passim	124
1:11	169
2	173
2:1–36	185
2:4	184
2:14–36	13
2:24	61, 157
2:32	157
2:38	210
3:2	31
3:7	61
3:11–26	13
3:12	31
3:15	157
3:26	157
4:10	157
7:1–53	13
9:1–19	220
10:1–11:18	219

(Romans continued)

15:13	171
16:20	137

1 CORINTHIANS

1:9	162
1:20	31
3:7	59
3:10–15	132
5:17	170
6:9–10	133
6:14	157
10:13	162
11:17–34	135
11:21	216
11:23–26	216, 223
11:23	41, 209
11:25	62
11:29–32	132
11:29	216, 224
12:4–11	186
12:6	59
12:9	215
12:27–31	186
13:4–7	186, 234
13:4–6	86
15	13
15:4	155
15:10	75, 142
15:15	187
15:21–22	198
15:22	204
15:24–25	114
15:42–49	204
15:44	156, 169
15:50	156
15:51	204
16:23	137

2 CORINTHIANS

1:9	59
1:18	162
3:6	62
4:18	15–16
5:1–5	178
5:8–10	132
5:17	62, 233
5:20	198
6:14–16	31
10:5	136
13:13	190

GALATIANS

1:1	61
1:11	134
2:11–14	130–31
2:16	58, 136, 199, 249
2:21	137
3–4	37
3	132
3:6	133, 249
3:22	136
3:24	249
3:25	130
3:28	134–35, 240
5:16	204
5:21	133
5:22–25	204
6:15	62

EPHESIANS

passim	14
1:20	61
2:15	62
4:2	105
4:24	62

PHILIPPIANS

1:19	98, 185, 190
2:3	105
2:5–11	164, 249
2:5	105
2:8	105, 136
2:12–13	133
2:12	136
2:13	59
3:9	58, 199

COLOSSIANS

1:4	58
1:16	170
1:24	169, 234
2:5	58
2:12	61, 210
2:23	106
3:10	62

1 THESSALONIANS

4	13, 168

2 THESSALONIANS

2:13	136

1 TIMOTHY

passim	14
3:1–13	212

TITUS

2:13	98–99

HEBREWS

passim	13, 162
1:8	99
4:14–5:10	200
4:14	156
4:15	101, 104, 109, 126
6:13–20	161–62
7:26–28	251
8:8	62
8:13	62
9:15	62
10:20	62
10:32–39	133
11:17–19	251
12:24	62
13:7–9	162
13:8	162–63
13:14	179, 237

JAMES

passim	14
1:17	161
1:18	161
2:1	136
4:6	139

1 PETER

passim	14
1:3	62
1:21	61
2:22	104
3:18	156

2 PETER

passim	14
1:1	98–99
3:13	62

1 JOHN

passim	14
2:8	62
2:15	15–16
4:8	95, 186
4:16	95

2 JOHN

5	62

JUDE

1:3	35

REVELATION

passim	213, 250
2:17	62
3:12	62
18	174
21:1–3	174
21:2	62
21:4	177

www.ingramcontent.com/pod-product-compliance
Lightning Source LLC
Chambersburg PA
CBHW071231230426
43668CB00011B/1384